The Hong Kong Legal System

Second Edition

This book provides an introduction to the legal system in Hong Kong. Understanding Hong Kong's legal system today requires an understanding of the British origins of many of its laws and legal institutions as well as of the uniquely Hong Kong developments in the application of the Basic Law under 'one country, two systems'. These features of the Hong Kong legal system are explored in this book, which takes into account developments in the two decades or so of the new legal framework in Hong Kong since the 1997 handover. In providing an exposition of the legal institutions in Hong Kong and legal method under Hong Kong's legal system (including practical guidance and examples on case law, statutory interpretation and legal research), this book is ideal for first-year law students, students of other disciplines who study law and readers who have an interest in Hong Kong's unique legal system.

Stefan H. C. Lo is Deputy Principal Government Counsel (Ag) at the Department of Justice, Hong Kong, where he has been advising the government on company and insolvency law reform. Dr Lo has published widely in the area of corporate law, including research on accountability of directors, shareholders and other responsible persons in the operation of corporate enterprises. Before joining the Department of Justice, Dr Lo was Assistant Professor in the School of Law, City University of Hong Kong.

Kevin Kwok-yin Cheng is Associate Professor and Assistant Dean (Research) in the Faculty of Law, The Chinese University of Hong Kong (CUHK), where he is the course leader for the Hong Kong Legal System and Legal System courses for the LLB and JD programmes respectively. His primary research interests are in the fields of criminal justice and socio-legal studies with a strong emphasis on empirical work in Hong Kong. Professor Cheng was the recipient of the CUHK Research Excellence Award (2015–16).

Wing Hong Chui is Professor in the Department of Social and Behavioural Sciences, City University of Hong Kong. He was formerly the Associate Dean (Undergraduate Education) of the Faculty of Social Sciences at The University of Hong Kong. Previously, he taught social work, criminology and law at the University of Exeter, University of Queensland and The Chinese University of Hong Kong. He has conducted socio-legal research on the impact of litigants in person in civil proceedings and young people's views on legal representation in Hong Kong.

The Hong Kong Legal System

Second Edition

Stefan H. C. Lo
Department of Justice, Government of the Hong Kong SAR

Kevin Kwok-yin Cheng
The Chinese University of Hong Kong

Wing Hong Chui
City University of Hong Kong

CAMBRIDGE
UNIVERSITY PRESS

University Printing House, Cambridge CB2 8BS, United Kingdom

One Liberty Plaza, 20th Floor, New York, NY 10006, USA

477 Williamstown Road, Port Melbourne, VIC 3207, Australia

314–321, 3rd Floor, Plot 3, Splendor Forum, Jasola District Centre, New Delhi – 110025, India

79 Anson Road, #06-04/06, Singapore 079906

Cambridge University Press is part of the University of Cambridge.

It furthers the University's mission by disseminating knowledge in the pursuit of education, learning, and research at the highest international levels of excellence.

www.cambridge.org
Information on this title: www.cambridge.org/9781108721820
DOI: 10.1017/9781108634687

First edition © McGraw-Hill, Education 2012
Second edition © Cambridge University Press 2020

This publication is in copyright. Subject to statutory exception and to the provisions of relevant collective licensing agreements, no reproduction of any part may take place without the written permission of Cambridge University Press.

First published 2012
Second edition 2020

A catalogue record for this publication is available from the British Library.

Library of Congress Cataloging-in-Publication Data
Names: Lo, Stefan H. C., author. | Cheng, Kevin Kwok-yin, 1985- author. | Chui, Wing Hong, author.
Title: The Hong Kong legal system / Stefan H C Lo, Kevin Kwok-yin Cheng, Wing Hong Chui.
Description: Second edition. | New york : Cambridge University Press, 2020. | Includes bibliographical references and index.
Identifiers: LCCN 2019038146 (print) | LCCN 2019038147 (ebook) | ISBN 9781108721820 (paperback) | ISBN 9781108634687 (epub)
Subjects: LCSH: Law–China–Hong Kong.
Classification: LCC KNQ9308 .L627 2020 (print) | LCC KNQ9308 (ebook) | DDC 349.5125–dc23
LC record available at https://lccn.loc.gov/2019038146
LC ebook record available at https://lccn.loc.gov/2019038147

ISBN 978-1-108-72182-0 Paperback

Cambridge University Press has no responsibility for the persistence or accuracy of URLs for external or third-party internet websites referred to in this publication and does not guarantee that any content on such websites is, or will remain, accurate or appropriate.

Contents

List of Figures	*page* vi
List of Tables	vii
Preface to the Second Edition	ix
Acknowledgements	xi
Table of Cases	xii
Table of Legislation	xxv

1	Introduction and Overview	1
2	Functions and Concepts of Law	34
3	√ Governance in Hong Kong	62
4	√ Sources of Law	90
5	√ The Court System and the Doctrine of Precedent	137
6	√ The Process of Legislation	183
7	√ Statutory Interpretation	200
8	√ Criminal Justice System	234
9	√ Civil Justice System	264
10	Alternative Methods of Resolving Disputes	287
11	√ Access to Justice	305
12	Finding and Citing Legal Materials	329
13	√ Interface between Hong Kong and International and Chinese Law	366
	Glossary	392
	Index	400

Figures

4.1	Different parts of a statute, as shown on the first page of the Pharmacy and Poisons Ordinance (Cap. 138)	*page* 105
4.2	Different levels of a section, as shown in s. 247 of the Securities and Futures Ordinance (Cap. 571)	106
4.3	Section 293 of the Securities and Futures Ordinance (Cap. 571)	107
4.4	Different meanings of the term 'common law'	108
4.5	Headnote from *Loyal Luck Trading Ltd* v. *Tam Chun Wah* showing the different parts of a reported case	115
5.1	Court system pre-1 July 1997	142
5.2	Court system post-1 July 1997	146
8.1	Criminal procedure in Hong Kong	240
9.1	Civil litigation in Hong Kong	267

Tables

6.1 Number of member's bills passed   *page* 194
8.1 Conviction and guilty plea rates, 2014–2017   254

Preface to the Second Edition

Hong Kong's legal system is unique in that the common law system that operated prior to the return of sovereignty to China in 1997 continues to operate today under a constitutional framework (Hong Kong's Basic Law) created under the civil law system of China. The purpose of this book is to provide readers with an introduction to the basic precepts of the law and legal institutions in Hong Kong, derived as they are from both the British legacy and the new constitutional underpinnings of the legal order under the Basic Law. Although the book is written in a way that is most beneficial for first-year law students, offering practical guidance in legal research and reading statutes and case law, we hope that it will be useful for students from other disciplines who study law as well. We also hope that this book will appeal to general readers, both in Hong Kong and abroad, who are seeking an understanding of Hong Kong's legal system. Developments relating to Hong Kong's legal system are not only relevant to lawyers but should also be of interest to others.

Since the first edition of this book was published in 2012, there have continued to be developments in the operation of Hong Kong's legal system. A prime illustration of this is the recent 'co-location arrangement', which we have included in this new edition (see Chapter 4). The Hong Kong and Mainland customs, immigration and quarantine arrangements of the Hong Kong section of the Guangzhou–Shenzhen–Hong Kong Express Rail Link, referred to as the co-location arrangement, which was opened in September 2018, has sparked controversy in Hong Kong. This rail link forms part of the 20,000-kilometre national high-speed rail network and aims to increase the connectivity between Hong Kong and other Mainland cities. It is argued by Hong Kong officials that to realise its full potential, a quarter of the West Kowloon Station located in Hong Kong (referred to as the Mainland Port Area) needs to be leased to Mainland authorities so that passengers can have their travel documents checked by both Hong Kong and Mainland officers in one terminus instead of separately (once before departing Hong Kong and again upon arrival in the Mainland). As the Mainland Port Area is subject to the laws of the Mainland and is regarded as outside the territorial boundary of the Hong Kong Special Administrative Region for the above purposes, the arrangement gives Mainland authorities unprecedented jurisdiction over an area that is geographically within Hong Kong. The co-location arrangement, seemingly concerned with the convenience of travel, goes to the heart of the issues arising from the principles of 'one country, two systems' and Hong Kong's 'high degree of autonomy' under the Basic Law.

The interconnectivity between Hong Kong and the rest of China will continue to increase while Hong Kong continues to strive to maintain its status as 'Asia's World City'. We have added a new chapter on the interface between Hong Kong and international and Chinese law (Chapter 13). Aside from legal issues concerning the relationship between Hong Kong and Mainland China, there have also been other important developments. The judiciary has drawn greater attention to the need to enhance access to justice for litigants in civil proceedings as well as defendants in criminal proceedings. In response, we have added a new chapter on access to justice (Chapter 11) and have provided an overview of Hong Kong's criminal and civil justice systems (Chapter 8 and Chapter 9 respectively). A Competition Tribunal was established in August 2013 and we have also included this in our discussion of the court system (see Chapter 5). In this book, the law is generally stated to be that in force as at 31 March 2019.

We would like to thank Becky Leung, Victor Tai and Zenith Lai for their assistance in this project. Whatever errors that may remain are entirely our own responsibility. We are also grateful to our publisher, Cambridge University Press, and especially to our acquisitions editor Joe Ng for his enthusiasm and commitment. This book would not have been completed without the unwavering support of our families.

Acknowledgements

The views in this book are the authors' own and do not necessarily represent those of the Department of Justice.

The authors thank Thomson Reuters Sweet and Maxwell for their permission for reproduction of pages from [2007] 4 HKLRD 917. Copyright in Hong Kong legislation reproduced in this book belongs to the Government of the Hong Kong Special Administrative Region and the legislation is reproduced under licence granted by the Government.

Stefan H. C. Lo, Kevin Kwok-yin Cheng
and Wing Hong Chui

Table of Cases

The following is a list of the cases that are cited in this book.

Name of Case

A Solicitor (24/07) v. *Law Society of Hong Kong* (2008) 11 HKCFA 117, [2008] 2 HKC 1,   163, 166, 168, 170–171, 177–180
AG v. *Kong Chung-Shing* [1980] HKLR 533,   238
Akai Holdings Ltd v. *Ernst & Young* (2009) 12 HKCFAR 376, [2009] 5 HKLRD 804,   212
Alderson v. *Booth* [1969] 2 QB 216,   241
Amalgamated Society of Engineers v. *Adelaide Steamship Co. Ltd* (1920) 28 CLR 129,   201
American Cyanamid Co. Appellants v. *Ethicon Ltd* [1974] AC 396,   274
An Application by the Official Solicitor (No. 1), Re [1983] 2 HKC 259,   219
Anandarajah v. *Lord Chancellor's Department* (1984) IRLR 131,   175
Anns v. *Merton LBC* [1978] AC 728,   131
Antonelli v. *Secretary of State for Trade and Industry* [1998] 1 All ER 997,   225
Assam Railways and Trading Co. v. *Commissioners of Inland Revenue* [1935] AC 445,   224
Association of Expatriate Civil Servants of Hong Kong v. *Chief Executive* [1998] 1 HKLRD 615,   88
Attorney General for Hong Kong v. *Reid* [1994] 1 AC 324,   180
Attorney General v. *Gardiner* [1987] HKLR 22,   174–175
Attorney General v. *George Wimpey International Ltd* [1986] HKLR 325,   207
Attorney General v. *Lau Chiu-tak* [1984] HKLR 23,   171
Attorney General v. *Ng Kwan* [1987] 1 HKC 183,   214
Attorney General v. *Prince Ernest Augustus of Hanover* [1957] AC 436,   208

Attorney General v. *Sham Chuen* [1986] HKLR 365,   176
Attorney-General v. *Ngan Kam Ming* [1996] 2 HKC 176,   220
Auburntown Ltd v. *Town Planning Board* [1994] 2 HKLR 272,   207
Australian Agricultural Co. v. *Federated Engine Drivers and Firemens' Association of Australasia* (1913) 17 CLR 261,   166
Australian Consolidated Press Ltd v. *Uren* [1969] 1 AC 590,   178

Baker v. *R* [1975] AC 774,   176
Balfour v. *Balfour* [1919] 2 KB 571,   342–343
Balogh v. *Crown Court at St Albans* [1974] 3 All ER 283,   141
Bank Mellat v. *Nikpour (Mohammed Ebrahim)* [1985] FSR 87 CA,   275
Bank of East Asia Ltd v. *Tsien Wui Marble Factory Ltd* (1999) 2 HKCFAR 349, [2000] 1 HKLRD 268,   220, 265
Bank of England v. *Vagliano Brothers* [1891] AC 107,   100
Barleycorn Enterprises Ltd, Re [1970] 2 WLR 898,   343–344
Barras v. *Aberdeen Steam Trawling and Fishing Co. Ltd* [1933] AC 402,   221
Behrens v. *Bertram Mills Circus Ltd* [1957] 1 All ER 583,   129
Black-Clawson International Ltd v. *Papierwerke Waldhof-Aschaffenburg AG* [1975] AC 591, [1975] 1 All ER 810,   201, 224
Bourne v. *Keane* [1919] AC 815,   176
Bowardley Enterprises Ltd v. *Millennium Group Ltd* [2006] 4 HKC 329,   168–169
Brandy v. *Human Rights and Equal Opportunities Commission* (1994-5) 127 ALR 1,   152
Brutus v. *Cozens* [1973] AC 854,   124
Building Authority v. *Business Rights Ltd* [1999] 3 HKC 247,   173

C v. *Director of Public Prosecutions* [1995] 2 All ER 43,   167
C and Others v. *Director of Immigration* [2008] 2 HKC 165,   374
Cabaya v. *Kwan So Han Sandy* [2004] 3 HKC 87,   173–174
Cackett v. *Cackett* [1950] P 253,   170
Campbell v. *Hall* (1774) 1 Cowp 204, 98 ER 1045,   17
Caparo Industries plc v. *Dickman* [1990] 1 All ER 568,   132
Chan Chun Shing v. *Chang Chen Chin* [2009] HKCU 639 (unreported, CFI, HCPI 395/2008, 4 May 2009),   283
Chan Fung Lan v. *Lai Wai Chuen* [1997] 1 HKC 1,   231

Chan Pun Chung v. *HKSAR* (2000) 3 HKCFAR 392, [2000] 3 HKLRD 498,   207, 212
Chan Sang v. *Chan Kwok and others* [2016] HKCU 401,   378
Chan Yuen Yee v. *Chan Chuck Kwong* [2005] 2 HKLRD 416,   172
Chappell & Co. Ltd v. *Nestle Co. Ltd* [1959] 2 All ER 701,   35
Cheng Kai Nam Gary, Re [2002] 1 HKC 41,   133
Cheung Kong (Holdings) Ltd v. *Chan Wai Yip Albert* [2000] 4 HKC 591,   133
Cheung Lai Wah v. *Director of Immigration* [1998] 1 HKLRD 772,   171
Cheung Sou-yat v. *R* [1979] HKLR 630,   171
Chief Executive of HKSAR v. *President of the Legislative Council* [2017] 1 HKLRD 460 (CA),   95
Chief Supplementary Benefit Officer v. *Leary* [1985] 1 All ER 1061,   175
China Field Ltd v. *Appeal Tribunal (Buildings) (No. 2)* (2009) 12 HKCFAR 342, [2009] 5 HKLRD 662,   180, 212
Chow Ching Man v. *Sun Wah Ornament Manufactory Ltd* [1996] 2 HKC 460,   268
Christie v. *Leachinsky* [1947] AC 573,   241
Chu Wai Ha, Re [2005] 2 HKC 36,   86, 88
Chung Chi Cheung v. *R* [1939] AC 160,   374
CKJW, Re (unreported, CFI, HCMP 5231/001,10 Dec 2001),   171, 176
Collector of Customs v. *Pozzolanic (1993)* 43 FCR 280,   124
Collins v. *Wilcock* [1984] 3 All ER 374,   225
Colquhoun v. *Brooks* (1887) 19 QBD 400,   217
Commissioner of Inland Revenue v. *Indosuez W I Carr Securities Ltd* [2002] 1 HKLRD 308,   170, 173
Commissioner of Rating and Valuation v. *Agrila Ltd* (2001) 4 HKCFAR 83, [2001] 2 HKLRD 36,   223
Cormack v. *Cope* (1974) 131 CLR 432,   189
Corocraft Ltd v. *Pan American Airways Inc.* [1969] 1 QB 622,   202
Courtauld v. *Legh* (1869) LR 4 Ex 126,   219
Craig v. *Kanssen* [1943] 1 All ER 108,   269
Craig v. *State of South Australia* (1995) 184 CLR 163,   140
Crawley v. *Attorney General* [1987] HKCU 160,   241
Curtis v. *Chemical Cleaning and Dyeing Co. Ltd* [1951] 1 KB 805,   35
Cushing v. *Dupuy* (1880) 5 App Cas 409,   166
Customs and Excise Commissioners v. *Barclay Bank plc* [2007] 1 AC 181,   132

Davis v. *Johnson* [1979] AC 264, 172
De Lasala v. *De Lasala* [1980] AC 546, 178
Dembele Salifou v. *Director of Immigration* [2015] 4 HKC 294, 273
Derby & Co. Ltd v. *Weldon (No. 3)* [1989] 3 All ER 118, 173
Dewhurst v. *Feilden* (1845) 7 M & G 182, 222
Director of Immigration v. *Chong Fung Yuen* (2001) 4 HKCFAR 211, [2001] 2 HKLRD 533, 67, 85, 95–96, 229, 230
Director of Lands and Survey and Universal Patents v. *Industrial Designs Ltd* [1977] HKLTLR 81, 216
Donoghue v. *Stevenson* [1932] AC 562, 125–126, 128–131
DPP v. *Ottewell* [1970] AC 642, 225
DPP v. *Ping Lin* [1976] AC 574, 243
Dragon House Investment Ltd v. *Secretary for Transport* (2005) 8 HKCFAR 668, [2005] 4 HKLRD 480, 84

Excel Concrete Ltd v. *The Concrete Producers Association of Hong Kong Ltd & Ors* [2014] HKCU 1520, 272

Faith Bright Development Ltd v. *Ng Kwok Kuen* [2010] 5 HKLRD 425, 282
Farr v. *Butters Brothers and Co.* [1932] 2 KB 606, 128
Fatuma Binti Mohamed Bin Salim Bakhshuwen v. *Mohamed Bin Salim Bakhshuwen* [1952] AC 1, 178
FG Hemisphere Associates LLC v. *Democratic Republic of the Congo* [2010] 2 HKC 487, 94–95, 374
Fielding v. *Morley Corporation* [1899] 1 Ch 1, 219
First National Securities Ltd v. *Hegerty* [1985] QB 850, 170
Fisher v. *Raven* [1964] AC 210, 219
Foshan Hua Da Industrial Co. v. *Johnson Stokes & Master* [1999] 1 HKLRD 418, 120, 123
Fourth South Melbourne Building Society, Re (1883) 9 VLR (Eq) 54, 213

Gensburger v. *Gensburger* [1968] HKLR 403, 23
Geoffrey L. Berman v. *SPF CDO I, Ltd. And Others* HCMP 1321/2010, 325
Gilmerton Ltd v. *Polywin Holdings Ltd* [2005] HKLT 1, 155
Gold v. *Essex County Council* [1942] 1 KB 293, 128
Golden Eagle International (Group) Ltd v. *GR Investment Holdings Ltd* [2010] 5 HKC 317, 291
Good Success Catering Group Ltd, Re [2007] 1 HKLRD 453, 244
Goodrich v. *Paisner* [1957] AC 65 122, 123

Grand Pacific Equity Ltd v. *RSH Sports (HK) Ltd* [2006] HKCU 1816,   268
Grant v. *Australian Knitting Mills* [1936] AC 85,   129
Grey v. *Pearson* (1857) 10 ER 1216,   204
Gu Chu Kwong v. *R* (1952) 36 HKLR 353,   174

Ha v. *New South Wales* (1997) 189 CLR 465,   165
Hebei Import and Export Corp. v. *Polytek Engineering Co. Ltd.* (1999) 2 HKCFAR 111,   381
Hemens v. *Whitsbury Farm and Stud Ltd* [1988] 1 AC 601,   214
Herrington v. *British Railways Board* [1972] AC 877,   167
Hing Sheung Fung Investment Co. Ltd v. *Incorporated Owners of Man Kee Mansion* [2008] HKEC 217, [2008] HKCU 205,   363
HKFE Clearing Corp. Ltd v. *Yicko Futures Ltd* [2006] 2 HKC 233,   273
HKSAR v. *Abdou Maikido Abdoulkarim* [2016] HKCA 397,   256
HKSAR v. *Chan Yuk Ling* [2013] 1 HKLRD 1093,   242
HKSAR v. *Cheung Kwun Yin* (2009) 12 HKCFAR 568,   208, 223
HKSAR v. *Chiu Kwok Ho* [2004] HKEC 179,   242
HKSAR v. *Hung Chan* (2006) 9 HKCFAR 614. [2006] 3 HKLRD 841,   163–164
HKSAR v. *Lam Kwong Wai* (2006) 9 HKCFAR 574, [2006] 3 HKLRD 808,   138–139, 207, 212, 258
HKSAR v. *Lau San Ching* [2004] 1 HKLRD 683,   230–231
HKSAR v. *Luk Kin Peter Joseph* (2016) 19 HKCFAR 619,   216
HKSAR v. *Ma Wai Kwan David* [1997] 2 HKC 315, [1997] HKLRD 761,   100, 111
HKSAR v. *Mui Kwok Keung* [2013] HKEC 610,   326
HKSAR v. *Ngai Yiu Ching* [2011] 5 HKLRD 690,   259
HKSAR v. *Ng Kung Siu & Another* [1999] 3 HKLRD 907,   187
HKSAR v. *Ng Po On* (2008) 11 HKCFAR 91, [2008] 4 HKLRD 176,   212
HKSAR v. *Ngo Van Nam* [2016] HKCA 396,   256
HKSAR v. *Tam Yuk Ha* [1997] HKLRD 1031,   230
HKSAR v. *Tang Hoi On Barry* [2003] 3 HKC 123,   225
HKSAR v. *Tse Yee Ping* (2016) 19 HKCFAR 427,   208
HKSAR v Wang Ping Shui [2001] 1 HKC 600,   219
HKSAR v. *Yau Mee Kwan* [2004] 1 HKLRD A6,   223
Ho Choi Wan v. *Hong Kong Housing Authority* (2005) 8 HKCFAR 628, [2005] 4 HKLRD 706,   205
Ho Po Chu v. *Tung Chee Wah* [2006] 1 HKC 527,   169

Hoi Kong Container Services Co. Ltd v. *Bewise Motors Co. Ltd* [1997]
   2 HKC 615,   177
Hollier v. *Rambler Motors (AMC) Ltd* [1972] 2 QB 71,   177
Hong Kong Clays & Kaolin Co. Ltd v. *Director of Lands* [1999]
   1 HKLRD 527,   223
Hong Kong Racing Pigeon Association Ltd v. *Attorney General* [1995]
   2 HKC 201,   213
Hong Lok School Ltd v. *Chow Sai Yiu* [2003] HKCU 819,   273
Huddart Parker and Co. Pty Ltd v. *Moorehead* (1909) 8 CLR 330,   138,
   152
Huddersfield Police Authority v. *Watson* [1947] KB 842,   172, 174
Hung Chan Wa v. *HKSAR* [2005] 3 HKLRD 291,   225

Ibrahim v. *R* [1914] AC 599,   243
INA Mueller v. *Hung Fat Cheung Investors Ltd* [2004] HKLT 50,   155
Incorporated Owners of Tropicana Gardens v. *Tropicana Gardens
   Management* [2001] 4 HKC 90,   174–175
Ind Coope & Co. v. *Emmerson* (1887) LR 12 App Cas 300,   111
Invercargill City Council v. *Hamlin* [1996] 1 All ER 756,   178–179

Jade City International Ltd v. *Director of Lands* [2002] 3 HKLRD 33,   201,
   207–209, 215
John v. *Federal Commissioner of Taxation* (1989) 166 CLR 417,   166
Julita F Raza v. *Chief Executive in Council* (unreported, CA, Civ App 218 of
   2005, 19 Jul 2006),   80, 86
Julita F Raza v. *Chief Executive in Council* (unreported, CFI, HCAL
   30/2003, 4 Jan 2005),   86

Kleinwort Benson Ltd v. *Lincoln City Council* [1998] 4 All ER 513,   167
Kong Kam-Piu v. *R* [1973] HKLR 120,   205
Koo Sze Yiu v. *Chief Executive of HKSAR* (2006) 9 HKCFAR 441, [2006]
   1 HKLRD 455,   86, 88, 102
Kutner v. *Phillips* [1891] 2 QBD 267,   199
Kwong Kwan-Nang Louis v. *Commissioner of Inland Revenue* [1989]
   2 HKLR 326,   214
Kwong Pak-yom v. *R* [1965] HKLR 931,   174

L'Office Cherifien des Phosphates v. *Yamashita-Shinnihon Steamship Co.
   Ltd* [1994] 1 All ER 20,   225

Lam Woo Shang (No. 2) v. *Commissioner of Inland Revenue* [1961] HKLR 609,   221
Lau Cheong v. *HKSAR* (2002) 5 HKCFAR 415, [2002] 2 HKLRD 612,   84, 86, 88, 260
Lau Chu v. *Lau Tang Su-ping* [1989] HKLR 470,   176
Lau Kong Yung v. *Director of Immigration* (1999) 2 HKCFAR 300, [1999] 3 HKLRD 778,   67, 94–96, 176, 230
Lau Kwai Yin v. *Tack Hsin Restaurant (London) Ltd* [2016] 4 HKC 460,   272
Lau Kwok Fai v. *Secretary for Justice* (unreported, CFI, HCAL 177 and 180 of 2002, 10 Jun 2003),   86
Lau Kwok Fai v. *Secretary for Justice* [2004] 3 HKLRD 570,   86
Lau Wai Chau, Re [2000] 1 HKLRD 924, (2000) 3 HKCFAR 98,   134
Lee Fred (Trustee in Bankruptcy of the Property of Leung Chin Yeung) v. *Leung Chin Yeung* [2007] 1 HKC 164,   208–209
Lee Fuk Hing v. *HKSAR* (2004) 7 HKCFAR 600,   242
Lee Yih Jen v. *Chung Newspapers Ltd* [1983] 2 HKC 550,   174
Leung Chung Hang Sixtus v. *President of Legislative Council* [2018] HKCFI, [2019] 1 HKLRD 292,   96, 136
Leung Kwan-fu v. *R* [1977] HKLR 175,   23
Leung Kwok Hung v. *Chief Executive of HKSAR* (unreported, CA, CACV 73 and 87 of 2006, 10 May 2006),   86, 88
Leung Kwok Hung v. *Chief Executive of HKSAR* (unreported, CFI, HCAL 107 of 2005, 9 Feb 2006),   88
Leung Kwok Hung v. *HKSAR* (2005) 8 HKCFAR 229, [2005] 3 HKLRD 164,   85, 101
Leung Sai Lun Robert v. *Leung May Ling* (1999) 2 HKCFAR 94, [1999] 1 HKLRD 649,   200, 203
Leung Sai Lun Robert v. *Leung May Ling* [1998] 1 HKC 26,   203
Leung T C William Roy v. *Secretary for Justice* [2005] 3 HKC 77,   101
Leung T C William Roy v. *Secretary for Justice* [2006] 4 HKLRD 211,   101
Lindley v. *Rutter* [1981] QB 128,   241
Lisbeth Enterprises Ltd v. *Mandy Luk* (2006) 9 HKCFAR 131, [2006] 1 HKLRD 1005,   213
Liu Chi Cheung v. *Tsang Wai Choi* [1958] HKDCLR 165,   175
Liu Sing Lee v. *Luk Fong Chun Richard* [1995] 1 HKC 499,   203
Liu Ying Lan v. *Liu Tung Yiu* [2003] 3 HKLRD 249,   134
London Tramways v. *London County Council* [1898] AC 375,   166

London Transport Executive v. *Betts (Valuation Officer)* [1959] AC 213,   215
London Transport Executive v. *Betts* [1959] AC 213,   123
Loyal Luck Trading Ltd v. *Tam Chun Wah* [2007] 4 HKLRD 917,   114–115, 360
Lui Hau Man v. *Director of Immigration* (unreported, CFI, HCAL134/2002, 21 Jan 2003),   174
Lui Tat Hang Louis v. *The Post-Release Supervision Board, Commissioner of Correctional Services* (unreported, CFI, HCAL154/1999, 14 Feb 2000),   175
Luk Ka Cheung v. *The Market Misconduct* Tribunal [2009] 1 HKC 1,   88, 138, 151

Mabo v. *Queensland (No. 2)* (1992) 175 CLR 1,   167
Marblesum Ltd v. *Poon Shu Pang* (unreported, CFI, HCCW 628/2001, 10 Jun 2005),   362
Mareva Compania Naviera SA v. *International Bulk Carriers SA* [1980] 1 All ER 213,   274
Matheson PFC Ltd v. *Jansen* [1994] 2 HKC 250,   217, 221
Maunsell v. *Olins* [1974] 3 WLR 835,   202
Medical Council of Hong Kong v. *Chow Siu Shek David* (2000) 3 HKCFAR 144, [2000] 1 HKLRD 674, [2000] 2 HKC 428,   204, 207–209, 219, 221, 226
Mercantile Bank of India v. *Central Bank* [1938] AC 287,   166
Merribee Pastoral Industries Pty Ltd v. *Australia and New Zealand Banking Group Ltd* (1998) 28 ASCR 103,   140
Miliangos v. *George Frank (Textiles) Ltd* [1976] AC 443,   171, 173
Millar v. *Taylor* (1769) 4 Burr 2303; 98 ER 201,   222
Miller v Minister of Pensions [1947] 2 All ER 372,   257, 275
Ming Pao Newspapers Ltd v. *Attorney General* [1998] AC 906,   187
Minister of Pensions v. *Higham* [1948] 2 KB 153,   173
Mita Kogyo Kabushiki Kaisha v. *Mitac Inc.* [1993] 1 HKC 207,   199
Mobil Petroleum Co. Inc. v. *Registrar of Trade Marks* [2000] 4 HKC 670,   171, 174
Morelle v. *Wakeling* [1955] 2 QB 379,   171
Myers v. *United States* 272 US 106, 71 L Ed 160 (1926),   82

Nanyang Commercial Bank Ltd v. *Lam Man Ki* [2003] 2 HKLRD 432,   223
Nauthum Chau Ching Kay v. *HKSAR* (2002) 5 HKCFAR 540,   243

Ng Chun Fai Stephen & Anor v. *Tamco Electrical & Electronics (HK) Ltd*
   [1993] 1 HKC 160,   275
Ng Fung Hong Ltd v. *ABC* [1998] 1 HKC 213,   380
Ng Ka Ling v. *Director of Immigration* (1999) 2 HKCFAR 4, [1999]
   1 HKLRD 315,   85, 95, 101
Ng Ka Ling v. *Director of Immigration (No. 2)* (1999) 2 HKCFAR 141,
   [1998] 1 HKLRD 577,   94–96, 176
Ng Siu Tung v. *Director of Immigration* (2002) 5 HKCFAR 1, [2002]
   I HKLRD 561,   95
Ng Yuen-Shiu v. *Attorney General* [1981] HKLR 352,   172
North Sea Continental Shelf cases *(Germany* v. *Demark, Germany* v.
   The Netherlands), ICJ Rep (1969) 3,   373
Numeric City Ltd v. *Lau Chi Wing* [2016] 5 HKC 448,   284

Oceania Manufacturing Co. v. *Pang Kwong-hon* [1979] HKLR 445,   23
Ogden Industries Pty Ltd v. *Lucas* [1970] AC 113,   176
Ormond Investment Ltd v. *Betts* [1928] AC 143,   221
Owen John Inglis v. *Loh Lai Kuen* (unreported, CFI, HCAL 74/2004,
   15 Oct 2004),   174

Pacific Electric Wire & Cable Co. Ltd v. *Harmutty Ltd & Ors* [2009]
   2 HKC 330,   271
Parkin v. *Thorold* (1852) 16 Beav 59, 51 ER 698,   110
Payne v. *Cave* (1789) 3 TR 148,   42
PCCW-HKT Telephone Ltd v. *Telecommunications Authority* (2005)
   8 HKCFAR 337, [2005] 3 HKLRD 235,   223
Peart v. *Stewart* [1983] 2 AC 109,   215
Pepper (Inspector of Taxes) v. *Hart* [1993] AC 593,   222–224
Pharmaceutical Society of Great Britain v. *Boots Cash Chemists Ltd*
   [1953] 1 QB 401,   42
Poon Hau Kei v. *Hsin Cheong Construction Co. Ltd* [2004] 2 HKC 235,   272
Pratt v. *Attorney General for Jamaica* [1993] 4 All ER 769,   166
Pun Jong-sau v. *Poon Wing-kong* [1979] HKLR 662,   219

Qualcast (Wolverhampton) Ltd v. *Haynes* [1959] AC 743,   123
Quazi v. *Quazi* [1980] AC 744,   215

Randall v. *R* [2002] 1 WLR 2237,   247
R v. *Allen* [1985] AC 1029, [1985] 2 All ER 641,   224–225

R v. *Bates* [1952] 2 All ER 842,   219
R v. *Bathurst* [1968] 2 QB 99,   258
R v. *Brosch* [1988] Crim LR 734,   241
R v. *Chandra Thanwardas Mirchandani* [1992] 2 HKCLR 174,   310
R v. *Cunningham* [1959] 1 QB 288,   56
R v. *Dudley and Stephens* [1881-85] All ER 61,   40
R v. *Edgehill* [1963] 1 QB 593,   221
R v. *Edmundson* (1859) 28 LJ (MC) 213,   215
R v. *Fu Yan* [1992] 2 HKCLR 59,   310
R v. *Gould* [1968] 1 All ER 899, 2 QB 65,   171–172
R v. *Hallstrom, ex parte W (No. 2)* [1986] QB 1090,   225
R v. *Horseferry Road Metropolitan Stipendiary Magistrate ex parte Siadatan* [1991] 1 All ER 324,   224
R v. *Jackson* [1974] QB 802,   171
R v. *Kwong Kui Wing* [1996] 6 HKPLR 125,   175
R v. *Kwong Lung Co. Ltd* [1986] 1 HKC 199,   217
R v. *L* (1991) 174 CLR 379,   167
R v. *Marais* [1902] AC 51,   22
R v. *Parole Board ex parte Wilson* [1991] 1 QB 740,   172
R v. *Patterson* [1962] 2 QB 429,   171
R v. *Pope* [2001] EWCA Crim 972,   171
R v. *Porter* [1949] 2 KB 128,   170
R v. *R* [1991] 4 All ER 481,   167
R v. *Secretary of State for the Home Department (ex parte Khawaja)* [1983] 2 WLR 321,   167
R v. *Soo Fat-ho* [1992] 2 HKCLR 114,   207
R v. *Spencer* [1985] QB 771,   170
R v. *The District Judge of Hong Kong; ex parte the Attorney General* (1955) 39 HKLR 8,   140
R v. *Trade Practices Tribunal, ex parte Tasmanian Breweries Pty Ltd* (1969-70) 123 CLR 361,   82
R v. *Turner* [1970] 2 WLR 1093,   253
R v Tyrone Justices [1917] 2 IR 437,   141
R v. *West Yorkshire Coroner; ex parte Smith (No. 2)* [1985] 1 QB 1096,   141
R v. *Yu Man Wu* [1995] 2 HKCLR 202,   256
Re China Star Enterprise Hong Kong Ltd [2013] 5 HKLRD 271,   227
Ridsdale v. *Clifton* (1877) 2 PD 306,   166

Sea Legend Holdings Ltd v. *China Taiping Insurance (HK) Co. Ltd & Ors* [2013] HKCU 2391, 268
Secretary for Justice v. *Lam Tat Ming* [2000] 2 HKLRD 431, 243
Secretary for Justice v. *Lau Kwok Fai* (2005) 8 HKCFAR 304, [2005] 3 HKLRD 88, 84, 86
Secretary for Justice v. *Lau Suk Han* [1998] 2 HKC 263, 218
Secretary for Justice v. *Oriental Press Group Ltd* [1998] 2 HKC 627, 225
Secretary for Justice v. *Tang Bun* [1999] 3 HKC 647, 218
Secretary for Justice v. *To Kan Chi* (2000) 3 HKCFAR 481, [2000] 3 HKLRD 756, 134, 139
Secretary for Justice v. *Wong Chi-fung and Others* [2018] 2 HKC 50, 259
Secretary for Justice v. *Wong Sau Fong* [1998] 3 HKC 544, 170–172, 176
Secretary for Justice v. *Yau Yuk Lung and Another* [2006] 4 HKLRD 196, 361
Secretary for Justice v. *Yau Yuk Lung* (2007) 10 HKCFAR 335, [2007] 3 HKLRD 903, 85, 101, 188, 191
Secretary of State for Defence v. *Guardian Newspapers Ltd* [1985] AC 339, 225
Setaffa Investments Ltd, Re [1998] 2 HKLRD 236, 225
Shun Kai Finance Co. Ltd v. *Japan Leasing (HK) Ltd (in liq) (No. 2)* [2001] 1 HKC 636, 180
Singway Ltd v. *Attorney General* [1974] HKLR 275, 217
Siu Yin Kwan v. *Eastern Insurance Co. Ltd* [1994] 1 All ER 213, 219
Society for the Protection of the Harbour Ltd v. *Chief Executive in Council* [2004] 2 HKLRD 902, 86
Spectrum Plus Ltd (in liq), Re [2005] 2 AC 680, 139, 163, 165, 182

T v. *Commissioner of Police* (2014) 17 HKCFAR 593, 201, 208, 212, 225
Tai Hing Cotton Mill Ltd v. *Liu Chong Hing Bank Ltd* [1985] 2 All ER 947, 179
Tam Nga Yin v. *Director of Immigration* (2001) 4 HKCFAR 251, [2001] 2 HKLRD 644, 229
Tang Kai-chung v. *Tang Chik-shang* [1970] HKLR 276, 23
Tang Kam-Yip v. *Yau Kung School* [1986] HKLR 448, 128, 181
Texas v. *Johnson* (1989) 491 US 397, 187
The Incorporated Owners of Phase One of Whampoa Estate v. *The Bank of Communications* [2004] HKLT 95, 155
Thompson v. *Goold & Co.* [1910] AC 409, 204

Tong Kin Hing v. Autron Mauritius Corp & Ors [2010] 1 HKLRD 77,   285
Tourmaline Ltd, Re [2000] 4 HKC 348,   361
Town Planning Board v. Town Planning Appeal Board (2017)
    20 HKCFAR 196,   228
Trade Practices Commission v. CC (NSW) Pty Ltd (1995) 58 FCR 426,   273
Tsang Shiu Tim v. Hang Fong [1959] HKLR 308,   175
Tse Wai Chun Paul v. Solicitors Disciplinary Tribunal [2002] 4 HKC
    1,   140–141
Tsoi Shun-hing v. R [1977] HKLR 408,   216
Tyler, Re ex parte Foley (1994) 181 CLR 18,   128
Tyrone Crystal Ltd v. European Asian Bank [1985] 2 HKC 762,   214

Ubamaka Edward Wilson v. Secretary for Security & Another
    [2013] 2 HKU 75,   372
United States v. Eichman (1990) 496 US 310,   187
Unruh v. Seeberger (2007) 10 HKCFAR 31,   325
Urban Parking Ltd v. The Commissioner of Rating and Valuation
    [2003] HKLT 50,   155

Vacher & Sons Ltd v. London Society of Compositors [1913] AC 107,   203
Vallejos v. Commissioner of Registration (2013) 16 HKCFAR 45,   208, 210
Victoria Sporting Club Ltd v. Hannam [1970] AC 55,   203
Victorian Stevedoring & General Contracting Co. Pty Ltd v. Dignan
    (Dignan's Case) (1931) 46 CLR 73,   197
Viro v. R (1978) 141 CLR 88,   178
Viscountess Rhondda's Claim [1922] 2 AC 339,   201

W v. Registrar of Marriages [2013] 3 HKLRD 90,   212
Wan v. Director of Agriculture, Fisheries and Conservation
    [2017] 5 HKLRD 141,   224
Wells v. Derwent Plastics Ltd [1978] ICR 424,   175
Whitley v. Stumbles [1930] AC 544,   219
Wing Hang Bank Ltd v. Crystal Jet International Ltd [2005] 2 HKC
    638,   271
Winnie Lo v. HKSAR [2012] HKEC 263,   326
Wong Kam-ying v. Man Chi-tai [1967] HKLR 201,   22
Wong Tze Yam v. Commissioner of Police [2009] 5 HKLRD,   238
Wong Yu Hing v. Tong Pak Wing [1995] 1 HKC 160,   225

Wong Yu-Shi v. *Wong Ying-Kuen* [1957] HKLR 420,   134
Woolmington v. *DPP* [1935] AC 462,   60, 257

Yau Kwong Man v. *Secretary for Security* [2002] 3 HKC 457,   86, 138
Yau Shun-po v. *Oriental Fire Insurance Co. Ltd* [1986] HKLR 72,   173
Yau Wai Ching v. *Chief Executive of HKSAR* (2017) 20 HKCFAR 390,   67, 95–96, 176, 230
Yeung Wing v. *VSL Engineers (Hong Kong)* [1981] HKLR 130,   180
Yew Bon Tew v. *Kenderaan Bas Mora* [1982] 3 All ER 833,   225
Young v. *Bristol Aeroplane Co. Ltd* [1944] KB 718,   168, 170–171
Yuen Sha v. *Tse Chi Pan* [1999] 2 HKLRD 28,   340
Yung Chi Keung v. *Protection of Wages on Insolvency Board* (2016) 19 HKCFAR 469,   212

Z v. *Director of Legal Aid and another* [2011] HKCU 1358,   310
ZN v. *Secretary for Justice* [2017] 1 HKC 340,   180

Table of Legislation

The following is the list of legislation, including treaties and arrangements, that are cited in this book:

Name of Legislation

Act of Settlement 1701, 6
Adaptation of Laws (Courts and Tribunals) Ordinance 1998, 101
Adaptation of Laws (Interpretative Provisions) Ordinance 1998, 101
Agreement between the Mainland and Hong Kong on Achieving Basic Liberalization of Trade in Services in Guangdong, 384
Agreement on Trade in Services, 384
Air Pollution Control Ordinance (Cap. 311), 155
Airport Authority (Amendment) Ordinance 2004, 353
Application of English Law Ordinance (Cap. 88), 22–23, 112, 134
Apprenticeship Ordinance (Cap. 47), 156
Arbitration Ordinance (Cap. 341), 298
Arbitration Ordinance (Cap. 609), 294–296, 298, 299–302, 380–381
Arbitration (Appointment of Arbitrators and Mediators and Decision on Number of Arbitrators) Rules (Cap. 609C), 300
Arrangement Concerning Mutual Enforcement of Arbitral Awards Between the Mainland and the Hong Kong Special Administrative Region, 380
Arrangement for Mutual Service of Judicial Documents in Civil and Commercial Proceedings between the Mainland and Hong Kong Courts, 376
Arrangement on Mutual Taking of Evidence in Civil and Commercial Matters between the Courts of the Mainland and the Hong Kong Special Administrative Region, 379
Arrangement on Reciprocal Recognition and Enforcement of Judgments in Civil and Commercial Matters by the Courts of the Mainland and of the Hong Kong SAR Pursuant to Choice of Court Agreements between Parties Concerned, 377

Arrangement on the Establishment of a Reciprocal Notification Mechanism between the Mainland Public Security Authorities and the Hong Kong Police, 389

Bankruptcy Rules (Cap. 6A), 360
Barristers (Qualification for Admission and Pupillage) Rules (Cap. 159AC), 16
Basic Law of the Hong Kong Special Administrative Region, 4–5, 7–10, 12–14, 24–26, 31, 35, 37–38, 42, 47–48, 59, 62–76, 82–101, 111–112, 133–138, 141, 145, 147, 152, 165–166, 176, 178, 180, 185–196, 198, 210, 228–230, 237, 239, 245, 247, 257, 305, 329, 332, 337, 366–368, 370–372, 375
Bills of Exchange Ordinance (Cap. 19), 184
Building Management Ordinance (Cap. 344), 155
Buildings Ordinance (Cap. 123), 155

Charter of the Colony of Hong Kong 1843, 99
Chinese Medicine Ordinance (Cap. 549), 247, 353
Chief Executive Election Ordinance (Cap. 569), 73
Commonwealth of Australia Constitution Act (Cth), 197
Community Service Orders Ordinance (Cap. 378), 262
Companies Ordinance (Cap. 622), 123, 332, 335, 347
Companies (Amendment) Ordinance 2018, 332
Companies (Forms) Regulations, 360
Companies (Winding Up and Miscellaneous Provisions) Ordinance (Cap. 32), 123
Competition Ordinance (Cap. 619), 140–141, 157–158
Constitutional Reform Act 2005, 111, 179
Consumer Goods Safety Ordinance (Cap. 456), 39
Control of Obscene and Indecent Articles Ordinance (Cap. 390), 159
Convention for the Suppression of the Illicit Traffic in Dangerous Drug 1936, 39
Convention of Peking 1860, 17, 63
Convention on the Marking of Plastic Explosives for the Purpose of Detection, Montreal 1991, 371
Convention on the Service Abroad of Judicial and Extrajudicial Documents in Civil or Commercial Matters 1965, 376

Convention on Third Party Liability in the Field of Nuclear Energy, Paris 1960, 371
Convention Relating to the Status of Refugees (Persecution) 1951, 322
Copyright Ordinance (Cap. 39), 360
Coroners (Fees) Rules (Cap. 504D), 197
Costs in Criminal Cases Ordinance (Cap. 492), 218
Crimes Ordinance (Cap. 200), 27, 35, 37, 40, 42, 59, 85, 352
Criminal Code Act 1975 (Cth), 184
Criminal Code Act 1879 (Qld), 184
Criminal Code Act Compilation Act 1913 (WA), 184
Criminal Procedure Ordinance (Cap. 221), 148–151, 241, 251, 258, 260–261
Custom and Excise Ordinance (Cap. 342), 247

Dangerous Drugs Ordinance (Cap. 134), 164, 218, 237, 247, 360
Demolished Buildings (Redevelopment of Sites) Ordinance (Cap. 337), 155
Dentists Registration Ordinance (Cap. 156), 221
District Court Ordinance (Cap. 336), 14, 141, 143, 149–150, 171, 265, 277, 280, 285
Domestic and Cohabitation Relationships Violence Ordinance (Cap. 189), 213
Drug Addiction Treatment Centres Ordinance (Cap. 244), 261
Dutiable Commodities Ordinance (Cap. 98), 247

Elections (Corrupt and Illegal Conduct) Ordinance (Cap. 554), 38, 42, 245
Electoral Affairs Commission Ordinance (Cap. 541), 37–38
Employees' Compensation Ordinance (Cap. 282), 149, 314
Employment Ordinance (Cap. 57), 35, 42, 55, 156
Employment (Amendment) Ordinance 2007, 185
English Arbitration Act 1950, 298
Estate Agents (Licensing) Regulation (Cap. 511A), 197

Firearms and Ammunition Ordinance (Cap. 238), 247, 258
First International Opium Convention 1912, 39
Foreign Judgments (Reciprocal Enforcement) Ordinance (Cap. 319), 377

Government Rent (Assessment and Collection) Ordinance (Cap. 515), 155
Guangzhou-Shenzhen-Hong Kong Express Rail Link (Co-Location) Ordinance (Cap. 632), 97

Heung Yee Kuk Ordinance (Cap. 1097), 192
High Court Ordinance (Cap. 4), 14, 111, 140–141, 147–149, 265, 274, 276–277, 280, 285
Hong Kong Act 1985, 101
Hong Kong Bill of Rights Ordinance (Cap. 383), 92, 171, 188, 240–242, 257–258, 305, 309, 372
Hong Kong Court of Final Appeal Ordinance (Cap. 484), 14, 140–141, 145
Hong Kong Letters Patent 1917, 17, 81, 99
Hong Kong Royal Instructions 1917, 17, 82
Hong Kong Reunification Ordinance 1997, 101
Housing Ordinance (Cap. 283), 155

Immigration Ordinance (Cap. 115), 92, 210, 237–239, 247, 322
Immigration Service Ordinance (Cap. 331), 247
Import and Export Ordinance (Cap. 60), 247
Independent Commission Against Corruption Ordinance (Cap. 204), 244–246
International Air Services Transit Agreement, Chicago 1944, 371
International Convention relating to the Simplification of Customs Formalities, and Protocol of Signature, Geneva 1923, 371
Independent Police Complaints Council Ordinance (Cap. 604), 243–244
Inland Revenue Ordinance (Cap. 112), 39
Interception of Communications and Surveillance Ordinance (Cap. 589), 86
International Covenant on Civil and Political Rights 1966, 59, 187, 312, 372
International Covenant on Economic, Social and Cultural Rights 1966, 59
International Labour Conventions, 59
Interpretation and General Clauses Ordinance (Cap. 1), 103–104, 112, 196, 198, 203, 206, 208, 213, 219–220, 225, 230–231, 331, 334, 336, 359

Joint Declaration 1984, 24–25, 63–65, 67–70, 83, 91, 188, 229
Judicial Committee Act 1833, 145

Jury Ordinance (Cap. 3), 14–15
Juvenile Offenders Ordinance (Cap. 226), 151, 184
Juvenile Offenders (Amendment) Ordinance 2003, 184

Labour Tribunal Ordinance (Cap. 25), 141, 144, 156, 156, 221, 233
Land Acquisition (Possessory Title) Ordinance (Cap. 130), 155
Land (Compulsory Sale for Redevelopment) Ordinance (Cap. 545), 155
Landlord and Tenant (Consolidation) Ordinance (Cap. 7), 154, 185
Lands Tribunal Ordinance (Cap. 17), 141, 144, 148, 154–155
Laws (Loose-leaf Publication) Ordinance 1990, 331
Legal Aid in Criminal Cases Rules (Cap. 221D), 311, 315
Legal Aid Ordinance (Cap. 91), 11, 311–314, 316
Legal Aid Services Council Ordinance (Cap. 489), 316
Legal Practitioners Ordinance (Cap. 159), 15–16, 221, 306, 308–309
Legislation Publication Ordinance (Cap. 614), 331, 337
Legislative Council Ordinance (Cap. 542), 9, 75
Legislative Council (Powers and Privileges) Ordinance (Cap. 382), 9, 75
Limitation Ordinance (Cap. 347), 220, 269, 382

Mainland Judgments (Reciprocal Enforcement) Ordinance
  (Cap. 597), 377–378
Magistrates Ordinance (Cap. 227), 14, 143–144, 148–151, 218, 241,
  251–253, 261, 311
Marriage Ordinance (Cap. 181), 201
Mass Transit Railway By-Laws (Cap. 556B), 197
Mass Transit Railway Ordinance (Cap. 556), 197
Mass Transit Railway Regulations (Cap. 556A), 197
Matrimonial Proceedings and Property Ordinance (Cap. 192), 149
Mediation Ordinance (Cap. 620), 288–290
Medical Registration Ordinance (Cap. 161), 221, 226
Mental Health Ordinance (Cap. 136), 262
Minor Employment Claims Adjudication Board Ordinance
  (Cap. 453), 144, 156

National Flag and National Emblem Ordinance 1997, 187
New Territories Ordinance (Cap. 97), 134
New York Convention on the Recognition and Enforcement of Foreign
  Arbitral Awards 1958, 295, 380

Offences Against the Person Ordinance (Cap. 212), 260
Official Languages Ordinance (Cap. 5), 102, 133, 230

Personal Data (Privacy) Ordinance (Cap. 486), 333
Pharmacy and Poisons Ordinance (Cap. 138), 104–105, 247
Pneumoconiosis and Mesothelioma (Compensation) (Assessment of Levy) Regulations (Cap. 360A), 197
Police Force Ordinance (Cap. 232), 235, 237–239, 241, 243, 251
Prevention of Bribery Ordinance (Cap. 201), 48, 205, 216, 245–246
Private Bills Ordinance (Cap. 69), 193
Probate and Administration Ordinance (Cap. 10), 148
Probation of Offenders Ordinance (Cap. 298), 262
Probation of Offenders Rules (Cap. 298A), 262
Protection of Children and Juveniles Ordinance (Cap. 213), 319
Public Order Act 1936, 124
Public Order Ordinance (Cap. 245), 85, 231, 237–238

Rating Ordinance (Cap. 116), 155
Reformatory Schools Ordinance (Cap. 225), 184
Regional Flag and Regional Emblem Ordinance, 187
Rehabilitation Centres Ordinance (Cap. 567), 261
Revised Edition of the Laws Ordinance 1965, 330
Road Traffic (Driving Licences) Regulations (Cap. 374B), 41
Road Traffic Ordinance (Cap. 374), 41, 237, 262
Roads (Works, Use and Compensation) Ordinance (Cap. 370), 41
Rules of the District Court (Cap. 336H), 268–274, 276–277, 280–285
Rules of the High Court (Cap. 4A), 158, 268–274, 276–277, 280–285, 287, 290, 376

Sale of Goods Act 1893, 23
Sale of Goods Ordinance (Cap. 26), 23, 39
Second Convention of Peking 1898, 17, 24
Second International Opium Convention 1925, 39
Securities and Futures Ordinance (Cap. 571), 99, 105–107, 158, 214, 333, 336, 360
Sewage Tunnels (Statutory Easements) Ordinance (Cap. 483), 209
Sex Discrimination Ordinance (Cap. 480), 149
Single Convention on Narcotic Drugs 1961, 39
Small Claims Tribunal Ordinance (Cap. 338), 35, 141, 144, 148, 153–154

Summary Offences Ordinance (Cap. 228), 215, 232
Supreme Court Ordinance 1844, 18, 21, 23, 142, 306
Supreme Court Ordinance 1845, 21, 142
Supreme Court Ordinance 1846, 21, 142
Supreme Court Ordinance 1873, 21–22, 111, 134
Supreme Court Ordinance 1975, 143–144, 147
Supreme Court (Summary Jurisdiction) Ordinance 1873, 143
Surviving Spouses' and Children's Pensions Ordinance (Cap. 79), 39

The Mainland and Hong Kong Closer Economic Partnership Arrangement, 382
Trainee Solicitors Rules (Cap. 159J), 16
Training Centres Ordinance (Cap. 280), 261
Treaty of Nanking 1842, 17, 63
Town Planning Ordinance (Cap. 131), 217

Unconscionable Contracts Ordinance (Cap. 458), 39
United Nations Commission on International Trade Law Rules of Arbitration, 296, 298
United Nations Convention Against Torture and Other Cruel, Inhuman or Degrading Treatment or Punishment 1984, 321
United States Constitution, 77

Vienna Convention on Consular Relations 1963, 370
Vienna Convention on Diplomatic Relations 1961, 370

Wills Ordinance (Cap. 30), 200–201
Wills, Probate and Administration Act 1898 (NSW), 204

Introduction and Overview 1

Chapter Highlights

- Aims of the Book 1
- Elements of the Legal System 3
- Historical Development of Hong Kong's Legal System 16
- The Enterprise of Studying Law 27
- Structure of the Book 30

Aims of the Book

For a society to function, there must be some system for the regulation of interactions between individuals in society. More primitive societies may have largely relied on customs and moral norms to regulate such interactions. Across much of the modern world today, law has taken on a fundamental role in governing human behaviour. While law is not, even in modern societies, the sole mechanism for regulating human conduct, the creation and maintenance of a functioning legal system has been of prime importance in providing for social stability and the well-being of humans in advanced societies. Indeed, the subjection of individuals and governments to law can be seen to be one of the major achievements of the human race.

For Hong Kong, the legal system established by the British during the period of colonisation is widely seen as one of the more positive legacies of British rule over the territory. With the return of sovereignty over Hong Kong to China on 1 July 1997, the common law legal tradition in Hong Kong is regarded as a major asset of the Special Administrative Region which is vital not only in preserving the freedoms and existing way of life of Hong Kong residents but also in placing Hong Kong on strong foundations as the city strives to preserve and enhance its regional and international significance in the wake of competition from other major metropolises both in Mainland China and elsewhere in Asia.

The transfer of sovereignty over Hong Kong in 1997 has sought to largely preserve the existing laws and legal system of Hong Kong, but the legal constitutional framework and the social and political landscape within which the legal system exists have been vastly altered after 1997. Hong Kong is unique in that under the concept of 'one country, two systems', the territory is able to maintain a common law legal system, underpinned by liberal ideology, within a country that operates under a socialist and civil law tradition. The period leading to the handover was beset with disputes and debate over the design of the new system, with concerns as to the extent to which the existing legal system in Hong Kong could survive the handover and remain independent from the Mainland. There have been various controversies since the handover concerning the operation of the concept of 'one country, two systems', including controversies within or affecting the legal sphere. While the worst fears have not to date been realised, continuing controversies highlight the tensions in the system.

This book aims to provide an introduction to the Hong Kong legal system for first-year students who are coming into contact with studying law, as well as students of other disciplines, and practitioners and scholars from other jurisdictions who are looking for a comprehensive and user-friendly overview of Hong Kong's legal system. More specifically, it highlights major issues and tensions across different aspects of the legal system under the new constitutional framework, especially after the return of sovereignty of Hong Kong to the People's Republic of China (PRC).

The book also seeks to provide students with a basic understanding of the main institutions in the Hong Kong legal system and with basic skills in finding, understanding and interpreting the law. As an introductory text for students studying the law in Hong Kong for the first time, the book does not aim to be comprehensive or to provide a detailed or advanced understanding of all aspects of Hong Kong's legal system. It is intended to equip first-year law students with the basic knowledge and skills which are needed for their further learning of the law. The book is also intended to provide an introduction to the Hong Kong legal system for non-law students. The law reaches into all facets of society and thus some understanding of the legal system may also be important for students whose core discipline is in another area. This book therefore provides an introduction to the legal system in Hong Kong for both first-year law students, students of other disciplines and those from other jurisdictions interested in learning more about Hong Kong's legal system.

Elements of the Legal System

Before discussing the historical development of the legal system of Hong Kong, this section introduces what a study of a legal system involves. The Hong Kong legal system is an amalgamation of principles, institutions, personnel and processes.[1] The system is the aggregate of the complex web of functions performed by these different elements. These different areas are not bound together by a central entity or department, and how they work together can be difficult to ascertain. Some aspects of these elements will be discussed further in subsequent chapters in order to articulate the workings of the contemporary legal system in Hong Kong.

When one thinks about what a legal system is, many things may come to mind, including the ideologies (such as the rule of law and human rights), the procedures (such as the law-making and trial processes) and the actors (such as lawmakers, judges, police and lawyers). It can be said with certainty that Hong Kong possesses a legal system, and other jurisdictions do as well. They may be similar, like Hong Kong with other common law jurisdictions, or connected but different, like the relationship of 'one country, two systems' that Hong Kong shares with Mainland China. What is difficult is to provide an overarching and convenient definition of what a legal system is. Rather, several building blocks are needed to provide a framework for the understanding of the term 'legal system'.[2]

First and foremost, a legal system embodies the institutions that create, operate and carry out the laws of the jurisdiction. In Hong Kong, the Legislative Council is responsible for enacting its laws.[3] Law enforcement agencies, most notably the Hong Kong Police Force, ensure that the public complies with the law. The courts also play an important role in operating and upholding the legal system. There are less known and less visible legal

---

[1] P. Wesley-Smith, *An Introduction to the Hong Kong Legal System*, 3rd ed. (Oxford: Oxford University Press, Hong Kong 1998), chapter 2.
[2] Ibid.
[3] The process of legislation will be discussed in Chapter 6.

institutions or departments, including the Court Interpreters' Office, the Land Registry, the Labour Department, the Customs and Excise Department, the Independent Commission Against Corruption and so on. In this sense, the legal system can be viewed as a part of the system of government.

Aside from creating and operating the law, a legal system also contains the laws themselves. In Hong Kong, statutory law is mainly in the form of ordinances and to a lesser extent regulations and by-laws.[4] The other main source of law is case law, namely the judicial decisions made by the courts.[5] Therefore the legal system from this vantage point is a collection of laws.

A legal system cannot be completely appreciated without recognising the ideologies, philosophies and jurisprudence behind the legal system. This is essentially why some legal systems are similar while others differ so greatly. These aspects of the legal system are discussed next.

Rules and Principles

The law itself is comprised of particular legal rules as contained in legislation and case law. Apart from these specific rules, there are fundamental doctrines or basic principles which underpin the law and the legal system. Such fundamental principles include the rule of law, separation of powers and judicial independence.

Rule of Law

The rule of law is arguably the foundation of Hong Kong's legal system. It has survived the return of sovereignty over Hong Kong to China[6] and is guaranteed to remain for at least fifty years.[7] The rule of law contains important principles upon which the system functions.

The rule of law has its foundations in the notion of Aristotle that government is best when it is done by law and not by man.[8] This requires

---

[4] The sources of law will be discussed in Chapter 4.
[5] The courts and doctrine of precedent will be discussed in Chapter 5.
[6] Basic Law, art. 8.
[7] Basic Law, art. 5.
[8] C. A. Bates, *Aristotle's 'Best Regime': Kingship, Democracy and the Rule of Law* (Baton Rouge, LA: Louisiana State University Press 2003).

that individual liberties are ensured by the regulation of behaviour by means of law only and punishment only in accordance with the law.[9] It is the body of principle often represented by Aristotle's famous quotation: 'he is a better ruler who is free from passion than he who is passionate. Whereas the law is passionless, passion must ever sway the heart of man.'[10] There are five basic principles under the modern understanding of the rule of law:

- *Law is the antithesis of arbitrary power.*
  This is the key principle of the rule of law, as it prevents government from exercising tyrannical whims, in particular the whim to punish a person who has not breached the law. This principle is famously stated as 'the absolute supremacy or predominance of regular law as opposed to the influence of arbitrary power'.[11] Moreover, the law should be certain and consistently applied. The law cannot apply unless it has been created by a legitimate constitutional process.
- *Law is not biased in its application.*
  This means that the law should be protected from the partisan interests of its administrators. Judges, therefore, are usually appointed with life tenure to ensure that their decisions are free from political interference. It also contemplates equal access to the judicial system,[12] which entails the provision of services such as legal aid and duty lawyers to people with low income.
- *All persons are equal before the law.*
  The traditional symbol for equality before the law is the Greek goddess of justice, Themis.[13] Themis is usually depicted as holding a pair of scales (signifying the tempering of justice with mercy) and wearing a blindfold. Equality before the law is represented by the blindfold. The law should perform its function in a way that is blind to individual characteristics of wealth, gender, class, education, race, religion, creed and political persuasion.

---

[9] R. Huxley-Binns, J. Martin and T. Frost, *Unlocking the English Legal System*, 5th ed. (London: Routledge 2017).
[10] Aristotle (384–322 BCE), *Politics* (Chicago, IL: Chicago University Press 1984).
[11] A. V. Dicey, *Introduction to the Study of Law of the Constitution*, 10th ed. (Basingstoke: Macmillan Education 1959), p. 202.
[12] Basic Law, art. 35; see also Chapter 11.
[13] See 'Justice' at the Old Bailey. Barnaby's Picture Library.

- *Law must be effective.*
  The law must be able to affect the conduct of the persons it is governing. It is logical that to do this, the obligations imposed by the law must be capable of being understood and obeyed by all the persons it attempts to regulate.
- *Law must be of benefit to society.*
  In order for the law to have longevity and be obeyed, it must be perceived as being advantageous. There must be a careful tempering of law between civil and political rights and duties so that the law is perceived as a desirable vehicle for order in society instead of being interfering and oppressive.

Separation of Powers

Montesquieu is credited as the founder of the doctrine of the separation of powers,[14] and it is the legacy of his political theory that developed in the tumultuous political climate of revolutionary France.[15] The basic precept of the doctrine is that to prevent the abuse of state power, power should be shared among the executive (Executive Council as well as the Chief Executive), the legislature (Legislative Council) and the judiciary (the courts). This system provides checks and balances on each of the arms of government. The doctrine of the separation of power and its application to both colonial and present day Hong Kong is dealt with in much more detail in Chapter 3.

Independent Judiciary

The independence of the judiciary is vital to provide the courts and arbiters with immunity and protection from interference by other governmental organisations. In England, the Stuarts were renowned for interference, by threats and bribery of members of the judiciary, and that instigated the Act of Settlement in 1701.[16] This Act introduced some very important provisions for an independent judiciary, and these are now commonplace in most common law jurisdictions. The provisions included life tenure for

---

[14] The doctrine of the separation of powers will be discussed in detail in Chapter 3.
[15] M. Ritcher (ed.), *The Political Theory of Montesquieu* (M. Ritcher, trans.) (Cambridge: Cambridge University Press 1977).
[16] Act of Settlement 1701 (UK).

judges, inability of anyone to dismiss a judge on anything other than legal grounds, and immunity of salaries from government interference.[17]

In Hong Kong, judicial independence is maintained by the constitutional precepts contained in Chapter IV of the Basic Law. The Basic Law provides that the courts of Hong Kong exercise their power independently, the application of this being that members of the judiciary are immune from legal action in the performance of their judicial function.[18] The Basic Law also provides that members of the judiciary are free from political interference by guaranteeing their tenure (their appointment to the judiciary). Judges are only to be removed for misbehaviour or inability to perform, and that can only be achieved through a tribunal of judges, including the Chief Justice.[19] Therefore, the judiciary regulates itself. It is both the intention and the consequence of this system that the regulation of the judiciary also remains independent of legislative or executive interference.[20]

Judicial independence is also protected by the Basic Law, which vests the power of final adjudication in the Court of Final Appeal,[21] although this is the subject of much academic and legal debate. Many argue that the Basic Law contains an inconsistency regarding where this power of final adjudication is actually vested. As mentioned above, art. 82 vests this power in the Court of Final Appeal, yet a conflict potentially exists with art. 158, which vests the final power of interpretation of the Basic Law itself with the Standing Committee of the National People's Congress (NPCSC) of the PRC. Many argue that the final power of adjudication is then effectually that of the NPCSC, is delegated by them to the Court of Final Appeal and such delegated power exercisable by the Court of Final Appeal is limited to those cases within the autonomy of the HKSAR, not including those cases that concern the responsibilities of the Central People's Government or the relationship between the central authorities and the HKSAR.[22] This raises key questions about the legitimacy of claims to the effectual independence of the Hong Kong judiciary in practice.

---

[17] P. S. Atiyah, *Law and Modern Society*, 2nd ed. (New York, NY: Oxford University Press 1995), p. 13.
[18] Basic Law, art. 85.
[19] Basic Law, art. 89.
[20] For further reading, see B. F. C. Hsu, 'Judicial Independence under the Basic Law' (2004), *Hong Kong Law Journal* 34, 279.
[21] Basic Law, art. 82.
[22] L. Feng, 'The Development of Jurisprudence of the Court of Final Appeal in Basic Law Litigation' (2001–2), *Journal of Chinese and Comparative Law* 5, 21. See further G. Zhu, 'Inter-Regional Conflict of Laws under "One Country, Two Systems": Revisiting Chinese

The judiciary, however, does enjoy independence in certain respects. The members of the judiciary enjoy security of commission (salary), security of tenure (appointment) and immunity from civil litigation in the performance of their duties. All of these provisions are constitutionally protected and assist in the maintenance of many fundamental characteristics of an independent judiciary.

Legal Institutions

There are three main categories of legal institutions in Hong Kong: legislative, judicial and executive institutions.[23] These institutions have the functions of enacting, enforcing, administering, interpreting, applying, amending and repealing laws. To understand these functions, it is necessary to understand how these institutions operate in their particular constitutional context.

Legislative Institutions

The Basic Law provides for the primary legislative body in Hong Kong to be the Legislative Council.[24] The establishment of the Legislative Council and its powers and functions are detailed in arts. 66 to 79 of the Basic Law. There are ten specific heads of power outlined in art. 73. and they include the making, amending and repealing of laws in accordance with the Basic Law and legal procedure;[25] fiscal responsibilities (such as budgets[26] and taxation[27]); enforcing the idea of responsible government (by asking questions about the work of the government,[28] debating matters of public interest,[29] keeping check on the policy initiatives of the Chief Executive[30] and being available to Hong Kong residents with complaints[31]); the

---

Legal Theories and Chinese and Hong Kong Law with Special Reference to Judicial Assistance' (2002), *Hong Kong Law Journal* 32, 615.
[23] Basic Law, Chapter IV.
[24] Basic Law, art. 66.
[25] Basic Law, art. 73(1).
[26] Basic Law, art. 73(2).
[27] Basic Law, art. 73(3).
[28] Basic Law, art. 73(5).
[29] Basic Law, art. 73(6).
[30] Basic Law, art. 73(4).
[31] Basic Law, art. 73(8).

appointment and dismissal of members of the judiciary[32] (in accordance with procedure); and a legal procedure for the dismissal of members of the Legislative Council held not to possess the confidence of the other members.[33] The detailed powers and functions of the Legislative Council are defined in the Legislative Council Ordinance[34] and the Legislative Council (Powers and Privileges) Ordinance.[35] The most significant restriction on the Legislative Council involves matters that may be the subject of legislation initiated by the legislature.[36] The process of legislation in Hong Kong is detailed in Chapter 6.

Not all law is, in practice, created by the Legislative Council or the extended legislative institutions which have jurisdiction to do so. For efficacy of government, the Legislative Council is able to delegate its powers to make law by creating subsidiary legislation which assigns this power to an authorised body from the executive branch.[37]

Judicial Institutions

The main institution engaged in the exercise of judicial power in Hong Kong is the courts. This is in accordance with the structure[38] outlined by the Basic Law which provides that the courts at all levels will be the judiciary of the region.[39] It is the main function of the courts to administer justice in the region in both criminal and civil matters.

The highest court in Hong Kong is the Court of Final Appeal (CFA), which enjoys the power of final adjudication.[40] The CFA was established after the handover, replacing the Privy Council as Hong Kong's highest appellate court. The legitimacy of its power is derived from art. 82 of the Basic Law and is practised in accordance with the Court of Final Appeal

---

[32] Basic Law, art. 73(7).
[33] Basic Law, art. 73(9).
[34] Legislative Council Ordinance (Cap. 542).
[35] Legislative Council (Powers and Privileges) Ordinance (Cap. 382).
[36] Y. Ghai, *Hong Kong's New Constitutional Order: The Resumption of Chinese Sovereignty and the Basic Law* (Hong Kong: Hong Kong University Press 1997), p. 252.
[37] Basic Law, art. 62(5).
[38] Chapter IV of the Basic Law defines the political structure of the Hong Kong Special Administrative Region.
[39] Basic Law, art. 80.
[40] Basic Law, art. 82.

Ordinance.[41] Other courts in Hong Kong include the Court of Appeal, the Court of First Instance, the District Court and the Magistrates' Courts. Besides the courts, Hong Kong has established certain tribunals to deal with specific matters. The court system in Hong Kong as well as the doctrine of precedent is discussed in Chapter 5.

Executive Institutions

The executive institution in Hong Kong is the Hong Kong Special Administrative Region (HKSAR) Government.[42] This includes the Department of Administration, Department of Finance, Department of Justice and various bureaus, divisions and commissions.[43] The structure of this government will be examined in greater detail in subsequent chapters which follow the legislative and political process of law-making in Hong Kong. This section will look at some of the executive institutions that are particularly relevant to the legal system.

The most relevant of these executive authorities to a study of the legal system of Hong Kong is the Department of Justice. The head of the Department of Justice is the Secretary for Justice. The Secretary for Justice is a member of the Executive Council and the principal legal adviser to the Chief Executive, the government and various individual governmental departments and agencies. The Department of Justice comprises six divisions:[44]

- The Prosecutions Division is headed by the Director of Public Prosecutions. The main duties of this division are to appear for the government in the prosecution of criminal offenders and to advise government law enforcement agencies.
- The Civil Division is responsible for providing legal advice on civil law matters to all government bureaus and departments. It is also responsible for representing the government in civil litigation and arbitrations.

---

[41] Court of Final Appeal Ordinance (Cap. 484).
[42] Basic Law, art. 59.
[43] Basic Law, art. 60.
[44] Refer to the homepage of the Department of Justice of the Government of the Hong Kong Special Administrative Region, available at www.doj.gov.hk/eng/about/organisationtoc.html.

- The Law Drafting Division is responsible for the drafting of government legislation. The drafting counsel is required to attend the meetings of both the Legislative and Executive Councils in the final stages of the legislative process.
- The Legal Policy Division is primarily responsible for giving legal policy advice to the government. This advice will extend to issues such as the administration of justice, human rights and other issues of constitutionality. This division also contains a special unit that is devoted to the understanding of the laws of the PRC.
- The International Law Division provides legal advice on public international law to the government and assists in its negotiation of bilateral and international agreements.
- The Administration and Development Division deals with all the administrative matters of the Department.

The Legal Aid Department also plays an important part in the legal system in both a procedural and a substantive role. It is a government institution which was established to provide legal representation in both civil and criminal cases to any person who has reasonable grounds for pursuing or defending a legal action, but is prevented from doing so by lack of means.[45] Other institutions such as the Hong Kong Police Force, the Independent Commission Against Corruption and the Correctional Services Department are law enforcement authorities that are integral parts of the Hong Kong legal system. Their purpose is to enforce the laws of Hong Kong, though their specific roles and methods differ in accordance with their specific missions. Further discussion on these law enforcement agencies and the prosecution can be found in Chapter 8.

Legal Personnel

The normal operation of any legal system requires the function and co-operation of a large number of personnel. Some of their roles are political, such as the Chief Executive, and others are administrative, such

---

[45] The Legal Aid Ordinance (Cap. 91) sets out the criteria that the Department considers when assessing a candidate's eligibility for legal aid.

as a jury member or court bailiff. Some of the key players in the Hong Kong legal system are discussed below.

The Chief Executive

The Chief Executive is the head of the HKSAR government.[46] Because of this political position, the Chief Executive has a high degree of involvement in the legal system, particularly in the law-making process. According to the Basic Law, the Chief Executive can exercise the powers and functions of his/her office to implement the Basic Law and other laws in Hong Kong.[47] The Basic Law also affords the Chief Executive the power to refuse and return any bills passed by the Legislative Council which, at the discretion of the Chief Executive, are deemed to be incompatible with the overall interests of the government.[48] The Chief Executive, therefore, holds a significant power in the law-making process: an effectual veto power. The Chief Executive enjoys some influence on the application and enforcement of laws. The Basic Law vests powers in the Chief Executive to appoint and remove (on legal grounds) judges from the courts at all levels[49] as well as to nominate principal officials including the Secretary for Justice and Commissioner of Police for appointment by the Central People's Government.[50] This power is, however, by no means unlimited and unchecked. According to the Basic Law, the Department of Justice can control criminal proceedings free from any interference,[51] and the Chief Executive's power to appoint and remove judges is restricted and cannot be exercised arbitrarily.[52]

Secretary for Justice

The Secretary for Justice is the head of the Department of Justice and must be nominated by the Chief Executive for appointment.[53] The role of the

---

[46] Basic Law, art. 43.
[47] Basic Law, art. 48(2).
[48] Basic Law, art. 49.
[49] Basic Law, art. 48(6).
[50] Basic Law, art. 48(5).
[51] Basic Law, art. 63.
[52] Basic Law, arts. 88, 89.
[53] Basic Law, art. 48(5).

Secretary for Justice is multifarious and includes acting as the principal legal adviser to the government; having the sole responsibility in deciding to prosecute criminal cases; and being the nominal defendant in all civil actions against the government. The Secretary for Justice is the 'guardian of the public interest'. This means that where necessary, the Secretary for Justice may act for the public and apply for judicial review of issues affecting public or civil rights. The Secretary for Justice is also the Protector of Charities and thus is able to bring an action for a charitable or public trust.[54]

Legislators

The legislators in Hong Kong are the members of the Legislative Council. The Basic Law restricts this membership to Chinese citizens, who are permanent residents of Hong Kong with no right of abode in any other foreign country.[55] Permanent residents of Hong Kong who are not of Chinese nationality or who have the right of abode in another country may be elected to the Legislative Council, provided that the proportion of such members does not exceed 20 per cent of the total composition of the Legislative Council.[56] The method of Legislative Council election is specified in Annex II of the Basic Law, 'Method for the Formation of the Legislative Council of the Hong Kong Special Administrative Region and Its Voting Procedures'.

Judges and Members of the Judiciary

Judges are the arbiters in the legal system. This role includes the hearing of cases before them, application of the relevant law and the direction of juries, among many other functions. In Hong Kong, all judges are appointed by the Chief Executive[57] on the recommendation of an independent commission composed of local judges, members of the legal profession and eminent persons from beyond the legal sector.[58] In Hong Kong, the highest-ranking

---

[54] Department of Justice, *The Legal System in Hong Kong* (Hong Kong: Department of Justice 2008) p. 38.
[55] Basic Law, art. 67.
[56] Ibid.
[57] Basic Law, art. 48(5).
[58] Basic Law, art. 88.

judge is the Chief Justice of the Court of Final Appeal and he/she is ultimately responsible for all judicial matters. The Chief Justice must be a Chinese citizen who is a permanent resident of Hong Kong with no right of abode in any foreign country.[59]

Judges to the High Court are appointed by the Chief Executive in accordance with the High Court Ordinance.[60] The Court of Appeal consists of the Chief Judge of the High Court and Justices of Appeal appointed by the Chief Executive.[61] Under the same ordinance, the Court of First Instance shall consist of the Chief Judge of the High Court, judges appointed by the Chief Executive and the deputy judges appointed by the Chief Justice.[62] Appointment to the District Court is similarly qualified under the District Court Ordinance.[63] The appointment of magistrates is regulated by the Magistrates Ordinance.[64]

Juries

The Basic Law provides that the principle of trial by jury should be maintained in Hong Kong.[65] The jury does not directly apply the law to factual situations; rather they are the arbiters of fact in a trial, determining the most probable fact scenario from competing accounts. This determination is based on evidence put to them at the trial. Jurors are private citizens who have been sworn to hear and pass verdict on an accused person in criminal trials (which are conducted in the Court of First Instance) and in some civil actions.

In Hong Kong, a jury typically consists of seven members of the community. The qualifications for jury service are found in the Jury Ordinance and include qualifications based on age, language and character.[66] Every person who is qualified under the ordinance has an obligation to serve unless they can prove they fall into one of the exceptions to jury service

---

[59] Basic Law, art. 90; Hong Kong Court of Final Appeal Ordinance (Cap. 484), s. 6.
[60] High Court Ordinance (Cap. 4).
[61] High Court Ordinance (Cap. 4), s. 5.
[62] High Court Ordinance (Cap. 4), s. 4.
[63] District Court Ordinance (Cap. 336).
[64] Magistrates Ordinance (Cap. 227).
[65] Basic Law, art. 86.
[66] Jury Ordinance (Cap. 3), s. 4.

(also found in the ordinance).[67] Exceptions exist for the Chief Executive, members of the Legislative Council, certain public officers (including legal officers and public officers in law enforcement agencies), barristers and solicitors, medical practitioners, full-time students and so forth.

Each week, the Registrar of the High Court draws at random a number of jurors from the List of Common Jurors. If a person is selected, the court will send him/her a summons and request his/her assistance in court on a particular day. The court officials then select seven jurors by ballot on the first day of the trial for service and the balance of jurors are excused.[68] Legal counsel for either party are allowed to object to a particular selection of jury in order to protect the interests of their party.[69] Jurors are given immunity from having their employment terminated due to their performance of jury service[70] and are entitled to monetary compensation for their service in a trial.[71]

Barristers and Solicitors

Legal practitioners perform a variety of professional legal duties for their clients. Some of these include representing litigants during a trial, giving legal advice, drafting contracts, performing conveyancing work in transactions and administering wills and estates. In Hong Kong, the Legal Practitioners Ordinance[72] regulates the administration and registration of these professionals. The legal profession of Hong Kong is further discussed in Chapter 11.

The legal profession in Hong Kong is split between barristers and solicitors, and each has a separate requirement for admission. The legal academic training for both barristers and solicitors is the same in Hong Kong. Admission into either field is possible after obtaining a Bachelor of Laws degree (LLB) from the University of Hong Kong, City University of Hong Kong or The Chinese University of Hong Kong and completion of the Postgraduate Certificate in Laws (PCLL) programme at any of these institutions. Graduates who hold a Bachelor of Laws degree from a university other than one of these three universities in Hong Kong may also seek to complete the PCLL in order to be admitted as either a barrister or solicitor. However, they are required to

---

[67] Jury Ordinance (Cap. 3), s. 5.
[68] Jury Ordinance (Cap. 3), s. 21.
[69] Jury Ordinance (Cap. 3), s. 29.
[70] Jury Ordinance (Cap. 3), s. 33.
[71] Jury Ordinance (Cap. 3), s. 31.
[72] Legal Practitioners Ordinance (Cap. 159).

demonstrate competence in five core subjects, Civil Procedure, Criminal Procedure, Commercial Law, Evidence and Business Associations, and three top-up subjects, Hong Kong Constitutional Law, Hong Kong Legal System and Hong Kong Land Law before they can undertake the PCLL programme.[73] Those who have an undergraduate degree from another faculty (non-law degree) can choose to either complete the Juris Doctor (JD) programme offered by the above educational institutions or obtain the Graduate Diploma in English and Hong Kong Law (Common Professional Examination) offered by HKU Space in association with Manchester Metropolitan University, before admission to the PCLL programme. Once a PCLL is obtained, admission to the Bar (as a barrister) requires at least a twelve-month pupillage in Hong Kong.[74] For admission as a solicitor, a graduate must work as a trainee solicitor at a qualified law firm for two years.[75] Once admitted to either side of the profession, it is possible to switch over, provided it is done so in compliance with the Legal Practitioners Ordinance.[76]

Academic Personnel

This category involves all the professors, lecturers and researchers of law at the universities. These academics educate the future lawyers and conduct research into developing and new areas of the law. They are also invaluable in contributing to jurisprudence and in critiquing of the legal system.

Historical Development of Hong Kong's Legal System

This section gives a brief account of the historical development the legal system of Hong Kong. It helps to illustrate how the common law system was imported from England to Hong Kong.

The Legal System upon Colonisation

Prior to the British colonisation of Hong Kong in 1841, the territory, with only a few thousand inhabitants (villagers and fishermen), existed as part

---

[73] For details, please refer to the information prepared by the PCLL Conversion Examination and Administration Limited, available at www.pcea.com.hk/package.html.
[74] Barristers (Qualification for Admission and Pupillage) Rules (Cap. 159AC), s. 10.
[75] Trainee Solicitors Rules (Cap. 159J), s. 6.
[76] Legal Practitioners Ordinance (Cap. 159).

of the Chinese Empire under the Qing Dynasty, with Chinese laws (under the imperial code) and customs applying in the territory. Following the First Opium War between China and Britain, Hong Kong Island was ceded to Britain under the Treaty of Nanking 1842. Kowloon was ceded under the Convention of Peking 1860 after the Second Opium War, while the New Territories was acquired by the British for a ninety-nine-year lease under the Second Convention of Peking 1898.

Upon acquisition of sovereignty over Hong Kong, the British took steps to set up its own legal system and to apply English law in Hong Kong. Under English legal principles, the acquisition of a colony by conquest or cession does not automatically lead to the application of English law in the colony. The existing legal system of the colony applies unless altered by the British Crown.[77] In Hong Kong, this was first effected (to a degree) by two proclamations of Captain Charles Elliot, the Chief Superintendent of Trade and Plenipotentiary in China, declaring that the local Chinese were to be governed by 'the laws and customs of China',[78] while British subjects and other foreigners would be governed by 'the principles and practice of British law'.[79] The reception of English law was formalised following the proclamation of the Charter of the Colony of Hongkong by the Queen of England on 5 April 1843 pursuant to the Crown's prerogative powers. Under that Charter, the Governor of the Colony of Hong Kong, with the advice of the Legislative Council, was granted 'power and authority to make and enact all such Laws and Ordinances as may from time to time be required for the peace, order, and good government of the said Colony of Hongkong'.[80] The Charter (and its successor instrument, the Hong Kong Letters Patent 1917, supplemented by the Hong Kong Royal Instructions 1917[81]) formed the written constitution[82] for Hong Kong under British rule.

---

[77] *Campbell* v. *Hall* (1774) 1 Cowp 204, 98 ER 1045.

[78] Proclamations dated 1 February 1841 (issued jointly by Commodore Sir Bremer and Captain Elliot) and 2 February 1841 (issued by Captain Elliot); see J. W. Norton-Kyshe, *History of the Laws and Courts of Hong Kong: From the Earliest Period to 1898: Volume 1*, revised ed. (Hong Kong: Vetch and Lee Ltd 1971), pp. 3–6. See also D. M. E. Evans, 'Common Law in a Chinese Setting' (1971), *Hong Kong Law Journal* 1, 9.

[79] Proclamation dated 2 February 1841.

[80] Charter of the Colony of Hongkong, reproduced in Norton-Kyshe (n. 78), p. 21.

[81] These documents are reproduced in P. Wesley-Smith, *Constitutional and Administrative Law in Hong Kong*, 2nd ed. (Hong Kong: Longman 1994), Appendices 1 and 2.

[82] On the concept of a constitution, see Chapter 4.

The dominant motive for British acquisition of Hong Kong was trade, as the British wished to establish a base for the protection and expansion of British economic interests in China.[83] Order and stability were necessary to facilitate British trade, and the introduction of English law into Hong Kong was done predominantly for the purpose of protecting the private and commercial interests of the British. Application of English law in the colony was seen to be important to ensure that British subjects were governed by laws familiar to them.[84] Yet although initially English law was only applied to the British and foreign persons in Hong Kong, the Supreme Court Ordinance (No. 15 of 1844) extended the application of English law to all persons in Hong Kong, including the local Chinese population. Munn has suggested that major factors leading to this policy included the following: the need to assert British sovereignty over the colony; rapid immigration and uncontrolled crime; and the view that Chinese methods of justice were inferior.[85] Thus, the extension of English law to the Chinese in Hong Kong is said to have been premised on both the element of control of the local population and the benevolent purpose of improving the conditions of the locals.[86]

Legal Institutions and the Rule of Law in Colonial Hong Kong

The generally held view today is that the laws and legal system imported from the British constitute one of the more important and positive legacies of British rule in Hong Kong. It is not doubted that the legal system set up under British rule has provided for stability and public safety, and has facilitated the economic developments which have led the territory to become one of the major international commercial centres by the end of

---

[83] R. Buckley, *Hong Kong: The Road to 1997* (Cambridge: Cambridge University Press 1997), p. 1; A. Y. S. Cheung, 'The Paradox of Hong Kong Colonialism' (1996), *Canadian Journal of Law and Society* 11, 63.
[84] E. Marcks, 'English Law in Early Hong Kong: Colonial Law as a Means for Control and Liberation' (2000), *Texas International Law Journal* 35, 265.
[85] C. Munn, *Anglo-China: Chinese People and British Rule in Hong Kong, 1841–1880* (Surrey: Curzon 2001), pp. 165–166.
[86] Marcks (n. 84), p. 274; C. Jones and J. Vagg, *Criminal Justice in Hong Kong* (London: Routledge-Cavendish 2007), p. 3.

the twentieth century.[87] However, academics and commentators have also pointed out that behind the popular image of the beneficence of the legal system inherited from the British and of its importance in securing the prosperity of Hong Kong, there were also authoritarian and repressive aspects of the legal system and significant flaws and defects which have created inequality and injustice in Hong Kong.[88]

Certainly, the formal institutions of the English legal system and the formal aspects of the rule of law were effectively transplanted to Hong Kong in the early days of colonial rule. The 1843 Charter that imported English law into Hong Kong also created the Legislative Council, which, acting together with the Governor, had the function of making laws for the colony. The court and penal system were quickly established, with a Chief Magistrate appointed in 1841, a police force set up and the Supreme Court created in 1844.[89] Yet despite the creation of the formal institutions necessary for a legal system and the rule of law, the reality on the ground left much to be desired. Professionalism and competence was lacking, with the police force unreliable and corrupt,[90] and judicial officers and lawyers often having less than adequate knowledge of the law.[91] The practice of the law in the courts looked far different from that in their English counterparts,[92] with the procedural protections and rules of evidence present in the English courts often being ignored.[93] Moreover, there was much bias against the Chinese in both the court system and the laws themselves. Repressive laws directed at control of the Chinese were enacted and policed heavily; there was bias in the jury and judges; and harsh forms of punishments were co-opted from the Chinese legal system to punish Chinese offenders.[94]

---

[87] Marcks (n. 84), p. 269; Jones and Vagg (n. 86), p. 8; M. K. Chan, 'The Imperfect Legacy: Defects in the British Legal System in Colonial Hong Kong' (1997), *University of Pennsylvania Journal of International Economic Law* 18, 133.
[88] See, e.g., Chan (n. 87).
[89] See Munn (n. 85), pp. 113–203.
[90] Munn (n. 85), pp. 120–121; Jones and Vagg (n. 86), pp. 52–56.
[91] Jones and Vagg (n. 100), pp. 132, 135.
[92] Munn (n. 85), p. 169.
[93] Ibid., p. 118.
[94] Ibid., pp. 125–251; Jones and Vagg (n. 86), pp. 133–168; Marcks (n. 84); R Klein, 'Law and Racism in an Asian Setting: An Analysis of the British Rule of Hong Kong' (1995), *Hastings International & Comparative Law Review* 18, 223.

As Munn notes, though, there were probably few legal systems in the world at that time that were entirely impartial or free from abuse;[95] moreover, there were humanitarian and liberal forces which occasionally restrained some of the illiberal tendencies of British rule.[96] Nonetheless, the use of repressive laws as a tool of political control continued well into the twentieth century. In response to worker unrest, political dissent and the riots of the 1950s and 1960s, laws were enacted and applied giving the government wide powers to deport 'undesirable' persons, impose curfews, outlaw demonstrations, censor criticism of the colonial government, and prosecute and imprison political protestors.[97] There also continued to exist institutional defects in the legal system. For example, there were limitations in the separation of powers in providing checks and balances on government power, with the Legislative Council, consisting solely of appointed members until the 1990s, largely being subservient to the executive.[98] Police corruption also remained problematic throughout much of the century.[99] Moreover, there continued to be systemic biases in the legal system against the Chinese. With the law expressed in the English language and with court proceedings conducted in English, difficulties would inevitably arise for the majority of the population for whom English was not their mother tongue or language of everyday use.[100] In addition, legal concepts imported from England and the application of the law by foreign judges in Hong Kong could sometimes give rise to injustice due to cultural biases and conflicts in values between the law and the judge on the one hand and the local population coming into contact with the law and court system on the other.[101]

Significant reforms and improvements were, however, effected in the decades following the Second World War. It has been observed, for example,

---

[95] Munn (n. 85), p. 203.
[96] Jones and Vagg (n. 86), p. 8.
[97] R Klein, 'The Empire Strikes Back: Britain's Use of the Law to Suppress Political Dissent in Hong Kong' (1997), *Boston University International Law Journal* 15, 1. See also Jones and Vagg (n. 86), pp. 307–343, 375–408.
[98] Chan (n. 87), pp. 139–140.
[99] See Jones and Vagg (n. 86), pp. 369–374.
[100] Chan (n. 87), pp. 134–138; A. H. Y. Chen, 'The Legal System' in R. Y. C. Wong and J. Y. C. Cheng (eds.), *The Other Hong Kong Report: 1990* (Hong Kong: Chinese University Press 1990), p. 65.
[101] Chan (n. 80), pp. 135–136; W. M. Sin and Y. W. Chu, 'Whose Rule of Law? Rethinking (Post-)Colonial Legal Culture in Hong Kong' (1998), *Social & Legal Studies* 7, 147.

that the social and economic reforms by the government in this period necessitated improvements in the rule of law as this was essential for improved governance and success of the social and economic changes.[102] Importantly, corruption was successfully tackled in the years following the establishment of the Independent Commission Against Corruption in 1974.[103] The enactment of the Bill of Rights Ordinance in 1991 led to the repeal of the more repressive laws in the statute books. Greater use of the Chinese language in the legal system was also brought about from the late 1980s, with existing legislation translated into Chinese and new legislation enacted in both English and Chinese, and with the increasing use of Chinese in court proceedings (at least in the lower courts).[104] The legal system and rule of law as a legacy of the British may be imperfect, but nonetheless have been of fundamental importance in contributing to the development of Hong Kong into a modern metropolis whose residents by 1997 enjoyed essential freedoms and lived in relative safety and stability.

The Law in Colonial Hong Kong

Following the establishment of the Legislative Council of Hong Kong pursuant to the 1843 Charter, the Supreme Court Ordinance (No. 15 of 1844) was enacted, which provided, subject to certain provisos, that 'the law of England shall be in full force in the said Colony of Hongkong, except where the same shall be inapplicable to the local circumstances of the said Colony, or of its inhabitants'.[105] The 1844 ordinance was replaced in the following years,[106] and under the Supreme Court Ordinance (No. 3 of 1873), the provision (s. 5) setting out the law in Hong Kong was re-worded as follows: 'Such of the laws of England as existed when the Colony obtained a local legislature, that is to say, on the 5th day of April, 1843, shall be in force in the Colony, except so far as the said laws are inapplicable to the

---

[102] B. T. Y. Tai, 'The Development of Constitutionalism in Hong Kong' in R. Wacks (ed.), *The New Legal Order in Hong Kong* (Hong Kong: Hong Kong University Press 1999), p. 46.
[103] Jones and Vagg (n. 86), pp. 435–447.
[104] See generally A. S. Y. Cheung, 'Hong Kong and the Unprecedented Transfer of Sovereignty: Towards a Bilingual Legal System – The Development of Chinese Legal Language' (1997), *Loyola of Los Angeles International and Comparative Law Review* 19, 315.
[105] Supreme Court Ordinance 1844, s. 3.
[106] Supreme Court Ordinance (No. 6 of 1845); Supreme Court Ordinance (No. 2 of 1846).

local circumstances of the Colony or of its inhabitants, and except as they have been modified by laws passed by the said legislature.' The English law that became the law in Hong Kong was comprised of both statute law (law made by the legislature) and common law (law as set out by the courts). The subject matter of the law ranged from matters of criminal law (murder, theft, etc.) to matters of civil law regulating private interactions between persons, including, for example, laws in the area of business or commerce (such as contract law). Much of that English law transplanted to Hong Kong still applies today in Hong Kong or at least formed the origins of the present law in Hong Kong.

The above formulation in the Supreme Court Ordinance importing English law into Hong Kong had the effect that English statutes before 5 April 1843 applied in Hong Kong. Principles of the common law, however, were not frozen as at that date;[107] that is, English court decisions after that date setting out common law principles could still be applicable in Hong Kong pursuant to the 'fiction' of the declaratory theory of the common law.[108] The common law to be applied in Hong Kong would not be affected, though, by changes brought about in England via post-5 April 1843 legislation, as only the statutes before that date applied in Hong Kong.

Under s. 5 of the Supreme Court Ordinance 1873, the Hong Kong legislature could enact legislation modifying both the common law principles and the law under English statutes pre-5 April 1843 that would otherwise have applied in Hong Kong. English Acts could have been effectively repealed in Hong Kong by implication,[109] and thus, over time, difficulties arose in determining precisely which English Acts remained part of the law in Hong Kong.[110]

Such difficulties led to the enactment of the Application of English Law Ordinance in 1966. Under s. 4 of that ordinance, the English Acts which would remain part of the law in Hong Kong were those set out in the Schedule to the ordinance and other Acts which applied by virtue of any Order in Council, any express provision in the enactment or necessary implication, or any ordinance in Hong Kong. It is important to note that

---

[107] *Wong Kam-ying* v. *Man Chi-tai* [1967] HKLR 201, 211.
[108] On the declaratory theory, see Chapter 4.
[109] *R* v. *Marais* [1902] AC 51, 54.
[110] P. Wesley-Smith, *The Sources of Hong Kong Law* (Hong Kong: Hong Kong University Press 1994), pp. 115–116.

although the application of English statutes in Hong Kong was effectively limited both under the 1966 ordinance and the earlier Supreme Court Ordinance (since post-5 April 1843 Acts were not imported into Hong Kong under that ordinance), much legislation enacted by the Hong Kong legislature has been modelled on English statutes. Thus, for example, the Sale of Goods Ordinance (Cap. 26), enacted in Hong Kong in 1896, was modelled on the former Sale of Goods Act 1893 (UK).

The Application of English Law Ordinance also replaced the previous Supreme Court Ordinance provisions importing English law into Hong Kong. Section 3(1) provided that 'The common law and the rules of equity shall be in force in Hong Kong – (a) so far as they are applicable to the circumstances of Hong Kong or its inhabitants; (b) subject to such modifications as such circumstances may require; (c) subject to any amendment thereof (whenever made) by – (i) any Order in Council which applies to Hong Kong; (ii) any Act which applies to Hong Kong; or any Ordinance.' Section 3(2) was inserted into the ordinance in 1971, which provided that 'The common law and the rules of equity shall be in force in Hong Kong as provided in subsection (1) notwithstanding any amendment thereof as part of the law of England made at any time by an Order in Council or Act which does not apply to Hong Kong.'[111] The effect of s. 3, as amended, largely (but not entirely!)[112] preserved the position as that under the Supreme Court Ordinance with respect to the reception of English common law into Hong Kong.

Chinese Law in Colonial Hong Kong

In the early days of colonisation, the intention had been for Chinese law to continue to apply to the local Chinese population, but this policy was soon altered with the enactment of the Supreme Court Ordinance in 1844, as noted earlier. The legislative provisions importing English law into Hong Kong did leave room for the continued operation of Chinese laws, as

---

[111] Inserted by Ordinance No. 58 of 1971.
[112] For the difficulties arising from imperfections in the drafting of the new provisions, which led to some modification of the application of English common law in Hong Kong, see *Gensburger* v. *Gensburger* [1968] HKLR 403, 413; *Tang Kai-chung* v. *Tang Chik-shang* [1970] HKLR 276; *Leung Kwan-fu* v. *R* [1977] HKLR 175; *Oceania Manufacturing Co* v. *Pang Kwong-hon* [1979] HKLR 445; Wesley-Smith (n. 110), pp. 121–128.

English laws were only to be applied in so far as they were applicable to the local circumstances. However, difficulties arising from interpretation by expatriate judges led to a distortion of the meaning and effect of Chinese laws and customs as applied in Hong Kong.[113] The erosion of Chinese laws and customs also occurred as a result of the courts applying Chinese laws in very narrow circumstances only, such that by the second half of the twentieth century, Chinese customary law only had significance in limited areas of marriage and property law.[114]

Hong Kong under Chinese Sovereignty: Common Law System under the Basic Law

With the British lease over the New Territories expiring in 1997 under the Second Convention of Peking, concerns were raised by the business community in the 1970s over the validity of land leases following 1997.[115] Such concerns led to negotiations in the early 1980s between the United Kingdom (UK) and the PRC over the future of Hong Kong, culminating in the signing of the Sino-British Joint Declaration[116] in 1984. The Joint Declaration binds the UK and the PRC as an international treaty under the principles of international law. China's firm intention had been to recover sovereignty over Hong Kong, and there was little that the British could do but concede.[117] The Joint Declaration laid down the blueprint for the existence of Hong Kong after 1997 as a Special Administrative Region of the PRC, setting out the principles under which the territory would be governed. The basic concept embodied in the Joint Declaration is the doctrine of 'one country, two systems'. Under this concept, the territory would be under the sovereignty of the PRC, being a part of China, but it would have a high degree of autonomy, with its existing legal, social and economic systems and way of life preserved and remaining unchanged for

---

[113] Cheung (n. 104).
[114] See Chapter 4.
[115] S. Shipp, *Hong Kong – China* (Jefferson, NC: McFarland & Co 1995), pp. 17–23.
[116] Joint Declaration of the Government of the United Kingdom of Great Britain and Northern Ireland and the Government of the People's Republic of China on the Question of Hong Kong (19 December 1984).
[117] Shipp (n. 115), pp. 29–50; Buckley (n. 83), pp. 104–115.

fifty years. Importantly, the Joint Declaration also sets out requirements for the legal protection of rights and freedoms of persons in Hong Kong under the new regime.

The Joint Declaration stipulated that a Basic Law would be enacted by the National People's Congress (NPC) of the PRC, which would embody the policies as set out in the Joint Declaration. The process of drafting the Basic Law commenced soon after the coming into effect of the Joint Declaration in May 1985, and the finalised version was approved by the NPC in April 1990.[118] While the Basic Law was to follow the policies of the Joint Declaration, there was much controversy over the precise provisions of the Basic Law in areas including the extent and pace of democratisation, the independence of the judiciary and the right of interpretation of the Basic Law, and the relationship between the PRC Constitution and the Basic Law.[119] There was considerable concern in Hong Kong over the extent to which the Basic Law would protect the existing freedoms and way of life in Hong Kong given the powers reserved to the PRC, such as in the appointment of the Chief Executive, the power to invalidate Hong Kong laws, to interpret and amend the Basic Law, and in declaring a state of emergency in Hong Kong.[120] None of the Hong Kong members of the Basic Law Drafting Committee had voted in favour of the final version before its submission to the NPC for approval and enactment.[121]

At the same time that the Basic Law was adopted, the NPC also provided for the establishment, as of 1 July 1997, of the Hong Kong Special Administrative Region (HKSAR) pursuant to art. 31 of the PRC

---

[118] Decision of the National People's Congress on the Basic Law of the Hong Kong Special Administrative Region of the People's Republic of China (adopted at the Third Session of the Seventh National People's Congress on 4 April 1990).

[119] F. Ching, 'Toward Colonial Sunset: The Wilson Regime, 1987–92' in M. K. Chan (ed.), *Precarious Balance: Hong Kong Between China and Britain, 1842–1992* (New York, NY: Sharpe 1994), pp. 176–177. On the drafting of the Basic Law, see further M. K. Chan and D. J. Clarke (eds.), *The Hong Kong Basic Law: Blueprint for 'Stability and Prosperity' under Chinese Sovereignty?* (Hong Kong: Hong Kong University Press 1991); Shipp (n. 115), pp. 81–87; Y. Ghai, *Hong Kong's New Constitutional Order: The Resumption of Chinese Sovereignty and the Basic Law*, 2nd ed. (Hong Kong: Hong Kong University Press 1997), pp. 57–64.

[120] Chan and Clarke (n. 119), p. 21, pp. 41–45; Shipp (n. 115), p. 67. Ghai has pointed out that the Basic Law departs from the Joint Declaration in a number of respects: see Ghai (n. 119), pp. 67–69.

[121] Shipp (n. 115), p. 82.

Constitution.[122] The transfer of sovereignty from the UK to the PRC took effect on 1 July 1997, and with the coming into existence of the HKSAR on that date, the Basic Law also came into operation. The Basic Law sets out the relationship between the HKSAR and the central authorities of the PRC, the political structure of Hong Kong, the laws and legal system of the territory, basic rights of individuals in Hong Kong, provisions on the policies governing the economy and other aspects of Hong Kong society giving effect to the principle of 'one country, two systems', as well as provisions on the interpretation and amendment of the Basic Law.

Articles 8 and 18 of the Basic Law largely ensure that the pre-existing laws and legal system in Hong Kong continue to exist following the handover. The major alteration is the constitutional framework, with the source of Hong Kong laws today flowing from the Basic Law and PRC Constitution.

The years following the handover have not been without controversy surrounding the Hong Kong legal system. The litigation over the right of abode of Mainland children of Hong Kong parents in 1999 saw the Standing Committee of the NPC (NPCSC) assert its powers and its supremacy over the Court of Final Appeal in the interpretation of the Basic Law. There was also controversy in 2003 over the Hong Kong government's plans to introduce new laws on treason, secession, sedition, subversion, etc., to implement art. 23 of the Basic Law, with the draft laws shelved following the public demonstrations of over 500,000 people on 1 July 2003. Confidence in the strength of the rule of law in Hong Kong has also been shaken in some quarters as a result of events such as the various NPCSC interpretations of the Basic Law.[123]

---

[122] Decision of the National People's Congress on the Establishment of the Hong Kong Special Administrative Region (adopted at the Third Session of the Seventh National People's Congress on 4 April 1990).

[123] Please consult the Special Issue (2018, Vol. 50, Issue 1) of *Chinese Law & Government* for the five cases of the HKSAR Basic Law Interpretations by the PRC NPCSC in 1999, 2004, 2005, 2011 and 2016; D. Rezvani, 'Dead Autonomy, A Thousand Cuts or Partial Independence? The Autonomous Status of Hong Kong', *Journal of Contemporary Asia*, 42(1), 93; Hong Kong Bar Association, *The Hong Kong Bar Association's Statement Concerning the Interpretation Made by the National People's Congress Standing Committee of Article 104 of the Basic Law* (7 November 2016), available at www.hkba.org/sites/default/files/20161107%20-%20Statement%20re%20NPCSC%20interpretration%20BL104%20%28Eng%20Version-web%29.pdf; K. Cheung, 'China's Power to Interpret Hong Kong's Basic Law "Greatest Threat to Rule of Law," Bar Assoc. Head', *Hong Kong Free Press*

It is important for the legal community and society generally to remain vigilant to ensure that the legal system remains robust in protecting rights and freedoms in Hong Kong. At the broader level, there are still certain institutional limitations in the rule of law today, which can potentially give rise to abuses in the future. In addition, there are many aspects of the laws and legal system which need improvement or reform, such as improving access to justice, affording greater protection to minorities and strengthening consumer protection laws, just to name a few areas. Law reform, though, is something that takes place in other modern legal systems as well. The quest for better laws and legal institutions will always be an ongoing one.

The Enterprise of Studying Law

For those coming to the study of law, many might picture it as a process of learning the legal rules (the 'black letter law') in the statute books and law reports that tell us what is lawful and what is not, and what the penalty may be for contravening the law. This is certainly a fundamental aspect of learning about the law. However, it is not the only aspect.

Studying the law is not only a process of reading what the rules are and attempting to memorise the rules. Law students need to learn to think like a lawyer or a judge would. The rules in the law books do not always give a definitive answer when determining whether someone has infringed the law or whether someone is entitled to exercise a legal right as against another in the particular circumstances that have arisen. This is one factor that gives rise to legal disputes which may need to be resolved by the courts, with judges called upon to determine what the law is and how the law applies to the facts of the case. For example, the criminal offence that prohibits sex workers from 'soliciting'[124] clients was developed or enacted before the internet age to deal with perceived problems of harassment of, or offence to, passers-by in the streets where sex workers might tout for customers. Would advertising for clients on a web forum today amount to 'soliciting' such that there is commission of a criminal offence? Lawyers

---

(6 March 2018), available at www.hongkongfp.com/2018/03/06/chinas-power-interpret-hong-kongs-basic-law-greatest-threat-rule-law-bar-assoc-head/.

[124] See Crimes Ordinance (Cap. 200), s. 147.

need to be able to provide answers to such questions when advising their clients so that their clients can know their chances of succeeding in court. In a sense, lawyers need to be able to predict how the courts might decide. Law students, then, need to learn the skills of how a lawyer would predict the outcome of court cases. This in turn requires the law student to learn how judges might arrive at their conclusions. This process of how a judge arrives at a decision is the process of legal reasoning,[125] a vital skill for law students to acquire. In beginning this learning process, first-year students in law must start to learn to read case judgments to see how judges have actually resolved cases in ascertaining what the legal rules are and which party to the litigation is to win the case. It must be borne in mind that in reading case judgments, students should not only try to remember what the judge decided in the particular case. It is just as important for students to learn the reasoning process of judges so that when faced with a novel factual scenario that raises a legal question, students can themselves engage in legal reasoning to predict how a judge might resolve the legal issue.

Another important skill that law students must acquire is the skill of researching or finding the law. Students who have completed their law degree will have studied major subject areas of law (e.g., tort law, contract law, criminal law) and the main legal rules and principles in those areas. Yet the body of law in existence in Hong Kong or any other jurisdiction is much larger than the laws that can be studied in a law degree. Moreover, the law can change over time, so the law that a student learns at law school may well be different from the law that they need to advise upon when in practice years down the track. Lawyers must have the skills to find out what the legal rules are for themselves. As the old saying goes, give a man a fish and you feed him for a day; but teach him to fish, and you feed him for a lifetime. Law students will be assigned textbooks to read to know what the law is in a subject area (say, contract law) at law school, but it will be necessary for law students to have the legal research skills to be able to find out for themselves what the law is in any subject area, whether they have studied it at university or not.

---

[125] Scholars have written various theories on legal reasoning or judicial decision-making, the major ideas of which students should, in time, become familiar with. See, e.g., D. N. MacCormick, *Legal Reasoning and Legal Theory* (Oxford: Clarendon Press 1994); R. Dworkin, *Law's Empire* (Oxford: Hart Publishing 1998).

Aside from learning the legal technical skills of a lawyer, it is also vital for law students to understand the wider context of the law. What is the purpose of a legal rule? Why did the legislature or the courts lay down a rule or principle as law? Why is certain conduct prohibited as a criminal offence? Why is particular behaviour or conduct in society regulated by the law rather than by some other means of social control (e.g., through morality or social mores)? What is or should the role of law be? What is the connection between law and justice? Can law be used or abused for sinister purposes? What factors in society shape what the laws are in the particular society? What is the effect of laws on individuals and on society as a whole? Do particular laws successfully achieve their goals? These are just some of the questions that students should be asking as they learn about the law and the legal system. Jurisprudential or legal theories explore or provide the framework for exploring these types of questions. Chapter 2 contains a brief introduction to some legal theories though it is beyond the scope of this book to discuss such theories in detail.[126] However, students should, from the outset of their legal studies, be aware of these wider issues and understand that law does not exist in a vacuum or in isolation from the rest of society. Law both is affected by and shapes society. To properly understand law and the legal system, the wider social, cultural, political and economic context in which the law exists must also be understood. These are not simply matters for legal philosophers but are also vital for law students and practising lawyers. Understanding the context in which a law was created, and the purpose of the law can be crucial to understanding the meaning and proper scope of the law. In addition, those in the legal profession must understand the power of the law and how the law is or can be used to affect real people. As Coleman has observed,

A lawyer stands between the individual, her client, and the coercive machinery of the state ... Other times the lawyer seeks to have the machinery of the state employed for the purposes of coercing others or forcing wealth transfers.

---

[126] For an introduction, see, e.g., B Bix, *Jurisprudence: Theory and Context*, 7th ed. (London: Sweet & Maxwell 2015); M. Freeman, *Lloyd's Introduction to Jurisprudence*, 9th ed. (London: Sweet & Maxwell 2014); J. W. Harris, *Legal Philosophies*, 2nd ed. (Oxford: Oxford University Press 2004); N. E. Simmonds, *Central Issues in Jurisprudence: Justice, Law and Rights*, 5th ed. (London: Sweet & Maxwell 2018).

A lawyer who never put[s] herself in a position to reflect meaningfully on what it mean[s] to be a lawyer in this respect shows little respect for the power of the law and even less for herself.[127]

Moreover, if lawyers (and law students) themselves – as experts or practitioners of the law – do not understand what the meaning and significance of law is, then who *can* we expect to have such an understanding?

Structure of the Book

The book begins with looking at law on an abstract level. The fundamental questions of 'What is law?' and 'Why have law?' will be answered by discussing the function and concept of law (Chapter 2). This is certainly not an easy task, and with the limited scope and introductory nature of this book, one cannot hope to answer these jurisprudential issues that have been debated by jurists, scholars and political theorists for centuries. What Chapter 2 does is to provide students with a framework of the purposes of law in the Hong Kong context both at a macro and a micro level and to outline the major perspectives on law from the leading schools of thought. This way, law students and law practitioners may come to a greater understanding of the 'spirit of the law' and will be able to hone their skills in legal reasoning, which is the ultimate aim of this book. Chapter 2 concludes with the various classifications of law, so that students will have a better understanding of the chapters to come and in further law (or law-related) courses.

Chapter 3 is concerned with the system of governance in Hong Kong. The balance of the three branches of government (the legislative, the executive and the judiciary) demonstrates the complexity of a legal system and the unique arrangement of 'one country, two systems'. It also reviews the doctrine of the separation of powers which provides that not all power can be concentrated in a single entity or in the office of a few and how the doctrine is applicable to Hong Kong.

Moving away from theories and concepts, Chapter 4 looks at the sources of law in Hong Kong. As mentioned above, it is vital for students and practitioners to be able to find the law and know how to read it. But

---

[127] J. Coleman, 'Legal Theory and Practice' (1995), *Georgetown Law Journal* 83, 2579.

learning what the sources of laws are should not only be for legal (and prospective legal) practitioners. It is beneficial for those not in legal practice in Hong Kong to understand the laws of the region given how laws affect so many areas of our everyday lives. An overview of the sources of law in Hong Kong, namely the Basic Law, legislation, case law, customary Chinese law and national laws of the PRC, is given.

The court system and the doctrine of precedent are examined in Chapter 5. It is not difficult to appreciate that the courts are one of the most fundamental legal institutions in a legal system. Chapter 5 leads readers through the hierarchical structure of the courts and its historical development during the pre- and post-1997 periods. The second section of this chapter deals with judicial precedent, an essential feature of the common law. It would be an understatement to say that students will come across and be asked to read and comprehend case law in their further studies and future practice. This chapter would be useful for lay persons to understand the court system as they may become involved in judicial proceedings.

Chapter 6 discusses how laws are made in Hong Kong by studying the process of legislation. Issues surrounding how the Basic Law limits the scope of certain legislation as well as who has the authority to create legislation will be discussed. In the last part, readers are taken through the passage of legislation to see how a proposed bill achieves status as law in Hong Kong. Again, the interactions and balance between branches of government and between governments (the HKSAR and the PRC) will be illustrated in the process of legislation.

After legislation is enacted and in force, it is up to the courts to interpret them. Chapter 7 turns our attention to the judiciary and focuses on statutory interpretation. The various approaches to interpretation will be reviewed. Recognising how judges interpret laws will help hone the skills in legal reasoning (to think like judges), and as previously said, this skill is a must to ensure a successful and lasting career as a legal professional. Also, the common law approaches to statutory interpretation would be useful for readers from other jurisdictions, especially Mainland China and civil law jurisdictions, from a comparative standpoint.

Chapter 8 provides a general picture of the criminal justice system in Hong Kong. In particular it examines the roles and powers of key criminal justice agencies including the police, the Independent Commission Against Corruption and the prosecution. It goes through the criminal procedure in Hong Kong highlighting key decision points such as bail, court venue, the plea and the standard of proof. It concludes by looking at the various sentencing options at the court's disposal.

Chapter 9 focuses on the civil justice system in Hong Kong. It provides readers with an overview of civil litigation and its processes from starting an action to remedies. Similar to the previous chapter, key stages of civil procedure such as summary judgment, discovery and injunctions are highlighted and discussed. The chapter also looks at the Civil Justice Reform that occurred in Hong Kong in 2009, discussing the changes that were implemented in the civil justice system.

With the increasing popularity of alternative methods of resolving disputes to lessen the burden on courts, a separate chapter must be dedicated to this topic. One may not typically think of alternative methods of resolving disputes as part of the legal system, but Chapter 10 shows otherwise. Particularly with the Civil Justice Reform in 2009,[128] alternative dispute resolution will play an even larger role in resolving legal disputes in Hong Kong. The two main methods of alternative dispute resolution (mediation and arbitration) are examined.

Chapter 11 examines the various schemes of how individuals can obtain legal advice and representation in Hong Kong. The chapter discusses the split legal profession in Hong Kong and then focuses on legal aid and its various schemes and the schemes operated by the Duty Lawyer Service. Besides a descriptive account, this chapter also looks at the reforms that have been proposed with respect to legal aid and the challenges that litigants in persons may face and the problems that they may pose to the court system.

Chapter 12 seeks to equip students with the ability to find law and conduct legal research. Tips and techniques on finding the law quickly in both hard copy and online databases will be provided. The last part of Chapter 12 offers a manual for legal citation. Consistent with the aim of this book, this chapter guides students in bestowing them with the skill set necessary to start their legal studies and subsequent legal careers.

Finally, Chapter 13 examines the interface between Hong Kong law and International law and Chinese law. It looks at the distinct international legal personality that Hong Kong possesses, Hong Kong's engagement with international entities and the application of international law in Hong

---

[128] See Civil Justice Reform, available at www.civiljustice.hk/eng/home.html.

Kong. Although previous chapters have discussed certain aspects of the interface between Hong Kong and the PRC legal system, this chapter furthers this by centring on mutual legal assistance between the two legal systems, access to the Mainland market for legal services from Hong Kong and cross-border crime.

2 Functions and Concepts of Law

Chapter Highlights

- Functions of Law   36
- Major Perspectives on Law   43
- Classifications of Law   56

No one can deny that the law is everybody's business and that it affects our everyday behaviour and decision-making in many respects. This chapter provides a brief definition of law and examines how it functions in society. As Miller argues, 'What is law?' is a fundamental question that every individual must ask. But a simple or obvious answer is hard to come by, and the most fundamental legal concepts are often subject to differing perspectives.[1] The multifaceted nature of law is then illustrated. The earlier sections of this chapter briefly comment on the meaning and functions of law, while subsequent sections are concerned with the classification of law, including criminal and civil law, private and public law, and procedural and substantive law. At the outset, it is important to emphasise that this chapter highlights some of the most important and interesting points that have been raised by various commentators in respect of the law. It is simply impossible to give a complete answer to the question 'What is law?' in the context of this introductory textbook.

Law is defined as a body of rules of conduct prescribed by the authorities or the state; in the event of its breach, sanctions or legal penalties will be imposed. Law usually takes a written form. The law pervades almost every aspect of our daily lives. Every contract, marriage, divorce, crime or

---

[1] J. Miller, *Getting into Law* (Chatswood, NSW: Butterworths 2002), p. 3.

purchase places individuals face to face with the law.² The law also regulates conduct and the relationships between 'persons' in a society, not only 'natural' persons but 'legal' persons as well, including groups, companies and the government.³ The types of conduct regulated by law are quite broad, ranging from minor transactions, such as the terms of entry in a competition⁴ or a contract for dry cleaning,⁵ to the right to vote in Legislative Council elections⁶ and the protection of life, liberty and property through sanctions of the criminal law.⁷ But the divisions and classifications of law regulating all the diverse activities of persons within a society can be confusing, indeed overwhelming, to the lay person. For example, whether we work as an employee or employer, our conduct is governed by employment law,⁸ contract law and ultimately the relevant provisions and principles of the Basic Law.

Learning how the law is organised and classified is useful to anyone engaged in business or social activities in Hong Kong and elsewhere. Knowledge of the law and the legal system will also lead to a greater awareness of our legal rights and responsibilities, and most importantly 'help guide you towards [a] happier and more financially successful [life]'.⁹ This is becoming increasingly relevant, since developments in the legal system are now encouraging lay people to participate instead of its being the exclusive preserve of legal professionals. For example, the Small Claims Tribunal requires the hearing of matters to be conducted in an informal manner,¹⁰ and it does not allow any qualified barrister or solicitor to appear on behalf of any party in the tribunal;¹¹ it also gives the right of audience to lay people.¹² Thus, if we have some basic knowledge about the

---

² E. T. McMahon, L. P. Arbetman and E. L. O'Brien, *Street Law: A Course in Practical Law*, 3rd ed. (St Paul, MN: West Publishing 1986), p. 3.
³ M. Partington, *Introduction to the English Legal System 2019–2020*, 14th ed. (Oxford: Oxford University Press 2019), chapter 2.
⁴ *Chappell & Co. Ltd v. Nestle Co. Ltd* [1959] 2 All ER 701.
⁵ *Curtis v. Chemical Cleaning and Dyeing Co. Ltd.* [1951] 1 KB 805.
⁶ Basic Law, art. 26.
⁷ Crimes Ordinance (Cap. 200).
⁸ Employment Ordinance (Cap. 57).
⁹ D. L. Carper and B. W. West, *Understanding the Law*, 4th ed. (Mason, OH: Thomson/South-Western West 2004), p. 2.
¹⁰ Small Claims Tribunal Ordinance (Cap. 338), s. 16.
¹¹ Ibid., s. 19.
¹² Ibid.

law and the legal system, we can make better use of our legal rights in this and other situations.

If one wants to practise as a lawyer or judicial officer, or become a member of one of the many law enforcement agencies, one must have a thorough appreciation of the laws of Hong Kong. Learning how to read and interpret the law is the starting point of a successful legal or law-related career. A good lawyer will also understand the dynamic nature of the law and its sources and functions. This involves appreciating the law as subject to multifarious political and moral perspectives, and recognising the sometimes uneasy relationship between law and justice, and between 'law' and 'morality'. It is also important that the law not be static but change with time and with the changing definitions of concepts such as justice and morality. For example, whereas homosexuality has been considered both immoral and illegal, in the last few decades there has been a move towards decriminalisation. In this respect, 'everything that is considered immoral is not necessarily illegal'.[13]

Functions of Law

Law has many faces and is defined differently according to different points of view. More specifically, 'law, like happiness, poverty and good music, is different things to different people. Politicians may see it as the expression of current government policy, accommodating the recurrent tensions between such groups as employees and employers, conservationists and developers, and so on ... Lawyers may see law as a familiar tool, to be manipulated to get the best results for their clients. Poor people may see law as hostile and inaccessible.'[14] Broadly speaking, the role of law in society is best understood by observing its separate functions for society at large (the macro functions), and for persons within the society (the micro functions).[15]

---

[13] McMahon, Arbetman and O'Brien (n. 2), p. 4.
[14] R. Chisholm and G. Nettheim, *Understanding Law*, 6th ed. (Chatswood, NSW: Butterworths 2002), p. 1.
[15] For full details, please read Partington (n. 3), chapter 2.

Macro Functions of the Law

The salient feature of the macro functions of the law is order. Aristotle first said, 'Law is order, and good law is good order.'[16] The order contemplated here by Aristotle remains the most fundamental function of the law for the many different spheres of modern society.

Public Order

Law is essential to maintaining a peaceful public order, and a successful legal system will achieve this by various means. The Basic Law provides public order through structure and stability. The various ordinances in Hong Kong disperse the provision of that order to specific areas of regulation. For instance, the Crimes Ordinance (Cap. 200) creates criminal sanctions for conduct detrimental to the public order. As an example, it is an offence under this ordinance[17] to raise and train a private armed force, because this falls outside the legitimate provision of state-operated armed forces; the consequent chaos and danger of several competing forces of privately owned and operated militia is obvious.

Political Order

Political order is established in a society by the law that creates and regulates political systems and processes. This is usually done by a constitution[18] (the ultimate law in a jurisdiction) and by other legislation that governs the specific and logistical aspects of the political and electoral processes. In Hong Kong, the ultimate law that establishes the structure of government is the Basic Law, while the specific aspects of the process, such as elections, are governed by specific ordinances such as the Electoral

---

[16] Aristotle (384 BCE–322 BCE), *Politics* (Chicago, IL: Chicago University Press 1984).
[17] Crimes Ordinance (Cap. 200), s. 18: The offence contemplated in this section is called 'unlawful drilling' which makes it an offence to train or drill any other person in the use of arms or military exercise.
[18] For further reading on Hong Kong's constitutional position see: Y. Ghai, *Hong Kong's New Constitutional Order: The Resumption of Chinese Sovereignty and the Basic Law*, 2nd ed. (Hong Kong: Hong Kong University Press 1997).

Affairs Commission Ordinance (Cap. 541) and the Elections (Corrupt and Illegal Conduct) Ordinance (Cap. 554).

The political order of a place or a country is also achieved through regulation of the government. In Hong Kong this is accomplished through multiple avenues. It is a legacy of the British political system that the Legislative Council creates and enforces its own rules and is immune from judicial interference under the doctrine of the separation of powers.[19] But judicial review may be available through constitutional law if the government fails to adhere to the Basic Law; or through administrative law if the conduct of the government or individual members is proven to be unreasonable, illegal or unconscionable.[20]

Social Order

A consequence of both capitalist and other economic systems is the social disparity that occurs between classes of people. These classes may be determined by wealth, education, race, ethnicity, religion or some other differential capacity to succeed in the capitalist pursuit. The law's function to maintain social order is twofold. Firstly, it protects the rights of the majority by providing a mechanism for the pursuit of wealth and capital. For example, contract law permits persons to enter into business transactions, and the courts will do little to extend the law's principles to interfere with these arrangements, especially if this will affect the efficacy of business.[21] Second, modern law provides a social order that serves to protect the interests of the less powerful party. As in the above example of contract law, which provides for commercial agreements, the law also seeks to protect the interests of less powerful parties in such transactions through both equitable doctrines[22] and various ordinances such as the

---

[19] The doctrine of the separation of powers will be discussed in Chapter 3.
[20] Judicial review is taken from the broad interpretation of art. 35 of the Basic Law, which provides Hong Kong residents a right to institute legal proceedings in the courts against acts of the executive authorities and their personnel. See A. Cheung and M. Wong, 'Judicial Review and Policy Making in Hong Kong: Changing Interface between the Legal and the Political' (2006), *The Asian Pacific Journal of Public Administration* 28(2), 117.
[21] G. Velijanovski, 'The Economic Approach to Law: A Critical Introduction' (1980), *British Journal of Law and Society* 7, 158.
[22] Equity is an area of law arising from the British Courts of Chancery and is commonly involved in disputes resulting from unfairness in contractual relations.

Unconscionable Contracts Ordinance (Cap. 458), the Sale of Goods Ordinance (Cap. 26) and the Consumer Goods Safety Ordinance (Cap. 456).

Economic Order

In a market economy like Hong Kong's, it is necessary for the law to provide a consistent regulation of the market. The order and stability provided by the law creates both confidence in the market and a successful economy. Law also functions to redistribute wealth in society. The government collects money through the salary tax based on an individual's income and other revenue,[23] part of which is then distributed through the welfare system[24] to ensure a minimum economic standard for society.

International Order

The law functions to promote international order both domestically and in international co-operation. The cumulative effect of the law's provision of social and economic order in many individual countries is to facilitate a cohesive international order. The co-operation among individual countries on specific issues of law and justice also works to facilitate international order. For example, the modern understanding of drug offences has been the result of many international conferences and conventions[25] that have, to some extent, created internationally understood goals in the policing of drugs; these goals have been effective because many countries have incorporated the decisions of these conventions into their domestic law. The law also has specific functions that attempt to create international order beyond the jurisdiction of the domestic law of individual countries.

International bodies such as the United Nations and the institutions of the European Union function to consult with the international community and to develop policies for it. Rogue countries face the possibility of

---

[23] Inland Revenue Ordinance (Cap. 112).
[24] See, for example, Surviving Spouses' and Children's Pensions Ordinance (Cap. 79).
[25] These conventions include the First International Opium Convention 1912, the Second International Opium Convention 1925, the Convention for the Suppression of the Illicit Traffic in Dangerous Drugs 1936, and the Single Convention on Narcotic Drugs 1961.

sanctions and trade boycotts. An example is the controversial sanctions against Iraq under the Saddam Hussein regime for its alleged production of nuclear, biological and chemical weapons.[26]

International relations are also regulated through international law. This may be done through customary rules or through treaties and conventions.[27] Much of international law stems from maritime law, which historically held jurisdiction over the major ways in which nation states communicated and traded.

Moral Order

Law is also an instrument of morality, and this function has survived revolutions and protests against the government's secularisation. For example, Hong Kong and many other jurisdictions consider sexual slavery[28] and living off the earnings of prostitutes ('pimping') as offences.[29] The law reflects contemporary moral values and aims to guide the conduct of citizens through this moral enterprise.

The English House of Lords' decision in the case of *R* v. *Dudley and Stephens*[30] illustrates the difficulties the law faces in creating this moral order. In this case, the accused were the surviving two members of a three-member crew of a shipwrecked vessel who were cast adrift in a small lifeboat. Their food supplies had become depleted, and the two accused decided to accelerate the death of the youngest crew member, whose health was ailing, by killing him; they survived by eating his body. After several days they were rescued and were later tried in England for the crime of murder. The judgment in that case recognised that the accused had faced an extraordinarily urgent situation, but that ultimately the law could not draw a line beyond which the killing of another human being was justified. One reason was the inability to determine a universal morality that would be able to decide in such a situation which life was more valuable, the youngest, the smartest, the strongest, or the weakest, the sickest or most

---

[26] See A. Downer, 'The Spread of Nuclear, Chemical and Biological Weapons: The Sum of All Our Fears' (2003), *Sydney Papers* 15(1), 30.
[27] See S. Hall, *Foundations of International Law*, 3rd ed. (Hong Kong: LexisNexis 2016).
[28] Crimes Ordinance (Cap. 200), s. 134.
[29] Ibid., s. 137.
[30] [1881-85] All ER 61.

vulnerable. Consequently, both of the accused were convicted. This case has become a well-known example of the moral function of the law.[31]

Micro Functions of the Law

The micro functions of the law affect the conduct of all persons within a society on an individual level. The law prescribes the boundaries of conduct and the consequences for defying those boundaries. These boundaries and consequences apply to all 'persons', and it is an important principle of the rule of law that no person, natural or legal, is immune from these sanctions.[32] 'Laws are partly formed for the sake of good men, in order to instruct them how they may live on friendly terms with one another, and partly for the sake of those who refuse to be instructed, whose spirit cannot be subdued, or softened, or hindered from plunging into evil.'[33] The micro functions of the law are as follows:[34]

- **Law defines the limits of acceptable behaviour.**
  Although most people do not think about it while performing their day-to-day activities, the law governs nearly everything we do every day. Driving, for example, is regulated by the licensing of drivers,[35] road and traffic rules,[36] and ordinances commissioning the money and work needed for building and maintaining roads;[37] criminal sanctions further define what we can or cannot do when driving, such as being under the influence of drugs or alcohol.[38] The law has the responsibility of setting these limits to prevent individuals from harming themselves or others, and consequently of preventing harm to society.

---

[31] For further reading relating to the law, morality and the case of *Dudley and Stephens*, see L. Fuller, 'The Case of the Speluncean Explorers' (1949), *Harvard Law Review* 6a, 616.
[32] The definition of the rule of law has been discussed in Chapter 1.
[33] Plato (427 BCE–347 BCE).
[34] P. Wesley-Smith, *An Introduction to the Hong Kong Legal System*, 3rd ed. (Hong Kong: Oxford University Press 1998), chapter 1.
[35] Road Traffic (Driving Licences) Regulations (Cap. 374B), r. 10.
[36] See, e.g., Road Traffic Ordinance (Cap. 374).
[37] See, e.g., Roads (Works, Use and Compensation) Ordinance (Cap. 370).
[38] Road Traffic Ordinance (Cap. 374), s. 39.

- **Law defines the consequences of certain forms of behaviour.**

  The law prescribes punishment for persons when they do not conform to the limits of conduct that it permits. The best example is in criminal law. If a person intentionally kills another human being and is convicted for the crime of murder, he or she will be punished with life imprisonment.[39]

- **Law defines the processes for the transaction of business and other activities.**

  The law provides facilities for private business arrangements between individuals. This may be as simple as a contract formed when purchasing medicine[40] or determining the precise point in an auction where the sale has occurred.[41] Another example is the Employment Ordinance (Cap. 57) which requires notice to be given for the termination of employment.[42] It also provides for rest days[43] and maternity leave.[44] These are important provisions that employers may seek to avoid in the absence of any law defining them as mandatory.

- **Law creates regulatory frameworks.**

  The law not only functions to regulate our behaviours and settle our disputes but also regulates its own creation and application. In Hong Kong, the Basic Law governs which laws will apply in the region.[45] It also regulates how new laws should be reported to the Standing Committee of the National People's Congress[46] and places other restrictions on new laws.[47]

- **Law prevents the abuse of official powers.**

  Just as the law functions to prescribe the boundaries and consequences of conduct for everyday activities, special laws function to prescribe these boundaries and consequences for the behaviour of our officials and lawmakers in their official capacities.[48] In this respect, it makes

---

[39] Crimes Ordinance (Cap. 200), s. 159J.
[40] *Pharmaceutical Society of Great Britain* v. *Boots Cash Chemists Ltd* [1953] 1 QB 401.
[41] *Payne* v. *Cave* (1789) 3 TR 148.
[42] Employment Ordinance (Cap. 57), s. 6.
[43] Employment Ordinance (Cap. 57), s. 17.
[44] Employment Ordinance (Cap. 57), s. 12.
[45] Basic Law, art. 8.
[46] Basic Law, art. 17. See Chapter 6, 'The Process of Legislation'.
[47] Basic Law, art. 18.
[48] See, e.g., Elections (Corrupt and Illegal Conduct) Ordinance (Cap. 554).

sure that no one is above the law, and all members of a society should be treated equally.

Major Perspectives on Law

The question 'What is law?' is difficult to answer. It is indeed a philosophical question, and the philosophical study of law is generally known as jurisprudence.[49] Some believe that law comprises a set of universal moral principles defined by nature; some see the law as man-made rules and commands; and some interpret the law as protecting individual rights and providing justice.[50] The notion of law is inextricably linked with social, political, moral and religious perspectives. Reaching a definition of law has been the life work of many philosophers and legal theorists, yet we are still no closer to a generally acceptable working definition. This section explores the basics of the major traditions of legal theory.[51] It should be emphasised that the following provides only a brief overview of the major perspectives on law.[52]

Natural Law

Ideas of natural law can be traced back to the times of the ancient Greeks – to the time of Plato and Aristotle, over 2,000 years ago. But ideas of natural law have not been static, and different theorists have put forward different versions of natural law theory in different times. Notwithstanding the diversity of natural law theories, a basic tenet of natural law theory is the idea that there is a necessary connection between law and morality. That is, the notion of law itself connotes certain moral values and principles.

---

[49] M. D. A. Freeman, *Lloyd's Introduction to Jurisprudence*, 9th ed. (London: Sweet & Maxwell 2014).
[50] R. Wacks, *Philosophy of Law: A Very Short Introduction*, 2nd ed. (Oxford: Oxford University Press 2014), introduction.
[51] A very useful article on the subject of the major legal traditions is S. Ratnapala, 'What is Law?' in J. F. Corkery (ed.), *A Career in Law*, 2nd ed. (Annandale, NSW: Federation Press 1989), 8.
[52] For details, please refer to textbooks on jurisprudence such as R. Wacks, *Understanding Jurisprudence: An Introduction to Legal Theory* (Oxford: Oxford University Press 2005); and B. Bix, *Jurisprudence: Theory and Context*, 4th ed. (London: Sweet & Maxwell 2006).

The Roman theorist Cicero stated that 'True law is right reason in agreement with nature; it is of universal application, unchanging and everlasting ... And there will not be different laws at Rome and at Athens, or different laws now and in the future, but one external and unchangeable law will be valid for all nations and all times.'[53] This statement reflects the basic ideas of natural law theorists within the classical tradition. Such classical theories put forward the view that there is a set of principles of law – called natural law – which are universal and immutable. They are universal in that they are applicable to all persons in different countries and in different eras, and they are immutable in that they do not change over time. This natural law is sometimes also said to be a 'higher law' in that it is superior to the black letter law made and enforced by the state. The actual laws promulgated by a state (termed 'positive law') would not be 'good' laws or 'true' laws if they are inconsistent with the natural law. The principles of natural law are fundamental and should be the source of the positive laws of the state, and provide a model against which the positive laws of a state can be measured.

But while the basic premise of classical natural law theories is that the law must accord with morality, the question arises as to whose morality it is. There is much controversy over the existence of a universal moral code which defines right and wrong in all contexts. Classical Greek scholars maintained that universal law is discoverable by reason, that is, by inquiry into the patterns of nature, and that morality is all that follows that pattern.[54] Catholic scholars such as St Thomas Aquinas[55] asserted that human law is subject to the law of God and that divine law is superior. For Aquinas, the universal principles of the law of God are revealed to humans both through scriptures and through human reasoning. Aquinas thus continued the Greek notions of natural law as being discoverable by human rationality but he located natural law firmly with Christianity.

A secular version of natural law comes from social contract theorists, whose heavy influence on modern history is undeniable. The basic notion of a social contract is that individuals relinquish their autonomy to the

---

[53] Cicero, *De Re Publica*, in J. W. Harris, *Legal Philosophies* (Oxford: Oxford University Press 2004), pp. 7–8.
[54] Aristotle, *Politics* (Chicago, IL: Chicago University Press 1984), pp. 1–2.
[55] T. Aquinas, *Summa Theologica I-II, Q96, The Political Ideas of St Thomas Aquinas* (D. Bigongiari, ed.) (New York, NY: Hafner 1953), p. 2.

state, and in return the State protects their natural rights such as those relating to life, liberty and property. When the people, as the collective entity of individuals, are dissatisfied with the state's protection, they have the right to revolt. The key figures of this movement were John Locke,[56] Jean-Jacques Rousseau[57] and Charles de Montesquieu.[58] Modern ideas of fundamental universal human rights can in part be traced back to the natural rights ideas of these political theorists of the Enlightenment era.

One of the more notable adherents of natural law theory in modern times is John Finnis.[59] In his theory, Finnis starts by considering what is good for human flourishing; that is, what is good for humans, given our nature. For Finnis, these universal 'basic goods' are knowledge, life, play, aesthetic experience, sociability/friendship, practical reasonableness (the ability to use intelligence to choose your own actions) and religion (which means not only accepted or established religions but simply the ability or freedom to reflect on the universal order of things). Coupled with these basic goods are what Finnis refers to as 'methodological requirements of practical reasonableness', which are ways of acting in order to achieve the basic goods. The most fundamental of these principles is the principle of choosing in a way that is compatible with the basic goods. From the basic goods and principles of practicable reasonableness, it is possible to derive a set of moral principles of what people ought or ought not to do. These moral principles can then be used to determine what the positive law should be.

Another contemporary natural law theorist is Lon L. Fuller,[60] who provides a different version of natural law as being not a 'higher law' but simply a set of principles that should generally exist in order for there to be something that can be described as a legal system. For Fuller, law is the enterprise of subjecting human conduct to the governance of rules. So, for there to be law, there must be rules in place which are publicly known, understandable, not contradictory, workable and enforced in practice. Moreover, the rules must not have retrospective effect, and there must be

---

[56] J. Harrison and P. Laslett, *The Library of John Locke*, 2nd ed. (Clarendon Press, Oxford 1971).
[57] J. J. Rousseau, *A Discourse upon the Origin and Foundation of the Inequality Among Mankind* (New York, NY: B. Franklin 1971).
[58] Charles de Montesquieu, *On the Spirit of Laws* (1748).
[59] J. Finnis, *Natural Law and Natural Rights* (Oxford: Clarendon Press 1980).
[60] L. L. Fuller, *The Morality of Law*, revised ed. (New Haven, CT: Yale University Press 1969).

some stability to the rules. Fuller refers to these principles as the 'inner morality of law', to reflect the idea that these principles are innate or intrinsic to the notion of law.

Legal Positivism

Legal positivism is often regarded to be the polar opposite of natural law. It gives no consideration to morality or to what the law should be. Its sole consideration is what the law positively *is*. Whether something is law is a matter of social fact. This is referred to as the social thesis in legal positivism. A second tenet of legal positivism (the separation thesis) states that what the law actually *is* may be completely disconnected from concepts of morality and justice. The question of 'What is the law?' and the question of whether the law is good or 'What should be the law?' are separate.

Inspired by the writings of Thomas Hobbes,[61] Jeremy Bentham became one of the first positivists, drawing a distinction between the law of 'expositors', who lay down the law, and the law of 'censors', who appraise the law and theorise about what it ought to be. Bentham's perception of law is that it is only, and strictly, the law as it is laid down, and the law of the censors is nothing but a critical appraisal that might become law only if it is incorporated into the law of the expositors.[62] Law, as advocated by Bentham, is 'the command of him that have the legislative power'.[63]

The theories of legal philosopher John Austin succeeded Bentham and furthered his ideas of the law as strictly limited to the command of the legislator.[64] For Austin, a command involves a wish expressed by a person that another will or will not do some act. Also, the person making the command has the power to inflict harm if the wish is not obeyed; that is,

---

[61] Thomas Hobbes (1588–1679) was an influential legal philosopher whose theories on parliamentary sovereignty had major impact on the Glorious Revolution in England. For further bibliographic reading on Hobbes, see J. Laird, *Hobbes* (London: Benn 1934).

[62] J. Bentham, *An Introduction to the Principles of Morals and Legislation* (Oxford: Clarendon Press 1907).

[63] *Dialogue of the Common Laws* (1681) in *Works*, vol. VI 26, cited in Ratnapala (n. 51), pp. 8–9.

[64] J. Austin, *Lectures on Jurisprudence: Of the Philosophy of Positive Law* (London: Murray 1885).

there are sanctions imposed if the wish is not compiled with. The legislator or the person making the command must be the sovereign. The sovereign is a person whom others generally obey and who does not have to follow anyone else.

The ideas of the early positivists, as represented by the command theory of law, sought to treat the study of what law is as a scientific enterprise, based on empirical observations of fact in determining whether something is or is not law. The most notable modern proponent of legal positivism, H. L. A. Hart, moved the analysis away from a strict empirical approach that followed the hard sciences towards an approach reflective of social sciences. This approach takes into account not only observations of actions but also the meaning of the actions to participants in the legal system.[65] Hart sees law as a species of social rules.[66] What characterises the legal species of rules from other social rules is not simply that they carry an obligation, but also that there is a systemic quality in the interrelationship between the categories of legal rules.[67] For Hart, the legal system involves two categories of rules, primary and secondary rules. Primary rules impose duties, such as in criminal law or tort law, while secondary rules are power-conferring rules, namely rules which confer power on law enforcement agencies, rules which allow individuals to structure their legal relations with others (such as contract law) and rules regulating law-making procedures. The last type of secondary rule constitutes what Hart refers to as the rule of recognition. Hart states that the basic rule of recognition in England is the rule that what the Queen in Parliament enacts is law. For Hong Kong, the basic rule of recognition comes from the PRC Constitution, as it is that constitution which provides the legal validity for the Basic Law and other laws in Hong Kong. The validity of the basic rule of recognition itself does not come from any other legal rule but is simply assumed or accepted to be valid by officials. Apart from the legal rules, Hart also emphasises the element of the internal aspect or internal point of view of law. By this, Hart is referring to the notion of obligation on the part of the people who themselves consider that there is an obligation to abide by the rules. This internal aspect distinguishes between acting in accordance with rules and acting by reason of habit.

---

[65] Bix (n. 52) p. 36.
[66] H. L. A. Hart, *The Concept of Law*, 2nd ed. (Oxford: Oxford University Press 1994).
[67] N. MacCormick, *H. L. A. Hart*, 2nd ed. (Stanford, CT: Stanford Law Books 2008), p. 31.

By noting the internal aspect of law, Hart's elucidation of law takes into account the normative nature of law. A norm is a standard of conduct, a standard that sets out what persons ought to do. Hans Kelsen, another relevant modern positivist, emphasised further the normative aspect of law.[68] For Kelsen, the legal order is a normative system. Law consists of a system of hierarchical norms which provides a chain of validity for the laws in a particular state. For example, consider the offence of bribery under s. 4 of the Prevention of Bribery Ordinance (Cap. 201). This provision is part of the law in Hong Kong because the provision was enacted by the Legislative Council. What is enacted by the Legislative Council is law because it has the power to make laws under the constitution in Hong Kong (the Basic Law). What the Basic Law prescribes is a valid law in Hong Kong because the Basic Law was enacted in accordance with the PRC Constitution. So, s. 4 of the ordinance constitutes a legal norm, the validity of which is provided for by another legal norm higher up in the hierarchy. The validity of each legal norm is provided for by a higher legal norm in the chain. According to Kelsen, each of the legal norms involves a primary norm directing the judges or officials to impose some sanction on a person who contravenes the secondary norm that proscribes the particular conduct (such as not to engage in bribery). The chain of validity must come to a stop at some point, and this will occur at the stage where it is not possible to find any higher legal norm that confers validity on all other legal norms in the particular legal system. For example, there is no further legal norm that gives validity to the PRC Constitution. At the top of the hierarchy is what Kelsen refers to as the *Grundnorm* or the basic norm. The basic norm is not a legal norm as its validity does not depend on another legal norm. The validity of the basic norm is presupposed. There has to be a basic norm as a matter of logical necessity. For each legal system, the content of the basic norm is simply that the constitution ought to be obeyed.

While legal positivism and natural law have traditionally been regarded as being in opposition to each other, the degree of conflict between the two theories depends on the particular version of positivism or natural law that is put forward. For example, while legal positivism rejects that there is a necessary connection between law and morality, some positivists (such as Hart) accept that particular legal systems can be constructed so that

---

[68] H. Kelsen, *The Pure Theory of Law* (M. Knight, trans.) (Berkeley, CA: University of California Press 1967).

the question of what is valid law can be shaped by morality (with such approaches referred to as soft positivism). Also, while some positivists might conclude that a positive law is binding even if it is supremely immoral, other positivists argue that whether something is law is one thing but whether there is an obligation to obey a validly made law is a separate question.[69] Conversely, while some natural law theorists might consider that a positive law that conflicts with the natural law is not true law and hence need not be obeyed, other theorists such as Finnis accept that although a positive law might not be a good law if it conflicts with the natural law, it is not a nullity as such and may still need to be obeyed to preserve the integrity of the legal system as a whole.

Sociology of Law

As summarised by Wacks, 'A sociological account of law normally rests on three closely related claims: that law cannot be understood except as a "social phenomenon", that an analysis of legal concepts provides only a partial explanation of "law in action", and that law is merely one form of social control.'[70] The sociology of law incorporates many elements from a variety of legal traditions, but specifically acknowledges the fact that law can change society at the same time that society changes law. It touches on critical perspectives on law, such as the Marxist and the feminist accounts which are discussed below. It also emphasises the importance of studying law in action as opposed to law in textbooks.

In saying that law must be understood as an entirely social phenomenon, sociologists seek to emphasise that law can only be understood as an aspect of social relationships, dealing with the co-existence of individuals in society.[71] While natural law theorists might conceive of a set of universal objective values underpinning law that transcend the distinctiveness of any particular society, sociologists tend to see law as being socially constructed and as a product of the particular circumstances of a society.

---

[69] See, e.g., F. Schauer, 'Positivism as Pariah', in R. P. George (ed.), *The Autonomy of Law: Essays on Legal Positivism* (Oxford: Clarendon Press 1996).
[70] Wacks (n. 52), p. 75.
[71] R. Cotterrell, 'Why Must Legal Ideas Be Interpreted Sociologically?' (1998), *Journal of Law and Society* 25, 171.

Max Weber,[72] for example, took the view that there is a matrix of forces which affects the development of law in any particular society. Weber described modern Western legal systems as formal rational law – formal in the sense that the legal system is internally self-sufficient where the rules and procedures necessary for decision-making are available within the system (as opposed to being sourced from outside the law, for example from religion); and rational in that decisions are made logically from the established rules and principles. For Weber, this type of legal system developed in the West as a result of the rationalism in Western philosophy (with the emphasis on logic and reasoning), the growth of government and bureaucracy (a strong centralised government can provide for the systematisation of law; moreover, with bureaucratic government comes the need for rational means of administration based on fixed rules) and the rise of capitalism (as capitalist economies depend on the existence of fixed and certain rules).

Other sociologists have examined other features of law. For example, Roscoe Pound[73] considered that law operates to reconcile the conflicting interests in society. There are conflicting interests arising from different claims by different persons with different wants, not all of which can be satisfied. In Pound's view, law is used to achieve a proper balance between the different interests. This balancing of interests results in a cohesive society with shared values and traditions. Other sociologists reject this type of consensus model of society, adopting instead a conflict model.[74] Under the latter model, it is said that law takes into account the interests of only particular parts of the population. Further, law is not a compromise between the different interests, but supports only certain interests at the expense of others. Proponents of the conflict model make the point that the consensus model overlooks systemic inequalities and the exclusion of certain groups from law-making.

Sociologists emphasise that law is an agent of social control, and this feature of law is revealed by both the consensus and conflict models of law. Under Pound's consensus model, law is used to order conduct to

---

[72] M. Rheinstein (ed.), *Max Weber on Law in Economy and Society* (Cambridge, MA: Harvard University Press 1954); A. Hunt, *The Sociological Movement in Law* (London: Macmillan 1978), chapter 5.

[73] R. Pound, *Contemporary Juristic Theory* (Claremont, CA: Claremont Colleges 1940).

[74] For example, R. Quinney, *The Social Reality of Crime* (Boston, MA: Little, Brown and Co. 1970).

satisfy the various interests in society as far as possible. For Durkheim,[75] another adherent of the consensus model, law is a measure of shared social values but at the same time law also operates to reinforce these social values in order to maintain social cohesion. Under the conflict model, law operates to coerce and constrain segments of society in the interests of the powerful. The ways in which law operates as a form of social control are diverse. The control of behaviour under criminal law provides an obvious example. However, other areas of law also effect social control, perhaps in subtler ways, for example employment law governs the dynamics between employers and employees, and licensing laws restrict and regulate particular activities in societies.[76]

Sociological approaches to law emphasise the importance of studying law in action as opposed to simply law in books. This entails a study of the actual social effects of legal institutions and legal rules and principles, and a study of the ways in which the purposes of law can be effectively achieved in the real world. Such an empirical approach to the study of law can be aided by the use of social science research techniques, such as surveys, case studies and other qualitative and quantitative research methods.

Law in action is the key principle of the tradition of legal realism, which attempts to identify the law at the point of enforcement, as opposed to the positivist perception of law at the point of its writing.[77] The American legal realism movement consisted of various American writers from the early part of the twentieth century, most notably Oliver Holmes,[78] Jerome Frank[79] and Karl Llewellyn.[80] There are differences between the works of the different theorists grouped as legal realists, but some major themes of realism include the following, as noted by Llewellyn:[81]

---

[75] E. Durkheim, *The Division of Labour and Society* (W. D. Halls, trans.) (Basingstoke: Macmillan 1984).
[76] See generally S. Vago and S. E. Barkan, *Law and Society*, 11th ed. (New York, NY: Routledge 2017).
[77] See Ratnapala (n. 51), p. 16.
[78] O. W. Holmes, 'The Path of the Law' (1897), *Harvard Law Review* 10, 457.
[79] J. Frank, *Law and the Modern Mind* (Gloucester: Peter Smith 1970).
[80] K. Llewellyn, *The Common Law Tradition: Deciding Appeals* (Boston, MA: Little, Brown and Co 1960).
[81] K. Llewellyn, 'Some Realism about Realism' (1931), *Harvard Law Review* 44, 1222.

- The idea that law is not static, and that there is judicial creation of the law. That is, judges do not simply apply or find the existing law, but actually make new law when deciding cases.
- Law is a means to social ends and not an end in itself. Thus, the law needs to be constantly examined for its purpose and for its effect, and to be judged in the light of the purpose and effect.
- Society is constantly in flux; that is, society is always changing and values are not static. There must be constant re-examination of the law to determine how far it fits the society which the law purports to serve.
- Focus is taken away from the legal rules so far as they purport to describe what either the courts or people are actually doing. Tied in with this idea is a distrust of the theory that the rules are *the* operative factor in producing court decisions.

Legal realists and those who appreciate the broader sociology of law recognise that a study of the legal rules in isolation is not sufficient. To have a proper understanding of both legal institutions and legal doctrines, it is necessary to examine the social, historical and cultural context of the law, including the social origins and effects of the law.[82]

Critical Legal Theory

Critical legal theorists hold that law is not an objective and value-free set of rules. This tradition holds that every legal system and legal rule has its own underlying political context, and that legal rules are used to consolidate and further the values and goals of political influence.

Critical scholars emphasise that every legal rule is based on political choice. In Western legal systems such as the common law system, underpinning the laws are values derived from liberal ideology or liberal concepts, such as values based on notions of freedom of the individual and individual rights. For example, property rights may be considered fundamental, but the concept of property rights is part of a political ideology based on notions of private property, and property law protects the interests of those who hold property. Critical scholars point out that problems

[82] See further Cotterrell (n. 71).

can occur in society when the political values upheld by the law protect certain segments of society at the expense of others. Taking property rights as an example again, the notion of property rights means that people who have property will be able to exercise rights, while those who do not will be marginalised and disadvantaged. This can lead to problems of poverty and inequality for those who do not have property.

The problem in law from this critical perspective is not only that injustice exists, but that the law itself upholds the relationships which cause injustice and thereby legitimates the oppression. The problem of legitimation of oppression arises because the legal system is presented under traditional legal theories (and by those in power) as being objective, fair and just, and inevitable and natural. But critical scholars argue that the law that exists in any particular society is not neutral and inevitable, but is something that is contingent and constructed.[83] Any particular legal system that exists is just a system that has been built by those in power over time. It may have been built in an attempt to consolidate their own power, or it may have been built in a genuine attempt to try to govern relationships between persons in a just and fair way. In either case, the system is one that has been constructed. But as the system becomes entrenched, the fact that it is one that has been constructed over time is no longer emphasised. People accept it as the way things are, thereby externalising the system – treating it as an objective system independent of human choice. The portrayal of the law as neutral and natural can mask exploitation. It is not simply a matter of the class in power using law as an instrument to oppress the weaker class. The focus of critical scholars is not on the obvious injustices or the obvious ways in which particular laws oppress the underprivileged. Rather, the concern is on how the image of the law itself is presented in a manner that even the underprivileged may not question the fundamental aspects of the law which are accepted by all as being fair and just but which in reality are underlying causes of injustice. As Robert Gordon has noted, 'the most effective kind of domination takes place when both the dominant and the dominated classes believe that the existing order, with perhaps some marginal changes, is satisfactory, or at least represents the most that anyone could expect,

---

[83] R. Gordon, 'New Developments in Legal Theory', in D. Kairys (ed.), *Politics of Law: A Progressive Critique* (New York, NY: Pantheon Books 1982), pp. 288–290.

because things pretty much have to be the way they are'.[84] Critical scholars, then, seek to highlight the underlying injustices to unmask the problems.

For example, when students learn about contract law, the underlying doctrines of contract law (such as freedom of contract) are presented as objective, fair and just. It seems to make sense to hold persons to contractual terms on which they have agreed. This seems 'natural'. However, critical scholars point out that contract law principles are not neutral and inevitable, but are a product of liberal and capitalist ideologies. Moreover, the apparent fairness of contract law is misleading, as there is almost always an imbalance of power between persons who enter into a contract. For example, consider the position of most employees vis-à-vis the employer under employment contracts, and consumers vis-à-vis businesses under consumer contracts. The inequality of bargaining power leads to disadvantage and oppression of the weaker segments of society. Yet the image of contract law as neutral and natural 'serves to provide a cloak of legitimacy to the underlying structural inequalities of power in society, such as those of class, gender and race'.[85] Against the critical scholars, it might be countered that contract law does provide protections and remedies for weaker parties – such as principles of undue influence and unconscionability. However, the critical scholar would argue that the scope of protection under these remedies is limited and fail to address the wider inequalities, and the existence and utilisation of such limited remedies actually reinforce the wider injustices. This is because the existence of undue influence or unconscionability is regarded as an exception to the norm, and so these remedies reinforce the picture of contract law as generally being fair and that 'normal' marketplace relations are unproblematically voluntary, informed, non-coercive and efficient.[86]

A number of different schools of critical legal theory have been developed by scholars. Post-colonial legal theory is an example. Under post-colonial perspectives of Hong Kong law, it is said that the apparent neutrality of Hong Kong's legal system masks and reinforces injustices that

---

[84] Ibid., p. 286.
[85] H. McCoubrey and N. D. White, *Textbook on Jurisprudence*, 3rd ed. (London: Blackstone Press 1999), p. 238.
[86] R. Gordon, 'Law and Ideology' (1988), *Tikkun* 3, 14.

arise from conflicts between local Chinese values and the Western values underlying the British laws imported into Hong Kong.[87]

Two other major examples of critical legal theory are the Marxist and feminist perspectives. These theories have had a significant impact on the modern understanding of law and are briefly introduced here.

The Marxist Perspective

Basic Marxist theory argues that law is an instrument of the powerful that is aimed at suppressing the masses.[88] A Marxist would argue that employment law, for example, is nothing more than a mechanism used by those in power, namely the capitalist bourgeoisie, to legitimise the oppression and exploitation of the proletariat, or working class. To many, the Marxist perspective seems dramatic and unrealistic, particularly in the light of existing employment laws that contain provisions to protect employees against late payment of wages[89] and to protect women from employment termination during pregnancy to avoid maternity leave payments.[90] But in practice the cost of legal fees and court filings in Hong Kong makes it quite difficult for an employee to bring action against an employer. It is not the law relevant to the dispute that functions to oppress the proletariat in this example; rather, a Marxist would argue that it is the laws governing the system itself that protect the bourgeoisie from legitimate proletariat dissent.

Feminist Legal Studies

Feminist legal theory holds similar views about law as an instrument of domination, but specifically focuses on law as an instrument of male domination. However, feminist legal theory is an extremely broad sociological enterprise, and it is impossible to outline the many different schools of feminist socio-legal perspectives. The basic premise shared by most schools is the existence of a social organisation in which men dominate women; this patriarchy forms the basis of institutions within the social

---

[87] W. M. Sin and Y. W. Chu, 'Whose Rule of Law? Rethinking (Post-)Colonial Legal Culture in Hong Kong' (1998), *Social & Legal Studies* 7(2), 147.
[88] L. J. Siegel, *Criminology*, 8th ed. (Belmont, CA: Wadsworth Thomson Learning 2003), p. 259.
[89] Employment Ordinance (Cap. 57), ss. 23, 25A.
[90] Employment Ordinance (Cap. 57), s. 15.

framework, including the legal system and particularly the criminal justice system. For example, an empirical study conducted by the Australian Institute of Criminology found that the main factor considered by Crown prosecutors in deciding whether to pursue a rape charge is the credibility of the victim.[91] It is doubtful whether in the case of a male victim of robbery, the prosecution would give much consideration to the sexual history and personal characteristics of the victim, or whether a prosecutor would decide to pursue a charge based on a judgment of the man's believability as a 'real victim'.

A similar phenomenon exists in much of the Commonwealth around the issue of battered woman syndrome. This syndrome applies to women who typically are physically abused over a long period of time and finally retaliate with violence and kill their partners; it is usually treated as a form of diminished responsibility for the crime of murder, although this varies across jurisdictions. Men who are provoked by their partners and retaliate with homicide only need to prove the provocation, and this will usually mitigate a murder charge.[92] But in the case of battered woman syndrome, women need to prove that the provocation of physical abuse has generated an actual psychological syndrome and require medical experts to attest to this; the provocation of sustained abuse is simply not enough. The inequality is obvious: to be granted some mitigation for 'human frailty' under the law, men need only to prove provocation, while women need a quantifiable psychological and medical dysfunction in addition.[93]

These are two specific examples of attention paid to the law by feminist legal theory, and they assist in orienting the beginner to the types of issues addressed by feminist theorists.

Classifications of Law

The law is classified according to its function and the context in which it is being used. These divisions and classifications can be puzzling at first,

---

[91] Australian Institute of Criminology, 'The Importance of Victim Credibility in Prosecuting Adult Sexual Assault Cases' (2005), *Crime Facts Information* 91, 1.

[92] See *R* v. *Cunningham* [1959] 1 QB 288.

[93] For further reading on battered woman syndrome, see 'Gender-Specific Response Patterns in Criminal Defences: Editorial' (1996), *Criminal Law Journal* 20, 185.

since some of the terms are used in different contexts to mean vastly different things. Legal systems are also classified according to their tradition and organisation; the system of a jurisdiction has an inextricable effect on the function of the law. This section explores some of the classifications of legal systems and the way in which the law is divided within them.

Common Law System and Civil Law System

The common law system is the underlying tradition of the English legal system. It comprises judge-made law, called common law, (including the rules of equity) and statute law (or legislation). Common law is created through the decisions of the superior courts[94] in a court hierarchy. It is made through the reporting of these decisions and by courts interpreting and applying the binding legal principles in a case. In doing so, a judge will look for the reason behind the judgment. This reason is called the *ratio decidendi* and is the portion of a judgment that is binding. The other portion of the judgment is known as *obiter dicta*, which are comments that are influential and instructive but not necessarily binding. Common law is also referred to as judge-made law, case law, precedent or unenacted law. Central to common law is the doctrine of *stare decisis*, which is covered in Chapter 5 as the doctrine of precedent.

Equity is an area of law arising from the English Court of Chancery and was developed in disputes resulting from unfairness for which a remedy was not available through the strict boundaries of the writ system of the common law. Equitable doctrines are principles of this fairness and justice that evolved from the precedents of the Court of Chancery: once the Chancellor made a decision on a subject matter in the Court of Chancery, similar petitions could be made. Such equitable doctrines include unconscionability and undue influence, which prevent parties to contracts from pressuring or tricking less powerful parties into unfair consumer or business agreements.[95]

The civil law system, originating from Roman law, is different and comprises most of the European nations' legal systems. This law is derived entirely from statutes that state the law exhaustively. No judge is needed to interpret the law and apply precedents, as the statutes in a civil law

---

[94] The structure of the court hierarchy of Hong Kong will be discussed in detail in Chapter 5.
[95] Partington (n. 3), chapter 2.

jurisdiction are already complete and instructive. These exhaustive statutes are called codes.

Other major legal systems of the world include the Sino-Soviet system, based on the writings of Karl Marx, the Hindu legal system, and Islamic law, or Sharia.[96]

Inquisitorial System and Adversarial System

The distinction between an inquisitorial system and an adversarial system is based on how matters are heard before a judge. In an inquisitorial arrangement, the judge will intervene, ask questions, direct counsel on legal matters and generally take an active role in the pre-trial investigation of a matter. In an adversarial system, a judge has no knowledge of the matter pre-trial and is passive and impartial throughout the proceedings. It is the task of counsel for the different parties in the matter to be 'adversaries' and battle it out in front of a judge, and maybe a jury. Sometimes a country that maintains an adversarial system will, for special reasons, create a proceeding where a judge or someone in place of a judge will act in an inquisitorial manner.[97] This type of arrangement is usually called an inquiry or a commission and is often used to investigate government or major business conduct, such as the Enron example in the United States,[98] or a coronial inquiry performed by a coroner into the cause of death in a suspected homicide case.

National and International Law

The sources of law in Hong Kong will be discussed in detail in Chapter 4; at this stage it is necessary to appreciate the distinction between national and international law. National,[99] or domestic (or municipal), law is enacted by

---

[96] R. David and J. E. C. Brierley, *Major Legal Systems in the World Today: An Introduction to the Comparative Study of Law*, 3rd ed. (London: Stevens 1985); W. Menski, *Comparative Law in a Global Context: The Legal Systems of Asia and Africa*, 2nd ed. (New York, NY: Cambridge University Press 2006).

[97] K. Malleson and R. Moules, *The Legal System*, 4th ed. (New York, NY: Oxford University Press 2010), chapter 1.

[98] P. H. Dembinski, C. Lager, A. Cornford and J.M. Bonvin (eds.), *Enron and World Finance: A Case Study in Ethics* (New York, NY: Macmillan Palgrave 2005).

[99] Wesley-Smith classifies national law as laws made by the PRC while the laws of Hong Kong fall under the category of municipal or local law. Wesley-Smith (n. 34), p. 18.

the legislature of a jurisdiction and is enforceable and applicable to that jurisdiction. For example, the Crimes Ordinance[100] of Hong Kong makes certain conduct criminal in the jurisdiction of Hong Kong. This jurisdiction does not usually extend to acts performed outside Hong Kong. National law in Hong Kong comprises the Basic Law, common law, rules of equity and statutes in the form of ordinances. National law also includes those laws made under delegated powers. This type of statute law is called delegated legislation and usually comprises regulatory details to assist in implementing statutory schemes and programmes.

International law, on the other hand, is usually an agreement between sovereign states and members of international organisations to co-operate on certain matters. These agreements are usually called treaties or conventions. Hong Kong is signatory to over 200 treaties and agreements with members of the international community.[101] These covenants and agreements become part of the domestic (or municipal) law of Hong Kong once they are implemented by laws passed by the Legislative Council.

Substantive and Procedural Law

Law is also classified according to its function as either substantive or procedural. The basic distinction involves the operational function of a provision of law. If a law creates an offence or regulation in itself, then it is usually substantive. If the law is descriptive or prescribes the function of a substantive or operative law, then it is procedural.

A related distinction in jurisprudence is that between substantial and procedural justice. Substantial justice, in this context, is created when the law functions to create a result that is in accord with traditional notions of justice, equality before the law, prompt and fair inquiry and the exercise of law as fair and equitable. Procedural justice is limited to the area of curial due process. The trial in South Africa of Nelson Mandela,[102] which led to his political imprisonment for nearly two decades before his freedom and subsequent presidency, was in accord with procedural justice. Mandela

---

[100] Crimes Ordinance (Cap. 200).
[101] For example, the International Covenant on Civil and Political Rights, the International Covenant on Economic, Social and Cultural Right and the International Labour Conventions.
[102] For more details on the trial of Nelson Mandela, see P. Limb, *Nelson Mandela: A Biography* (Westport, CT: Greenwood Press 2008), pp. 63–78.

had curial due process for the trial of his 'crimes', but it was the substantive law, or the 'crimes' themselves, that created the case for outrage in the area of substantial justice.

Public and Private Law

The distinction between public and private law is based on the law's control of both private parties and the state (government) in different ways, or by different means. Private law is defined as 'the body of law regulating the rights and duties that exist between private persons ("persons" being a term that includes corporations)'.[103] Areas of private law include matters of equity, tort, contract, property, family, commercial, succession, intellectual property and corporate law. On the other hand, public law is 'the body of law directly concerned with public rights and obligations'.[104] Public law consists of constitutional and administrative, criminal and taxation law. These laws have traditionally placed substantive duties on public authorities with regard to fairness and equity in the discharge of their business; for example, the provision of free public health services as based on need, not means.

Civil and Criminal Law

Civil law here has a different meaning from that above, where the civil law systems were considered. The distinction between this type of civil law and criminal law is based on the parties in the matter and what the matter concerns. Criminal jurisdiction involves an accused or defendant who has committed a crime. This crime, whether it has a complaining witness (i.e., a victim) or not, is against society. Society, including any victim of the offence, is represented by the prosecution. To be successful, the prosecution has an onus to prove 'beyond a reasonable doubt'[105] that the accused party is guilty of the offence. If the prosecution is able to discharge that onus, the consequence for the accused is punitive, in the form of fines or incarceration.

---

[103] Carper and West (n. 9), p. 21.
[104] Ibid.
[105] See *Woolmington* v. *DPP* [1935] AC 462.

A civil dispute involves two or more persons (legal or natural), who are represented by counsel or self-represented. In a civil case, the party bringing the matter to court is called the plaintiff and the other party is the defendant. The plaintiff's onus is to prove its complaint 'on the balance of probabilities', which is a more relaxed requirement than 'beyond a reasonable doubt'. The consequences for the defendant if the plaintiff is successful are compensatory, and usually financial, by way of damages, costs and possibly an injunction.[106]

Review Questions

(1) Why does society need laws?
(2) Make a list of your day-to-day activities (such as dining in a restaurant, shopping, travelling, posting photographs on the Internet). Are there laws that affect these activities? What is the major function of each law that you identify?
(3) What is the relationship between law and justice?
(4) In your opinion, can law protect the interests of the poor? Give examples to justify your answer.

---

[106] See Chapters 8 and 9 on Hong Kong's criminal justice system and civil justice system, respectively.

3 Governance in Hong Kong

Chapter Highlights

- 'One Country, Two Systems'   62
- High Degree of Autonomy   67
- Executive, Legislature and Judiciary   71
- Separation of Powers   76

This chapter provides an overview of the system of governance in Hong Kong. The discussion introduces the fundamental concepts of 'one country, two systems' and 'high degree of autonomy' under the Basic Law, which provide the framework for the allocation and exercise of responsibilities over Hong Kong by the central authorities and the Hong Kong government. Within the sphere of Hong Kong's autonomy, the Basic Law provides for the exercise of governmental powers by three arms of government: the executive, the legislature and the judiciary. The powers and functions of these three arms are outlined in this chapter, together with discussion of the doctrine of 'separation of powers'.

'One Country, Two Systems'

The concept of 'one country, two systems' provided the framework for China's resumption of sovereignty over Hong Kong and constitutes a core principle underpinning the Basic Law. The broad concept was presented by the PRC to the British in June 1984 during negotiations for the return of sovereignty, with the details subsequently fleshed out with British input on the text to be adopted in the Joint

Declaration.¹ The genesis of the proposal of the concept was to give assurance to the people of Hong Kong that their economic and social system would be preserved to ensure peaceful reunification of Hong Kong with Mainland China.² While the phrase 'one country, two systems' does not itself appear in the Joint Declaration, the basic principles under the concept are set out in article 3 of the Joint Declaration and elaborated upon in Annex I of the document. Under the Basic Law, the preamble expressly refers to the application of the principle of 'one country, two systems' in Hong Kong. In *Ng Ka Ling* v. *Director of Immigration*,³ the Court of Final Appeal ('CFA') affirmed that the Basic Law is based on that principle.

One Country

The notion of 'one country' in the concept underlies the sovereignty of the PRC over Hong Kong. The Joint Declaration, which operates as an international treaty between the UK and the PRC,⁴ provides the legal basis for China's resumption of sovereignty as a matter of international law. The two articles on the issue of sovereignty reflect, however, the different views of the PRC and the UK on the historical question of sovereignty during the period of colonisation.⁵ The PRC considered that the nineteenth century treaties⁶ leading to British rule over Hong Kong were imposed through force, 'unequal' and hence invalid.⁷ Article 1 accordingly declares the PRC's decision to resume the exercise of sovereignty over Hong Kong. On the other hand, the British had regarded the nineteenth-century treaties

---

¹ Y. Ghai, *Hong Kong's New Constitutional Order*, 2nd ed. (Hong Kong: Hong Kong University Press 1999), pp. 48–51.
² Ibid., p. 140.
³ (1999) 2 HKCFAR 4 at 28.
⁴ See *Home Restaurant* v. *Attorney General* [1987] HKLR 237; *Tang Ping-hoi* v. *Attorney General* [1987] HKLR 324.
⁵ Ghai (n. 1), p. 53.
⁶ Treaty of Nanking, 1842; Convention of Peking, 1860; Convention of Peking, 1898. See Chapter 1.
⁷ Ghai (n. 1), pp. 9–11; P. Wesley-Smith, *Unequal Treaty 1898–1997: China, Great Britain and Hong Kong's New Territories* (Hong Kong: Oxford University Press 1980), pp. 184–186. Ghai has observed that the widespread view is that the PRC position is not supported by international law, nor the 1969 Vienna Convention on Treaties (which invalidates treaties secured through force but does not apply retrospectively): Ghai (n. 1), pp. 11–12; see also Wesley-Smith, p. 187.

as giving full sovereignty of Hong Kong to Britain (subject to the ninety-nine-year term limit in the case of the New Territories),[8] and thus article 2 states the UK's declaration that it will restore Hong Kong to PRC with effect from 1 July 1997.

PRC's sovereignty over Hong Kong is emphasised in the Basic Law. The preamble to the Basic Law refers to the resumption of China's exercise of sovereignty over Hong Kong. Article 1 states that the Hong Kong SAR is an inalienable part of the PRC, while article 12 states that the Hong Kong SAR is a local administrative region directly under the Central People's Government (CPG). The sovereignty of the PRC over Hong Kong means that ultimate governmental authority over Hong Kong resides with the relevant governmental organs of the PRC pursuant to the PRC Constitution. Powers which may be exercised by the Hong Kong Government are powers as authorised by the PRC under the Basic Law. But while the PRC has sovereignty over Hong Kong, the exercise of governmental powers by the PRC authorities is to be in accordance with the restrictions set out under the Basic Law.

Two Systems

Crucial to the restrictions is the maintenance of a separate 'system' in Hong Kong. The 'two systems' in the concept of 'one country, two systems' denotes that the 'system' in Hong Kong is to be different to that operating on the Mainland. The original twelve points embodying the concept of 'one country, two systems' which the PRC proposed to the British[9] indicated that the economic, social and legal systems in Hong Kong would be separate from those in the rest of the PRC. This was subsequently provided for in the Joint Declaration.[10] Apart from independent judicial power being vested in the Hong Kong SAR, the Joint Declaration also specified that the Hong Kong SAR would be vested with executive and legislative power, that the Chief Executive of the Hong Kong SAR shall be selected by election or through consultations held locally (though appointment is to

---

[8] Ghai (n. 1), p. 7.
[9] See R. Cottrell, *The End of Hong Kong: The Secret Diplomacy of Imperial Retreat* (London: John Murray 1993), p. 112; Ghai (n. 1), p. 50.
[10] See Basic Law, art. 3(3), (5)–(10); and see also Annex I arts. II (legal system), III (judicial system), V (finance), VI (economic system), VII (monetary system), VIII (shipping), (IX) (civil aviation), X (education), XIII (basic rights and freedoms) and XIV (right of abode, travel, immigration).

be made by the CPG) and that the legislature of the Hong Kong SAR shall be constituted by elections.[11] In this sense, the Joint Declaration also provided for a separate political system in Hong Kong.

In accordance with the Joint Declaration, the Basic Law sets out the systems to be practised in Hong Kong that are different to the systems on Mainland China. Hong Kong has, under the Basic Law, its own political,[12] legal,[13] social[14] and economic systems.[15]

One of the core premises of the 'one country, two systems' principle is that Hong Kong is to retain its own capitalist system.[16] This is expressly provided for in the Basic Law with a clear demarcation of the two different economic systems: the socialist system and policies of the PRC are not to be practised in Hong Kong,[17] while the previous capitalist system in Hong Kong will remain unchanged for fifty years.[18] The Basic Law also stipulates specific aspects of the economic sphere where Hong Kong would have its own separate systems. For example:

- Rights of private ownership of property are to be protected.[19]
- There is to be an independent taxation system.[20]
- Hong Kong is to have its own currency.[21]
- There is to be a free flow of capital and no foreign exchange control policies may be applied.[22]
- Hong Kong is to remain a free port and a policy of free trade must be maintained.[23]
- Hong Kong is to be a separate customs territory.[24]
- The previous shipping and civil aviation systems are to be maintained.[25]

---

[11] Arts. 2(3) and (4), and Annex art. I.
[12] Basic Law, chapter IV.
[13] Basic Law, arts. 8, 18; and see also chapter III (fundamental rights), chapter IV section 3 (legislature) and section 4 (judiciary).
[14] Basic Law, art. 5; chapter VI.
[15] Basic Law, arts. 5, 6; chapter V.
[16] See Ghai (n. 1), p. 49.
[17] Basic Law, preamble and art. 5.
[18] Basic Law, art. 5.
[19] Basic Law, arts. 6, 105.
[20] Basic Law, art. 108.
[21] Basic Law, art. 111.
[22] Basic Law, art. 112.
[23] Basic Law, art. 115.
[24] Basic Law, art. 116.
[25] Basic Law, arts. 124, 129.

In terms of Hong Kong's separate social system, article 5 of the Basic Law states that the previous 'way of life' in Hong Kong must remain unchanged for fifty years. Hong Kong is also to have its own systems and policies in areas including education,[26] the medical and health sector,[27] science and technology,[28] culture,[29] religion,[30] sports,[31] social welfare[32] and labour.[33]

In the political sphere, Hong Kong has its own executive[34] and legislature,[35] with the method of appointment as stipulated in the Basic Law. In the legal sphere, the common law system continues to apply in Hong Kong,[36] and Hong Kong has its own independent judiciary.[37]

It might be said that while Hong Kong's economic and social systems are largely separate from those of the Mainland under the Basic Law, there are aspects of the political and legal systems which are interlinked with Mainland systems or which come under the power of Mainland authorities. Some of these aspects are discussed below in the context of the principle of 'high degree of autonomy'. Here, we briefly mention the interaction of Hong Kong and the PRC's systems in the legal sphere.[38]

First, there are certain (limited) Mainland laws which apply in Hong Kong.[39] Second, although the Hong Kong courts are authorised under article 158(2) of the Basic Law to interpret, when adjudicating cases, the provisions of the Basic Law, the ultimate power of interpretation of the Basic Law lies with the Standing Committee of the National People's Congress (NPCSC) under article 158(1). The Hong Kong courts have accepted that when the NPCSC gives an interpretation of a provision of

---

[26] Basic Law, art. 136.
[27] Basic Law, art. 138.
[28] Basic Law, art. 139.
[29] Basic Law, art. 140.
[30] Basic Law, art. 141.
[31] Basic Law, art. 143.
[32] Basic Law, art. 145.
[33] Basic Law, art. 147.
[34] Basic Law, chapter IV, sections 1 and 2.
[35] Basic Law, chapter IV, section 3.
[36] Basic Law, arts. 8, 18.
[37] Basic Law, chapter IV, section 4.
[38] See also Chapter 13.
[39] Basic Law, annex III; and see Chapter 4.

the Basic Law, it is entitled to do so pursuant to the principles of interpretation under the PRC legal system.[40]

Sir Anthony Mason NPJ has made the following extrajudicial observations on article 158:

> Because art. 158 is the point of intersection between two systems, it is the source of tension. The tension arises not merely from the co-existence of two interpreters – the courts of the [HKSAR] and the [NPCSC] – and the possibility that different systems of law will yield different interpretations, but also from different concepts of what constitutes interpretation.[41]

Under the Mainland system, interpretation of a law by the NPCSC can involve supplementing the text (instead of simply ascertaining the meaning of the existing text).[42] Mason has further observed that the Mainland approach to interpretation of statutes is more policy-oriented than the common law approach.[43]

High Degree of Autonomy

The notion of Hong Kong having a 'high degree of autonomy' is derived from the original twelve points proposed by the PRC when setting out the concept of 'one country, two systems' in negotiations with the British in 1984.[44] It was stated, among other matters, that Hong Kong would not be run by emissaries from Beijing but would run its own affairs without central interference (except for matters of defence and foreign affairs). The Joint Declaration expressly refers to HKSAR being able to 'enjoy a high degree of autonomy', for the HKSAR to be vested with executive,

---

[40] See *Lau Kong Yung* v. *Director of Immigration* (1999) 2 HKCFAR 300; *Director of Immigration* v. *Chong Fung Yuen* (2001) 4 HKCFAR 211; *Yau Wai Ching* v. *Chief Executive of HKSAR* (2017) 20 HKCFAR 390, at [35]; and see further Chapters 4 and 7.

[41] A. Mason, 'The Rule of Law in the Shadow of the Giant: The Hong Kong Experience' (2011), *Sydney Law Review* 33, 623, at 628.

[42] *Director of Immigration* v. *Chong Fung Yuen* (2001) 4 HKCFAR 211; [2001] 2 HKLRD 533, at 554–555; *Yau Wai Ching* v. *Chief Executive of HKSAR* (2017) 20 HKCFAR 390, at [35]; Mason (n. 41), at 630.

[43] Mason (n. 41), p. 630. See also Y. Ghai, 'The Intersection of Chinese Law and the Common Law in the Hong Kong Special Administrative Region: Question of Technique or Politics?' (2007), *Hong Kong Law Journal* 37, 363.

[44] See Cottrell (n. 9), p. 112; Ghai (n. 1), p. 50.

legislative and independent judicial power, and for the Government of the HKSAR to be composed of local inhabitants.[45]

The Basic Law also expressly provides that the HKSAR is authorised to exercise and enjoy a 'high degree of autonomy'.[46] This is spelt out in more detail in specific provisions of the Basic Law. Thus, for example:

- The HKSAR is to enjoy its own executive, legislative and judicial powers.[47]
- Although the land and natural resources in Hong Kong are State property, the Hong Kong Government is responsible for their management, use and development.[48]
- In economic matters, the HKSAR has independent finances[49] and sets its own monetary and financial policies,[50] and trade and economic policies generally.[51] The CPG must not levy taxes in Hong Kong.[52]
- In other matters regulating Hong Kong society, the HKSAR is to formulate, on its own, policies relating to labour,[53] education,[54] health,[55] science and technology,[56] culture,[57] the professions,[58] sport[59] and social welfare.[60]
- The HKSAR is authorised to conduct relevant external affairs on its own.[61]

Hong Kong is not fully autonomous, however. There are limits to Hong Kong's autonomy, underscored by specific provisions in the Basic Law that set out the powers of Mainland authorities in Hong Kong. For example:

---

[45] Joint Declaration, arts. 3(2)–(4), Annex I, arts. I, IV.
[46] Basic Law, arts. 2, 12.
[47] Basic Law, art. 2; and see also chapter IV.
[48] Basic Law, art. 7.
[49] Basic Law, art. 106.
[50] Basic Law, art. 110.
[51] Basic Law, arts. 118, 119.
[52] Basic Law, art. 107.
[53] Basic Law, art. 147.
[54] Basic Law, art. 136.
[55] Basic Law, art. 138.
[56] Basic Law, art. 139.
[57] Basic Law, art. 140.
[58] Basic Law, art. 142.
[59] Basic Law, art. 143.
[60] Basic Law, art. 145.
[61] Basic Law, arts. 13, 151, 152, 156. 'External affairs' relates to international relations concerning, for example, trade, culture, sports and tourism (see art. 151) and is different to 'foreign affairs' (as to which, see below).

- The CPG is responsible for foreign affairs[62] and defence[63] of Hong Kong.
- The CPG appoints the Chief Executive and the principal officials of the executive authorities of Hong Kong.[64]
- The NPCSC has power to invalidate legislation made by Hong Kong's legislature on the ground that the legislation is not in conformity with the Basic Law.[65]
- The NPCSC has power to add to or delete from the list of laws in Annex III, containing national laws of the PRC which are to apply in Hong Kong.
- The NPCSC has power to interpret[66] the Basic Law while the National People's Congress (NPC) has power to amend[67] the Basic Law.

While the Basic Law follows the Joint Declaration in stating that Hong Kong is to have a high degree of autonomy, Ghai has pointed out that '"autonomy" suffered something of a sea change in the transformation of the Declaration into the Basic Law'.[68] This is because the Joint Declaration referred to Hong Kong having 'a high degree of autonomy, except in foreign and defence affairs' (article 3(2)). This could be taken as implying a 'neat division of powers' between the PRC (defence and foreign affairs) and the HKSAR (all internal affairs).[69] On the other hand, this juxtaposition is not found in the Basic Law. Although the Basic Law sets out powers that may be exercised by the HKSAR 'on its own', it has been said that the scope of autonomy of the HKSAR is not clearly delineated in the Basic Law.[70]

Gittings has observed that existing research on the notion of autonomous regions within a state or country indicates that the following characteristics are commonly present in autonomous areas:

- a locally chosen chief executive, with responsibility for administering local laws (though certain powers may be reserved for the national government);

---

[62] Basic Law, art. 13. 'Foreign affairs' relate to matters of state and international diplomacy: Ghai (n. 1), p. 461.
[63] Basic Law, art. 14.
[64] Basic Law, art. 15.
[65] Basic Law, art. 17.
[66] Basic Law, art. 158.
[67] Basic Law, art. 159.
[68] Ghai (n. 1), p. 146.
[69] Ghai (n. 1), p. 146.
[70] Ghai (n. 1), pp. 146, 176; and see also D. Gittings, *Introduction to the Hong Kong Basic Law*, 2nd ed. (Hong Kong: Hong Kong University Press 2016), p. 55.

- a locally elected legislature with the power to make law on local matters;
- an independent local judiciary with jurisdiction over local matters; and
- an independent body with responsibility for dispute resolution between local and central authorities (for example concerning who has power over particular matters).[71]

Gittings takes the view that although Hong Kong broadly satisfies the first three of these characteristics, the fourth characteristic is absent.[72]

In 2014, the Information Office of the State Council of the PRC issued a White Paper on the practice of the 'one country, two systems' policy in Hong Kong, which stated that

the central government exercises overall jurisdiction over the HKSAR, including the powers directly exercised by the central government, and the powers delegated to the HKSAR by the central government to enable it to exercise a high degree of autonomy in accordance with the law. The central government has the power of oversight over the exercise of a high degree of autonomy in the HKSAR.[73]

The White Paper raised concerns in some quarters of increased interference from the PRC authorities in governance in Hong Kong, thereby encroaching on the scope of Hong Kong's autonomy as provided for under the Joint Declaration and the Basic Law.[74] On the other hand, it has been said that the reference to 'overall jurisdiction' in the White Paper simply reflects the position under the Basic Law that the powers of the HKSAR are delegated from the central authorities.[75] That is, the Basic Law does not provide for a 'division of powers' between the central authorities and the HKSAR as such. Rather, Hong Kong's autonomy is authorised or delegated from the sovereign.[76]

Be that as it may, it seems that a critical issue is the extent to which the autonomy provided to Hong Kong under the Basic Law would be treated as

---

[71] Gittings (n. 70), p. 58; and see H. Hannum and R. B. Lillich, 'The Concept of Autonomy in International Law' (1980), *American Journal of International Law* 74, 858.
[72] Gittings (n. 70), p. 91.
[73] State Council Information Office, 'The Practice of the "One Country, Two Systems" Policy in the Hong Kong Special Administrative Region' (June 2014).
[74] See, e.g., M. C. Davis, 'The Basic Law, Universal Suffrage and the Rule of Law in Hong Kong' (2015), *Hastings International and Comparative Law Review* 38, 275, at 290.
[75] See P. Y. Lo and A. H. Y. Chen, 'The Judicial Perspective of "Separation of Powers" in the Hong Kong Special Administrative Region of the People's Republic of China' (2018), *Journal of International and Comparative Law* 5, 337, at 358.
[76] Ibid., p. 358; P. Y. Lo, *The Judicial Construction of Hong Kong's Basic Law: Courts, Politics and Society after 1997* (Hong Kong: Hong Kong University Press 2014), pp. 30–32.

'hard law' by the central authorities[77] that restrains the exercise of power by the central authorities over areas where Hong Kong is conferred with, or delegated with, autonomy under the Basic Law. Central to this question is the exercise of the power of interpretation of the Basic Law by the NPCSC. The exercise of the NPCSC's power binds, and cannot be questioned by, the Hong Kong courts.[78] As such, it has been observed that:

> if the high degree of autonomy vested in the HKSAR is to be respected, then it becomes imperative that the NPCSC exercises constitutional self-restraint and develops constitutional conventions that will preclude itself from interpreting provision within the autonomy of the HKSAR lest the plenary power of interpretation of the NPCSC be turned into 'a control of expedience', enabling it to legislate directly for the HKSAR on matters which would otherwise have been left to the HKSAR to do on its own as mandated by the Basic Law.[79]

Executive, Legislature and Judiciary

Under the Basic Law, the political structure of the HKSAR involves division of governmental power into three branches: the executive, the legislature and the judiciary.[80] Broadly, the legislature has the function of making laws, the judiciary has the functions of interpretation of the law and adjudication of legal disputes, while the executive performs the other functions of government, including the formation and implementation of government policy, the enforcement and execution of laws, and the administration of government services for the public.

Executive

Executive Authorities and Powers of the Executive

The Government of the HKSAR is constituted by the executive authorities,[81] which includes a Department of Administration, Department of

---

[77] Ghai (n. 1), p. 186.
[78] Ghai (n. 1), pp. 179–180; see also Chapter 4.
[79] D. Chang, 'The Imperatives of One Country, Two Systems: One Country before Two Systems?' (2007), *Hong Kong Law Journal* 37, 351, at 360.
[80] Basic Law, chapter IV.
[81] Basic Law, art. 59.

Finance, Department of Justice and various bureaus, divisions and commissions.[82]

The Government (executive authorities) exercise the following powers and functions:

- to formulate and implement policies;
- to conduct administrative affairs;
- to conduct external affairs as authorised by the CPG under the Basic Law;
- to draw up and introduce budgets and final accounts;
- to draft and introduce bills, motions and subordinate legislation; and
- to designate officials to sit in on the meetings of the legislature and to speak on behalf of the Government.[83]

Chief Executive and the Executive Council

The Chief Executive is head of both the Government[84] and the HKSAR.[85] The Chief Executive is accountable to both the CPG and the HKSAR in accordance with the provisions of the Basic Law.[86] The Chief Executive is assisted in policy-making by the Executive Council,[87] the members of which are appointed by the Chief Executive from among the principal officials of the executive authorities, members of the legislature and public figures.[88] The Chief Executive is required to consult the Executive Council before making important policy decisions, introducing bills to the legislature, making subordinate legislation or dissolving the legislature.[89]

Method for Selection of Chief Executive

Article 45(1) of the Basic Law states that the Chief Executive shall be selected by election or through consultations held locally and be appointed by the CPG. Article 45(2) states:

---

[82] Basic Law, art. 60(2).
[83] Basic Law, art. 62.
[84] Basic Law, art. 60(1).
[85] Basic Law, art. 43(1). For the powers and functions of the Chief Executive, see art. 48.
[86] Basic Law, art. 43(2).
[87] Basic Law, art. 54.
[88] Basic Law, art. 55(1).
[89] Basic Law, art. 56(2).

The method for selecting the Chief Executive shall be specified in the light of the actual situation in the Hong Kong Special Administrative Region and in accordance with the principle of gradual and orderly progress. The ultimate aim is the selection of the Chief Executive by universal suffrage upon nomination by a broadly representative nominating committee in accordance with democratic procedures.

The Chief Executive is elected by an Election Committee before appointment by the CPG. The Committee is required to be 'broadly representative' and is presently composed of 1,200 members drawn from the following:

- industrial, commercial and financial sectors (300 members);
- the professions (300 members);
- labour, social services, religious and other sectors (300 members); and
- members of the Legislative Council, representatives of members of the District Councils, representatives of the Heung Yee Kuk, Hong Kong deputies to the NPC, and representatives of Hong Kong members of the National Committee of the Chinese People's Political Consultative Conference (300 members).[90]

Candidates may be nominated by at least 150 members of the Election Committee. Members of the Committee then vote on a one-person-per-vote basis by secret ballot. The candidate who obtains more than 600 votes is returned at the election.[91] Once elected, there must still be appointment by the CPG in accordance with Basic Law article 45(1). It has been said that the power of appointment by the CPG 'is a substantive power and not merely a ceremonial procedure or formality'.[92]

As noted above, article 45(2) of the Basic Law envisages that the method for selection of the Chief Executive would be reformed so as to ultimately allow universal suffrage. The reforms required to introduce a democratic model for election of the Chief Executive have proved to be controversial and divisive in Hong Kong. In 2003, there had been public pressure to introduce universal suffrage for the 2007 election. However, this did not

---

[90] Basic Law, art. 45(3) and Annex I; and see also the Chief Executive Election Ordinance (Cap. 569).
[91] Chief Executive Election Ordinance (Cap. 569) ss. 26A, 27. Annex I was amended in 2010 to increase the size of the Election Committee from 800 to 1,200: see Instrument 1 – Decision of the NPCSC on Approving the Amendment to Annex I (28 August 2010); and Instrument 2 – Amendment to Annex I (28 August 2010).
[92] A. H. Y. Chen, 'The Constitutional Controversy of Spring 2004' (2004), *Hong Kong Law Journal* 34, 215, at 224.

eventuate following the NPCSC interpretation of Annex I, article 7 on the procedure for amending the method for selecting the Chief Executive[93] and the NPCSC decision[94] in 2004 which stated that the earliest date for selection of the Chief Executive by universal suffrage would be 2017.[95] The Government's proposals for reform in 2014[96] and the NPCSC decision of 2014[97] (that the reform model must be based on 'two to three candidates' nominated by a committee identical in composition to the Election Committee) sparked the 'Occupy Central' protests in September to December of 2014, with critics arguing that the restrictions under the proposals were inconsistent with genuine universal suffrage as understood under international norms.[98] Subsequently, the Government's final proposal[99] in 2015 failed to be endorsed by the required two-thirds majority of all seventy Legislative Council members.[100]

Legislature

Constitution and Powers of the Legislative Council

The Basic Law provides for the primary legislative body in Hong Kong to be the Legislative Council.[101] This council is currently composed of seventy members: thirty-five are elected according to geographical constituencies through direct elections (organised on the basis of residence)

---

[93] Instrument 18 – Interpretation of the NPCSC on art. 7 of Annex I and art. III of Annex II (6 April 2004).

[94] Instrument 21 – Decision of the NPCSC on Issues Relating to the Methods for Selecting the Chief Executive and Forming the Legislative Council (29 December 2007).

[95] See further Chen (n. 92).

[96] HKSAR, 'Report on the Public Consultation on the Methods for Selecting the Chief Executive in 2017 and for Forming the Legislative Council in 2016' (July 2014).

[97] Instrument 23 – Decision of the NPCSC Issues Relating to the Methods for Selecting the Chief Executive and Forming the Legislative Council (31 August 2014).

[98] See, e.g., Davis (n. 74).

[99] HKSAR, 'Method for Selecting the Chief Executive by Universal Suffrage: Consultation Report and Proposals' (April 2015).

[100] See further S. N. M. Young, 'Rethinking the Process of Political Reform in Hong Kong' (2015), *Hong Kong Law Journal* 45, 381; G. S. Gordon, 'When "One Country Two Systems" Meets "One Person, One Vote": The Law of Treaties and the Handover Narrative Through the Crucible of Hong Kong's Election Crisis' (2015), *Melbourne Journal of International Law* 16, 122; F. Lin, 'Interaction between International Standards and Domestic Constitutional Norms: A Case Study of the Chief Executive Election in Hong Kong' (2016), *Hong Kong Law Journal* 46, 193.

[101] Basic Law, art. 66.

and thirty-five according to functional constituencies[102] (organised on the basis of occupation).[103] The term of office is four years.[104]

The establishment of the Legislative Council and its powers and functions are detailed in articles 66–79 of the Basic Law.[105] Article 73 sets out various powers, including:

- the making, amending and repealing of laws in accordance with the Basic Law and legal procedure;
- fiscal responsibilities (to approve budgets, taxation and public expenditure);
- enforcing the idea of responsible government (by asking questions about the work of the government, debating matters of public interest, keeping check on the policy initiatives of the Chief Executive and being available to Hong Kong residents with complaints);
- the appointment and dismissal of members of the judiciary (in accordance with procedure); and
- impeachment of the Chief Executive for serious breach of law or dereliction of duty.

The role of the Legislative Council is discussed in further detail in Chapter 6 in relation to the process of making legislation.

Judiciary

The judiciary of the HKSAR is constituted by the courts of the Region at all levels.[106] The main function of the courts is to administer justice in the adjudication of cases in both criminal and civil matters. Article 81 specifies the courts to be established in Hong Kong: the Court of Final Appeal, the High Court (comprising the Court of Appeal and the Court of First Instance), district courts, magistrates' courts and other special courts.

---

[102] See further C. Loh and Civic Exchange (eds.), *Functional Constituencies: A Unique Feature of the Hong Kong Legislative Council* (Hong Kong: Hong Kong University Press 2006).
[103] Basic Law, art. 68(3), Annex II. Annex II was amended in 2010 to increase the size of the Legislative Council from sixty to seventy: Instrument 3 – Proclamation of the NPCSC No. 15 (28 August 2010); Instrument 4 – Amendment to Annex II for the Formation of the Legislative Council (28 August 2010). See also the Legislative Council Ordinance (Cap. 542).
[104] Basic Law, art. 69.
[105] See also the Legislative Council (Powers and Privileges) Ordinance (Cap. 382).
[106] Basic Law, art. 80.

Judges of the various courts are appointed by the Chief Executive on the recommendation of an independent commission composed of local judges, persons from the legal profession and eminent persons from other sectors.[107]

The court system is discussed in detail in Chapter 5.

Separation of Powers

The doctrine of separation of powers is a theory relating to government, dealing with the separation of government into different branches, each with its own independent areas of responsibility. The adoption of the doctrine in the constitutional framework of a state has implications for which government organs have powers to make laws, to adjudicate on the legal rights of persons or to exercise other particular powers of government.[108] The doctrine is generally regarded as one that involves the separation of government into the executive, the legislature and the judiciary.

The concept of the doctrine of separation of powers is elaborated upon below, followed by discussion of the extent to which the separation of powers doctrine applies in Hong Kong.

Origins and Rationale of the Doctrine of Separation of Powers

In ancient Greece, Aristotle described government as operating via three branches: the deliberative, which discusses matters of common importance; the officials (i.e., the civil service, in modern terms); and the judicial.[109] In England, from the thirteenth century onwards, there came to be a division in government reflecting some form of separation of powers – with a distinction between the King's Council, Parliament and the courts of law.

---

[107] Basic Law, art. 88.

[108] For example, for discussion of controversy and debate over the application of the doctrine in the United States, see G. Casper, *Separating Power: Essays on the Founding Period* (Cambridge: Harvard University Press 1997); N. C. Bay, 'Executive Power and the War on Terror' (2005), Denver University Law *Review* 83, 335; J. L. Mashaw and D. Berke, 'Presidential Administration in a Regime of Separated Powers: An Analysis of Recent American Experience' (2018), *Yale Journal on Regulation* 35, 549.

[109] See H. Barnett, *Constitutional and Administrative Law*, 4th ed. (London: Cavendish Publishing 2002), p. 105.

English political philosopher John Locke wrote in the seventeenth century that because of human frailty, there is a risk that persons who both make the law and execute the law might exempt themselves from obedience to the law or might use the law for their own private advantage.[110] Accordingly, it is necessary for legislative and executive power to be separated. While Locke did not consider separation of the judicial power, other writers did, such as Viscount Bolingbroke, who advocated a balance of power between the executive, the legislature and the judiciary in a constitution in order to preserve 'the safety of the whole'.[111] French thinker Montesquieu was also concerned with the prevention of tyranny through a separation of powers. Montesquieu wrote:

> When the legislative and executive powers are united in the same person ... there can be no liberty; because apprehensions may arise, lest the same monarch or senate should enact tyrannical laws, to execute them in a tyrannical manner. Again, there is no liberty, if the judiciary power be not separated from the legislative and executive. Were it joined with the legislative, the life and liberty of the subject would be exposed to arbitrary control; for the judge would be then the legislator. Were it joined to the executive power, the judge might behave with great violence and oppression.[112]

The doctrine of the separation of powers found expression in the French Declaration of the Rights of Man of 1789,[113] and was relied upon by James Madison and others in the drafting of the United States Constitution of 1787.[114]

It can be seen, then, that the concern of the above political thinkers in the seventeenth and eighteenth centuries was to prevent tyrannical government. If one person or government body can exercise executive, legislative and judicial powers, there is a concentration of power that results in a greater risk of one person or body abusing its powers for its own advantage or for the oppression of the populace. The separation of

---

[110] J. Locke, *Two Treatises of Civil Government*, extracted in M. Rosen and J. Wolff (eds.), *Political Thought* (Oxford: Oxford University Press 1999), pp. 115–117.
[111] See C. R. Munro, *Studies in Constitutional Law*, 2nd ed. (London: Butterworths 1999), pp. 296–298.
[112] B. de Montesquieu, *The Spirit of the Laws* (T. Nugent, trans.), extracted in M. Rosen and J. Wolff (eds.), *Political Thought* (Oxford: Oxford University Press 1999), pp. 117–118.
[113] Art. 16.
[114] See Casper (n. 108), pp. 12–22.

power between three separate government organs, each acting independently, would mean the following:

- laws are not made purely to serve the executive, since law-making power resides with another body (the legislature);
- the powers of the executive are circumscribed if the executive is required to operate within laws as made by another body (the legislature);
- the law is not selectively enforced for the purposes of the lawmaker, since enforcement powers reside in the executive; and
- the law can be applied impartially to both the lawmakers and the executive, since there is an independent judiciary.

The following passage from T. R. S. Allan is incisive in highlighting the importance of a legislature separate from the executive:

> In view of its responsibilities for the public safety and efficient conduct of affairs, the executive will naturally be inclined to exaggerate the strength of government interests – or the needs of its own conception of the public good – at the expense of countervailing individual interests, especially the exercise of rights to criticize and organize opposition to current government policy. It is a matter of recent historical experience that the interests of national security or official secrecy or public order, for example, are likely to be accorded exaggerated weight if the executive is allowed a free hand in devising strategies for their protection. The role of the legislature is to review such executive concerns with a cautious scepticism, seeking a defensible accommodation of public and private interests, and attempting to preserve constitutional values against ill-considered departures induced by anxiety to resolve short-term problems or desire to frustrate or silence political enemies.[115]

Although the rationale widely given for the doctrine is to restrain the exercise of arbitrary power, some have argued that the importance of the doctrine lies in efficiency in government.[116]

Different Concepts of Separation

The basic idea of the separation of powers seems straightforward; however, the concept can be applied in different ways. Or put differently, there could

---

[115] T. R. S. Allan, *Constitutional Justice: A Liberal Theory of the Rule of Law* (Oxford: Oxford University Press 2001), p. 48.

[116] See N. W. Barber, 'Prelude to the Separation of Powers' (2001), *Cambridge Law Journal* 60, 59.

be different versions or notions of the separation of powers. The doctrine is sometimes analysed in terms of the following distinct but related aspects of separation:

- functional separation, which involves a conceptual division of the functions of government into the legislative, judicial and executive spheres;
- institutional separation, which requires that there are three institutions (the legislature, executive and judiciary) that operate independently and each free from interference from the other branches;
- personnel separation, which requires that no person should be a member of more than one of the three branches of government; and
- checks and balances, that is, certain powers of each branch are checked and balanced by powers of supervision conferred on the other branches in order to ensure that there is no concentration of power within any one branch.[117]

In discussions on the separation of powers, it is therefore important to be clear about which specific concept is being used in order to avoid confusion. Some constitutions might adopt only some of the above forms of separation but not others. It should also be noted that advocates of the doctrine generally do not argue for an absolute separation of functions into separate institutions operating in total isolation from each other, for otherwise there might be conflict and deadlock between the different institutions, potentially leading to paralysis in government.[118] Accordingly, the operation of the doctrine involves partial as opposed to absolute separation. There may be variances, then, in the extent to which a particular constitution adopts any one form of separation.

Critiques of the Doctrine

Various theorists have criticised the doctrine of the separation of powers on a number of grounds. One basis of criticism is that the doctrine is imprecise and incoherent because there is ambiguity between the notions

---

[117] See, e.g., G. Marshall, *Constitutional Theory* (Oxford: Clarendon Press 1971), p. 100.
[118] See, e.g., E. Barendt, 'Separation of Powers and Constitutional Government' (1995), *Public Law* 599, 605–609.

of executive, legislative and judicial functions.[119] For instance, is the power to make rules or regulations a legislative power, meaning that the legislature should not delegate such powers to the executive? Moreover, there is no clear line between 'judicial' and 'non-judicial' means of settling disputes, giving rise to uncertainty as to whether dispute resolution by tribunals or other adjudicatory bodies amounts to a usurpation of the judicial function by the executive.

In reply to such criticisms, Barendt, for example, has argued that although there may be uncertainties in borderline situations, it is possible to define in general terms the legislative, judicial and executive functions, and to draw a principled line between those functions in particular cases.[120] More importantly, since the aim of the doctrine of the separation of powers is to prevent arbitrary government arising from a concentration of power, it might not matter whether a particular function is allocated to one branch or the other in a borderline case, so long as the result does not lead to a concentration of power.[121]

Another criticism of the doctrine is that it leads to deadlock in the government, undermining the ability of the government to act quickly and decisively.[122] For instance, opposition in the legislature might mean that the executive is unable to implement policies in a timely manner or at all. The policy objectives of the executive or the legislature might be thought to be frustrated if their acts are struck down by the courts as being unconstitutional. Defenders of the doctrine have replied by arguing,[123] for example, that criticism over stalemates in government misses the point that the reason policies might not be implemented is that there is a lack of consensus on the issue. Moreover, greater government action does not necessarily mean that such action is optimal, and, in the words of

---

[119] See I. Jennings, *The Law and the Constitution*, 5th ed. (London: English Language Book Society 1979).

[120] E.g., see *Julita F Raza v. Chief Executive in Council* (unreported, CA, Civ App 218 of 2005, 19 Jul 2006), at paras. [31]–[46], where the Court of Appeal analysed the difference between an executive act and a legislative act in deciding that an order of the Chief Executive approving a labour importation scheme which involved imposition of a levy on employers of foreign domestic workers was an executive act.

[121] Barendt (n. 118), pp. 605–613.

[122] See, e.g., C. M. Hardin, *Constitutional Reform in America: Essays on the Separation of Powers* (Iowa City, IA: Iowa State University Press 1989), chapters 6 and 10.

[123] See, e.g., M. H. Redish, *The Constitution as Political Structure* (New York, NY: Oxford University Press 1995), pp. 108–113.

Redish, 'The most significant problem with the modern attacks on separation of powers is that they completely ignore the very real fears that led to adoption of the system in the first place.'[124]

Separation of Powers in Colonial Hong Kong

The governance structure in colonial Hong Kong was divided between the executive, legislature and judiciary, but there were significant limitations with respect to separation between the executive and the legislature. The executive[125] was composed of the Governor, the Executive Council, the civil service and so on. Primary legislation was enacted by the Legislative Council, as provided for under the constitution of colonial Hong Kong,[126] which to some extent indicated functional and institutional separation.

However, the degree of separation was limited under the 'executive-led gubernatorial government'.[127] The Governor was responsible to the British government rather than to the Legislative Council, and had the authority to govern through his appointment by the British Crown without any need to maintain the confidence of the Legislative Council. Although bills were passed by the Legislative Council, the Governor's assent was required for a bill to become law.[128] Furthermore, the Legislative Council contained members appointed by the Governor until 1995;[129] the Governor was President of the Legislative Council until reforms were implemented by Governor Chris Patten in 1993; and the Chief Secretary, the Attorney General and the Financial Secretary were *ex officio* members until 1995.

Moreover, there was no system of checks and balances between the executive and the legislature; the Legislative Council did not have

---

[124] Redish (n. 123), p. 111.
[125] On the constitutional structure of colonial Hong Kong, see generally P. Wesley-Smith, *Constitutional and Administrative Law in Hong Kong*, 2nd ed. (Hong Kong: Longman Asia 1994).
[126] Hong Kong Letters Patent 1917, arts. VI, VII.
[127] Wesley-Smith (n. 125), p. 20.
[128] Hong Kong Letters Patent 1917, arts. VII, X.
[129] When elections were first introduced in 1985, only a minority of the legislators were elected (and elected only from functional constituencies). Further changes to the composition of the legislative council were made in the following years, and by 1995, in the last colonial legislative council, thirty members were elected from functional constituencies, twenty were returned from direct elections in geographical constituencies, and ten were elected by the Election Committee constituency.

the power to remove the Governor from office, while the Governor could dissolve the legislature.[130] Thus, until the time of Governor Patten's reforms, the Legislative Council was largely subservient to the will of the Governor.[131] With the fully elected Legislative Council in 1995, though, the legislature did, in the final years of British rule, take on a greater role in scrutinising government policy.[132]

While the separation of the executive and the legislature was limited in colonial Hong Kong, there was for the most part separation of the judiciary.[133] The judiciary was largely independent, and the courts had a role in checking both the legislature and the executive, having powers to declare invalid any unconstitutional acts of the Governor[134] or unconstitutional laws[135] made by the Legislative Council.

Separation of Powers in the HKSAR

Chapter IV of the Basic Law is headed 'Political Structure', and divides government into the three branches of the executive, the legislature and the judiciary. Executive powers are conferred on the Chief Executive and the executive authorities (articles 48, 62, 63); legislative power is conferred on the Legislative Council (article 73); and judicial power is conferred on the courts (article 80). While the Basic Law does not contain the term 'separation of powers', courts overseas, such as in the United States[136] and Australia,[137] have been prepared to interpret their state's constitutions as

---

[130] Hong Kong Royal Instructions 1917, art. XXVIIIA.
[131] Wesley-Smith (n. 125), pp. 20, 161; M. K. Chan, 'The Imperfect Legacy: Defects in the British Legal System in Colonial Hong Kong' (1997), *University of Pennsylvania Journal of International Economic Law* 18, 133, 139–140.
[132] A. B. L. Cheung, 'The Changing Political System: Executive-Led Government or 'Disabled' Governance?', in S. K. Lau (ed.), *The First Tung Chee-Hwa Administration: The First Five Years of the Hong Kong Special Administrative Region* (Hong Kong: Chinese University Press 2002), p. 48.
[133] See Wesley-Smith (n. 125), pp. 20, 120, 142–148. However, for examples illustrating inadequate separation between the executive and the judiciary, see Chan (n. 131), pp. 138–139, 152–153.
[134] See Wesley-Smith (n. 125), pp. 114–120.
[135] See Wesley-Smith (n. 125), p. 186.
[136] See *Myers v. United States* 272 US 106, 71 L Ed 160 (1926); J. L. Fitzgerald, *Congress and the Separation of Powers* (New York, NY: Praeger 1986), pp. 29–43, 67–68.
[137] See *R v. Trade Practices Tribunal, ex parte Tasmanian Breweries Pty Ltd* (1969–70) 123 CLR 361, 389; see also, e.g., W. A. Wynes, *Legislative, Executive and Judicial Powers in Australia*, 5th ed. (Sydney, NSW: Law Book 1976).

implicitly incorporating the doctrine of the separation of powers on the basis of the constitutional division of power into different branches of government and a system of checks and balances.

It seems that this is also the position in Hong Kong. Apart from the structure of Chapter IV and the division of the three functions of government into three different branches, other provisions can also be regarded as reflecting the doctrine of the separation of powers, such as the following which protect each branch from interference or which provide a system of checks and balances:

- immunity conferred on legislators in respect of their statements at meetings of the legislature (article 77);
- protection of legislators from arrest when attending meetings of the legislature (article 78);
- independence of the judiciary (article 85);
- security of the tenure of judges (article 89);
- the executive to be accountable to the legislature (article 64);
- taxation and public expenditure to be approved by the legislature (article 64);
- the legislature having the power to pass a motion of impeachment of the Chief Executive for a serious breach of law or dereliction of duty (following investigation by the Chief Justice of the Court of Final Appeal) (article 73);
- the Chief Executive having the power to dissolve the legislature if he refuses to sign a bill passed twice by the legislature or if the legislature refuses to pass a budget or any other important bill introduced by the government (article 50); and
- the requirement for the Chief Executive to resign if he still refuses to sign a bill passed by a new legislature (in place of a legislature dissolved under article 50) or if the new legislature still refuses to pass the budget or other important bill (article 52).

Although the PRC system is not based on the doctrine of the separation of powers and although Deng Xiaoping did not intend the adoption of the principle of the separation of powers in the Joint Declaration,[138] the Court of Final Appeal has affirmed the view that the Basic Law provides for a

---

[138] Cheung (n. 132), p. 43.

separation of powers. The court has observed that the separation between the executive, legislature and the judiciary is a fundamental doctrine that is reflected in both the Basic Law and the common law in Hong Kong.[139]

The view of the Hong Kong courts that the doctrine of separation of powers applies in Hong Kong is largely supported by the literature in Hong Kong[140] and also by some Mainland scholars.[141] On the other hand, Mainland authorities and other Mainland scholars have emphasised that Hong Kong remains an 'executive-led government' and that the separation of powers doctrine does not apply in Hong Kong.[142]

In *Leung Kwok Hung* v. *President of the Legislative Council*,[143] Hartmann J recognised that Hong Kong has an executive-led government in the sense that:

- it is the function of the Chief Executive to lead the Government, to decide on Government policies and to approve the introduction of motions regarding revenues or expenditure to the Legislative Council;[144] and
- it is the function of the Government (the executive authorities, led by the Chief Executive) to formulate and implement policies, to conduct administrative affairs and to draw up and introduce (into the Legislative Council) budgets and final accounts.[145]

Yet while recognising the 'executive-led' nature of the Hong Kong governance structure, Hartmann J also accepted that the Basic Law

---

[139] See *Lau Cheong* v. *HKSAR* (2002) 5 HKCFAR 415 at [101]; *Secretary for Justice* v. *Lau Kwok Fai* (2005) 8 HKCFAR 304, [2005] 3 HKLRD 88 at 103; *Dragon House Investment Ltd* v. *Secretary for Transport* (2005) 8 HKCFAR 668, [2005] 4 HKLRD 480, at 497–498; *Leung Kwok Hung* v. *President of the Legislative Council (No 1)* (2014) 17 HKCFAR 689, at [27].

[140] See Ghai (n. 1), p. 262; P. Wesley-Smith, *Hong Kong's Basic Law: Problems and Prospects* (Hong Kong: University of Hong Kong 1990), pp. 72–73, 83; B. F. C. Hsu, 'Judicial Independence under the Basic Law' (2004), *Hong Kong Law Journal* 34, 279, at 283–284.

[141] See W. Xiao, 'Hong Kong Basic Law Bonds Two Leading Bodies', in M. K. Chan and D. J. Clarke (eds.), *The Hong Kong Basic Law: Blue Print for 'Stability and Prosperity' Under Chinese Sovereignty?* (Hong Kong: Hong Kong University Press 1991), pp. 242–244; S. Wang et al., *Introduction to the Basic Law of the Hong Kong Special Administrative Region* (Beijing: Law Press 2000), pp. 345–354, 379–383, 408–409, 466–471.

[142] See the discussion of Mainland views in Lo and Chen (n. 75), pp. 356–359. See also State Council Information Office, 'The Practice of the "One Country, Two Systems" Policy in the Hong Kong Special Administrative Region' (June 2014).

[143] [2007] 1 HKLRD 387, at [67].

[144] Basic Law, art. 48.

[145] Basic Law, art. 62.

enshrines the separation of powers.[146] Thus his Lordship did not consider that 'executive-led government' precluded the operation of the 'separation of powers' doctrine.[147] As the law currently stands, as declared by the Hong Kong courts, the separation of powers doctrine does apply under the Basic Law. However, the 'executive-led' nature of government, together with various other factors, does impact on the scope to which the doctrine applies in Hong Kong even if it does not displace the doctrine outright.[148]

In terms of application of the separation of powers doctrine in Hong Kong, the courts continue to have the role of checking the constitutionality of laws made by the legislature[149] and the constitutionality of the actions of the executive. For example, in *Leung Kwok Hung* v. *HKSAR*,[150] the Court of Final Appeal ruled that various provisions of the Public Order Ordinance (Cap. 245) regulating public processions were invalid for being contrary to the right of freedom of assembly protected under the Basic Law, while in *Secretary for Justice* v. *Yau Yuk Lung*,[151] certain provisions of the Crimes Ordinance (Cap. 200) dealing with homosexual activity were held by the court to be unconstitutional and invalid.

As for court supervision over the powers of the executive, the controversy in 2006 over police powers of secret interception of communications in investigating crimes provides an illustration. The controversy arose following two District Court decisions that held that covert surveillance conducted without a legislative basis contravened article 30 of the Basic Law. As an interim measure before the enactment of appropriate legislation, the Chief Executive promulgated an executive order pursuant to Basic Law article 48, purportedly to ensure that investigating agencies could in the meantime exercise covert surveillance lawfully. The Court of Appeal, however, held that the executive order could not be effective for this purpose as the executive did not have the constitutional power to make

---

[146] [2007] 1 HKLRD 387, at [66].
[147] Lo and Chen (n. 75), p. 360.
[148] See the discussion below.
[149] *Ng Ka Ling* v. *Director of Immigration* (1999) 2 HKCFAR 4, [1999] 1 HKLRD 315, [1999] 1 HKC 291, at 322; *Director of Immigration* v. *Chong Fung Yuen* (2001) 4 HKCFAR 211, [2001] 2 HKLRD 533, at 545–546.
[150] (2005) 8 HKCFAR 229, [2005] 3 HKLRD 164.
[151] (2007) 10 HKCFAR 335, [2007] 3 HKLRD 903.

law and that Basic Law article 30 required that covert surveillance be authorised only pursuant to law.¹⁵²

Other examples of the courts applying the separation of powers doctrine include the striking down of any action of the executive that has improperly infringed upon the judicial sphere,¹⁵³ observing the limits of the role of the judiciary¹⁵⁴ and examining whether the legislature has overstepped its boundaries and taken on a judicial role.¹⁵⁵

Yet while it can be accepted that the Basic Law incorporates the doctrine of the separation of powers, a further question arises concerning the scope and meaning of the doctrine as applied in Hong Kong. The constitutional limits on judicial independence under the Basic Law arising from the power of interpretation of the NPCSC (article 158) means that there are some limitations to the degree of separation of the judicial function. Moreover, there may be certain practices presently in existence, such as the appointment of temporary and part-time judges, that might be regarded as infringements of the Basic Law provisions for judicial independence.¹⁵⁶

As between the executive and the legislature, there are also limits on the degree of separation in the various aspects of institutional and personal separation and the scope of checks and balances on each branch. Firstly, members of the Legislative Council can also be members of the Executive Council (see article 55). Secondly, the continuation of the 'executive-led' system of the colonial era could be said to lead to an imbalance in

---

¹⁵² *Leung Kwok Hung* v. *Chief Executive of HKSAR* (unreported, CA, CACV 73 and 87 of 2006, 10 May 2006). There was no appeal on this point when the matter went to the Court of Final Appeal: *Koo Sze Yiu* v. *Chief Executive of HKSAR* (2006) 9 HKCFAR 441, [2006] 3 HKLRD 455. See now the Interception of Communications and Surveillance Ordinance (Cap. 589).

¹⁵³ *Yau Kwong Man* v *Secretary for Security* [2002] 3 HKC 457.

¹⁵⁴ *Re Chu Wai Ha* [2005] 2 HKC 36; *Society for the Protection of the Harbour Ltd* v. *Chief Executive in Council* [2004] 2 HKLRD 902, at para. [38]; *Julita F Raza* v. *Chief Executive in Council* (unreported, CFI, HCAL 30/2003, 4 Jan 2005), at para. [11]; on appeal, see *Julita F Raza* v. *Chief Executive in Council* (unreported, CA, Civ App 218 of 2005, 19 Jul 2006).

¹⁵⁵ *Lau Cheong* v. *HKSAR* (2002) 5 HKCFAR 415, [2002] 2 HKLRD 612 (mandatory sentencing); *Lau Kwok Fai* v. *Secretary for Justice* (unreported, CFI, HCAL 177 and 180 of 2002, 10 Jun 2003), at paras. [114]–[124] (legislation imposing pay cut on civil servants) (on appeal, see *Lau Kwok Fai* v. *Secretary for Justice* [2004] 3 HKLRD 570, CA; *Secretary for Justice* v. *Lau Kwok Fai* (2005) 8 HKCFAR 304, [2005] 3 HKLRD 88, CFA).

¹⁵⁶ E.g., see Hsu (n. 140).

power between the Chief Executive and the Legislative Council. It has been observed that dominance by the executive was clearly preferred by both the PRC leaders and the local civil service, as well as conservatives in the business and professional sectors who wished to preserve the status quo, so that 'Hong Kong remain[ed] bureaucratically controlled and governed in much the same way as it had been during the more typical British colonial days'.[157]

The greater power of the Chief Executive can be seen from a number of provisions of the Basic Law. For example, the legislative programme of the Legislative Council is driven by the executive (see article 62). While this is similar to the principles of overseas constitutions such as those of the United States and the United Kingdom, there is a greater restriction under the Basic Law on the introduction of private members' bills, with the consent of the Chief Executive required before legislators can introduce bills relating to government policies (article 74). Moreover, it has been argued that the Legislative Council's role in the scrutiny and review of government proposals is hampered by factors such as the rules on voting and the support that the government is likely to receive from the functional constituency members.[158] Executive dominance is also reflected in that, although the Basic Law specifies that the executive is accountable to the legislature (article 64), the Chief Executive is also accountable to the CPG (article 43) and impeachment of the Chief Executive by the Legislative Council results in the removal of the Chief Executive only if the CPG so decides (article 73).[159]

Nonetheless, while there is an imbalance between the executive and the legislature, we saw earlier that there is still a system of checks and balances in the Basic Law, and the Legislative Council's role in checking the power of the executive as set out in the Basic Law should not be ignored or marginalised.

---

[157] Cheung (n. 132), pp. 43-44.
[158] Ghai (n. 1), pp. 281-282, 291-292. Note Cheung's comments that the introduction of functional constituencies in 1985 were less a development towards representative government than a legitimation of the reservation of Legislative Council seats for the business and professional sectors from which previous appointed members came: Cheung (n. 132), p. 43.
[159] For further discussion of the relationship between the executive and the legislature, see Ghai (n. 1), pp. 262-300.

Under any constitution that adopts a separation of powers, it becomes necessary to ascertain the correct delineation between the different branches under the particular constitution. It was observed earlier that, on occasion, the courts in Hong Kong have been required to determine whether there has been a contravention of the doctrine under the Basic Law. The matters dealt with by the courts have included the following: the scope of the ability of the courts to review the prosecutorial discretion of the executive;[160] whether mandatory sentencing laws that take away the discretion of the courts involve the legislature exercising judicial power;[161] and the scope of the law-making power of the Chief Executive via executive orders.[162] There is a range of other circumstances as well that give rise to questions of whether there is a contravention of the Basic Law, such as whether judges can exercise non-judicial functions (in, say, tribunals or commissions of inquiry), whether it is permissible for particular tribunals to exercise judicial power[163] and the permissible scope of the delegation of law-making functions by the legislature.[164]

Review Questions

(1) Is there any conflict between the notions of 'one country' and 'two systems' in the concept of 'one country, two systems'?
(2) To what extent does Hong Kong have autonomy in self-governance under the Basic Law?
(3) To what extent is the doctrine of the separation of powers reflected in the constitutional framework of Hong Kong?

---

[160] *Re Chu Wai Ha* [2005] 2 HKC 36.
[161] *Lau Cheong* v. *HKSAR* (2002) 5 HKCFAR 415, [2002] 2 HKLRD 612.
[162] *Leung Kwok Hung* v. *Chief Executive of HKSAR* (unreported, CFI, HCAL 107 of 2005, 9 Feb 2006), confirmed on appeal: see *Leung Kwok Hung* v. *Chief Executive of HKSAR* (unreported, CA, CACV 73 and 87 of 2006, 10 May 2006), *Koo Sze Yiu* v. *Chief Executive of HKSAR* (2006) 9 HKCFAR 441, [2006] 3 HKLRD 455. Cf. *Association of Expatriate Civil Servants of Hong Kong* v. *Chief Executive* [1998] 1 HKLRD 615.
[163] See *Luk Ka Cheung* v. *The Market Misconduct Tribunal* [2009] 1 HKC 1.
[164] See P. Wesley-Smith, 'Judges and Judicial Power under the Hong Kong Basic Law' (2004), *Hong Kong Law Journal* 34, 83.

(4) To what extent do you think that it is vital for courts to have the power to check the constitutionality of legislation and of acts of the executive?
(5) Do you think that a law that provides for a mandatory sentence of life imprisonment for murder would infringe the separation of powers doctrine?

4 Sources of Law

Chapter Highlights

- The Basic Law   90
- Legislation   98
- Case Law and Common Law   107
- Chinese Customary Law   134
- National Laws of the PRC   135

Where do lawyers look to when they wish to ascertain what the law is on a particular matter? To answer this question, we must know what the sources of law are. The law in Hong Kong is mainly composed of statute law (the Basic Law and legislation enacted by the Legislative Council) and common law (judgments rendered by the courts), as set out under the Basic Law.

The Basic Law

The Basic Law as Hong Kong's Constitution

The constitution of a nation is composed of the rules and practices which set out the system of government for the nation, including the laws and legal system of the country. Commonly, the constitution is embodied in a written document, such as in the PRC. For the Hong Kong Special Administrative Region, there is the Basic Law, which came into effect on 1 July 1997 upon the transfer of sovereignty over Hong Kong to China from the British, and which is generally regarded as the constitution of Hong Kong. The Basic Law is sometimes referred to as a 'mini-constitution', which signifies that Hong Kong is not actually an independent country of its own, and accordingly the status of the Basic Law as a constitution must be qualified to a certain extent. However, the Basic Law operates in the nature of a constitution in that it sets out the political, legal and other structures that exist in Hong Kong following the return of sovereignty to China. The Basic Law implements, and as law,[1] provides legal backing to the operation, and doctrine, of 'one country, two systems' in Hong Kong. Thus, while specifying that Hong Kong is a part of the PRC,[2] the Basic Law prescribes that Hong Kong is to enjoy a high degree of autonomy with its own political, economic and legal system[3] which is in significant respects independent and different from the systems which operate on the Mainland. The Basic Law is a piece of legislation, as well as being a source of law in Hong Kong, with articles 8 and 18 prescribing what the laws in force in Hong Kong are to be. Similar to other constitutions generally, the Basic Law is also a 'higher law' whereby other laws of the HKSAR cannot contravene the Basic Law.[4]

Legal Validity of the Basic Law

Generally speaking, the legal validity of the constitution of the nation is simply assumed or accepted by the populace. That would appear to be the case for the PRC Constitution. In Hong Kong, however, the validity and authority of the Basic Law is derived from the PRC Constitution, as the Basic Law was enacted by the NPC as a PRC statute pursuant to article 31 of the PRC Constitution, which allows for the creation of Special Administrative Regions. The Basic Law is also underpinned by treaty obligations of the PRC in accordance with international law, as the Basic Law was enacted to implement the 1984 Sino-British Joint Declaration.[5]

---

[1] Basic Law, art. 18.
[2] Basic Law, art. 1.
[3] Basic Law, art. 2.
[4] Basic Law, art. 8.
[5] Joint Declaration of the Government of the United Kingdom of Great Britain and Northern Ireland and the Government of the People's Republic of China on the Question of Hong Kong, 19 December 1984. On the international law implications of the Joint Declaration, see Y. Ghai, *Hong Kong's New Constitutional Order: The Resumption of Chinese Sovereignty and the Basic Law*, 2nd ed. (Hong Kong: Hong Kong University Press 1999), pp. 70–72.

Contents of the Basic Law

The Basic Law contains the following:

- Preamble, which expressly states, among other matters, the principle of 'one country, two systems'.
- Chapter I – General principles. Article 1 provides that Hong Kong is an inalienable part of the PRC. Article 2 confers on the Hong Kong SAR a 'high degree of autonomy'. Other articles in Chapter I flesh out the concept of 'one country, two systems'.[6] For example, article 8 provides for the continued application of the laws previously in force in Hong Kong (prior to 1 July 1997), including the common law.
- Chapter II – Relationship between the Central Authorities and the Hong Kong SAR. Chapter II contains articles vesting the Hong Kong SAR with executive, legislative and independent judicial power. Article 18 sets out the laws in force in Hong Kong. Chapter II also provides for the powers that are to be exercised by the Central People's Government.
- Chapter III – Fundamental rights and duties of the residents. Article 24 defines 'residents' to be both permanent and non-permanent residents and also states the persons who are permanent residents[7] of Hong Kong. Articles 25 to 40 set out fundamental rights (including human rights[8]) of both residents and other persons in Hong Kong.[9] Article 42 states that residents and other persons in Hong Kong have the obligation to comply with the laws in force in Hong Kong.
- Chapter IV – Political structure. Chapter IV deals with the three arms of government, namely the executive, the legislature and the judiciary, including provisions on the powers of each.[10] Chapter IV also contains provisions on district organisations and public servants.
- Chapter V – Economy. This chapter contains provisions on the economy, including protections for private property rights, provisions setting out the autonomy of the Hong Kong SAR in respect of its finances and economic policies, and entrenchment of principles of free trade

---

[6] On 'one country, two systems' and 'high degree of autonomy', see further Chapter 3 of this book.
[7] On 'permanent residents', see also Immigration Ordinance (Cap. 115), Sch. 1.
[8] For human rights protections, see also Hong Kong Bill of Rights Ordinance (Cap. 383).
[9] See Basic Law, art. 41.
[10] On the branches of the Government, see further Chapter 3 of this book.

and free markets. There are also provisions on land leases, shipping and civil aviation.
- Chapter VI – Education, science, culture, sports, religion, labour and social services. Chapter VI provides for the autonomy of the Hong Kong SAR to set its own policies in relation to the foregoing. Certain protections are also set out in this chapter, including freedom of religious belief under article 141.
- Chapter VII – External affairs. While the Central People's Government is responsible for 'foreign affairs' under article 13, the Hong Kong SAR is authorised to conduct external affairs on its own, pursuant to article 13 and Chapter VII.[11]
- Chapter VIII – Interpretation and amendment of the Basic Law. Article 158 sets out the respective powers of the Standing Committee of the National People's Congress and of Hong Kong courts in interpretation of the Basic Law. Article 159 states the power of the National People's Congress to amend the Basic Law, as well as setting out the procedures to be followed.
- Chapter IX – Supplementary provisions. Article 160 supplements articles 8 and 18 in providing for the continued application of the laws previously in force in Hong Kong (prior to 1 July 1997) and also sets out the basis for invalidity of any previous laws which contravene the Basic Law.
- Annex I sets out the method for selection of the Chief Executive.
- Annex II sets out the method for formation of the Legislative Council and procedures for voting in the Legislative Council.
- Annex III lists the national laws to be applied in Hong Kong.

Interpretation of the Basic Law

The reading of any piece of written text can potentially give rise to different interpretations as to its meaning. With legal texts (i.e., laws), there is a practical necessity for there to be some person or body who has the power to authoritatively interpret the meaning of the legal text, in order for the legal system to work. Under the separation of powers doctrine

---

[11] See also Chapter 3 of this book.

as applied in common law systems, the function of interpretation of laws is given solely to the judiciary. However, under the system in Mainland China, the NPCSC, a non-judicial body, is given power under the PRC Constitution to interpret laws.[12]

A hybrid system was adopted under the Basic Law in relation to its interpretation. Under article 158, ultimate power to interpret the Basic Law is vested in the NPCSC. The courts in Hong Kong are, however, authorised pursuant to the article to interpret the provisions of the Basic Law when adjudicating cases.[13] The Hong Kong Court of Final Appeal is required to seek an interpretation from the NPCSC, though, when there is a need to interpret provisions of the Basic Law concerning affairs which are the responsibility of the Central People's Government, or concerning the relationship between the central authorities and the HKSAR.[14] Generally, in any situation, whether a matter is brought before the courts or not, the NPCSC would have the power to interpret any provision of the Basic Law on its own initiative[15] or on request[16] from the Chief Executive of the HKSAR.[17] Interpretations by the NPCSC are binding on Hong Kong courts and so constitute a source of law on the meaning of the Basic Law,[18] as do the judgments of the courts in Hong Kong in interpreting the Basic Law.

---

[12] See generally H. Wen, 'Interpretation of Law by the Standing Committee of the National People's Congress', in J. Chan, H. L. Fu and Y. Ghai (eds.), *Hong Kong's Constitutional Debate: Conflict Over Interpretation* (Hong Kong: Hong Kong University Press 2000), pp. 183–197.

[13] On the general approach of the Hong Kong courts to interpretation of the Basic Law, see Chapter 9.

[14] For a case where the CFA sought an interpretation from the NPCSC, see *Democratic Republic of the Congo* v. *FG Hemisphere Associates LLC (No. 1)* (2011) 14 HKCFAR 95; *Democratic Republic of the Congo* v. *FG Hemisphere Associates LLC (No. 2)* (2011) 14 HKCFAR 395.

[15] A. H. Y. Chen, 'Constitutional Adjudication in Post-1997 Hong Kong' (2006), *Pacific Rim Law and Policy Journal* 15, 627, at 646.

[16] This was implicitly accepted by the Court of Final Appeal in *Lau Kong Yung* v. *Director of Immigration* (1999) 2 HKCFAR 300, [1999] 3 HKLRD 778.

[17] Query whether art.158 effectively limits judicial independence in Hong Kong. See Chapter 3 regarding the separation of powers in Hong Kong.

[18] *Ng Ka Ling* v. *Director of Immigration (No. 2)* (1999) 2 HKCFAR 141, [1999] 1 HKLRD 577; *Lau Kong Yung* v. *Director of Immigration* (1999) 2 HKCFAR 300, [1999] 3 HKLRD 778.

Interpretation by the NPCSC

To date, the NPCSC has interpreted provisions in the Basic Law on five occasions:

- Instrument 17: Interpretation of the NPCSC on arts. 22(4) and 24(2), (3) (26 June 1999), relating to the right of abode in Hong Kong.[19]
- Instrument 18: Interpretation of the NPCSC on article 7 of annex I and art III of annex II (6 April 2004), relating to universal suffrage and the election of the Chief Executive and members of the Legislative Council.[20]
- Instrument 20: Interpretation of the NPCSC on article 53 (27 April 2005), relating to the length of the term of office of a replacement Chief Executive.[21]
- Instrument 22: Interpretation of the NPCSC on articles. 13 and 19 (26 August 2011), relating to state immunity.[22]
- Instrument 25: Interpretation of the NPCSC on article 104 (7 November 2016), on oath-taking in swearing to uphold the Basic Law and swearing allegiance to the HKSAR and PRC.[23]

---

[19] See *Ng Ka Ling v. Director of Immigration* (1999) 2 HKCFAR 4; *Ng Ka Ling v. Director of Immigration (No. 2)* (1999) 2 HKCFAR 141; *Lau Kong Yung v. Director of Immigration* (1999) 2 HKCFAR 300; *Director of Immigration v. Chong Fung Yuen* (2001) 4 HKCFAR 211; *Ng Siu Tung v. Director of Immigration* (2002) 5 HKCFAR 1; A. H. Y. Chen, 'Ng Ka Ling and Article 158(3) of the Basic Law' (2001–2), *Journal of Chinese and Comparative Law* 5, 221.

[20] See A. H. Y. Chen, 'The Constitutional Controversy of Spring 2004' (2004), *Hong Kong Law Journal* 34, 215.

[21] See A. H. Y. Chen, 'The NPCSC's Interpretation in Spring 2005' (2005), *Hong Kong Law Journal* 35, 255.

[22] See *Democratic Republic of the Congo v. FG Hemisphere Associates LLC (No. 1)* (2011) 14 HKCFAR 95; *Democratic Republic of the Congo v. FG Hemisphere Associates LLC (No. 2)* (2011) 14 HKCFAR 395; C. L. Lim, 'Absolutely Immunity for Sovereign Debtors in Hong Kong' (2011), *Law Quarterly Review* 127, 495; P. Y. Lo, 'The Congo Case: The Gateway Opens Wide' (2011), *Hong Kong Law Journal* 41, 385.

[23] See *Chief Executive of HKSAR v. President of the Legislative Council* [2017] 1 HKLRD 460 (CA); leave to appeal refused: *Yau Wai Ching v. Chief Executive of HKSAR* (2017) 20 HKCFAR 390; and see also Po Jen Yap and Eric Chan, 'Legislative Oaths and Judicial Intervention in Hong Kong' (2017), *Hong Kong Law Journal* 47, 1; P. Y. Lo, 'Enforcing an Unfortunate, Unnecessary and "Unquestionably Binding" NPCSC Interpretation: The Hong Kong Judiciary's Deconstruction of Its Construction of the Basic Law' (2018), *Hong Kong Law Journal* 48, 399.

In *Yau Wai Ching* v. *Chief Executive of HKSAR*,[24] the CFA summarised the legal position regarding the NPCSC's power to interpret the Basic Law:[25]

- The NPCSC's power to interpret the Basic Law derives from article 67(4) of the Constitution of the PRC and is provided for expressly in the Basic Law itself in article 158(1) and is in general and unqualified terms.
- The exercise of interpretation of the Basic Law under PRC law is one conducted under a different system of law to the common law system, and includes legislative interpretation which can clarify or supplement laws.
- An interpretation of the Basic Law issued by the NPCSC is binding on Hong Kong courts.
- Such NPCSC interpretations declare what the law is and has always been since the coming into effect of the Basic Law on 1 July 1997.[26]

Apart from actual interpretations of the Basic Law exercised pursuant to article 67(4) of the PRC Constitution and article 158(1) of the Basic Law, the NPCSC also has powers to issue 'decisions' in the exercise of its powers to supervise the implementation of the PRC Constitution, including article 31 of the Constitution which implements the 'one country, two systems' as applied in Hong Kong under the Basic Law.[27] An issue arises as to whether such decisions are binding on Hong Kong courts under Hong Kong law.

The issue was discussed in *Leung Chung Hang Sixtus* v. *President of Legislative Council*,[28] though the Court of First Instance considered that it was unnecessary to resolve the issue for the purposes of the case. The decision dealt with the dispute over the constitutionality of the co-location arrangement of the Express Rail Link. The Express Rail Link is a high-speed rail system linking Hong Kong with the Mainland. A 'co-location arrangement' has been established whereby customs, immigration and quarantine clearance procedures of both Hong Kong and the Mainland are undertaken at the West Kowloon Station in Hong Kong.

---

[24] (2017) 20 HKCFAR 390, at para. 35.
[25] For earlier decisions setting out these principles, see *Ng Ka Ling* v. *Director of Immigration (No. 2)* (1999) 2 HKCFAR 141; *Lau Kong Yung* v. *Director of Immigration* (1999) 2 HKCFAR 300; *Director of Immigration* v. *Chong Fung Yuen* (2001) 4 HKCFAR 211. See also Lin Feng, 'The Duty of Hong Kong Courts to Follow the NPCSC's Interpretation of the Basic Law: Are There Any Limits?' (2018), *Hong Kong Law Journal* 48, 167.
[26] That is, NPCSC interpretations have retrospective effect.
[27] *Leung Chung Hang Sixtus* v. *President of Legislative Council* [2018] HKCFI, [2019] 1 HKLRD 292, at para. 53.
[28] [2018] HKCFI, [2019] 1 HKLRD 292.

The application of Mainland clearance procedures in Hong Kong is implemented by the creation of a Mainland Port Area at the West Kowloon Station (together with train compartments of trains in operation on the Express Rail Link in Hong Kong). Laws of the Mainland apply in the Mainland Port Area to the exclusion of Hong Kong laws (except certain 'reserved matters') and the Mainland exercises jurisdiction within the Mainland Port Area. The Mainland Port Area was created following a Co-operation Arrangement made between Hong Kong and the Mainland, a decision of the NPCSC endorsing the Arrangement and affirming that the Arrangement is consistent with the Basic Law, and implementation of the Arrangement under the procedures of both jurisdictions, including, in the case of Hong Kong, enactment of the Guangzhou–Shenzhen–Hong Kong Express Rail Link (Co-location) Ordinance 2018.

Various parties instituted judicial review proceedings, arguing that the Ordinance is unconstitutional as it is inconsistent with the Basic Law, including articles 8 and 18, which provide to the effect that only Mainland laws specified in Annex III can apply in Hong Kong. One of the issues argued in the case was on the effect of the NPCSC decision under Hong Kong law. The decision was not made pursuant to a specific provision in the Basic Law but was made pursuant to the NPCSC's supervisory powers under the PRC Constitution.

The applicants argued, inter alia, that the decision cannot be binding under Hong Kong law because it was not made within the framework of the Basic Law.[29] The Hong Kong Government countered that the decision must be taken into account by Hong Kong courts because: (1) the NPCSC has power to interpret the Basic Law under article 158 and even if the decision is not strictly binding because the decision was not formally made in accordance with article 158, the decision should be regarded as being of great persuasive value; (2) the decision was 'in substance' an interpretation of the Basic Law and hence should be regarded as binding; and (3) the issue of consistency of the Ordinance with the Basic Law is one that is at the interface of the 'one country, two systems' doctrine and ought to be determined on the basis of the position under PRC law.[30]

The Court of First Instance considered that it was unnecessary to resolve the above issue as the court in the end did not decide the case on the basis

---

[29] [2018] HKCFI, [2019] 1 HKLRD 292, at para. 59.
[30] [2018] HKCFI, [2019] 1 HKLRD 292, at para. 60.

of the NPCSC decision. Instead, the court held that, as a matter of the court's interpretation of the Basic Law, the establishment of the Mainland Port Area under the Ordinance was constitutional.[31]

Laws in Force in Hong Kong: Basic Law art. 18

Article 18 of the Basic Law sets out four categories of law in Hong Kong: (1) the Basic Law, (2) the laws previously in force in Hong Kong under article 8, (3) laws enacted by the legislature of the HKSAR and (4) certain national laws of the PRC.

The phrase 'laws previously in force in Hong Kong' refers to the laws in force prior to the transfer of sovereignty over Hong Kong in 1997. These are specified in article 8 to be the common law, rules of equity, ordinances, subordinate legislation and customary law. Thus, article 8 covers essentially three categories of law: judge-made law (common law and equity), legislation and customary Chinese law. Article 8 is significant in preserving to a large extent the pre-existing laws which applied in Hong Kong prior to the handover, and provides an important pillar for the preservation of the separate legal system which exists in Hong Kong under the 'one country, two systems' principle.

Legislation

Definition

Legislation or statute law refers to law made by or under the authority of the legislature.

---

[31] The court held that the question of consistency with the Basic Law should not be approached 'in a literal or mechanistic manner' (at para. 68). The court took a broad-brush approach to interpretation instead and considered that the Basic Law did not prohibit the creation of a port within Hong Kong subject to the jurisdiction and laws of the Mainland for the purposes of customs, immigration and quarantine control. Rather, the establishment of the Mainland Port Area is a manifestation of the exercise of a high degree of autonomy by Hong Kong (at paras. 69–73). On the debate over the constitutionality of the co-location arrangement, see also Hong Kong Bar Association, 'Statement of the HKBA on the Decision of the NPCSC of 27 December 2017 on the Co-operation Agreement' (28 December 2017), available at www.hkba.org/sites/default/files/20171228%20-%20Bar%20Co-Location%20Arrangement%20Statement%20%28English%29%20FINAL_0.pdf; Lin Feng, 'Constitutionality of the Co-Location Arrangement at the West Kowloon High-Speed Rail Terminus' (2017), *Hong Kong Law Journal* 47, 699; Po Jen Yap and Jiang Xixin, 'Co-Location Is Constitutional' (2018), *Hong Kong Law Journal* 48, 37.

Primary and Secondary Legislation

Legislation is divided into two categories: (1) primary legislation and (2) delegated or subsidiary legislation.

Primary legislation refers to statutes, which in Hong Kong are the ordinances enacted by the Legislative Council (being the legislature of the HKSAR).[32] In England and various other jurisdictions, primary legislation is composed of statutes referred to as Acts, which are created, in the case of England, with the assent of the Crown in Parliament. The Crown (i.e., the King or Queen) also has a limited power to legislate pursuant to the royal prerogative, and ordinances are one form of legislation so made by the Crown without the assent of Parliament. Statutes made by the governments of the British colonies were often in the form of ordinances. This was the situation in Hong Kong under colonial rule, where the local legislature was given the power to enact laws in the form of ordinances pursuant to letters patent[33] issued by the Crown, and accordingly local statutes have been referred to as ordinances. The terminology has not been altered following the 1997 change in sovereignty.

Delegated or subsidiary or subordinate legislation refers to legislation which is made by some person or authority who has been delegated or given power by the legislature to make such subsidiary legislation. Thus, an ordinance enacted by the Legislative Council might contain a section giving a certain government body the power to make subsidiary legislation. For example, section 376 of the Securities and Futures Ordinance (Cap. 571) allows the Chief Executive in Council to make regulations or rules for the matters set out in the section. Regulations and rules are two examples of subsidiary legislation, and are commonly used to deal with matters of detail in the practical implementation of the general provisions of an ordinance. Other categories of subsidiary legislation include by-laws, orders, notices, proclamations, notices and instruments made under the authority of an ordinance.

---

[32] Basic Law, art. 66.
[33] See the Letters Patent (Charter of the Colony of Hong Kong) dated 5 Apr 1843; and the Hong Kong Letters Patent 1917.

Consolidations

A consolidating statute is one which brings together provisions previously contained in different pieces of legislation in the one statute and which replaces the previous legislation. Consolidations do not usually amend or change the pre-existing law, but are enacted simply to bring the provisions together for ease of accessibility.

Codification

Codifying statutes are those which draw together the whole of the law in the particular subject area and which are intended to comprehensively set out the law in that area. The code might be based on existing statutory law or common law principles, and may effect some change to the existing law. Where a particular area of law is so codified, then usually it would not be necessary or appropriate to refer back to previous statements of the law set out in statutes or case authorities before the commencement of the codifying statute.[34]

Legislation as a Source of Law in Hong Kong

Legislation has the status of law in Hong Kong by reason of Basic Law articles 8 and 18. Legislation created by or under the authority of the Legislative Council following 1 July 1997 forms part of the law pursuant to article 18. Ordinances and subsidiary legislation in existence as at 30 June 1997 continue to be part of the law in Hong Kong pursuant to the combined operation of articles 8 and 18.[35]

The continuity of statutory law in Hong Kong following the transfer of sovereignty is qualified, however, in certain respects. First, article 8 does not include English statutes and prerogative instruments which applied in Hong Kong. But much of the content of those laws was necessary under the post-1 July 1997 legal system in Hong Kong (e.g., laws dealing with international matters such as extradition, maritime and shipping, civil aviation), and thus a process of localisation of the English

---

[34] See, e.g., *Bank of England* v. *Vagliano Brothers* [1891] AC 107.
[35] See *HKSAR* v. *Ma Wai Kwan David* [1997] 2 HKC 315, at 365.

Sources of Law   101

Localisation

statutes was required. This involved enactment of those laws as Hong Kong Ordinances.[36]

Second, article 8 contains a proviso that any prior laws that contravene the Basic Law would not be maintained. A process for adaptation of the previous laws to ensure compliance with the Basic Law was therefore undertaken. In 1997, the NPCSC exercised its power under article 160 to declare various laws as being contrary to the Basic Law,[37] and the Hong Kong Reunification Ordinance was enacted on 1 July 1997 to give effect to the NPCSC decision by repealing and amending various laws. Following the handover, the process of adaptation continued, for example, with the enactment of the Adaptation of Laws (Courts and Tribunals) Ordinance and the Adaptation of Laws (Interpretative Provisions) Ordinance in 1998.

Constitutional Invalidity of Legislation

It was mentioned earlier in this chapter that the Basic Law is superior to other law in Hong Kong. This means that all local legislation must be consistent with the Basic Law.[38] Where an ordinance is enacted, the NPCSC has the power to invalidate the ordinance where it considers that the ordinance is not in conformity with the provisions of the Basic Law regarding affairs within the responsibility of the central authorities or regarding the relationship between the central authorities and the HKSAR.[39] More generally, the courts in Hong Kong have the power to declare any part of an ordinance to be invalid as being contrary to the Basic Law.[40] If a legislative provision is declared to be unconstitutional, it is possible for the courts to order temporary validity of the statutory provision

1). Excluded provisions.

2) others.

not invalidity!

---

[36] The Hong Kong legislature was given power to repeal or amend English legislation by the Hong Kong Act 1985 (UK) and three Orders in Council passed under the Act.
[37] NPCSC's Decision on Previous Laws of 23 Feb 1997 (Decision of the Standing Committee of the National People's Congress on Treatment of the Laws Previously in Force on Hong Kong in Accordance with Article 160 of the Basic Law of the Hong Kong Special Administrative Region of the People's Republic of China).
[38] See Basic Law, arts. 8, 11.
[39] Basic Law, art. 17.
[40] *Ng Ka Ling* v. *Director of Immigration* (1999) 2 HKCFAR 4, [1999] 1 HKLRD 315; and see, e.g., *Leung Kwok Hung* v. *HKSAR* (2005) 8 HKCFAR 229, [2005] 3 HKLRD 164; *Leung T C William Roy* v. *Secretary for Justice* [2005] 3 HKC 77 at 94, on appeal *Leung T C William Roy* v. *Secretary for Justice* [2006] 4 HKLRD 211; *Secretary for Justice* v. *Yau Yuk Lung* (2007) 10 HKCFAR 335, [2007] 3 HKLRD 903.

or to suspend the operation of the court order for a specified period of time, for example where striking down of the provision poses a potential danger to the public or otherwise threatens the rule of law.[41]

Bilingual Legislation

There are both English and Chinese versions of all ordinances and subsidiary legislation in Hong Kong. Before 1989, legislation was enacted and published in English only; however, since then there has been enactment and publication in both English and Chinese. The Official Languages Ordinance (Cap. 5) requires all principal ordinances to be enacted and published in both the official languages in Hong Kong, that is, English and Chinese.[42] Both the English and Chinese enactments have the status of law.[43] In addition, a process was undertaken in the early 1990s to translate all pre-existing legislation into Chinese, and to have the Chinese translated versions reviewed and, once approved, gazetted as an 'authentic text' pursuant to section 4B of the Official Languages Ordinance.[44] Once declared and gazetted as an authentic text, the Chinese version also has the status of law at the same level as the pre-existing English version of the legislation. The authentic Chinese texts of all legislation are published together with the English versions in the loose-leaf edition of the *Laws of Hong Kong*[45] and on the Government legislation website.[46]

---

[41] See *Koo Sze Yiu* v. *Chief Executive of the HKSAR* (2006) 9 HKCFAR 441, [2006] 3 HKLRD 455.

[42] Section 4. There is no need to enact and publish in both languages where the Ordinance only amends an English Ordinance where no authentic text has been published in Chinese, or where the Chief Executive in Council determines that the bill is urgent and enactment in both languages will occasion unreasonable delay: ss. 4(2), (3). Subsidiary legislation is now also made and published in both official languages, as is allowed under s. 4A of the Official Languages Ordinance (Cap. 5).

[43] For resolution of conflict in meaning between the two versions, see Chapter 7.

[44] See A. S. Y. Cheung, 'Hong Kong and the Unprecedented Transfer of Sovereignty: Towards a Bilingual Legal System – The Development of Chinese Legal Language' (1997), *Loyola of Los Angeles International and Comparative Law Review* 19, 315, at 318–319.

[45] See Chapter 12. The 'Enactment history' in the pink sheets for each Ordinance in the loose-leaf edition shows when the authentic Chinese text was gazetted.

[46] Hong Kong e-legislation, www.elegislation.gov.hk/.

Operation, Amendment, Repeal and Expiry of Legislation

Commencement

Although an ordinance may be enacted or subsidiary legislation made, the particular piece of legislation does not have legal effect until it has commenced operation. The ordinance or subsidiary legislation itself would often specify the date of commencement (which might be a particular date or a date to be subsequently notified in the *Government Gazette*). If there is no provision in the ordinance or subsidiary legislation dealing with commencement, then the date of commencement is the day on which the ordinance or subsidiary legislation is published in the *Government Gazette*.[47]

Amendment

Legislation can be amended, that is, changed or altered by the addition, deletion or replacement of specific words or provisions in the legislation. It might be appropriate to amend legislation, for example, where the legislation has not worked well in the form originally enacted. Ordinances can be amended by a subsequent ordinance that is enacted. Subsidiary legislation can be amended either by the person with the power to make the subsidiary legislation in the first place or by a subsequent ordinance that is enacted.[48]

Repeal

If it is desirable to do away with an entire piece of legislation, then the legislation may be repealed. This might be done, for example, where the legislation is old and out of date. An ordinance can be repealed by a subsequent ordinance that is enacted. Subsidiary legislation may be repealed by the person with the power to make the subsidiary legislation in the first place or by a later ordinance.[49] Once the repeal of a piece of legislation takes effect, then that legislation no longer has the force of law.[50] Apart from repealing an entire piece of legislation, it is also possible to repeal particular provisions in an ordinance or subsidiary legislation.

---

[47] Interpretation and General Clauses Ordinance (Cap. 1), s. 20(2)(a).
[48] See ibid., ss. 28(1)(c), 37A.
[49] Cf. ibid., ss. 28(1)(c), 37A; and see s. 36.
[50] See ibid., ss. 23–25.

Expiry or Lapse

A piece of legislation can itself provide that it will expire or lapse on a particular date. Such provisions contained in the legislation are sometimes referred to as sunset clauses. The effect of the clause is that the piece of legislation will expire and no longer have legal effect from the date of expiry.[51] The inclusion of a sunset clause may be done where it is anticipated that the legislation will have served its purpose and no longer be useful by a certain date, or where the legislation is contentious (e.g., conferring greater police powers on the government in times of emergency) so as to provide an in-built mechanism to temporarily limit the operation of the legislation.

The Different Parts of a Statute

Figure 4.1 shows the different parts of a statute, which are as follows:

- A Chapter number: Ordinances are given chapter numbers, with each ordinance comprising a particular chapter in the *Laws of Hong Kong*.[52]
- B Short title: Ordinances can be referred to or cited by their short title – here, Pharmacy and Poisons Ordinance.
- C Long title: The long title of an ordinance gives a description of the subject matter or purpose of the ordinance.[53]
- D Commencement date: This is the date when the ordinance came into legal effect.
- E Gazettal information: This shows that the ordinance was, following enactment, published in the *Government Gazette* in Legal Notice 186 of 1969.
- F Section number: Legislative provisions are numbered by section.
- G Section heading: Headings are used to denote the subject matter of the section. Section headings, however, do not have legislative effect.[54]

---

[51] See also Interpretation and General Clauses Ordinance (Cap. 1), s. 27.
[52] Ordinances which only amend other Ordinances do not have a chapter number and are not published separately in the Laws of Hong Kong. The amendments are directly incorporated into the Ordinance being amended.
[53] As to the use of the long title in ascertaining the legislative intention when interpreting an Ordinance, see Chapter 9.
[54] See Interpretation and General Clauses Ordinance (Cap. 1), s. 18(3), and Chapter 9.

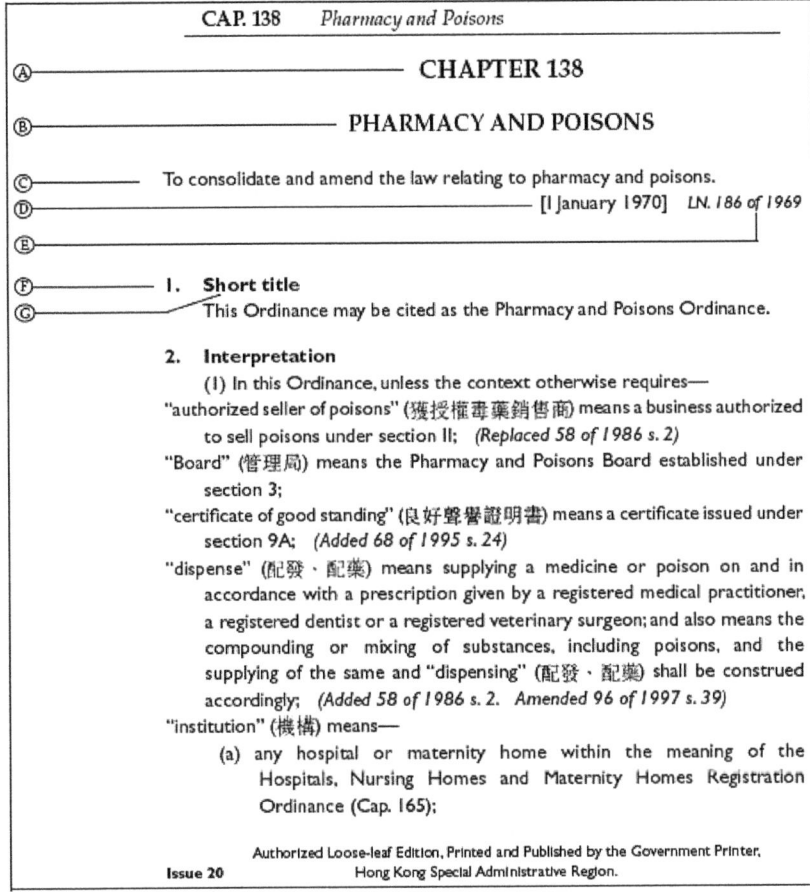

Figure 4.1 Different parts of a statute, as shown on the first page of the Pharmacy and Poisons Ordinance (Cap. 138)

See section 247 of the Securities and Futures Ordinance in Figure 4.2. The different levels of a section are referred to as follows:

- section 247
- subsection (1)
- paragraph (a)
- subparagraph (i)
- subsubparagraph (A)

> **247. Connected with a corporation (insider dealing)**
>
> (1) For the purposes of Division 4, a person shall be regarded as connected with a corporation if, being an individual—
>
> (a) he is a director or employee of the corporation or a related corporation of the corporation;
>
> (b) he is a substantial shareholder of the corporation or a related corporation of the corporation;
>
> (c) he occupies a position which may reasonably be expected to give him access to inside information in relation to the corporation by reason of— *(Amended 9 of 2012 s. 14)*
>
> (i) a professional or business relationship existing between—
>
> (A) himself, or his employer, or a corporation of which he is a director, or a firm of which he is a partner; and
>
> (B) the corporation, a related corporation of the corporation, or an officer or substantial shareholder of either corporation; or
>
> (ii) his being a director, employee or partner of a substantial shareholder of the corporation or a related corporation of the corporation;
>
> (d) he has access to inside information in relation to the corporation and— *(Amended 9 of 2012 s. 14)*
>
> (i) he has such access by reason of his being in such a position that he would be regarded as connected with another corporation by virtue of paragraph (a), (b) or (c); and
>
> (ii) the inside information relates to a transaction (actual or contemplated) involving both those corporations or involving one of them and the listed securities of the other or their derivatives, or to the fact that the transaction is no longer contemplated; or *(Amended 9 of 2012 s. 14)*
>
> (e) he was, at any time within the 6 months preceding any insider dealing in relation to the corporation, a person who would be regarded as connected with the corporation by virtue of paragraph (a), (b), (c) or (d).
>
> (2) For the purposes of Division 4, a corporation shall be regarded as a person connected with another corporation so long as any of its directors or employees is a person who would be regarded as connected with that other corporation by virtue of subsection (1).
>
> (3) In subsection (1), notwithstanding any other provisions of this Ordinance, substantial shareholder (大股東), in relation to a corporation, means a person who has an interest in 5% or more of the total number of shares comprised in the relevant share capital of the corporation. *(Amended 28 of 2012 ss. 912 & 920)*

Figure 4.2 Different levels of a section, as shown in s. 247 of the Securities and Futures Ordinance (Cap. 571).

> **293.Insider dealing offence–defences for certain trustees and personal representatives**
>
> Where a person who is a trustee or personal representative is charged with an offence under section 291(8) in respect of a contravention of section 291 taking place through his dealing in or counselling or procuring another person to deal in listed securities or derivatives, it is a defence to the charge for the person to prove that–
>
> (a) he acted on advice obtained in good faith from another person;
>
> (b) that other person appeared to him to be an appropriate person from whom to seek the advice; and
>
> (c) it did not appear to him that, had that other person dealt in the listed securities or derivatives in question, a contravention of section 291 would take place.

Figure 4.3 Section 293 of the Securities and Futures Ordinance (Cap. 571), which does not contain subsections, only paragraphs

Sometimes sections do not contain subsections but only paragraphs. An example is shown in Figure 4.3.

In section 293, the provision after the numbering (a) should be referred to as 'paragraph (a)' and not 'subsection (a)'.

Case Law and Common Law

Case law refers to the law as set out in written judgments handed down by the courts following the conclusion of cases adjudicated upon by the courts. Judicial pronouncements of legal rules and principles form part of the law in common law jurisdictions, including Hong Kong, pursuant to the doctrine of precedent.[55]

The term 'common law' has different meanings when used in different contexts (see Figure 4.4).

Common Law and Civil Law

At the broadest level when referring to families of legal systems, we talk of the common law system or a common law jurisdiction, which is contrasted with other families of legal systems in the world, such as the civil law system. In this sense, common law denotes the legal systems inherited from England where case law and the doctrine of binding judicial precedent form an important part of the system. Civil law systems, on the other hand, as exemplified by Western continental European systems and

---

[55] See Chapter 5.

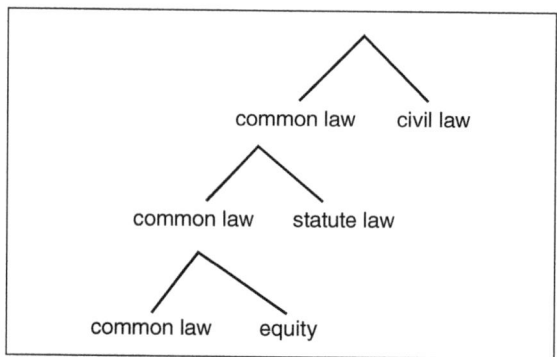

Figure 4.4 Different meanings of the term 'common law'

systems elsewhere that are modelled on such systems (such as Taiwan and Japan), have a Roman law tradition and are characterised by the existence of codes or statutes which comprehensively set out the law that applies in the country.

Common Law and Statute Law

At the next level of usage of the term, within the legal system in, say, Hong Kong, 'common law' is used to refer to case law or the judgments of the courts, as opposed to statute law. When a dispute or a case comes before a court, the court, in deciding the outcome of the case, may need to set out the relevant principles of law in a written judgment that the court hands down. There is then a body of legal principles contained in the written judgments of the courts, sometimes referred to as case law or decisional law. The term 'common law' used in the present context refers to this body of case law.

The common law, as a coherent body of legal principles, developed in England following the Norman conquest of England in 1066. While laws existed in England prior to the Norman reign, the Norman kings, on hearing complaints from subjects across the land, brought unity to the law that applied in the whole of the land. This law came to be known as the common law, being the law in accordance with which the king's courts handed out justice across the whole of England.[56]

---

[56] See further J. H. Baker, *An Introduction to English Legal History*, 3rd ed. (London: Butterworths 1990), chapters 1 and 2.

Common Law and Equity

Finally, in a narrower meaning of the term, 'common law' refers to the case law derived from the common law courts that existed in England prior to the Supreme Court of Judicature Acts 1873 and 1875,[57] namely, the King's Bench (or Queen's Bench), the Exchequer and the Court of Common Pleas. In this sense, common law is distinguished from equity, the latter referring to the principles and rules of law developed by the Court of Chancery. Principles of common law and equity are both principles of case law (as distinct from statute law); in this context, common law is one branch or one category of case law.

To properly understand the distinction between common law and equity, it is necessary to briefly venture back into English legal history.[58] By the thirteenth century, the common law courts were well established in England in applying the common law of the land to disputes which arose. Common procedures were also developed, embodied in the writ system. Historically, a writ was a written command given under the authority of the King requiring a person to be brought before the courts to answer a complaint.[59] Over time, writs became standardised in light of the common types of actions being brought in the courts. However, rigidity developed, where if a person's complaint did not come within existing writs (i.e., within one of the established forms of action), then the courts could not give any remedy for the person.

By the fifteenth century, rigidity in the writ system and in the application of substantive law in the common law courts resulted in a situation where there were increasing numbers of persons petitioning the King to complain about injustices in the common law courts. These petitions were dealt with by the Chancellor who headed the Chancery, which was originally a royal secretariat but became a court as its judicial activities increased. Regarded as a 'court of conscience', the Chancery was not constrained by formal procedures and the strict rules of the common law, but could hand out justice as

---

[57] The various courts were reorganised under this legislation to provide for the existence of the High Court and the Court of Appeal in England.
[58] On the history of the common law courts and the Court of Chancery, see further Baker (n. 56), Chapters 3, 4 and 6.
[59] C. Cook et al., *Laying Down the Law*, 5th ed. (Sydney, NSW: Butterworths 2001), p. 15.

appropriate to the particular facts of the case. Thus developed the notion of equity given by the Chancery to correct deficiencies in the common law.

By the seventeenth century, though, the jurisprudence that developed in the Court of Chancery had hardened into specific rules and principles. The flexibility that existed in earlier times in providing justice according to the particular circumstances gave way to strict rules which were applied to dictate the outcome of cases in largely the same way that the rules of common law operated. Thus, under the modern law of equity, the rules and principles of equity are ascertained from the decisions of the courts in the same way that principles of common law are ascertained; and the doctrine of precedent[60] applies to equitable principles just as much as it does to common law principles.

Nonetheless, the modern principles of equity do still reflect the 'equitable' nature of its origins from the Chancery as a court of conscience in various respects. For example, the rules and principles are underpinned by broad maxims of equity which are aimed towards fairness and justice in the circumstances of the case (e.g., 'equity looks to the intent, rather than to the form').[61] Also, equitable remedies are discretionary in that even if the elements of a cause of action are established, the court can decline to grant an equitable remedy, for example where the plaintiff had himself or herself engaged in improper or wrongful conduct.[62] Furthermore, notions of fairness are embodied in the concept of 'unconscionable conduct' which provides the basis for a number of doctrines in equity.

As a matter of procedure, equitable remedies could only be sought in the Court of Chancery, while common law remedies had to be sought in the common law courts. Difficulties arising from that situation were, however, removed by the Supreme Court of Judicature Acts 1873 and 1875, which, in addition to merging the common law courts and Chancery into the Supreme Court of Judicature (composed of the High Court and the Court of Appeal), fused the equitable and common law jurisdictions of the previous

---

[60] See Chapter 8.
[61] See *Parkin* v. *Thorold* (1852) 16 Beav 59, at 66, 51 ER 698, at 701. This maxim provides the basis for the doctrine of rectification which allows incorrect documents to be rectified or changed to reflect the original intentions of the parties drafting the document in certain circumstances.
[62] This is reflected by the maxims 'he who seeks equity must do equity' and 'he who comes into equity must come with clean hands'.

courts such that any judge sitting in the Supreme Court[63] could apply both the rules of equity and common law. The fusion of common law and equity jurisdiction was likewise provided for in the Supreme Court (now High Court) in Hong Kong.[64]

Despite the fusion of the jurisdictions, equitable principles and common law principles remain distinct, as the fusion only operates to provide the one court with jurisdiction to give both common law and equitable remedies. It is a fallacy to simply assume that common law and equitable doctrines can be combined or merged together at will;[65] for example, common law damages are not available as a remedy where the wrong is one which is actionable in equity only and not under any common law cause of action.

Common Law as a Source of Law in Hong Kong

Common law and the rules of equity are included under 'laws previously in force in Hong Kong' which are specified to remain part of the law in Hong Kong pursuant to Basic Law articles 8 and 18. The basic intention of these provisions is clear, namely to ensure that the case law or decisional law applying in Hong Kong as at 30 June 1997,[66] immediately before the handover, would still apply after the handover. However, it is necessary to comment on certain aspects of the operation of these articles.

First, article 8 covers not only decisions of the courts exercising the jurisdiction of the previous common law courts in England and the Court of Chancery, but also decisions of the courts exercising the jurisdiction of previous courts *other* than the common law courts and Chancery. For example, the former High Court of Admiralty in England dealt with maritime matters arising on the high seas, and so admiralty law can be

---

[63] Now referred to as the Senior Courts of England and Wales pursuant to the Constitutional Reform Act 2005 (UK).
[64] See, originally, ss. 7 and 8 of the Supreme Court Ordinance (No. 3 of 1873); see now ss. 12 and 16 of the High Court Ordinance (Cap. 4).
[65] *Ind Coope & Co* v. *Emmerson* (1887) LR 12 App Cas 300, at 308, per Lord Watson. The mistake of treating common law and equitable doctrines as being fused or combined substantively is referred to as 'fusion fallacy'; see further R. P. Meagher, W. M. C. Gummow and J. R. F. Lehane, *Equity: Doctrines and Remedies*, 3rd ed. (Sydney, NSW: Butterworths 1992), pp. 46–59.
[66] See *HKSAR* v. *Ma Wai Kwan David* [1997] 2 HKC 315.

distinguished from equity and the common law (under a narrow interpretation of the common law to refer to the decisions of the common law courts). Although article 8 does not refer to admiralty law, it would seem that it does cover all decisional law.[67]

Second, the common law (decisional law) in existence in Hong Kong as at 30 June 1997 was the common law of England previously incorporated into the law of Hong Kong pursuant to the former Application of English Law Ordinance of 1966.[68]

Third, although article 8 provides for the continued application of the common law as it stood at 30 June 1997, the common law that applies today is not frozen as at the date of the handover. This is so for two reasons: (1) the operation of the common law has always involved development and extension of the law by the courts[69] and (2) the Court of Final Appeal can overturn previous decisions of English courts as well as its own decisions.[70] These two factors are not inconsistent with articles 8 and 18 because those provisions, combined with the preservation of the pre-existing judicial system pursuant to articles 80 and 84 (and the preservation of the jurisdiction and authority of the courts in Hong Kong), should mean that the ways in which the courts interpret and apply the common law following the handover are the same as the approach that applied before the handover. Put differently, it is the nature of the common law itself that allows for its development, and the preservation of the common law and the court system administering the common law maintains that characteristic of the common law.

Fourth, the common law before the handover that applies today would be modified to the extent that it is inconsistent with the Basic Law; see Interpretation and General Clauses Ordinance (Cap. 1), s. 2A.

---

[67] This was the generally accepted view in relation to previous legislation (Application of English Law Ordinance) which had also only referred to 'the common law and the rules of equity' in relation to the non-statutory laws of England that were to be applied in Hong Kong; see P. Wesley-Smith, *The Sources of Hong Kong Law* (Hong Kong: Hong Kong University Press 1994), pp. 92–94.
[68] See Chapter 1.
[69] See the discussion later in this chapter.
[70] See Chapter 5.

Cases and Law Reports

Law Reporting

Case judgments or decisions of the courts are published in law reports. In Hong Kong,[71] the law reports produced include the following:

- *Hong Kong Law Reports and Digest* (HKLRD) (previously *Hong Kong Law Reports* or HKLR),
- *Hong Kong Cases* (HKC),
- *Hong Kong Court of Final Appeal Reports* (HKCFAR),
- *Hong Kong Family Law Reports* (HKFLR),
- *Hong Kong Conveyancing and Property Law Reports* (CPR).

These law reports today contain judgments mainly from the High Court (both the Court of First Instance and the Court of Appeal) and the Court of Final Appeal. From time to time, some decisions of lower courts are also reported, for example in the HKLRD, though previously there was a separate law report series for District Court decisions (*District Court Law Reports*).

Law reports are now published in hard-copy format as bound volumes, as well as electronically in case databases. For example, cases in the HKLRD are also available on Westlaw, while cases in the HKC are available on LexisNexis.[72]

Unreported Cases

Not all cases handed down are reported, and this is so even for the decisions of superior courts. Usually only cases which are significant in setting out some legal rule or principle would be published in a law report. However, sometimes it is still useful to look at unreported decisions, for example where the subject area is one where there are not many reported cases in Hong Kong.

---

[71] For English law reports, see, e.g., D. Raistrick, *Index to Legal Citations and Abbreviations*, 2nd ed. (London: Bowker-Saur 1993).
[72] See Chapter 12.

Different Parts of a Reported Case

Figure 4.5 shows the different parts of a reported case (*Loyal Luck Trading Ltd v. Tam Chun Wah* [2007] 4 HKLRD 917), as follows:

A These are the parties to the proceedings. Loyal Luck Trading Ltd is the plaintiff, that is, the party who commenced proceedings and sued for a remedy in the court. Tam Chun Wah is the defendant, that is, the party being sued. Where the case is one that was heard on appeal, then the first party named is the appellant (the party which brought the appeal), while the second party named is the respondent.

B This shows the court in which the matter was heard, in this case, the Court of First Instance.

C This is the matter number for the proceedings. Every action commenced in the courts is given a matter number by the court. The number assists in identification of the case in question, and is shown in all court documents relating to that action.

D This shows the judge or judges who heard the case. The case here was heard before a single judge (Barma J).

E These are the dates of the hearing. The case was heard in court over two days (18 and 19 January 2007). The other date (15 June 2007) is the date when the court's decision was handed down.

F These are the catchwords for the judgment. The publishers of the law report provide a list of words and phrases denoting the subject matter of the case. A perusal of the catchwords in the law report gives a quick indication as to the legal areas dealt with in the judgment.

G This is the first part of the headnote of the case. The publishers of the law report provide a summary of the case and the decision in the headnote. The first part of the headnote sets out briefly the facts of the case and perhaps the issues raised.

H This is the second part of the headnote. This section summarises the main points in the court's decision. The headnote usually sets out the important principles of law as set out in the judgment, as well as the court's conclusions on the facts of the case.

I This part of the headnote indicates that the case of *Wheeldon* v. *Burrows* (1879) LR 12 Ch D 31 was applied by Barma J in reaching the decision in the case at hand. Later in the headnote (at J), it is stated that the case of *Batchelor* v. *Marlow* [2003] 1 WLR 764 was distinguished. The terms 'applied' and 'distinguished' are examples of terms which describe how the court treated earlier case precedents in the particular case in

Sources of Law   **115**

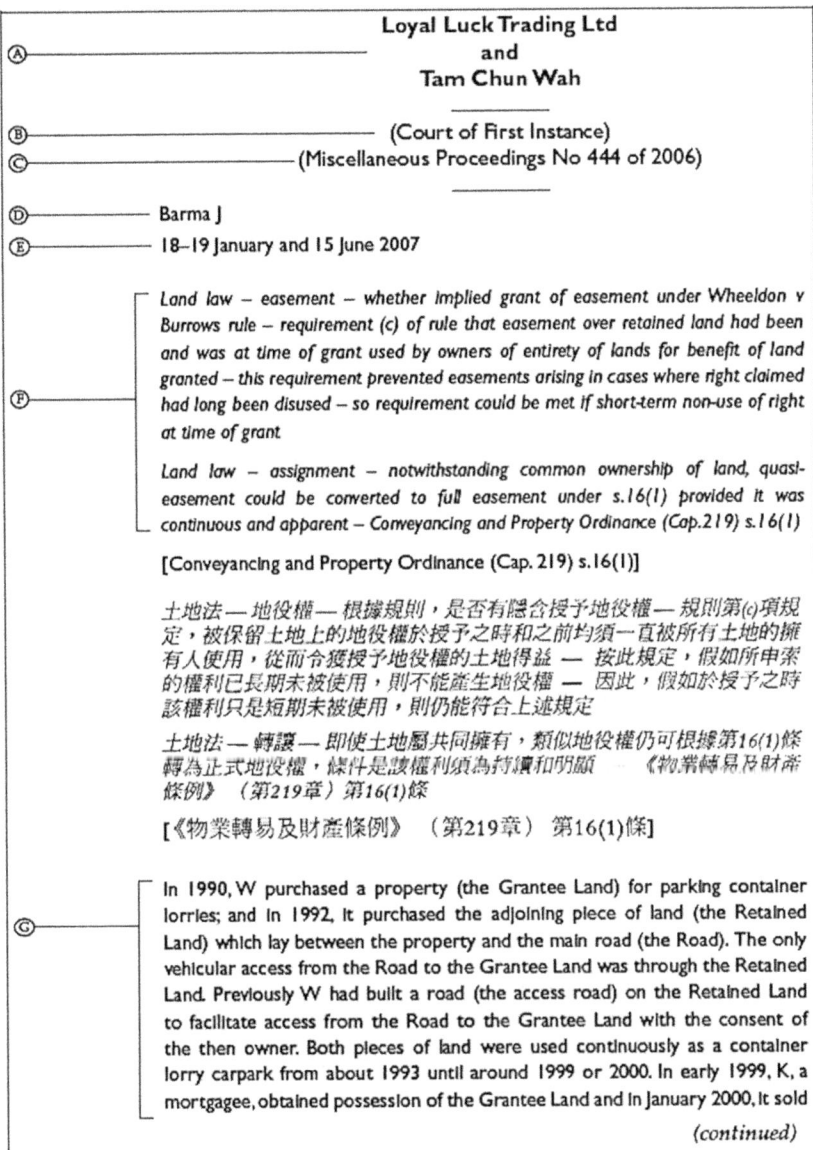

Figure 4.5 Headnote from *Loyal Luck Trading Ltd* v. *Tam Chun Wah* showing the different parts of a reported case

question. The meaning of these and other terms is summarised as follows:
- 'Applied' or 'followed': Where an earlier case is applied or followed, it means that the case at hand was decided in accordance with the

the Grantee Land to M. At this point, with K being in possession, the access road had probably not been in use for a short time as W was probably not using the Grantee Land at all. Subsequently, at the end of 2002, container lorries resumed parking on the Grantee Land. However, as this contravened town planning zoning regulations and permission for such use was recently denied, part of the Grantee Land was currently being used for the permitted use of open storage of vehicles other than container lorries. The Grantee Land was eventually assigned to P and the Retained Land sold to D. P claimed it was entitled to a right of way over the Retained Land, specifically the access road, for vehicular access to the Grantee Land. P argued that the right arose by implication or alternatively under s.16(1) of the Conveyancing and Property Ordinance (Cap.219). D denied that such right arose.

Held, granting the declaration and injunction sought by P, that:
Whether right of way arose by implication
(1) The rule in *Wheeldon v Burrows* (the Rule) implied in favour of a grantee of part of a land against the grantor, easements over the retained land where they: (a) were continuous, which meant permanent in nature, and apparent; (b) were necessary for the reasonable enjoyment of the land granted; and (c) had been and were at the time of the grant used by the owner of the entirety of the lands for the benefit of the land granted (*Wheeldon v Burrows* (1879) LR 12 Ch D 31 applied). (See para.14.)
(2) Here, an implied easement arose over the Retained Land under the Rule when K sold the Grantee Land to M in January 2000. As to requirement (a), the access road was permanent in nature and readily apparent, being a well-defined roadway that was concreted over, or gravelled. As to requirement (b), W's earlier purchase of the Retained Land was good evidence that it was necessary for P's reasonable use. Without the easement, P's property was essentially inaccessible by vehicle and its viable uses severely restricted. As to requirement (c), that the right of way probably was not in active use for a relatively short period of time before the assignment to M was not fatal to implying an easement as the non-use was probably because W was not using the Grantee Land at all and one purpose of requirement (c) was to prevent easements arising in cases where the right claimed had long been long disused, but that was not the case here (*Wheeldon v Burrows* (1879) LR 12 Ch D 31 applied). (See paras.17–19, 21.)
(3) (*Obiter*) So it was not necessary to decide whether the Rule operated when a mortgage was granted. (See para.22.)
(4) D's argument that the easement did not arise as the use to which the Grantee Land was being put was illegal as it contravened the Town Planning Ordinance (Cap.131) (the TPO), was rejected. P did not have to rely

(continued)

Figure 4.5 (cont.)

legal rules set out in the earlier case. This may be because the earlier case was binding as a matter of precedent or where the court takes the view that, although not strictly binding, the rules from the earlier decision should be used to determine the outcome of the present case.

on the use to which the land was put to assert its legal rights in respect of the easement claimed; P had only to establish that an implied easement arose under the Rule. Alternatively, given the heavy penalties under the TPO, it was unnecessary for the promotion of its objectives to deny P the benefit of the right of way claimed. Moreover, the right of way was necessary for access to and the reasonable enjoyment of part of the Grantee Land's present permitted uses, including the parking of vehicles other than container lorries (*Magistrates of Airdrie & Another v County Council of the County of Lanark* [1910] AC 286, *George Legge & Son Ltd v Wenlock Corp* [1938] AC 204, *Glamorgan County Council v Carter* [1963] 1 WLR 1 distinguished). (See paras. 31–33.)

(5) Finally, D's argument that the right of way claimed was excessive, rendering the Retained Land practically unusable was rejected. The right of way would not deprive D of the entire use of his land for a substantial part of each day. At least about 50% of that land was not subject to it and D was free to use this portion as he wished (*Batchelor v Marlow & Another* [2003] 1 WLR 764 distinguished). (See paras. 36–39.)

Section 16 of the Ordinance

(6) Notwithstanding common ownership of a land with no prior diversity of ownership and occupation, a quasi easement could still be converted into a full easement, by operation of s.16 of the Ordinance, upon an assignment of part of the land provided that it was continuous and apparent. Thus, here, an easement could also have arisen under s.16 on the mortgage of the property to K or on its assignment to M. In the former case, no issue about non-use of the right of way arose as W was then still carrying on business; and in the latter case, the relatively recent cessation of use would not be such as to prevent the easement from arising (*Long v Gowlett* [1923] 2 Ch 177 applied; *Sovmots Investments Ltd & Another v Secretary of State for the Environment & Others* [1979] AC 144 distinguished). (See paras. 28–30.)

Application

This was an application by the plaintiff for a declaration that it had a right of way over the defendant's land and an injunction to prevent the defendant from interfering with the use of this right. The facts are set out in the judgment.

Mr Robert Pang, instructed by Chow, Griffiths & Chan, for the plaintiff.

Mr Andy Hung, instructed by Hagon Wai & Partners, for the defendant.

(*continued*)

Figure 4.5 (cont.)

The term 'followed' is used where the facts in the present case are essentially similar to the earlier case. The term 'applied' is used where the facts are not quite the same, but where the rules from the earlier case should still dictate the outcome of the present case.

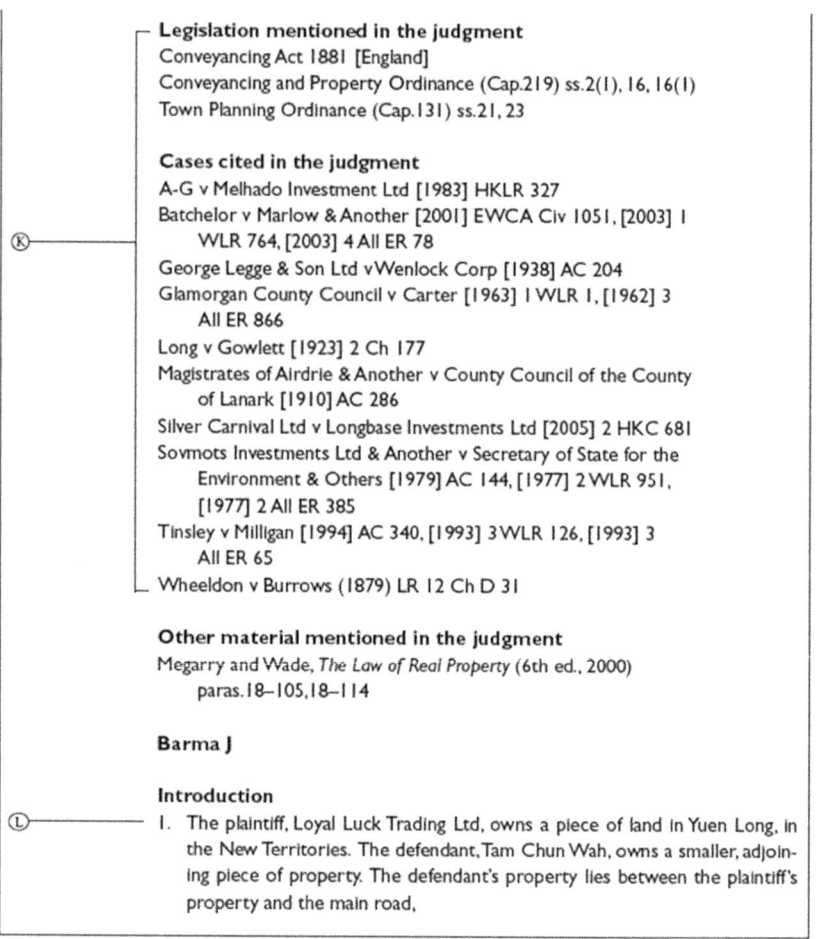

Figure 4.5 (cont.)

- ○ 'Approved': Where a (higher) court takes the view that the legal rules set out in the judgment of a lower court are correct, then the higher court is said to approve the earlier decision of the lower court.
- ○ 'Distinguished': Where the court decides that the rules set out in an earlier case should not determine the outcome of the present case because of some material difference in the facts, then the earlier case is distinguished.[73]

---

[73] See Chapter 5.

- o 'Overruled': A court higher up in the hierarchy can decide that the legal rules as set out in the judgment of a court lower in the hierarchy are wrong. Where this occurs, then the lower court's decision is overruled and is no longer good law. In some situations,[74] a court can also overrule an earlier decision of its own.
- o 'Not followed': This phrase is used in relation to earlier cases which are strictly speaking not binding on the court in the case at hand (e.g., because it is a decision in a different jurisdiction or different hierarchy of courts), and where the court decides that the legal rules in that earlier case were wrongly decided and hence should not be followed or applied in the case at hand. A case that is 'not followed' is strictly speaking not overruled, and so in principle remains as good law within its own jurisdiction.
- o 'Doubted' or 'disapproved': These terms are used where the court expresses the view that the earlier decision was incorrectly decided. Where these terms are used, the earlier decision would not have been strictly binding either because it is from a different jurisdiction or because it could have been distinguished. The use of the term 'doubted' or 'disapproved' indicates that the court in the present case is inclined to the view that the rules set out in the earlier decision are wrong; however, this does not strictly affect the status of the earlier decisions as precedents. A case can potentially still have binding effect until it is overruled.
- o 'Considered': Where a case is mentioned or discussed in the judgment but the court does not give any firm view as to whether the rules set out in the earlier case are correct or not, then the term 'considered' is used in referring to the court's treatment of the earlier case in the judgment.
- o 'Affirmed': Where a decision is on appeal and the appeal court decides that the lower court is correct, then the appeal court is said to affirm the lower court's decision. Where the appeal court considers that the lower court's decision is only correct in some parts, then it is said that the earlier decision is 'affirmed in part'.
- o 'Reversed': Where a decision is on appeal and the appeal court decides that the lower court's decision is wrong and should be overturned,

---

[74] Ibid.

then the lower court's decision is reversed. Where only part of the lower court's decision is held to be incorrect, then it can be said that the earlier decision is 'reversed in part'.
J The legislation and cases analysed or referred to in the judgment are listed here.
K This is the beginning of the actual judgment of the court. For this particular case, the judgment commences on page 920 and ends on page 934 of the particular volume of the law report.

Which Parts of a Court Judgment Constitute the Law?

Not every statement made by the court in a judgment handed down in a case constitutes the law. In other words, in order to know what the legal principles are which form case law under the doctrine of precedent, it is necessary to be able to ascertain the particular parts of a judgment which state the principles of binding law.

Distinction between Fact and Law

Matters of fact and matters of law are distinguished from each other for a variety of purposes in the legal system. In some contexts, and at various levels (both conceptual and practical), the distinction might be amorphous,[75] but the distinction nonetheless remains fundamental in the legal system. In the present context, the distinction is important as statements of fact in a judgment do not amount to law.

To illustrate, consider the case of *Foshan Hua Da Industrial Co v. Johnson Stokes & Master.*[76] This was a professional negligence case where the plaintiff company sued the defendant solicitors, alleging that the solicitors were negligent (and were liable either in tort or contract) in relation to a loan that the plaintiff had granted to another party. The plaintiff had received security for the loan by way of an equitable mortgage over certain shares in a company; however, the plaintiff subsequently suffered losses when the borrower failed to make the loan repayments. The plaintiff was unable to rely on the security pursuant to the mortgage due to

---

[75] See, e.g., Ronald J. Allen and Michael S. Pardo, 'The Myth of the Law–Fact Distinction' (2003), *Northwestern University Law Review* 97, 1769.
[76] [1999] 1 HKLRD 418.

the claims of another mortgagee who had priority over the plaintiff. The plaintiff argued that the solicitors were negligent in not having fully advised on the risks of the transaction and not having procured a legal mortgage for the plaintiff (which would have given the plaintiff greater protection). The court decided, among other matters, the following:

(1) The plaintiff retained the defendant solicitors under a contract to prepare documentation for the plaintiff to grant a loan, supported by security, to another party.
(2) The plaintiff did not seek advice from the solicitors as to whether the transaction which they wished to enter into was a safe one or not.
(3) The solicitors did advise the plaintiff generally on the desirability of obtaining a legal mortgage rather than an equitable one.
(4) Solicitors owe a duty to their clients, both in contract and tort, to exercise skill and care.
(5) The duty of a solicitor is to exercise that reasonable degree of skill and care to be expected of a competent and reasonably experienced solicitor.
(6) The failure of the defendant solicitors to spell out in detail all the differences between a legal mortgage and an equitable mortgage did not amount to negligence or a breach of contractual duty.
(7) The solicitors did not breach their duties owed to the plaintiff.

Statements (1) to (3) are findings of fact made by the court. In a judgment, the court sets out the facts which are relevant to the legal issues in the case. The court makes findings of fact based on what is agreed to by the parties to the litigation or on the basis of the evidence that the parties have presented to the court.

Statements (4) and (5) are statements of law. The court sets out and explains the principles of law that are relevant to the case. Statements of law made in a judgment can be binding or authoritative (under the doctrine of precedent), or they could be non-binding.[77]

Statements (6) and (7) involve the court's determination of the issues following an application of the law to the facts. These types of statement are sometimes referred to as statements of mixed law and fact, but in

---

[77] See the discussion of *ratio* and *obiter* later in this chapter.

the present situation would be regarded as statements of fact – as will be explained.

There is perhaps no consensus as to a failsafe test for distinguishing between fact and law, but a rough guide is provided here to introduce readers to the distinction. Statements (1) to (3) should be seen to be facts in the sense that they describe what events occurred. These findings of fact simply set out what happened as between the parties. Statement (4) can be distinguished from statements (1) to (3) in the sense that statement (4) clearly prescribes a norm; that is, it sets out what a person ought to do (as required by the law). The statement does not purport to describe what actually happened between the plaintiff and the defendant, only what the defendant should have done in order to comply with the law. Accordingly, the statement involves a statement of law. Similarly, statement (5) sets out a principle of law. It prescribes a norm (that the defendant ought to take reasonable care) through defining the meaning of the legal principle that forms an element of the cause of action (i.e., failure to take reasonable care).

Statements (1) to (3), on the one hand, and statements (4) and (5), on the other hand, can be seen as being at the two opposite ends of a continuum. Recognising these two categories of statements as being statements of fact and law respectively generally poses little problem in practice. Statements (6) and (7) lie more towards the middle of the continuum, and it is in situations like this that the difficulties in the fact/law distinction are most evident. The uncertainties as to whether a statement is one of fact or law can arise because the particular statement can be regarded as both a description of what happened as well as prescribing a legal norm or standard. For instance, statement (6) can be a statement describing what happened, namely that the defendant solicitors did not fail to take reasonable care in the provision of their services to the plaintiff. However, the statement can also be construed as setting out a legal principle that can be applied to others, namely that a solicitor who is retained only to provide documentation for a loan and equitable mortgage does not breach his or her duty of care owed to the client if the solicitor fails to advise in detail on all the differences between a legal and an equitable mortgage.

How then do we establish whether such a statement involves a matter of fact or law? Unfortunately, there is no clear test of general application, and often it is necessary to have regard to the case law to see what the judges have said on the issue. Thus, in the case of negligence, the courts have accepted that whether the conduct of the defendant amounts to a failure to take reasonable care in the circumstances is a question of fact.[78] Thus, we might look at the case of *Foshan Hua Da Industrial Co* v. *Johnson Stokes & Master*[79] as an example where the court found that the solicitors were not negligent; however, it does not establish a legal principle that solicitors would necessarily escape liability where they have advised generally that a legal mortgage would be beneficial but where they have not explained this in detail. Whether the solicitors would be negligent depends on the particular circumstances of the case.[80] The uncertainty here in the fact/law distinction is in some respects similar to the difficulty in distinguishing between the *ratio* and *obiter* of a case, and this will be discussed further.[81]

Interpretation of a Statute

A court's construction or interpretation of a statute is a question of law and thus a statement in a judgment as to the meaning of words in a piece of legislation can itself form part of the law that can be binding under the doctrine of precedent.[82] Although a court's interpretation of a statute itself amounts to law, it should be borne in mind that the words used in the statute always have primacy over the words used in the court's judgment, and that the interpretation given by a court cannot be treated rigidly as if it were words in the statute itself.[83]

Also, the courts distinguish between legal technical terms (or legal terms of art) from words which are to be given their ordinary meaning as a matter of common usage. Legal technical terms are terms which are specifically defined in the statute or which have an established legal meaning as set out by the courts.[84] On the other hand, courts might determine that particular words used in the statute should simply be given their ordinary, everyday

---

[78] *Qualcast (Wolverhampton) Ltd* v. *Haynes* [1959] AC 743.
[79] [1999] 1 HKLRD 418.
[80] In the above case, the court expressly stated that the failure to provide the detailed advice did not, 'in the circumstances of [the] case', constitute negligence.
[81] See the discussion below later in this chapter.
[82] *London Transport Executive* v. *Betts* [1959] AC 213, at 232. On the doctrine of precedent, see Chapter 5.
[83] *Goodrich* v. *Paisner* [1957] AC 65, at 88; see also Chapter 7.
[84] E.g., terms such as 'company', 'prospectus' or 'debenture' as understood in company law under the Companies Ordinance (Cap. 622)/Companies (Winding Up and Miscellaneous Provisions) Ordinance (Cap. 32) or the common law.

meaning.[85] Whether certain terms are to be given their ordinary meaning or have a special meaning in law is a question of law.[86] However, the ordinary meaning of words is a question of fact, and thus the application of the ordinary meaning of words to a particular factual situation is a matter of fact and would not strictly give rise to a principle of law that would be applied as a matter of precedent.[87] Putting the matter differently, the distinction is between the court construing or interpreting the statute (this gives rise to statements of law) and applying the ordinary meaning of the statute to the facts (the application of the law to the facts here does not constitute a statement of law).

Ratio and Obiter

Having identified the statements of law from a judgment, it is then necessary to distinguish between statements of law, which form the *ratio decidendi* of a judgment, and statements of law, regarded as the *obiter dictum*. When we talk of case law as being a source of law, we are strictly speaking referring only to the legal rules in a judgment which are authoritative statements of the law. Only the *ratio* of a case has this status of being an authoritative statement of the law, and only such statements can bind subsequent courts under the doctrine of precedent.

When a court sets out legal rules in a judgment, the court does not usually give an exposition of the entire area of law to which the particular dispute relates, but only discusses the specific legal rules which are relevant. For example, where a contractual dispute arises because of disagreement between the parties as to whether an exclusion clause was properly incorporated into the contract, the court would discuss legal principles in relation to exclusion clauses and incorporation of contractual terms. The court would not discuss all the general rules of contract law ranging from rules dealing with the formation of contracts to rules dealing with the measure of damages.

---

[85] E.g., the words 'insulting behaviour' as used in former s. 5 of the Public Order Act 1936 (UK): *Brutus* v. *Cozens* [1973] AC 854.
[86] *Collector of Customs* v. *Pozzolanic* (1993) 43 FCR 280.
[87] S. H. Bailey, J. P. L. Ching and N. W. Taylor, *Smith, Bailey and Gunn on The Modern English Legal System*, 5th ed. (London: Sweet and Maxwell 2007), para. 7-002.

However, having said that, the court does not necessarily confine its judgment only to the legal rules necessary for resolution of the case at hand. For instance, the court might give a summary of the particular area of law, setting out related legal rules even though not all those rules are of specific relevance to the case. Thus, in the above example, a court might perhaps summarise the different ways in which a term can be incorporated (e.g., by signature, by reference, by notice or by course of dealing) even though the dispute only relates to incorporation by notice.

A legal rule which is crucial to the court's decision on the facts of the case or which forms the essential basis of the court's decision is referred to as the *ratio decidendi* (or *ratio*, for short)[88] of the case. The Latin term *ratio decidendi* literally means 'reason for deciding'. A statement of law set out in a judgment which need not have been discussed by the court for the purposes of resolving the case is termed *obiter dictum* ('something said by the way').

It is not always easy to determine what the *ratio* of a case is. It has been said that ascertaining the *ratio* of a decision can be a creative enterprise involving a choice among different possibilities.[89] This uncertainty can be seen from looking at the seminal decision of *Donoghue* v. *Stevenson*[90] dealing with the tort of negligence. It will be recalled that the case looked at the liability of a manufacturer of a bottle of ginger beer to a person who consumed the drink allegedly containing the decomposed remains of a snail. The House of Lords held that the manufacturer was liable in tort for failing to take reasonable care that the drink was free from defects which were likely to cause injury or death. It is possible to express the legal rules dealing with a duty of care flowing from the case at different levels of particularity. For example:

(1) A manufacturer of ginger beer owes a duty to the consumer to take reasonable care to ensure that there are no decomposed snails in the drink.
(2) A manufacturer of any food or drink owes a duty to the consumer to take reasonable care to ensure that there are no defects in the product that are likely to cause death or injury.

---

[88] The plural is *rationes decidendi* (or *rationes*).
[89] I. McLeod, *Legal Method*, 4th ed. (New York, NY: Palgrave Macmillan 2002), p. 133.
[90] [1932] AC 562.

(3) A manufacturer of any product owes a duty to the consumer to take reasonable care to ensure that there are no defects in the product that are likely to cause death or injury.

(4) A person owes a duty of care to another where it is reasonably foreseeable that his or her acts or omissions could cause injury to the other person.

It is generally accepted that statement (3) forms the *ratio* of the case. However, how would a lawyer or a judge come to this conclusion? There is no precise formula,[91] but the following sets out some factors to be borne in mind when attempting to determine the *ratio* of a decision.[92]

First, it is important to look at the actual text in the judgment. How has the judge framed the rules in the judgment? Does the judge appear to be laying down a narrow rule or one of wider application? Sometimes the judge takes care to note that he or she is not intending to lay down a broad rule but is only intending to set out the legal rule as relevant to the particular facts of the case. However, on other occasions, the judgment might indicate that the specific circumstances in the case are but an illustration of the application of a more general rule that the court is laying down. A case might stand for a broader rule if, for example, the court has reviewed earlier cases which have applied the rule in different, but analogous, circumstances from which it is possible to distil a general rule of application that the court accepts to be a correct statement of the law.

For example, Lord Atkin in *Donoghue* v. *Stevenson* came to the conclusion that the manufacturer was liable after referring to previous cases imposing liabilities on manufacturers in respect of a range of different products, and not only food and drinks.[93] Lord Atkin noted in the judgment that 'There are other instances than of articles of food and drink where goods are sold intended to be used immediately by the consumer, such as many forms of goods sold for cleaning purposes, where the same liability must exist.'[94] Further, after noting the various case law on the different types of products where a duty of care was owed to consumers, Lord Atkin stated:

The nature of the thing may very well call for different degrees of care, and the person dealing with it may well contemplate persons as being within the sphere of

---

[91] R. Cross and J. W. Harris, *Precedent in English Law*, 4th ed. (Oxford: Clarendon Press 1991), p. 72.
[92] See also, e.g., ibid., chapter II.
[93] [1932] AC 562, at 584–595.
[94] Ibid., at 583.

his duty to take care who would not be sufficiently proximate with less dangerous goods; so that not only the degree of care but the range of persons to whom a duty is owed may be extended. But they all illustrate the general principle.[95]

Finally, in conclusion, Lord Atkin stated:

A manufacturer of products, which he sells in such a form as to show that he intends them to reach the ultimate consumer in the form in which they left him with no reasonable possibility of intermediate examination, and with the knowledge that the absence of reasonable care in the preparation or putting up of the products will result in an injury to the consumer's life or property, owes a duty to the consumer to take that reasonable care.[96]

Therefore, as a matter of interpretation of the text of Lord Atkin's judgment, it would seem that Lord Atkin was not distinguishing between the different types of products that might be manufactured and sold, and thus his Lordship's judgment should not be interpreted as stating a narrow *ratio* in the form of either statement (1) or (2). This conclusion is fortified not only by the express words in the judgment, but also because it can well be accepted that there is no material difference between situations of different products being manufactured with respect to the question of whether it is appropriate to impose a duty of care.

That still leaves the question of whether statement (3) or (4) sets out the *ratio* of the case. There is an argument that statement (4) forms the *ratio* in Lord Atkin's judgment,[97] as parts of the judgment appear to indicate that his Lordship was seeking to provide a broader rule as to the nature of the relationship between the parties so as to give rise to a duty of care.[98] However, the generally accepted view is that statement (4) does not state the *ratio* of the case.[99]

First of all, even if statement (4) forms the *ratio* of Lord Atkin's judgment, it is not the *ratio* of the case, because it appears that the other members of the House of Lords in the case did not accept this as the broad rule to be applied.[100] This point illustrates a further difficulty in the

---

[95] Ibid., at 596.
[96] [1932] AC 562, at 599.
[97] R. F. V. Heuston, 'Donoghue v. Stevenson in Retrospect' (1957), *Modern Law Review* 20, 1, at 7.
[98] See [1932] AC 562, at 578–581.
[99] See, e.g., Heuston (n. 97), p. 9.
[100] Ibid., p. 8.

determination of the *ratio* of a case where the decision is handed down by a court comprising more than one judge (as in appellate courts).

For example, say that two judges in the Court of Appeal allow an appeal, but the third judge dissents. Now the *ratio* of the case would be as set out by the majority, assuming that the two judges in the majority applied the same reasoning in reaching their decision. However, if the two judges stated separate legal rules, then there is a question as to which of the two judgments should be regarded as setting out the *ratio*. Where one of the judges set out the rule more broadly than the other judge, then it appears that the *ratio* of the case is the narrower rule.[101]

However, if the two judges arrived at their conclusion via different lines of reasoning, then there is some difference in view as to the proper approach to take. One view is to say that there are two *rationes* in the case and both can be binding.[102] On the other hand, it has been said that in these situations, there is no binding *ratio* in the sense that it would not be possible to extract and apply any legal rule from the case outside of factual circumstances which are exactly the same as that arising in the case. Put differently, the decision is confined to its own facts. Although the decision would be binding where the same facts arise, there is no statement of law from the case that can be applied to other factual circumstances.[103]

Returning to *Donoghue* v. *Stevenson*, it may be that even if the other Law Lords forming the majority who held against the manufacturer had agreed with Lord Atkin's wider proposition (comprising statement (4)), that wider statement of law would not be regarded as the *ratio* of the case in light of subsequent decisions. In determining the *ratio* of a decision, it is sometimes necessary to read the decision in the context of subsequent cases.[104] Subsequent decisions[105] have suggested that the *ratio* of *Donoghue* v. *Stevenson* is not the broad rule in statement (4), with the courts always careful not to interpret the *ratio* of a case too widely 'lest essential factors be omitted in the wider survey and the inherent adaptability of [the common] law be unduly restricted'.[106] So although statements of law in a particular judgment might be expressed broadly, a later court might

---

[101] See *Gold* v. *Essex County Council* [1942] 1 KB 293.
[102] McLeod (n. 89), p. 138.
[103] See *Tang Kam-Yip* v. *Yau Kung School* [1986] HKLR 448, 455 (CA); *Re Tyler, ex parte Foley* (1994) 181 CLR 18; Cook et al. (n. 59), at 90.
[104] See Cross and Harris (n. 91), pp. 45–47, 72–74.
[105] E.g., *Farr* v. *Butters Brothers and Co* [1932] 2 KB 606.
[106] *Donoghue* v. *Stevenson* [1932] AC 562, at 584.

confine or narrow the scope of the decision by interpreting the *ratio* more narrowly. This is not to suggest though that the *ratio* can only be narrowed by subsequent decisions. It is also possible that a wider formulation of the *ratio* can be accepted through looking at interpretations of later decisions. Cases subsequent to *Donoghue* v. *Stevenson* have imposed a duty of care on manufacturers of products other than food and drink,[107] confirming the view that statement (3) sets out the *ratio* of the case rather than the narrower rules in statements (1) and (2).

Apart from looking at subsequent cases to provide guidance in ascertaining the *ratio* of a decision, it might also be important to read the decision in the context of earlier cases.[108] A judge might not always be precise in laying down the correct scope of a legal rule, and therefore guidance may be obtained from looking at how the courts have expressed the principle in previous decisions – especially where those decisions are relied upon or approved of in the particular case in question.

The above discussion of different judgments of different judges in an appellate decision illustrates one situation where on its face there might be more than one *ratio* in the decision. A situation where there are two or more *rationes* can also arise in a judgment if the judge arrives at the same conclusion via more than one line of reasoning, that is, on alternative grounds. Prima facie, each of the *rationes* would be binding on later courts,[109] though there is always the possibility of subsequent decisions interpreting the earlier case to hold that only one of the different statements of law formed the 'true *ratio*' of the case.[110]

Judicial Reasoning and the Common Law Method

Declaratory Theory and Its Limitations

Under the separation of powers doctrine,[111] the task of making law is vested in the legislature while the courts' role is simply to adjudicate cases.

---

[107] E.g., *Grant* v. *Australian Knitting Mills* [1936] AC 85 (manufacturer of woollen underwear).
[108] Cross and Harris (n. 91), 45.
[109] *Behrens* v. *Bertram Mills Circus Ltd* [1957] 1 All ER 583.
[110] See J. Holland and J. Webb, *Learning Legal Rules*, 6th ed. (Oxford: Oxford University Press 2006), para. 6.8.2.
[111] See Chapter 3.

In common law countries, the courts are also involved in declaring or stating the legal rules and principles, and as discussed in this chapter, judgments of the courts are one of the sources of law. This raises the question of whether judges are actually involved in making law.

The traditional answer to this question was provided by the declaratory theory of law. Under this theory, judges do not make law but simply declare what the law is. The function of the judge is solely to ascertain the relevant rule or principle of the common law and apply it to the facts of the case. Where the existing law is clear and the facts of the particular case fall squarely within the existing precedents, the declaratory theory is accurate in describing the role of the judge. However, the theory fails to account for the role of the courts in developing the law and filling in the gaps of the existing law.

In the first half of the twentieth century, the American realists[112] revealed the difficulties of the declaratory theory by emphasising the existence of uncertainties in the law which are only resolved through a dynamic process whereby judges are in a sense involved in judicial law-making. The different mechanisms by which courts can decide not to apply particular precedents and the uncertainties in ascertaining the *ratio* of a case reveal that judges to some extent have a choice in deciding what the law is.

In addition, uncertainties in the law can arise where there are conflicting precedents in the law that could apply to the facts at hand, or where there are gaps in the law in that there are no existing legal rules which squarely cover the novel factual situation that has arisen before the court. For example, before the decision in *Donoghue* v. *Stevenson*, there were no cases precisely on point which held that a manufacturer of any article would owe a duty of care to any user of the product. There were decisions which held that persons in particular contexts or relationships would owe a duty of care to others, for example manufacturers of goods which were inherently dangerous (such as a handgun); however, the situation of the manufacturer of the ginger beer did not fall precisely within any existing categories where a duty of care arose.

In situations where the court may be faced with several conflicting precedents or where there are gaps in the law, it cannot be said that the judge simply declares what the existing law is. The judge needs to make a

---

[112] For an overview, see, e.g., B. Bix, *Jurisprudence: Theory and Context*, 7th ed. (London: Sweet and Maxwell 2015), chapter 17.

choice and perhaps set out a new principle. For this reason, the declaratory theory has been said to be a myth or a fairy tale[113] and is no longer accepted to be correct in legal circles.

Judicial Development of the Law

In dealing with conflicts or gaps in the law, the courts develop the law. The choice for the House of Lords in *Donoghue* v. *Stevenson* was either to confine the scope of negligence by deciding that a duty of care would arise only if the facts fell within the existing categories recognised in the precedents, or to expand the scope of the tort by extending the duty of care to other situations not precisely within the existing precedents. The minority Law Lords in the decision favoured the former approach while the majority held in favour of the latter.

Another aspect of the common law method which is illustrated by *Donoghue* v. *Stevenson* is the process by which a court distils general principles from the existing case law. Lord Atkin examined the existing precedents dealing with specific classes of relationships where a duty of care would arise, and took the view that there was a general principle based on the concept of reasonable foreseeability underlying all these situations.[114] Although this statement of general principle is not regarded as the *ratio* of *Donoghue* v. *Stevenson*, it has been instrumental in guiding the development of the law in this area.[115] Later cases have relied on this general principle to extend the duty of care to other situations not falling clearly within the existing precedents.

Moreover, the courts have, since 1932, sought to define the general principle with more precision in determining whether a duty of care would arise in a novel situation. Lord Atkin's neighbour principle was adopted for instance by Lord Wilberforce in *Anns* v. *Merton LBC*,[116] where his Lordship held that a duty of care arises where the element of reasonable foreseeability of loss is established and there are no countervailing considerations of policy which should deny the existence of the duty. Under this

---

[113] Lord Reid, 'The Judge as Lawmaker' (1972), *Journal of Society of Public Teachers of Law* 12, 23.
[114] [1932] AC 562, at 580.
[115] This also illustrates how *obiter dictum*, while strictly speaking not binding, can often still be influential in guiding the development of the law.
[116] [1978] AC 728, at 751–752.

approach, the categories of negligence as accepted by the courts expanded significantly.[117] More recently, though, the accepted approach is to apply the threefold test, which involves an examination of whether there was reasonable foreseeability of harm, proximity between the plaintiff and the defendant, and questions of policy as to whether it is fair, just and reasonable to impose a duty on the defendant in the circumstances.[118] This test appears to narrow the circumstances as to when a duty of care would arise in novel situations,[119] and if that is correct, then it can be said that under this test the courts have changed again the direction of the law of negligence.

Judicial Reasoning

Although there is an element of judicial law-making in the common law method, this does not mean that judges can decide arbitrarily on what the law is or decide cases purely on the basis of subjective notions of justice. Judges must give reasons for their decisions. For example, if there are two precedents which might be relevant to the particular facts at hand, then the judge needs to examine the factors or reasons why one precedent should be decisive but not the other. This reasoning might not be like links in a chain (deductive reasoning), but are like the legs of a chair. When all the reasons are put together, there is a sound basis for the conclusion.[120] Therefore the judge's decision cannot be arbitrary.

What types of factors *can* a court take into account in supporting the development of the law one way or another? Various scholars have suggested different theories of judicial reasoning.[121] For example, MacCormick argues that there must be coherency in the development of the law in that not only must legal rules and principles be developed in a way that is not contradictory, they must also be consistent with each other in a broader sense 'embodying the rational pursuit of a consistent set of values'.[122]

---

[117] J. Murphy, *Street on Torts*, 12th ed. (Oxford: Oxford University Press 2007), p. 27.
[118] *Caparo Industries plc* v. *Dickman* [1990] 1 All ER 568; *Customs and Excise Commissioners* v. *Barclay Bank plc* [2007] 1 AC 181.
[119] Murphy (n. 117), p. 33.
[120] M. D. A. Freeman, *Lloyd's Introduction to Jurisprudence*, 7th ed. (London: Sweet and Maxwell 2001), p. 1407.
[121] See generally, e.g., ibid., chapter 17.
[122] Ibid., pp. 1475–1478.

Dworkin likens the development of the common law to a chain novel.[123] In a chain novel, a different author develops the story by writing a new chapter in the one novel based on the existing characters and storyline. Similarly, judges develop the common law by writing new judgments which build upon the existing law. Yet, just as in the chain novel a new author is constrained to develop the story in a way consistent with the previous chapters, so a judge can only develop the law in a way which is consistent and coherent with the pre-existing case law.

It must be said, however, that this notion of coherency in the common law is an idealised notion. It may well be impossible to reconcile all the existing cases in many areas of the law. In other words, there are bound to be areas where cases are inconsistent or contradictory. Nonetheless, these theories may well describe what the courts strive to achieve.

Bilingual Judgments

Although both English and Chinese are official languages in Hong Kong, and there is now the possibility of using either language in judicial proceedings,[124] proceedings in the higher courts continue for the most part to be conducted in English, with judgments handed down and published in the law reports predominantly in the English language. Cases conducted in Chinese would have their judgments reported in Chinese in the first instance. Some judgments written in Chinese are translated into English by the judiciary, and where this is done, then the judiciary translation should be cited by parties in court.[125] If there is no judiciary translation, then parties who wish to cite the judgment in court would need to prepare an English translation in accordance with the court's requirements as set out in Practice Direction 10.3.

---

[123] R. M. Dworkin, *Law's Empire* (Oxford: Hart Publishing 1998), pp. 228–232.
[124] Basic Law, art. 9; Official Languages Ordinance (Cap. 5), s. 5. See also *Cheung Kong (Holdings) Ltd* v. *Chan Wai Yip Albert* [2000] 4 HKC 591; *Re Cheng Kai Nam Gary* [2002] 1 HKC 41; A. S. Y. Cheung, 'Hong Kong and the Unprecedented Transfer of Sovereignty: Towards a Bilingual Legal System – The Development of Chinese Legal Language' (1997), *Loyola of Los Angeles International and Comparative Law Review* 19, 315.
[125] Practice Direction 10.3 (19 Jan 2007), para. 3.

Chinese Customary Law

Under article 8 of the Basic Law, the laws previously in force in Hong Kong include Chinese customary law. The effect of this provision, together with article 18 of the Basic Law, is that the Chinese customary law that had been part of the law in Hong Kong prior to the 1997 handover continues to be part of the law today. The legislation before the handover which applied English common law to Hong Kong had been subject to the qualification that the English law would only be applicable 'so far as they are applicable to the circumstances of Hong Kong or its inhabitants'.[126] The courts interpreted this qualification restrictively, though,[127] and the scope of application of Chinese laws and customs was confined to matters such as marriage and property. Even within some of those areas where the courts accepted a continued application of Chinese laws and customs, there was significant erosion of such application through legislative amendments.[128] The main area of Chinese customary law which is relevant today deals with land law in the New Territories.[129] In addition, customary law still applies to some extent in relation to marriages and succession, for example the validity of pre-1971 customary marriages was preserved in the 1971 legislative amendments in this area.[130] Any one case might raise a number of issues – some to be dealt with under Chinese customary law, some under other principles of Hong Kong law. However, Chinese customary law cannot be fused together with other principles of Hong Kong law to create some new principle or customary rule that is a hybrid between Hong Kong law and Chinese customary law.[131]

---

[126] Former Application of English Law Ordinance, s. 3; and see also former Supreme Court Ordinance 1873, s. 5.
[127] The English laws would be inapplicable only if the particular legal rule or principle would lead to injustice or oppression by reason of the peculiar local circumstances: *Wong Yu-Shi v. Wong Ying-Kuen* [1957] HKLR 420, at 442–443.
[128] See D. J. Lewis, 'A Requiem for Chinese Customary Law in Hong Kong' (1983), *International and Comparative Law Quarterly* 32, 347.
[129] New Territories Ordinance (Cap. 97), s. 13. See, e.g., *Secretary for Justice v. To Kan Chi* [2000] 3 HKLRD 756 (CFA, ownership of a temple).
[130] See D. J. Lewis (n. 128); *Liu Ying Lan v. Liu Tung Yiu* [2003] 3 HKLRD 249 (CA).
[131] *Re Lau Wai Chau* (2000) 3 HKCFAR 98, [2000] 1 HKLRD 924, at 931.

National Laws of the PRC

Article 18 of the Basic Law is the primary provision dealing with the applicability of national laws of the PRC in Hong Kong. The article provides that national laws shall not be applied in Hong Kong subject to the qualifications set out in the article.

The first qualification is that national laws listed in Annex III of the Basic Law are applicable. Those laws, however, need to be incorporated into the law of Hong Kong by way of promulgation or legislation by the Hong Kong government.

Second, in the event of the NPCSC declaring a state of war or deciding that Hong Kong is in a state of emergency by reason of turmoil within Hong Kong which endangers national unity or security and is beyond the control of the HKSAR government, the Central People's Government may issue an order applying relevant national laws in Hong Kong. Where this proviso in article 18 is invoked, it appears that prima facie any national laws could be applied in Hong Kong; however, there is an argument that national laws applied in Hong Kong must still be consistent with the Basic Law, including article 39 protecting the rights and freedoms of Hong Kong residents.[132]

Apart from Basic Law article 18, there may be other situations where national laws are applicable in Hong Kong. For example, members of the PRC military stationed in Hong Kong are required to abide by both national laws as well as Hong Kong laws under article 14.[133] There has also been debate as to whether national criminal laws apply to Mainland residents who have committed an offence within Hong Kong.[134] More generally, it would seem that there are at least some provisions of the PRC Constitution which apply in Hong Kong.[135]

The PRC Constitution itself is not part of the laws of Hong Kong which the Hong Kong courts can directly apply in the adjudication of cases. However, the PRC Constitution can still be relevant in adjudicating

---

[132] See Ghai (n. 5), pp. 397–398.
[133] Ibid., pp. 394–397.
[134] See B. Ling, 'Applicability of the PRC Criminal Law in Hong Kong and the Prospect of a Rendition Agreement between Hong Kong and the Mainland' (1999), *Hong Kong Law Journal* 29, 393.
[135] See H. L. Cheung, 'Hong Kong SAR: Autonomy within Integration?' (1999), *UCLA Journal of International Law and Foreign Affairs* 4, 181, at 190–193.

cases in certain situations. For example, various concepts in the Basic Law (e.g., the NPC, NPCSC, State Council, national flag, national emblem) can only be understood by reference to the PRC Constitution.[136]

As for the application of PRC laws in the Mainland Port Area at the West Kowloon Station under the 'co-location arrangement, see the discussion earlier in this Chapter.

Review Questions

(1) To what extent has the Basic Law preserved the continuity of laws in Hong Kong following the 1997 transfer of sovereignty?
(2) To what extent do the courts in Hong Kong have power to interpret the Basic Law? When can the NPCSC exercise power to interpret the Basic Law?
(3) What is the difference between statutory law and case law?
(4) What are the different meanings of the term 'common law'?
(5) Where the application of common law principles in a case might be thought to lead to an unjust outcome, is it always possible for the courts to override the common law principles to arrive at a just outcome by invoking the courts' equitable jurisdiction?
(6) What is meant by the terms *ratio decidendi* and *obiter dictum*?
(7) Read the case *Carlill* v. *Carbolic Smoke Ball Co* [1893] 1 QB 256. Answer the following in relation to the case:
  (a) What are the material facts of the case?
  (b) What are the issues raised in the case?
  (c) What are the legal rules or principles forming the *ratio* (or *rationes*) of the case?
(8) In common law jurisdictions, do judges make law or simply declare the existing law?

---

[136] *Leung Chung Hang Sixtus* v. *President of Legislative Council* [2018] HKCFI 2657, (2019) 1 HKLRD 292, at para. 42.

The Court System and the Doctrine of Precedent 5

Chapter Highlights

- Judicial Power of the Court   138
- Meanings of the Term 'Jurisdiction'   139
- Superior and Inferior Courts   140
- The Court System: Pre-1 July 1997   141
- The Court System: Post-1 July 1997   145
- Tribunals   151
- Doctrine of Judicial Precedent   159
- Vertical and Horizontal *Stare Decisis* in the Hong Kong Courts   165
- Avoiding Precedents   176
- Status of English and Overseas Decisions under the Basic Law   177
- Persuasive Authorities   179

Courts are venues where parties with a legal dispute can have their dispute settled and their rights and liabilities determined, and where persons accused of committing a crime have their innocence or guilt established. This chapter outlines the system and structure of courts in Hong Kong and discusses the concept of judicial precedent.

The courts in Hong Kong are established in accordance with the provisions of the Basic Law that deal with the judiciary, namely s. 4 of Chapter IV. Article 80 provides that the courts in the HKSAR exercise the judicial power of the region. Article 81 sets out the courts that comprise the judiciary: the Court of Final Appeal, the High Court (comprising the Court of Appeal and the Court of First Instance), the District Court, Magistrates' Courts and other special courts.

Judicial Power of the Court

Judicial power, as vested in the courts under articles 80 and 81 of the Basic Law, is distinguished from legislative power and executive power. Under the separation of powers doctrine, issues may arise in relation to, for example, whether a certain body is improperly exercising judicial power.[1] In this type of context, it has been said that judicial power refers to 'the power which every sovereign must of necessity have to decide controversies between its subjects, or between itself and its subjects, whether the rights relate to life, liberty or property. The exercise of this power does not begin until some tribunal which has power to give a binding and authoritative decision (whether subject to appeal or not) is called upon to take action'.[2]

The basic function of the courts in the exercise of judicial power is to adjudicate cases.[3] The court's adjudicative role includes determination of the legal rights of parties arising from disputes between private persons or between individuals and the government in civil cases. In setting out the rights of the parties, the court may make various types of orders, such as orders for one party to pay compensation to another, or orders restraining a party from doing some act. Apart from such civil cases, the courts also have a role in determining whether persons have violated the criminal law, and if so, what sentence is to be handed down.[4]

In the determination of such matters under either the civil or criminal law, the court applies the applicable law to events that have occurred in the past, and in doing so, the court may need to make a declaration of what the existing law is. In addition, the courts in Hong Kong have jurisdiction to determine whether legislation enacted by the legislature or acts of the executive authorities of the HKSAR are contrary to the Basic Law and therefore invalid as being unconstitutional.[5]

---

[1] See further Chapter 3.
[2] *Huddart Parker and Co Pty Ltd* v. *Moorehead* (1909) 8 CLR 330 at 357. As cautioned, however, by Hartmann J in *Yau Kwong Man* v. *Secretary for Security* [2002] 3 HKC 457, at 471, it might not be possible to frame an exhaustive definition of judicial power. See also *Luk Ka Cheung* v. *The Market Misconduct Tribunal* [2009] 1 HKC 1 (CA).
[3] *HKSAR* v. *Lam Kwong Wai* [2006] 3 HKLRD 808, at para. 67 (CFA).
[4] See Chapters 8 and 9 for a more through discussion of Hong Kong's criminal justice system and civil justice system respectively.
[5] See Chapter 3.

The powers of the courts are limited only by the concept of 'judicial power' and by any relevant legislative provisions confining the scope of the jurisdiction or powers of the particular court.[6] The grant of judicial power and the investing of jurisdiction in a court carries with them all those powers that are necessary or reasonably required to make effective the exercise of the judicial power and jurisdiction so granted.[7]

Meanings of the Term 'Jurisdiction'

There are different meanings of the term 'jurisdiction' when referring to a court's jurisdiction.

Jurisdiction can refer to the area of law or type of dispute in relation to which the court has power to hear a matter and to make a decision. The ordinance which creates a court would set out the jurisdiction of the court. For example, jurisdiction could be limited to criminal cases or civil cases, or jurisdiction could be limited by the amount of money being claimed by a plaintiff.

Jurisdiction is also classified as being original or appellate. Original jurisdiction refers to the jurisdiction of a court to hear a new matter which comes before the courts for the first time or 'at first instance', while appellate jurisdiction refers to the jurisdiction of a court to hear appeals from the decision of another court.

The jurisdiction of a court can also refer to the powers of a court, for example where the issue is whether the court has jurisdiction or the power to grant a particular remedy or to make particular orders.

In addition, the term 'jurisdiction' can be used in the context of referring to the geographical area in which a court can exercise power. For example, a court in Hong Kong might not have territorial jurisdiction to resolve disputes which have occurred in Italy and which have no connection at all with Hong Kong. Principles of constitutional law and international law would determine the scope of the territorial jurisdiction of a court in a particular state.

---

[6] *Re Spectrum Plus Ltd (in liq)* [2005] 2 AC 680, at para. 69.
[7] *HKSAR* v. *Lam Kwong Wai* [2006] 3 HKLRD 808, at para. 70 (Court of Final Appeal held that the judicial power as vested in the Hong Kong courts includes the making of a remedial interpretation of a statutory provision in order to preserve its constitutional validity); and see also *Re Spectrum Plus Ltd (in liq)* [2005] 2 AC 680, at paras. 70–74.

Superior and Inferior Courts

Courts are categorised as superior or inferior. The historical basis of the distinction is that the superior courts are said to have unlimited jurisdiction, while the inferior courts have limited jurisdiction and are subject to the supervision of the superior courts. In Hong Kong, the superior courts are the Court of Final Appeal,[8] the Court of Appeal, the Court of First Instance[9] and the Competition Tribunal.[10] The inferior courts are the District Court, the Magistrates' Courts, the Small Claims Tribunal, the Lands Tribunal and the Labour Tribunal.

Strictly speaking, the jurisdiction of the superior courts can be limited, as it is under the ordinances[11] establishing those courts in Hong Kong. However, being created as superior courts, the Court of Final Appeal, the Court of Appeal and the Court of First Instance have the inherent powers exercised by superior courts in the English common law tradition, such as the inherent power to punish for contempt of court committed outside of court[12] and the power to order security for costs of actions,[13] whether or not these powers are expressly provided for by way of statute.[14]

In addition, superior courts exercise a supervisory jurisdiction over inferior courts in that prerogative relief is available in the superior courts in relation to acts of, or proceedings in, an inferior court, such as via a writ of *certiorari* quashing a decision of an inferior court.[15] Such powers are exercised in the original jurisdiction of the superior court and not via an appellate procedure.[16] In other words, decisions of superior courts can only

---

[8] Hong Kong Court of Final Appeal Ordinance (Cap. 484), s. 3.
[9] See High Court Ordinance (Cap. 4), ss. 3, 12, 13.
[10] Competition Ordinance (Cap. 619), s. 134.
[11] See Hong Kong Court of Final Appeal Ordinance (Cap. 484), s. 4; High Court Ordinance (Cap. 4), s. 3; Competition Ordinance (Cap. 619), s. 142.
[12] *Tse Wai Chun Paul* v. *Solicitors Disciplinary Tribunal* [2002] 4 HKC 1.
[13] *Merribee Pastoral Industries Pty Ltd* v. *Australia and New Zealand Banking Group Ltd* (1998) 28 ASCR 103.
[14] In the case of the Competition Tribunal, since the tribunal is established as a superior court, it would seem that the tribunal can also exercise inherent powers. Section 142(2) of the Competition Ordinance confirms that in the exercise of jurisdiction over matters as set out in the ordinance, the tribunal has the same jurisdiction to grant remedies and relief, equitable or legal, as the Court of First Instance.
[15] See High Court Ordinance (Cap 4), s. 21I; *R* v. *The District Judge of Hong Kong; ex parte the Attorney General* (1955) 39 HKLR 8.
[16] See *Craig* v. *State of South Australia* (1995) 184 CLR 163.

be reviewed through the appellate system, while inferior courts are liable in all instances to supervisory jurisdiction through an application to a superior court for judicial review.

The courts of record in Hong Kong include the Court of Final Appeal,[17] the Court of Appeal,[18] the Court of First Instance[19] and the District Court.[20] The acts and judicial proceedings of a court of record are enrolled in its archives and are conclusive evidence of the matters so recorded.[21] In addition, courts of record have the power to fine or imprison for contempt committed in the face of the court (though not for contempt committed outside of court unless the court is also a superior court).[22]

The Court System: Pre-1 July 1997

Article 81 of the Basic Law provides that the judicial system previously practised in Hong Kong is to be maintained following 1 July 1997, with the exception of changes consequent upon the establishment of the Court of Final Appeal. To a significant extent, then, art. 81 maintains continuity between the court system under British rule and the current system. Accordingly, it is useful to outline the prior system which existed so that the current system can be seen and understood in context. In addition, an appreciation of the previous system is necessary for a proper understanding of how the doctrine of precedent is applied even today, since the decisions of the courts prior to 1 July 1997 still form part of the law in Hong Kong.

The hierarchy of courts in Figure 5.1 shows the court structure which existed and indicates the avenues of appeal from the lower courts and

---

[17] Hong Kong Court of Final Appeal Ordinance (Cap. 484), s. 3.
[18] High Court Ordinance (Cap. 4), s. 13.
[19] High Court Ordinance (Cap. 4), s. 12.
[20] District Court Ordinance (Cap. 336), s. 3. Various tribunals in Hong Kong are also declared by statute to be courts of record: see Lands Tribunal Ordinance (Cap. 17), s. 3; Small Claims Tribunal Ordinance (Cap. 338), s. 3; Labour Tribunal Ordinance (Cap. 25), s. 3; Competition Ordinance (Cap. 619), s. 134.
[21] *R* v. *Tyrone Justices* [1917] 2 IR 437; *R* v. *West Yorkshire Coroner; ex parte Smith (No. 2)* [1985] 1 QB 1096.
[22] *Tse Wai Chun Paul* v. *Solicitors Disciplinary Tribunal* [2002] 4 HKC 1; *Balogh* v. *Crown Court at St Albans* [1974] 3 All ER 283.

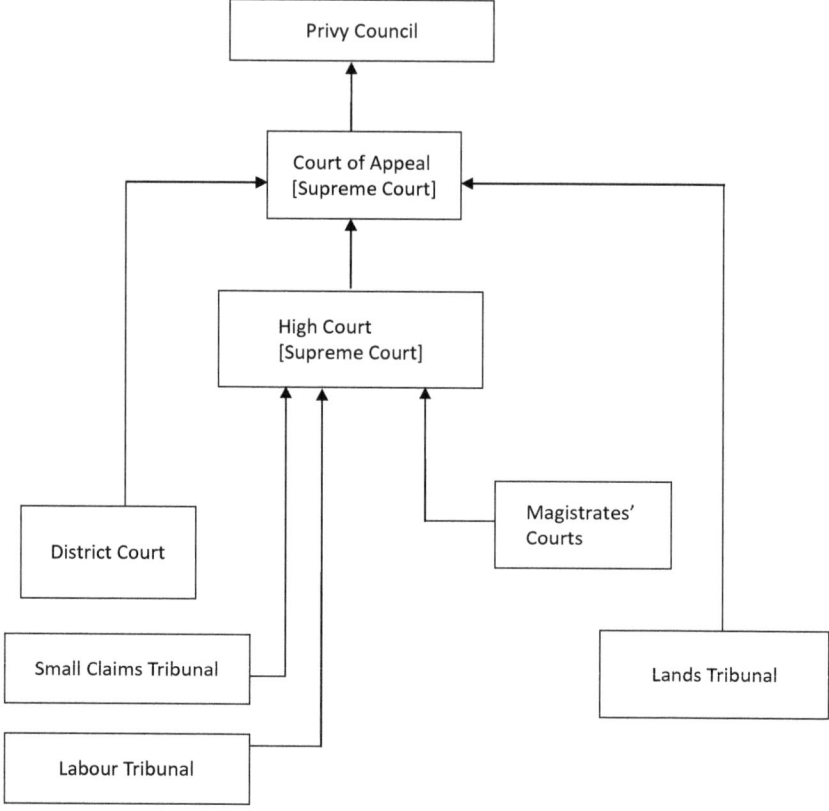

Figure 5.1 Court system pre-1 July 1997

tribunals to the higher courts. The different courts and tribunals in the system are briefly discussed here.

Supreme Court

The Supreme Court was established in 1844 pursuant to the Supreme Court Ordinance.[23] Under the ordinance, the Supreme Court was conferred with the same jurisdiction as the common law courts[24] in England, the Court of Chancery and the ecclesiastical courts. Thus, the court was vested with full common law and equitable jurisdiction in Hong Kong, including

---

[23] Ordinance 15 of 1844; and see Supreme Court Ordinance (No. 6 of 1845); Supreme Court Ordinance (No. 2 of 1846).

[24] Court of Common Pleas, Queen's Bench and the Exchequer.

jurisdiction in granting probate and letters of administration. The court was reconstituted in 1873 as the Supreme Court of Judicature of the colony under the new Supreme Court Ordinance enacted that year.[25] The jurisdiction of the court was exercised by a single judge sitting alone, or by two or three judges sitting as the Full Court. The Full Court also exercised appellate jurisdiction. In 1975, the Supreme Court was reorganised so that there would be a permanent appeal court similar to the system that developed in England. Under the Supreme Court Ordinance of 1975,[26] the Supreme Court was reconstituted to comprise the High Court of Justice and the Court of Appeal, both being superior courts of record. The High Court assumed generally the original jurisdiction of the Supreme Court, while the Court of Appeal essentially took over the previous Full Court's appellate jurisdiction.

District Court

The District Court was established in 1953 pursuant to the District Court Ordinance.[27] The court was established to relieve some of the load of the Supreme Court. It was created as an inferior court, having limited civil and criminal jurisdiction.

Magistrates' Courts

The first Chief Magistrate of Hong Kong was originally appointed in 1841 with criminal jurisdiction over the local population under Chinese laws, and over the British and foreigners 'according to the customs and usages of British Police Law'.[28] Formal appointment was made on 26 June 1843 pursuant to the Royal Charter of 1843, and in the ensuing years various ordinances varied the jurisdiction of the magistrates. The current Magistrates Ordinance was enacted in 1932 as Ordinance 41 of 1932, which replaced the Magistrates Ordinance of 1890 (Ordinance 3 of 1890).

---

[25] Ordinance 3 of 1873. See also Supreme Court (Summary Jurisdiction) Ordinance (No. 4 of 1873).
[26] Ordinance 92 of 1975.
[27] Ordinance 1 of 1953.
[28] J. W. Norton-Kyshe, *History of the Laws and Courts of Hong Kong: From the Earliest Period to 1898* (Hong Kong: Vetch and Lee Ltd 1971, reissue), p. 6.

By the early 1990s there were ten magistracies and about sixty-five magistrates appointed in Hong Kong.[29]

Tribunals

Some of the major tribunals were established in the 1970s, for example the Labour Tribunal in 1972, the Lands Tribunal in 1974 and the Small Claims Tribunal in 1976.[30] The various tribunals have jurisdiction to deal with specific matters as set out in the ordinance creating the tribunal. These tribunals are established as courts of record[31]; however, there are other tribunals in Hong Kong which are established to operate as administrative tribunals rather than courts exercising judicial power, for example the Minor Employment Claims Adjudication Board.[32] The diagram in Figure 5.1 does not include all the tribunals that exist in Hong Kong.

System of Appeals and the Privy Council

The ordinances establishing the courts and tribunals set out the appropriate avenues of appeal. The structure of the appeals system is broadly represented by the diagram in Figure 5.1. Rights of appeal are in some cases limited, though, and depending on the court and the nature of the proceedings, an appeal might not be possible or might be available only if leave is granted by the court.

Broadly, decisions in a Magistrates' Court could be appealed to the High Court[33]; and decisions of the District Court and of the High Court could be appealed to the Court of Appeal.[34] The Court of Appeal was the highest court in Hong Kong, but appeals from that court were possible to the Privy Council in England.

The Privy Council was originally established as a body of advisers to the King, as a part of the King's Council. By 1540, the Privy Council developed

---

[29] V. A. Penlington, *Law in Hong Kong: An Introduction*, 3rd ed. (Hong Kong: Federal Publications 1993), p. 55.
[30] Tribunals are discussed in more detail later in this chapter.
[31] Labour Tribunal Ordinance (Cap. 25), s. 3(1); Lands Tribunal Ordinance (Cap. 17), s. 3; Small Claims Tribunal Ordinance (Cap. 338), s. 3(2).
[32] Minor Employment Claims Adjudication Board Ordinance (Cap. 453).
[33] Magistrates Ordinance (Cap. 227), ss. 105, 113.
[34] Supreme Court Ordinance (No. 92 of 1975), ss. 13, 14.

as a separate body, and by the seventeenth century its function was predominantly to hear applications for redress in Britain's overseas colonies pursuant to the prerogative rights of the British Crown.[35] The Judicial Committee of the Privy Council was formally established in 1833 by the Judicial Committee Act of that year, giving the appeals body statutory footing and providing the body with a defined membership. The decisions of the Privy Council take the form of advice to the Crown. In practice the advice of the Privy Council is always accepted, and effect is given to the advice by the Queen through an Order in Council. The Privy Council stood at the apex of the court hierarchy in Hong Kong and was the final arbiter of legal disputes in the colony.

The Court System: Post-1 July 1997

A comparison of Figures 5.1 and 5.2 shows that, in accordance with article 81 of the Basic Law, the judicial system was largely kept intact following the transfer of sovereignty over Hong Kong to the PRC in 1997. The most important change was the creation of the Court of Final Appeal.

Court of Final Appeal

The Court of Final Appeal (CFA) was established pursuant to Basic Law article 81 and the Hong Kong Court of Final Appeal Ordinance.[36] The CFA is a superior court of record, and replaced the Privy Council as the highest court in Hong Kong, being vested with the final power of adjudication in the HKSAR under article 81. The CFA has civil jurisdiction to hear appeals from decisions of the Court of Appeal, and in certain defined circumstances, from the Court of First Instance.[37]

In civil cases, generally leave is to be obtained from either the Court of Appeal or the CFA before an appeal is possible.[38] Such leave may be granted where the question involved in the proceedings is one which, by

---

[35] See J. H. Baker, *An Introduction to English Legal History*, 3rd ed. (London: Butterworths 1990), pp. 136, 161–162.
[36] Hong Kong Court of Final Appeal Ordinance (Cap. 484), s. 3.
[37] Ibid., s. 22(1)(c).
[38] note 36., s. 23(1). In the specific cases involving appeals from the Court of First Instance as set out in s. 22(1)(c) or 27B, leave is to be sought from the CFA and not the Court of Appeal.

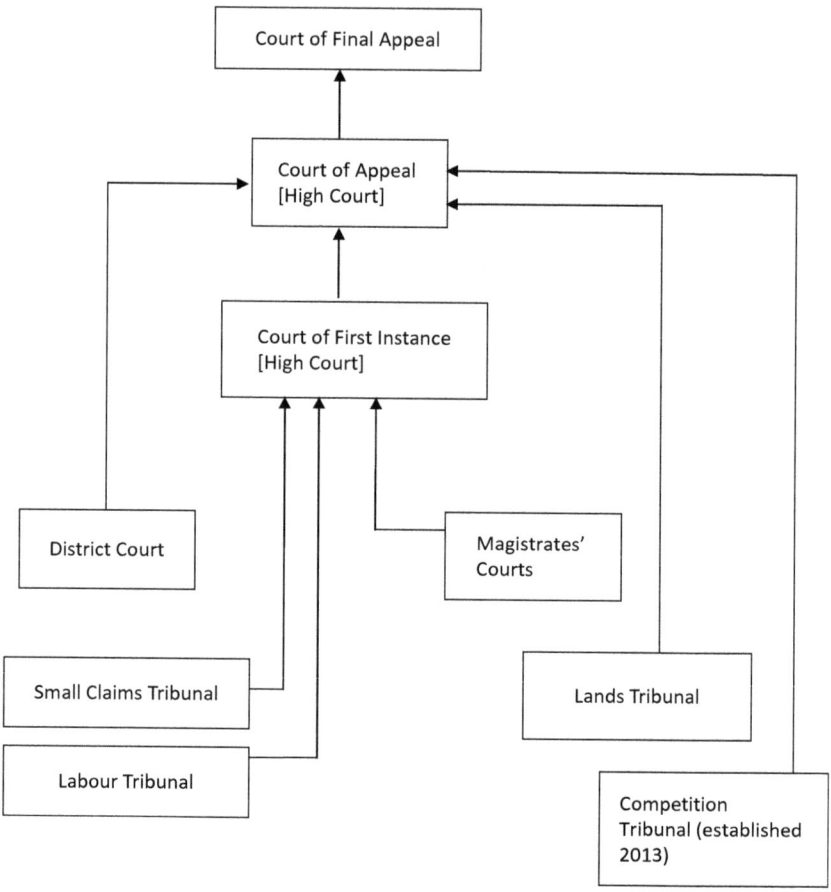

Figure 5.2 Court system post-1 July 1997

reason of its great general or public importance or otherwise, ought to be submitted to the CFA for decision.[39] As for the CFA's criminal jurisdiction, appeals from the Court of Appeal (and in certain limited situations from the Court of First Instance) lie to the CFA, at the CFA's discretion,[40] but again leave to appeal must first be granted. Such leave may be granted

---

[39] Ibid., s. 22(1)(b). See also ss. 22(1)(c) and 27B for certain appeals directly to the CFA from the Court of First Instance. Previously, where the matter involved a liquidated claim of HK$1 million or more, or a claim in respect of property with a value of HK$1 million or more, appeal to the CFA was provided for as of right under former s. 22(1)(a). However, this provision was repealed in 2014 by the Administration of Justice (Miscellaneous Provisions) Ordinance (20 of 2014).

[40] Ibid., s. 31.

if either the Court of Appeal (or Court of First Instance, if appeal is from that court) or the CFA certifies that a point of law of great and general importance is involved in the decision or it is shown that substantial and grave injustice has been done.[41]

The CFA, in hearing an appeal, is to consist of the Chief Justice, three permanent judges of the court and either one non-permanent judge or one judge from another common law jurisdiction selected by the Chief Justice.[42] The ordinance provides for the appointment of permanent judges to the court and the keeping of a list of non-permanent judges and a list of judges from other common law jurisdictions.[43] The possibility of inviting judges from other common law jurisdictions to sit on the CFA is enshrined in article 82 of the Basic Law, and it appears that this had been proposed to ensure that there would be available judges of the highest calibre to replace the Privy Council and to enhance the prospects of the court maintaining its independence.[44] A number of pre-eminent Law Lords of the UK Supreme Court (and previously, the House of Lords) and former Chief Justices of the High Court of Australia (the highest court in Australia) have, for example, been appointed as non-permanent judges to the CFA.

High Court

Following the handover in 1997, the Supreme Court was renamed the High Court of the Hong Kong Special Administrative Region. The previous High Court of Justice became the Court of First Instance, and the Court of Appeal is now the appeal court of the High Court rather than the Supreme Court.[45] Apart from a change in names, the functioning and jurisdiction of these courts remain the same.

---

[41] Ibid., s. 32.
[42] Ibid., s. 16.
[43] Ibid., ss. 7, 8, 9.
[44] See Y. Ghai, *Hong Kong's New Constitutional Order: The Resumption of Chinese Sovereignty and the Basic Law*, 2nd ed. (Hong Kong: Hong Kong University Press 1999), pp. 323–324. For more details on Hong Kong's Court of Final Appeal, see S. Young and Y. Ghai (eds.), *Hong Kong's Court of Final Appeal: The Development of the Law in China's Hong Kong* (New York, NY: Cambridge University Press 2014).
[45] High Court Ordinance (Cap. 4), s. 3. The Supreme Court Ordinance of 1975 was renamed the High Court Ordinance; see Ordinance No. 25 of 1998.

The Court of First Instance is a superior court of record having jurisdiction as set out in the High Court Ordinance,[46] including original jurisdiction in civil claims under the common law and equity, and original jurisdiction in criminal matters comparable with that of the High Court of Justice and the Crown Court in England. Larger civil claims, including those in contract or tort, which are above the jurisdictional limits of the District Court, are thus brought in the Court of First Instance. Other civil proceedings commenced in the Court of First Instance include judicial review proceedings,[47] proceedings for the winding-up of companies[48] and probate and administration of deceased estates.[49] In relation to criminal matters, the Court of First Instance deals with the more serious offences, which are not tried by a magistrate or by the District Court,[50] namely offences which can only be proceeded by way of indictment and which are set out in Part III of the Second Schedule to the Magistrates Ordinance, or offences to be tried on indictment where the sentence that is sought by the prosecution would be more than seven years' imprisonment. Examples of criminal matters tried by the Court of First Instance include murder, manslaughter, rape, armed robbery, trafficking in large quantities of dangerous drugs and complex commercial frauds. The court also has appellate jurisdiction covering appeals from the decisions of magistrates[51] as well as certain tribunals.[52] Civil proceedings in the Court of First Instance are generally heard by a judge sitting alone, while criminal proceedings are tried before a judge and jury.[53]

The Court of Appeal is also a superior court of record, and it exercises the appellate jurisdiction of the High Court. The court has jurisdiction to hear appeals from decisions of the Court of First Instance and of the District Court in both civil and criminal matters,[54] and also appeals from certain tribunals.[55] In the hearing of an appeal, there are generally three judges sitting in the Court of Appeal, but there can be more, as long as

---

[46] High Court Ordinance (Cap. 4), s. 12.
[47] See ibid., ss. 12, 21K.
[48] See Companies (Winding Up and Miscellaneous Provisions) Ordinance (Cap. 32).
[49] See Probate and Administration Ordinance (Cap. 10).
[50] See the discussion on the District Court below.
[51] Magistrates Ordinance (Cap. 227), ss. 105, 113.
[52] See, e.g., Small Claims Tribunal Ordinance (Cap. 338), ss. 28, 29.
[53] See High Court Ordinance (Cap. 4), ss. 32, 33A; Criminal Procedure Ordinance (Cap. 221), ss. 41, 42.
[54] Ibid., s. 13.
[55] See, e.g., Lands Tribunal Ordinance (Cap. 17), s. 11(2).

there is an uneven number of judges.[56] In certain situations, two judges can hear a matter (e.g., appeals against interlocutory orders).[57] If the members of the court are equally divided on the matter, then the judgment appealed from would not be disturbed,[58] though in civil cases, the appeal can be re-argued before an uneven number of judges of at least three.[59]

District Court

The District Court that existed before 1 July 1997 continues its existence following the handover, with the continued operation of the District Court Ordinance. The District Court is an inferior court of record.[60] The court's civil jurisdiction is set out in Part 4 of the ordinance, and includes jurisdiction to hear actions in contract and tort where the amount of the plaintiff's claim does not exceed $3 million,[61] and equitable jurisdiction, subject to monetary limits, in relation to various matters such as administration of deceased estates, proceedings enforcing mortgages or charges and proceedings in relation to trusts.[62] The court also has civil jurisdiction as conferred by other ordinances, for example jurisdiction to hear claims for employee compensation under the Employees' Compensation Ordinance,[63] claims under the Sex Discrimination Ordinance[64] and matrimonial cases under the Matrimonial Proceedings and Property Ordinance.[65]

Part 5 of the District Court Ordinance sets out the criminal jurisdiction of the District Court, which includes jurisdiction over certain indictable offences transferred to the District Court under either Part IV of the Magistrates Ordinance or section 65F of the Criminal Procedure Ordinance. Both the District Court and the Court of First Instance have jurisdiction to try offences proceeded by way of indictment; however, the jurisdiction

---

[56] See High Court Ordinance (Cap. 4), ss. 34, 34A, 34B, 35.
[57] See ibid., ss. 34(2A), 34B(4).
[58] In criminal cases, s. 34(5) provides that where the two judges sitting on the appeal differ, the judgment appealed from would be disturbed only in so far as it may be modified by any order which the judges make as to which they do not differ.
[59] High Court Ordinance (Cap. 4), s. 34B(5).
[60] District Court Ordinance (Cap. 336), s. 3.
[61] Ibid., s. 32.
[62] Ibid., s. 37.
[63] Employees' Compensation Ordinance (Cap. 282), s. 18A.
[64] Sex Discrimination Ordinance (Cap. 480), s. 76.
[65] Matrimonial Proceedings and Property Ordinance (Cap. 192), s. 2A.

of the District Court is limited in that certain serious offences cannot be transferred to the District Court by a magistrate under the Magistrates Ordinance,[66] and also in that the court does not have the power to impose a sentence of imprisonment of greater than seven years.[67]

Both civil and criminal proceedings in the District Court are heard by a judge sitting alone.[68] Appeals may be possible from a decision of the District Court to the Court of Appeal of the High Court.[69]

Magistrates' Courts

The system of magistracies which previously existed in Hong Kong continue to exist following 1 July 1997, and magistrates continue to exercise the same criminal jurisdiction[70] as they did previously. There are presently seven magistracies located in Hong Kong: Eastern, Kowloon City, Kwun Tong, West Kowloon, Fanling, Sha Tin and Tuen Mun Magistrates' Courts.

There are two types of magistrates: permanent and special magistrates.[71] Both are appointed by warrant by the Chief Executive; however, permanent magistrates have more extensive powers in terms of jurisdiction and in terms of the sentence that can be imposed. Special magistrates often deal with minor offences such as littering, hawking and less serious traffic offences. The Magistrates Ordinance does not create a court as such, but simply provides for the appointment of magistrates. Thus, the power of magistrates need not be exercised in a court, although in practice, most proceedings before a magistrate are conducted in court.

All criminal proceedings are commenced before a magistrate. Where the offence is a summary offence, the magistrate hears and decides the case in accordance with Part II of the Magistrates Ordinance. Magistrates may also hear and determine in a summary manner those indictable offences that can be dealt with by summary proceedings.[72] Where the prosecution

---

[66] See Magistrates Ordinance (Cap. 227), s. 88 and Second Schedule Pt III.
[67] District Court Ordinance (Cap. 336), s. 82.
[68] Ibid., s. 6.
[69] Ibid., ss. 63, 83, 84; and Criminal Procedure Ordinance (Cap. 221), ss. 80–83Y.
[70] There is also partial civil jurisdiction in the enforcement of civil debts; see Magistrates Ordinance (Cap. 227), s. 67.
[71] Magistrates Ordinance (Cap. 227), s. 5.
[72] See Magistrates Ordinance (Cap. 227), ss. 91, 92. Permanent magistrates are restricted from dealing with the offences set out in Pt I of the Second Schedule summarily, while special magistrates cannot deal with any of the offences set out in the Second Schedule summarily.

of an offence is to be proceeded by way of indictment, the matter is either transferred to the District Court under Part IV of the Magistrates Ordinance,[73] or committal proceedings are held before the magistrate, wherein the magistrate determines whether there is sufficient evidence to commit the accused person to trial.[74] If the magistrate commits the person to trial, then the trial would be heard in the Court of First Instance.

Proceedings before a magistrate are heard by the magistrate sitting alone, and there is no jury involved. The maximum penalties that can be imposed by magistrates are, in the case of special magistrates, six months' imprisonment and a HK$50,000 fine, and in the case of permanent magistrates, two years' imprisonment and a HK$100,000 fine.[75] A magistrate may review his or her own decision upon application by either the prosecution or the defendant, or upon the magistrate's own initiative.[76] Decisions of Magistrates' Courts can also be appealed to the Court of First Instance.[77]

Apart from hearing and determining prosecutions for offences, magistrates also have power in relation to, for example, the issuing of search or arrest warrants[78] and granting of bail.[79]

Furthermore, permanent magistrates sit in the Juvenile Court created under the Juvenile Offenders Ordinance (Cap. 226) for the purpose of dealing with criminal charges (other than homicide) brought against children below the age of sixteen.

Tribunals

The system of tribunals existing before 1 July 1997 have continued existence under the present system.[80] Since 1 July 1997, new tribunals

---

[73] However, the offences set out in Pt III of the Second Schedule cannot be transferred by a magistrate; see s. 88.
[74] See Magistrates Ordinance (Cap. 227), Pt III.
[75] Ibid., ss. 91, 92. Where there is conviction of more than one offence and two or more terms of imprisonment are ordered to run consecutively, the aggregate of those terms must not, in the case of a special magistrate, exceed twelve months and, in the case of a permanent magistrate, exceed three years: s. 57.
[76] Magistrates Ordinance (Cap. 227), s. 104.
[77] See ibid., ss. 105, 113.
[78] E.g. ibid., ss. 9, 72.
[79] See Criminal Procedure Ordinance (Cap. 221), Pt IA.
[80] For a discussion of the continuity of the system of tribunals, see *Luk Ka Cheung* v. *The Market Misconduct Tribunal* [2009] 1 HKC 1.

have also been established in Hong Kong, such as the Competition Tribunal. Tribunals are discussed in more detail below.

Tribunals in Hong Kong

At the lower level of the Hong Kong court system, there are various tribunals. There are four tribunals[81] included in the court hierarchy that exercise judicial power[82] (Small Claims Tribunal, Lands Tribunal, Labour Tribunal and the Competition Tribunal) as well as a number of administrative tribunals. Most of the tribunals focus on a specific area of law. Tribunals are also often designed to be a quick and less expensive method for resolving disputes without the need to go through the usual court system. Proceedings in tribunals tend to be less formal and in some cases, legal representation is not permitted.

Although there exist tribunals in Hong Kong which exercise judicial power, the common law system does not usually lend itself to the inclusion of tribunals functioning as courts within the judiciary. This is because tribunals lack many of the qualities and restrictions usually assigned to courts.[83] These qualities are important for maintaining the separation of powers, the separation of persons[84] and to promote the rule of law. The essential issue lies in ensuring that those people and bodies exercising the judicial power are independent and ensuring that the proper protections from political interference guaranteed by the Basic Law are afforded to them.[85] The curiosity of this point in Hong Kong law is described by Peter Wesley-Smith:

It [the Basic Law] vests the courts with 'the judicial power of the Region' (Article 80 of the Basic Law); after listing the primary 'courts' under the previous regime it refers to 'other special courts' (Art. 81), without telling us what these are; it then states that the courts shall exercise judicial power independently (Art. 85). All 'courts', that is, must be independent. Judges of the courts (somewhat confusingly,

---

[81] See also the text to n. 31 above.
[82] See Chapter 5 for a discussion on the relevance of judicial power under the doctrine of the separation of powers.
[83] This issue has been the source of many constitutional challenges in Australia: see *Brandy v. Human Rights and Equal Opportunities Commission* (1994–1995) 127 ALR 1; *Huddart Parker and Co Pty Ltd v. Moorehead* (1909) 8 CLR 330.
[84] The doctrine of the separation of powers is discussed in Chapter 3. The separation of persons follows that the different types of government power should not be exercised by the same person.
[85] See Basic Law, arts. 85, 89, 92 and 93.

the courts are also equated with the judiciary) are to be appointed by the Chief Executive on the recommendation of the Judicial Officers Recommendation Commission and may only be removed, on limited grounds, on the recommendation of a special tribunal; 'members of the judiciary other than judges', however, shall be appointed and removed in accordance with the previous system (Art. 91) ... What, then, is a 'court' and who are 'members of the judiciary other than judges'? ... These are important questions, at least if one accepts that judicial power is a particular species to be distinguished from legislative and executive power.[86]

In many respects, it is the legislated ordinances of the respective tribunals that fill any constitutional gaps in the tribunals' exercise of the judicial power.[87]

Small Claims Tribunal

The Small Claims Tribunal[88] was established to provide quick and informal resolution of monetary disputes between private parties. The tribunal hears monetary claims founded on contract, quasi-contract or tort.[89] The most common disputes are actions for debts, service charges, damage to property, faulty goods, consumer claims etc. However, particular matters are specifically excluded from the tribunal's jurisdiction. These include actions in respect of defamation, maintenance agreements (between parties to a marriage), actions by money lenders for the recovery of loans, and actions (such as claims for wages) within the jurisdiction of the Labour Tribunal or Minor Employment Claims Adjudication Board. As the tribunal's jurisdiction is confined to monetary claims, actions for possession of land are also not dealt with by the tribunal.[90] The Small Claims Tribunal's jurisdiction only extends to claims which are not more than HK$75,000; therefore, claims over this amount should not be submitted to the tribunal unless the claimant abandons the part of the claim above HK$75,000.

---

[86] P. Wesley-Smith, 'Judges and Judicial Power under the Hong Kong Basic Law' (2004), *Hong Kong Law Journal* 34, 83, p. 84.
[87] See Y. Ghai, *Hong Kong's New Constitutional Order: The Resumption of Chinese Sovereignty and Basic Law*, 2nd ed. (Hong Kong: Hong Kong University Press 1997), pp. 286–291.
[88] See Small Claims Tribunal Ordinance (Cap. 338).
[89] On the jurisdiction of the Small Claims Tribunal, see Small Claims Tribunal Ordinance (Cap. 338), s. 5 and Sch.
[90] This is within the jurisdiction of the Lands Tribunal.

Disputes brought before the tribunal between a claimant and defendant are adversarial in nature and are heard by an adjudicator. As one of the central aims of the tribunal is to provide a quick, informal and inexpensive judicial recourse for small claims, neither party in a dispute is allowed to instruct legal representatives.[91] Hearings are conducted in an informal manner[92] and the strict rules of evidence (which are ordinarily applicable in court proceedings) do not apply.[93] Each party has the opportunity to present and cross-examine witnesses and to summarise their arguments before the adjudicator.

If either party wishes to appeal the decision, they may do so by applying to the tribunal for a review of the decision within seven days of judgment.[94] On such a review, the tribunal will re-open and re-hear the claim either in part or *de novo*, and it has the discretion to hear fresh evidence. The tribunal will then alter or confirm the order. As an alternative to a review (or following a review, if a party is dissatisfied with the result of the review), a party may apply to the Court of First Instance for leave to appeal the decision of the tribunal.[95] The application must be made within seven days of the order being handed down by the tribunal. Application for leave to appeal may only be made on a ground involving a question of law alone or on the ground that the claim was outside the jurisdiction of the tribunal. If leave is granted, the powers of the Court of First Instance are limited. It is unable to vary or reverse any question of fact and is unable to consider new evidence.[96]

Lands Tribunal

The Lands Tribunal[97] performs four main judicial functions[98]:

(1) The making of orders for possession of premises and consequential relief. These are cases brought by landlords to obtain possession under the Landlord and Tenant (Consolidation) Ordinance (Cap. 7) or under

---

[91] Small Claims Tribunal Ordinance (Cap. 338), s. 19(2).
[92] Ibid., s. 16(1).
[93] Ibid., s. 23(2).
[94] Ibid., s. 27A.
[95] Ibid., s. 28.
[96] Ibid., s. 29.
[97] See Lands Tribunal Ordinance (Cap. 17).
[98] On the jurisdiction of the Lands Tribunal, see ibid., s. 8.

the common law. In such applications, the tribunal also has power, for example, to make orders as to the payment of rent or other money due under a tenancy agreement.[99]

(2) The determination of compensation payable by the government in cases of compulsory acquisition or where it is liable for the depreciation in value of premises under various land-related ordinances.[100] The Lands Tribunal will perform such functions as determination of the amount of compensation for the land under compulsory sale for redevelopment if the market price is in dispute.[101]

(3) The hearing and determination of appeals arising from the decisions of the Commissioner of Rating and Valuation and the Director of Housing.[102] An example of a matter arising in this category is a dispute over the rateable value of a property.[103]

(4) The hearing and determination of building management matters and disputes specified under the Building Management Ordinance.[104] These cases are usually matters of disputes concerning the cost of maintenance, repair, renovation and management of buildings.[105]

There is no limit as to the amount of compensation that the tribunal can award in cases brought before it. Both parties involved in a dispute are able to represent themselves, authorise a representative to act on their behalf (lay representation) or engage a lawyer to handle the proceedings. If either party is dissatisfied with the ruling, they are able to apply to the tribunal for a review of the decision within one month from the date of the ruling.[106] On a review, the tribunal may reverse, vary or confirm the

---

[99] Ibid., s. 8(8); *INA Mueller* v. *Hung Fat Cheung Investors Ltd* [2004] HKLT 50.

[100] These include the Buildings Ordinance (Cap. 123), Land Acquisition (Possessory Title) Ordinance (Cap. 130), Air Pollution Control Ordinance (Cap. 311), Demolished Buildings (Redevelopment of Sites) Ordinance (Cap. 337) and Land (Compulsory Sale for Redevelopment) Ordinance (Cap. 545).

[101] See *Gilmerton Ltd and Others* v. *Polywin Holdings Ltd and Others* [2005] HKLT 1.

[102] Rating appeals refer to those matters arising out of the following ordinances: the Rating Ordinance (Cap. 116), Housing Ordinance (Cap. 283) and Government Rent (Assessment and Collection) Ordinance (Cap. 515).

[103] See *Urban Parking Ltd* v. *The Commissioner of Rating and Valuation* [2003] HKLT 50.

[104] Building Management Ordinance (Cap. 344), s. 45: This section grants the tribunal jurisdiction to determine proceeding on certain matters. The matters justiciable under s. 45 are set out in Schedule 10 of this ordinance.

[105] See *The Incorporated Owners of Phase One of Whampoa Estate* v. *The Bank of Communications* [2004] HKLT 95.

[106] Lands Tribunal Ordinance (Cap. 17), s. 11A.

original decision. Parties also have a separate right to apply to the tribunal or to the Court of Appeal for leave to appeal a decision of the tribunal.[107] An appeal can only be made on the basis of an error of law in the tribunal's decision.[108]

Labour Tribunal

The main function of the Labour Tribunal is to offer a quick, informal and inexpensive way to resolve monetary disputes between employees and employers. The jurisdiction[109] of the Labour Tribunal arises from the Employment Ordinance (Cap. 57) and the Apprenticeship Ordinance (Cap. 47). Jurisdiction also extends to cases of breach of contract in employment and apprenticeship agreements. There is no upper limit on the amount of compensation that may be awarded. Some restrictions on standing do exist: the claim must be at least HK$8,000 or be a class claim of ten or more complainants.[110]

The common types of matters heard in the Labour Tribunal include wages due for work done, wages in lieu of notice of resignation or termination of a contract of employment, termination of a contract without the required notice having been served, pay for statutory holidays, compensation for unlawful dismissal and long-service leave payments.

Parties to a dispute are unable to have legal representation in a hearing before the Labour Tribunal.[111] This is partly because the rigid rules of evidence do not apply to these hearings[112] and trained legal practitioners may take advantage of this to exploit the other (less-resourced) party. A party may authorise an office bearer of a registered trade union or an association of employers to represent them. They are also allowed to question each other and the witnesses during the trial.

If either party is dissatisfied with the order of the tribunal after the hearing, they can apply for a review of the decision within seven days from

---

[107] Ibid., ss. 11, 11AA.
[108] Ibid., s. 11(2).
[109] See Labour Tribunal Ordinance (Cap. 25), s. 7 and Schedule.
[110] Claims where this threshold is not met may be brought before the Minor Employment Claims Adjudication Board: see Minor Employment Claims Adjudication Board Ordinance (Cap. 453), Sch.; Labour Tribunal Ordinance (Cap. 25), Sch. para. 1.
[111] Labour Tribunal Ordinance (Cap. 25), s. 23.
[112] Ibid., s. 27(2).

the date of the order.[113] The tribunal can also review a decision by its own motion within fourteen days of the date of the order. It is also open to both parties to appeal to the Court of First Instance on the grounds that the orders made are based on erroneous points of law or on the grounds that the tribunal has acted outside of its jurisdiction.[114] Further action exists beyond the Court of First Instance if leave is granted to appeal to the Court of Appeal within seven days of judgment. Leave to appeal will be granted on as question of law of general public importance.[115]

Competition Tribunal

The Competition Tribunal was established in 2013 to deal with legal proceedings concerning competition law under the Competition Ordinance (Cap. 619).[116] The Competition Tribunal is a specialist tribunal with economic and commercial expertise. This was thought to be necessary due to the complex nature of evidence in competition matters and the need to assess expert evidence on the economic impact of conduct which may affect competition in the marketplace.[117]

The tribunal has jurisdiction to hear various matters under that ordinance, including applications made by the Competition Commission or Communications Authority regarding contraventions of the competition rules, and private actions regarding contraventions of the conduct rules. 'Competition rules' means the conduct rules and merger rule under the Competition Ordinance.[118] There are two 'conduct rules' under the ordinance: the first prohibits agreements which restrict competition, and the second prohibits abuse of market power.[119] On applications made by the Competition Commission or Communications Authority, the Competition Tribunal has power to make various orders, including imposition of pecuniary penalties

---

[113] Ibid., s. 31.
[114] Ibid., s. 32.
[115] Ibid., s. 35A.
[116] Competition Ordinance (Cap. 619), s. 134. The tribunal is a superior court of record: s. 134(2).
[117] Commerce and Economic Development Bureau, *Detailed Proposals for a Competition Law – Public Consultation Paper* (Hong Kong: Commerce and Economic Development Bureau May 2008), para. 20.
[118] Competition Ordinance (Cap. 619), s. 2(1).
[119] Ibid., ss. 6, 21.

on persons who have contravened a competition rule.[120] Where it has been determined that there has been a contravention of a conduct rule, persons suffering loss or damage may bring a private action to seek various orders, including orders for compensation.[121]

The practice and procedure of the tribunal is as set out in the Competition Tribunal Rules,[122] the Competition Tribunal Practice Directions and also the Rules of the High Court if the matter is not provided for in the Competition Ordinance or the Competition Tribunal Rules. The tribunal is required to conduct its proceedings with as much informality as is consistent with attaining justice.[123] Except for certain proceedings for pecuniary or financial penalties, the tribunal is not bound by the strict rules of evidence.[124] Parties to proceedings may engage legal representation.

Subject to certain exceptions, an appeal lies as of right to the Court of Appeal against any decision of the tribunal.[125] On an appeal, the Court of Appeal has power to confirm, set aside or vary the tribunal's decision.

Other Tribunals

Aside from the four tribunals mentioned, there exist in Hong Kong other tribunals which are not established as courts. Such tribunals deal with appeals against different administrative decisions or with other matters. These tribunals are established by various ordinances and each is concerned with the specific ordinance that grants them jurisdiction.

For example, the Securities and Futures Appeals Tribunal ensures that decisions made by the Securities and Futures Commission, a securities regulatory body, are reasonable and fair. The Market Misconduct Tribunal rules on issues brought forth by the Financial Secretary regarding market misconduct, which includes insider dealing, price rigging and stock market manipulation.[126] Both of these tribunals were established under the Securities and Futures Ordinance (Cap. 571).

---

[120] Ibid., ss. 93, 94, Sch. 3.
[121] Ibid., ss. 110, 112, Sch. 3.
[122] Competition Tribunal Rules (Cap. 619D).
[123] Competition Ordinance (Cap. 619), s. 144.
[124] Ibid., s. 147.
[125] Ibid., s. 154.
[126] See Securities and Futures Ordinance (Cap. 571), s. 252.

Another example of a tribunal is the Obscene Articles Tribunal, which performs two main functions: to classify articles submitted by any person who commissions the design, production or publication of those articles, and to determine whether an article or a matter is obscene or indecent when a court or magistrate refers such an article or matter to the tribunal during the course of a proceeding.[127]

Doctrine of Judicial Precedent

The doctrine of judicial precedent (or *stare decisis* – 'keep to what has been decided previously') is a fundamental aspect of the common law, whereby judges decide cases in accordance with decisions handed down by the courts in prior cases. A case is said to be a precedent for a legal principle set out in the court's judgment, which would be followed or applied in later cases where the same or similar issue arises.

In most legal systems, courts look at previous decisions and would generally decide like cases in the same way, following decisions in the past by way of analogy. However, what distinguishes the common law system in the English tradition[128] from other systems is that in the former, a strict doctrine of precedent is applied such that the decisions of superior courts lay down authoritatively what the law is, and so judges in later cases are *bound* by those previous decisions. The decisions on points of law by the courts are themselves a source of law, and so judges in later cases must follow those principles as laid down by the courts.

On the other hand, courts in civil law jurisdictions, for example, do not lay down the law as such, and so their decisions do not strictly bind later courts. In those systems, courts apply the law as set out in the codes, and simply have resort to previous decisions of the courts as guidance on application of the law as set out in the codes.

---

[127] Control of Obscene and Indecent Articles Ordinance (Cap. 390).
[128] On the history of the development of the doctrine of precedent in England, see T. E. Lewis, 'The History of Judicial Precedent I' (1930), *Law Quarterly Review* 46, 207; 'The History of Judicial Precedent II' (1930), *Law Quarterly Review* 46, 341; 'The History of Judicial Precedent III' (1931), *Law Quarterly Review* 47, 411; 'The History of Judicial Precedent IV' (1932), *Law Quarterly Review* 48, 230.

Hierarchy of Courts

While broadly the doctrine of precedent requires courts to decide in accordance with principles set out in previous cases, the doctrine only applies in relation to a specific hierarchy of courts that exists in a particular legal system. Different jurisdictions will have their own hierarchy of courts, and the decisions in a particular hierarchy or jurisdiction are not strictly binding on a court of a different hierarchy or jurisdiction. For example, a Hong Kong court is not bound by the decision of a New Zealand court, even though both courts are applying common law, as New Zealand courts exist in a different jurisdiction and hierarchy from the courts in Hong Kong.

Another feature of the hierarchy of courts which affects how the doctrine of precedent applies is that while lower courts are bound by the decisions of courts higher up in the hierarchy, a higher court is not bound by the decisions of lower courts. For example, the Court of First Instance is bound by the decisions of the Court of Appeal, but the Court of Appeal is not bound by the decisions of the Court of First Instance.

The requirement for lower courts to follow the decisions of higher courts in the same hierarchy is sometimes referred to as vertical *stare decisis*. As for decisions of courts at the same level or standing in the hierarchy (i.e., courts of co-ordinate jurisdiction), the doctrine of precedent could require that earlier decisions of the courts bind later decisions of the same court or another court of equal standing. This aspect of the doctrine is sometimes referred to as horizontal *stare decisis*.

Decisions on Law as Precedent, Not on Facts

The doctrine of precedent only applies in relation to decisions of courts on legal principles. In other words, decisions on facts do not bind later cases; a court is only bound by the court's decision as to what the legal principle is.[129]

Rationale for Doctrine of Precedent

The main rationale for the doctrine of precedent is that it provides certainty and consistency in the law. Consistent application of the law is an

---

[129] See Chapter 4.

important aspect of fairness. It would be an affront to justice if laws were applied arbitrarily to reach different outcomes in different cases, though the factual circumstances may be the same. Moreover, if the law is to act as a guide for the behaviour of persons in society, then there must be certainty in the law so that individuals know in advance whether their conduct would be lawful or not.

That certainty and consistency are, generally speaking, desirable features of the law would not be contentious. What is more debatable is whether a strict doctrine of precedent is the only way (or necessarily the best way) for achieving certainty and consistency in the law. It has been pointed out, for example, that judges in continental Europe no doubt wish to achieve certainty in the law just as much as common law judges, yet *stare decisis* is not applied in civil law systems.[130] It is not necessarily the case that there is a greater degree of certainty in the law in common law systems compared with civil law systems. It may be that a rigid doctrine of precedent developed in England but not in continental Europe largely because of historical and structural factors.[131] For instance, the existence of codes in civil law systems may provide sufficient certainty to the law without the need for a doctrine of *stare decisis*. On the other hand, under the common law system, where much of the law is not sourced from statute but from judgments of the courts, a doctrine of precedent may be necessary to ensure that different courts are not saying different things at different times as to what precisely the law is.

Limitations and Disadvantages of the Doctrine

Although the basic rationale of the doctrine of precedent is that it provides certainty and consistency in the common law, it has often been said that this element of certainty in the law is more apparent than real. Like cases are to be treated alike, but as a practical matter, there may be difficulties in determining whether two cases are sufficiently alike such that the same legal principle should be applied.[132] Where the factual circumstances

---

[130] R. Cross and J. W. Harris, *Precedent in English Law*, 4th ed. (Oxford: Clarendon Press 1991), p. 11.
[131] See further Cross and Harris (ibid.), pp. 11–15.
[132] See further P. Wesley-Smith, *The Sources of Hong Kong Law* (Hong Kong: Hong Kong University Press 1994), p. 38.

giving rise to a legal dispute are precisely the same as those which have arisen in a previous case, the application of precedent is more straightforward. But often, a different mix of factual circumstances arises, or the situation before the courts may be entirely novel or new. In these circumstances, it is not always clear which existing legal principle and which existing precedent would be applicable. As will be seen later in this chapter, there are different ways in which a court can decide not to apply a particular precedent that might initially seem applicable. The possibility of courts choosing not to apply particular precedents in certain situations tends to show that there is a greater degree of flexibility to the system than what the doctrine of precedent may indicate at first sight.

The element of uncertainty can also be seen in the difficulty of accurately predicting the outcomes of cases before the courts, and in the not uncommon occurrence of judges having different views on the law and deciding cases differently (as can be seen from dissenting judgments and appeal courts overturning the decisions of lower courts).[133]

Nonetheless, while uncertainty in the common law clearly exists despite the doctrine of precedent, the degree of uncertainty should not be exaggerated, as the existing case law does provide important constraints on how a judge decides a case.

It should also be borne in mind that the desirability for certainty and consistency in the law sometimes conflicts with the desirability for flexibility to meet the demands of justice in any particular case. An existing legal principle as laid down in a case may lead to an unjust outcome if applied in a later case for a number of reasons. For example, the judge in the earlier case might have been mistaken as to the law and so the legal principle laid down was wrong; or the earlier legal principle might have been set down without the court realising the adverse consequences of applying the principle in different unforeseen circumstances; or it may be that social conditions and viewpoints have changed such that an earlier principle is now regarded as outdated and unjust. The doctrine of *stare decisis* may well require the existing precedent to be applied in the case

---

[133] The existence of uncertainty in the common law is one major theme of jurists categorised in the tradition of the American Realists: see, e.g., J. Frank, *Law and the Modern Mind* (Gloucester: Peter Smith 1970), viii–xvii; K. Llewellyn, 'Some Realism about Realism' (1931), *Harvard Law Review* 44, 1222, at 1233–1242. On the writings of the realists generally, see, e.g., B. Bix, *Jurisprudence: Theory and Context*, 7th ed. (London: Sweet and Maxwell 2015), chapter 17.

before the court even though it may lead to an outcome which the court or the public might view to be unjust.[134]

To address such concerns, a degree of flexibility is built into the system of precedent whereby the courts can in certain situations choose not to apply a particular precedent that might on its face seem applicable. It has been noted by the Court of Final Appeal that this flexibility demonstrates that 'the great strength of the common law lies in its capacity to develop to meet the changing needs of the society in which it functions'.[135] However, some judges are more willing than others to depart from precedent in order to provide what is regarded as a just result, and this difference in the approach of the courts perhaps reveals the tension in the doctrine of *stare decisis* that arises from the competing demands of certainty and flexibility.

Retrospective and Prospective Effect of Court Decisions

A court's decision has both prospective and retrospective effect.[136] It is prospective in that it applies to events that occur after the decision was handed down. It is retrospective in that the court's determination of the law applies to and is binding on both the persons who are party to the particular court case, and also others in relation to events that occurred prior to the decision. For example, if a Court of Final Appeal decision on a principle relating to the formation of contracts was handed down in 2009, the legal principles in that case would also apply in relation to events that occurred, say, in 2008.[137] Thus, where a dispute arises over the alleged contract formed in 2008 and the parties come to the court, say, in 2011, the law that was laid down in the 2009 case would apply to the events occurring in 2008.

There could be occasions where some might argue that retrospective application of the court's decision is unfair, because what was thought to be lawful at the time is now retrospectively rendered unlawful. An issue arises as to whether the court could order that its decision only have prospective effect. This issue has arisen in various cases in relation to

---

[134] See further Wesley-Smith (n. 131), p. 35.
[135] *A Solicitor (24/07)* v. *Law Society of Hong Kong* (2008) 11 HKCFAR 117, [2008] 2 HKC 1, at para. 19.
[136] *HKSAR* v. *Hung Chan* (2006) 9 HKCFAR 614, [2006] 3 HKLRD 841, [10] (CFA); *Re Spectrum Plus Ltd (in liq)* [2005] 2 AC 680, at paras. 7, 65.
[137] This will be the case so long as the 2008 dispute had not been finally resolved by the courts before the 2009 decision was handed down.

where the court has overruled earlier decisions. For example, in *HKSAR v. Hung Chan*,[138] the court considered the effect of Dangerous Drugs Ordinance (Cap. 134) section 47(2) which provides that:

> Any person proved or presumed to have had a dangerous drug in his possession shall, until the contrary is proved, be presumed to have known the nature of such drug.

The defendants were caught with dangerous drugs in their possession and were charged with the offence of trafficking in dangerous drugs.[139] As is common with criminal offences, it was necessary for a mental element (*mens rea*) to be established before a person could be convicted of the offence, and the requirement of *mens rea* in the present circumstances meant that it was necessary to show that the defendants knew they were in possession of the drugs. The prosecution relied on the reversal of the onus of proof under section 47(2), and the issue before the court was whether the provision imposed on the defendant a legal or persuasive burden of proof or only an evidential burden of proof.[140] Previously, the widely accepted view was that the provision created a legal or persuasive burden; however, the Court of Appeal[141] (affirmed on appeal by the Court of Final Appeal[142]) held against the prevailing view, concluding that it would be proper to treat the provision as imposing an evidential burden.

There were earlier cases where defendants were convicted under the ordinance after they were unable to discharge the legal burden of proof under section 47 (that had previously been applied). The government accordingly raised the concern that, if there was retrospective application of the above decision, there would be a flood of applications by previously convicted defendants to appeal against their convictions, resulting in gravely disruptive consequences for the criminal justice system.[143] The

---

[138] [2006] 3 HKLRD 841.
[139] Dangerous Drugs Ordinance (Cap. 134), s. 4.
[140] In the present context, if the defendants have the legal or persuasive burden of proving that they did not know the nature of the drug, then they must provide sufficient evidence to prove that to the requisite standard of proof (which, here, would be on the balance of probabilities). On the other hand, where there is only an evidential burden imposed on the defendants, the defendants would only be required to adduce some evidence to raise the matter as an issue, and once this is done, the burden falls back on the prosecution to prove (beyond reasonable doubt) that the defendants did know the nature of the drug.
[141] *Hung Chan v. HKSAR* [2005] 3 HKLRD 291.
[142] *HKSAR v. Hung Chan* (2006) 9 HKCFAR 614, [2006] 3 HKLRD 841.
[143] Ibid., at para. 20.

government therefore sought a court order for the decision to apply prospectively only and not retrospectively. In other words, the decision would not have effect in relation to events in the past, and would only apply to future circumstances from the date of the court order.[144] So the prior convictions would be treated as having been lawful, governed under the previous understanding of the law. The Court of Final Appeal left open the possibility of the courts in Hong Kong providing for prospective overruling but did not give any concluded view as to whether the courts did have this power, as it held that even if prospective overruling was within the power of Hong Kong courts, the present circumstances did not justify prospective overruling (on the grounds that the problem of a flood of applications was much smaller than apprehended by the government).

The House of Lords also considered the issue of prospective overruling in *Re Spectrum Plus Ltd.*[145] A majority of the Law Lords held that it was within the judicial power[146] of the courts to provide for prospective overruling and that such power may need to be exercised in order to administer justice fairly and to avoid gravely unfair and disruptive consequences in relation to past transactions or events. However, such power would only be exercised in exceptional circumstances, and on the facts of the case, it was held that prospective overruling would not be appropriate.

Vertical and Horizontal *Stare Decisis* in the Hong Kong Courts

Court of Final Appeal

Vertical Stare Decisis

As the power of final adjudication of the HKSAR is vested in the Court of Final Appeal (CFA),[147] the decisions of the CFA would be binding on all other courts in Hong Kong, while the CFA itself is not bound by the

---

[144] A modified form of retrospective overruling was actually sought, as the government accepted that it would be appropriate for the decision to apply retrospectively in relation to the particular defendants who were parties to the present proceedings.
[145] [2005] 2 AC 680.
[146] A different view has, however, been taken in Australia: see *Ha* v. *New South Wales* (1997) 189 CLR 465 (High Court of Australia).
[147] Basic Law, art. 82.

decisions of any other court. Although the CFA is the highest court in the hierarchy of courts in Hong Kong, it must be borne in mind that article 158 of the Basic Law reserves the final power of interpretation of the Basic Law to the NPCSC.[148]

Horizontal Stare Decisis

The Court of Final Appeal, being the final appellate court in Hong Kong, is not bound by its own decisions.[149] This is consistent with the approach adopted by final appellate courts in other common law jurisdictions[150] as well as by the Privy Council.[151]

The possibility of the highest appeal courts departing from their previous decisions indicates that the operation of the doctrine of precedent does allow for some flexibility so as to mitigate some of the problems mentioned earlier that can arise from a rigid application of precedent. Nonetheless, despite this freedom of the highest courts, it is clear that these courts would still generally follow their own earlier decisions and would only overrule their previous decisions on rare occasions. In *A Solicitor (24/07)* v. *Law Society of Hong Kong*,[152] the CFA noted that it would approach the exercise of its power to overrule its own decisions 'with great circumspection', and that the power would be exercised 'most sparingly'.

In England, the approach of the Supreme Court (previously House of Lords) looks at whether too rigid an adherence to precedent may lead to injustice in a particular case or would unduly restrict the proper development of the law.[153] The Supreme Court would be cautious in departing

---

[148] See the discussion on the NPCSC below.
[149] *A Solicitor (24/07)* v. *Law Society of Hong Kong* (2008) 11 HKCFAR 117, [2008] 2 HKC 1, at para. 18.
[150] In Australia, see *Australian Agricultural Co* v. *Federated Engine Drivers and Firemen's Association of Australasia* (1913) 17 CLR 261; *John* v. *Federal Commissioner of Taxation* (1989) 166 CLR 417. In England, the House of Lords previously considered that it was bound by its own decisions (see e.g., *London Tramways* v. *London County Council* [1898] AC 375), but the practice since 1966 was that the House of Lords, and now the UK Supreme Court, is free to depart from its prior decisions where appropriate: Practice Statement (Judicial Precedent) [1966] 1 WLR 1234.
[151] See, e.g., *Ridsdale* v. *Clifton* (1877) 2 PD 306; *Cushing* v. *Dupuy* (1880) 5 App Cas 409; *Mercantile Bank of India* v. *Central Bank* [1938] AC 287; *Pratt* v. *Attorney General for Jamaica* [1993] 4 All ER 769.
[152] (2008) 11 HKCFAR 117, [2008] 2 HKC 1, at para. 19.
[153] Practice Statement (Judicial Precedent) [1966] 1 WLR 1234.

from a previous decision, bearing in mind the danger of disturbing retrospectively the basis on which contracts, settlements of property and fiscal arrangements have been entered into and also the special need for certainty as to the criminal law.[154] Changed social circumstances might be a factor taken into account in determining whether to depart from an earlier decision.[155] However, the mere fact that the decision sought to be impugned is relatively recent does not necessarily mean that the court will invariably decline to depart from that decision.[156] In *C* v. *Director of Public Prosecutions*,[157] Lord Lowry stated the following considerations:

(1) if the solution is doubtful, the judges should beware of imposing their own remedy; (2) caution should prevail if Parliament has rejected opportunities of clearing up a known difficulty or has legislated while leaving the difficulty untouched; (3) disputed matters of social policy are less suitable areas for judicial intervention than purely legal problems; (4) fundamental legal doctrines should not be lightly set aside; (5) judges should not make a change unless they can achieve finality and certainty.

A situation where a long-accepted doctrine of the common law was abolished by the House of Lords is illustrated by the case of *Kleinwort Benson Ltd* v. *Lincoln City Council*,[158] where the rule that money paid under a mistake of law is not recoverable was abrogated in circumstances where (1) the rule had become inconsistent with other developments in the common law of restitution, based as it is now on the principle of unjust enrichment; (2) the rule had long been criticised as being unjust; (3) the rule had been rejected in other common law jurisdictions either by way of statute or judicial development; and (4) the Law Reform Commission had recommended abrogation of the rule. A majority of the House of Lords felt that there was no good reason for postponing the matter for legislation as it was unknown whether or, if so, when Parliament would legislate, and

---

[154] Ibid.
[155] See, e.g., *Herrington* v. *British Railways Board* [1972] AC 877; *R* v. *R* [1991] 4 All ER 481.
[156] See, e.g., *R* v. *Secretary of State for the Home Department (ex parte Khawaja)* [1983] 2 WLR 321.
[157] [1995] 2 All ER 43, at 52. See also B. V. Harris, 'Final Appellate Courts Overruling Their Own 'Wrong' Precedents: The Ongoing Search for Principle' (2002), *Law Quarterly Review* 118, 408. For the Australian approach, see e.g. *Mabo* v. *Queensland (No. 2)* (1992) 175 CLR 1, 29–30; *R* v. *L* (1991) 174 CLR 379 (rejection of principle that a husband could not be guilty of raping his wife).
[158] [1998] 4 All ER 513.

as it would be unjust to deprive the appellant of the benefit of the decision of the House in this instance.

Court of Appeal

Vertical Stare Decisis

The Court of Appeal (CA) is bound by decisions of the CFA, even if it regards decisions of the CFA as being wrong.

Horizontal Stare Decisis

Prior to the CFA decision in *A Solicitor (24/07)* v. *Law Society of Hong Kong*,[159] the Hong Kong Court of Appeal[160] followed the approach of its English counterpart under the principles in *Young* v. *Bristol Aeroplane Co Ltd*.[161] In the latter case, the English Court of Appeal had held that it was bound by its own decisions, subject to three exceptions: (1) where there are conflicting decisions of the CA, the court will need to decide for itself which decision is correct and which to follow; (2) the court is bound to refuse to follow a decision of its own which has been overruled by the higher appellate court (in Hong Kong, the CFA or the Privy Council pre-1 July 1997); and (3) the court is not bound to follow a decision of its own if given *per incuriam*. In relation to civil cases, the CFA has now held, in *A Solicitor (24/07)* v. *Law Society of Hong Kong*,[162] that the rule to be applied in place of *Young* v. *Bristol Aeroplane Co Ltd* is that the CA is bound by its previous decisions but it may depart from a previous decision where it is satisfied that it is plainly wrong.[163] The CFA stated the following points in explaining when an earlier decision should be regarded as 'plainly wrong'[164]:

- Where the arguments over whether the previous decision is wrong are finely balanced, the CA's mere preference for the view that it is wrong would plainly be insufficient to justify departure from it. Even where the

---

[159] (2008) 11 HKCFAR 117, [2008] 2 HKC 1.
[160] E.g., *Bowardley Enterprises Ltd* v. *Millennium Group Ltd* [2006] 4 HKC 329.
[161] [1944] KB 718.
[162] (2008) 11 HKCFAR 117, [2008] 2 HKC 1.
[163] Ibid., at para. 48.
[164] Ibid., at paras. 49–53.

CA is satisfied that the arguments against its previous decision are more substantial and cogent than the contrary arguments in its favour, this would still be insufficient. It is only where the CA is convinced that the contentions against its previous decision are so compelling that the decision can be demonstrated to be plainly wrong that the test is satisfied.

- Previous decisions reached in ignorance of an inconsistent statutory provision or a binding authority would satisfy the plainly wrong test. Further, decisions which involve a manifest slip or error[165] also satisfy the plainly wrong test. However, the category of decisions which are plainly wrong is not limited to these instances. The reasoning of a decision may be so seriously flawed that it should be regarded as plainly wrong.
- In examining whether a previous decision is plainly wrong, the CA is not confined to a consideration of the matters as they stood at the time the previous decision was made. It may take into account the development in jurisprudence in Hong Kong or elsewhere. What is contemplated here is that subsequent developments on the constitutional, statutory or case law fronts in the relevant area of the law or related areas may have so substantially impaired the previous decision that it should now be regarded as plainly wrong.
- A conclusion by the CA that its previous decision is plainly wrong does not necessarily mean that the court should depart from it. The court should also take into account other circumstances, including the nature of the issue involved, the length of time for which the previous decision has stood, the extent of its application, whether the issue is likely to be brought before the CFA or the legislature, whether the matter is best left to that court or the legislature, and whether and the extent to which failure to depart from it would occasion injustice in the case in question and similar cases. Where the CA is satisfied that its previous decision on a question of statutory interpretation is plainly wrong in failing to ascertain the true intent of the legislature, it may be more prepared to depart from its previous decision, having regard to the courts' responsibility to give effect to the legislative intent.

---

[165] See *Ho Po Chu* v. *Tung Chee Wah* [2006] 1 HKC 527; *Bowardley Enterprises Ltd* v. *Millennium Group Ltd* [2006] 4 HKC 329.

- The CA should approach the matter with great caution, having regard to the great importance of the doctrine of *stare decisis*. The possible ramifications of disturbing the basis on which property, commercial and other transactions have been entered into and rights have been acquired would have to be borne in mind. The plainly wrong test sets a high hurdle, and the departure from a previous decision in accordance with this test should be wholly exceptional and should occur very rarely.

The CFA also noted in the above case that the first two exceptions in *Young* v. *Bristol Aeroplane Co Ltd*, while correct, are not really exceptions to the general rule at all.[166] The principle under the second so-called exception applies both where the prior CA decision has been expressly overruled, as well as situations where the court's decision is impliedly overruled or undermined because its reasoning or conclusion is inconsistent with, or was rejected in, a later decision by the higher court.[167] However, the test of inconsistency is a stringent one, in that there must be a closeness of subject matter and a clear inconsistency of approach.[168] There has to be shown the enunciation by the final appellate court of a clear principle which is plainly inconsistent with the approach in the previous CA decision.[169]

In *A Solicitor (24/07)* v. *Law Society of Hong Kong*,[170] the CFA was only concerned with civil cases and thus the rejection of *Young* v. *Bristol Aeroplane Co Ltd* does not presently apply to criminal cases. Thus, for criminal cases, the general rule and the third exception (*per incuriam* decisions) in *Young* v. *Bristol Aeroplane Co Ltd*[171] would still be applicable.[172]

Per incuriam literally means 'through lack of care'. A decision is given *per incuriam* if it was made in ignorance of some statutory provision[173] or

---

[166] (2008) 11 HKCFAR 117, [2008] 2 HKC 1, at para. 42.
[167] *R* v. *Porter* [1949] 2 KB 128, at 132; *First National Securities Ltd* v. *Hegerty* [1985] QB 850; *Cackett* v. *Cackett* [1950] P 253; and see also *Commissioner of Inland Revenue* v. *Indosuez W I Carr Securities Ltd* [2002] 1 HKLRD 308.
[168] (2008) 11 HKCFAR 117, [2008] 2 HKC 1, at para. 43.
[169] Ibid.
[170] Ibid.
[171] [1944] KB 718.
[172] The rule has been applied to criminal cases as well: *R* v. *Spencer* [1985] QB 771; Cross and Harris (n. 131), p. 154.
[173] For example, in *Secretary for Justice* v. *Wong Sau Fong* [1998] 3 HKC 544, the Court of Appeal declined to follow an earlier decision of the court which had been given in

of some binding precedent, which if had been brought to the notice of the court, would have led to the court deciding differently.[174] A decision will not be regarded as having been given *per incuriam* simply because one of the parties did not appear before the court to argue its case,[175] or because the court did not have the benefit of the best or fullest argument[176] or where the authority ignored *might* only have affected the court's decision had it been taken into account.[177] However, the precise scope of the *per incuriam* doctrine is not clear, as it has been said that there could be exceptional circumstances outside the general definition which can come within the doctrine.[178]

In relation to criminal matters, there is also an exception in that the CA can refuse to follow its earlier decision if the earlier decision was wrong (i.e., where the law had been misapplied or misunderstood in the earlier case) and where the accused person would be imprisoned if the earlier decision was to be applied.[179] The rationale is to avoid the conviction or imprisonment of an innocent person. The precise scope of the exception is not entirely clear in a number of respects. First, there had been some indications that the exception applies whenever the earlier decision is wrong[180]; however, the weight of authority appears to be that the exception is not that wide and only applies where the liberty of the person is at stake.[181] Second, it might be arguable that the exception applies not only in criminal cases but also in civil or non-criminal proceedings where the

---

ignorance of s. 3 of the Hong Kong Bill of Rights Ordinance. If the earlier court had been cognisant of the provision, it would have been bound to give a different interpretation of the scope of the rights of appeal under s. 84 of the District Court Ordinance than it did in the case, so that the interpretation was consistent with article 11(4) of the Bill of Rights which guarantees every accused person an 'unfettered right' of appeal.

[174] See *Miliangos* v. *George Frank (Textiles) Ltd* [1976] AC 443, 477; *Cheung Lai Wah* v. *Director of Immigration* [1998] 1 HKLRD 772, at 779.
[175] *Morelle* v. *Wakeling* [1955] 2 QB 379, at 407.
[176] *Mobil Petroleum Co Inc* v. *Registrar of Trademarks* [2000] 4 HKC 670.
[177] *Re CKJW* (unreported, CFI, HCMP 5231/2001, 10 Dec 2001); *Miliangos* v. *George Frank (Textiles) Ltd* [1976] AC 443, at 477.
[178] See *Young* v. *Bristol Aeroplane Co Ltd* [1944] KB 718, 729. See also *A Solicitor (24/07)* v. *Law Society of Hong Kong* [2008] 2 HKC 1, at paras. 32–40.
[179] *R* v. *Gould* [1968] 1 All ER 899; *Cheung Sou-yat* v. *R* [1979] HKLR 630, at 635; *Secretary for Justice* v. *Wong Sau Fong* [1998] 3 HKC 544, at 550–552.
[180] *R* v. *Gould* [1968] 2 QB 65 at 69; and see *Cheung Sou-yat* v. *R* [1979] HKLR 630; *R* v. *Patterson* [1962] 2 QB 429; *R* v. *Jackson* [1974] QB 802.
[181] See *Attorney General* v. *Lau Chiu-tak* [1984] HKLR 23, 24; *R* v. *Spencer* [1985] QB 771, 779; *R* v. *Pope* [2001] EWCA Crim 972; and see further S. H. Bailey et al., *Smith, Bailey*

3) liberty of the person is in issue.[182] Third, it has been stated that an earlier decision should only be overruled on this ground where there is a Full Court convened for the purpose of reviewing the previous decision,[183] though it should be noted that there are examples in the case law where a three-member CA and not a Full Court has relied on this exception to depart from a previous decision.[184]

The rationale given for the general rule that the CA is bound by its own decisions is that it promotes certainty. Even if the CA is compelled to apply a precedent that is wrong, the problem can always be corrected on further appeal.[185] The opposing arguments, however, are that the losing party might not appeal the decision and so there may not be an opportunity for the higher appeal court to correct the matter. Further, it might be regarded as unjust for the losing party to have to bear the consequences of an incorrect application of the law, and to have to bear the risks and costs of launching a further appeal if the party wishes to be vindicated. In contrast with the position in Hong Kong and in England, the Courts of Appeal in a number of states in Australia do not regard themselves as strictly bound by their previous decisions and adopt a practice of convening a bench of five judges to review a decision of three judges.

Court of First Instance

Vertical Stare Decisis

The Court of First Instance (CFI) is bound by decisions of the CA[186] and the CFA.[187] Where an earlier decision of the CA has been overruled or undermined by a later decision of a higher court (Privy Council pre-July 1997, and now the CFA), then it appears that the CFI should follow the decision

---

and Gunn on the *Modern English Legal System*, 5th ed. (London: Sweet and Maxwell 2007), para. 7-024.

[182] *R* v. *Parole Board; ex parte Wilson* [1991] 1 QB 740, at 755. Cf *Ng Yuen-Shiu* v. *Attorney General* [1981] HKLR 352.

[183] *Secretary for Justice* v. *Wong Sau Fong* [1998] 3 HKC 544, at 552. A full court in this context refers to a court where more than the usual number of judges sit. Five judges sitting in the Court of Appeal would constitute a full court.

[184] E.g., *R* v. *Gould* [1968] 2 QB 65.

[185] See *Davis* v. *Johnson* [1979] AC 264.

[186] E.g., see *Chan Yuen Yee* v. *Chan Chuck Kwong* [2005] 2 HKLRD 416, at 422.

[187] Cf. *Huddersfield Police Authority* v. *Watson* [1947] KB 842, at 848.

of the higher court.[188] Where a judge in the CFI is of the opinion that the CA has wrongly interpreted or applied a decision of a higher court,[189] the judge is still required to apply the decision of the CA.[190] However, where the CA's decision was made without reference to the earlier decision of the higher court, there is a possibility that the *per incuriam* exception could be applied so that the CFI would not be bound by the CA's decision.[191] It appears that there is also an exception which can be applied in an application to strike out a claim where the application is based on a particular decision of the CA which is under appeal. In this situation, the CFI need not be bound by the CA's decision and can in its discretion refuse to strike out the claim on the basis that, having regard to the possibility that the CA's decision might be reversed on appeal, the facts do potentially give rise to a cause of action.[192]

Where there is conflict between two decisions of the CA (or conflict between two decisions of the CFA), it appears that the CFI would apply the general rule that where there are conflicting decisions of courts of co-ordinate jurisdiction, the later decision is to be preferred if it was reached after full consideration of the earlier decision.[193]

Horizontal Stare Decisis

In contrast to the position of the CA, the CFI is not bound by its own decisions.[194] The courts have not often stated the reason for the divergent practice, but such an approach reflects the fact that decisions of the appeal courts or higher courts are to command greater respect than decisions of trial judges or single judges at first instance. Although the CFI is not bound by its own decisions, judges in the court would, as a matter of judicial comity and to avoid problems of uncertainty, generally follow the previous

---

[188] *Commissioner of Inland Revenue* v. *Indosuez W I Carr Securities Ltd* [2002] 1 HKLRD 308, at 330–331.
[189] I.e., the Privy Council before 1 July 1997, and the CFA after that date.
[190] See the comments of Lord Simon in *Miliangos* v. *George Frank (Textiles) Ltd* [1975] 3 All ER 801.
[191] See the discussion of 'per incuriam' earlier in this chapter.
[192] *Derby & Co Ltd* v. *Weldon (No. 3)* [1989] 3 All ER 118.
[193] See *Minister of Pensions* v. *Higham* [1948] 2 KB 153; *Cabaya* v. *Kwan So Han Sandy* [2004] 3 HKC 87.
[194] See, e.g., *Yau Shun-po* v. *Oriental Fire Insurance Co Ltd* [1986] HKLR 72; *Building Authority* v. *Business Rights Ltd* [1999] 3 HKC 247, at 251.

decisions of other judges of the court,[195] and would only depart from a prior decision where the judge is convinced that the earlier decision is wrong.[196] Where there is conflict between two earlier judgments of the court where the second was given in ignorance of the first, then a judge in the instant case would need to choose between them and not start with any preference for one over the other; however, it has been said that where the later judgment was made after full consideration of the first, then the second decision should normally be followed, unless the third judge is convinced that the second judge was wrong not to follow the first (as where some binding or persuasive authority was not cited in either of the first two cases).[197]

In England, it has been suggested that where the court is exercising appellate jurisdiction, then its decisions are binding, similar to the position of the CA.[198] However, this approach has not been adopted in Hong Kong.[199]

Inferior Courts and the Tribunals
Vertical Stare Decisis

Magistracies are bound by decisions of the CFI,[200] CA and CFA.[201] The District Court would at least be bound by decisions of the CA and CFA. It is not entirely clear whether decisions of the CFI are binding on the District Court. In *Incorporated Owners of Tropicana Gardens* v. *Tropicana Gardens Management Ltd*,[202] it was noted that the District Court would be bound by the Court of First Instance. However, the District Court in *R* v. *Kwong Kui*

---

[195] See, e.g., *Lui Hau Man* v. *Director of Immigration* (unreported, CFI, HCAL134/2002, 21 January 2003).
[196] See *Mobil Petroleum Co Inc* v. *Registrar of Trade Marks* [2000] 4 HKC 670, at 681; *Lee Yih Jen* v. *Chung Newspapers Ltd* [1983] 2 HKC 550, at 552.
[197] See *Attorney General* v. *Gardiner* [1987] HKLR 22; *Cabaya* v. *Kwan So Han Sandy* [2004] 3 HKC 87.
[198] *Huddersfield Police Authority* v. *Watson* [1947] KB 842.
[199] *Attorney General* v. *Gardiner* [1987] HKLR 22; *Kwong Pak-yam* v. *R* [1965] HKLR 931.
[200] See, e.g., *Owen John Inglis* v. *Loh Lai Kuen* (unreported, CFI, HCAL 74/2004, 15 October 2004); affirmed on appeal (unreported, CA, CACV 341/2004, 21 July 2005). If two decisions of the court conflict, then the later decision would be preferred: *Attorney General* v. *Gardiner* [1987] HKLR 22.
[201] See *Gu Chu Kwong* v. *R* (1952) 36 HKLR 353.
[202] [2001] 4 HKC 90, at 95.

Wing[203] was inclined towards the view that the court is not so bound by reason that appeals from the court go to the CA rather than the CFI.[204]

Tribunals are generally bound by the decisions of all the superior courts on the basis that the superior courts have supervisory jurisdiction over the tribunals.[205] Where the inferior court or tribunal is faced with conflicting decisions of the superior courts of co-ordinate jurisdiction, then the general rule is to apply the later decision if that had been reached after full consideration of the earlier decision.[206]

Horizontal Stare Decisis

Inferior courts[207] and the tribunals[208] are not bound by their own decisions. It has been said, though, that the decision of a District Court judge made in the exercise of appellate jurisdiction would be binding, similar to the approach of the CA[209]; however, this would be inconsistent with the approach of the CFI in relation to that court's appellate jurisdiction. In any event, the judicial comity principle should also be applicable to inferior courts and tribunals.

---

[203] [1996] 6 HKPLR 125, at 130–131. The court did accept though that judicial comity would still require the District Court to follow decisions of the High Court (now CFI), unless convinced that they were wrong.

[204] Cross and Harris have stated that the prevailing view is that the inferior courts are bound by the High Court (English equivalent of the Court of First Instance). The learned authors do accept that the opposing view might be arguable, but observe that 'the argument has only been advanced most tentatively': see Cross and Harris (n. 131), p. 123.

[205] See, e.g., *Lui Tat Hang Louis* v. *The Post-Release Supervision Board, Commissioner of Correctional Services* (unreported, CFI, HCAL154/1999, 14 February 2000); *Chief Supplementary Benefit Officer* v. *Leary* [1985] 1 All ER 1061 (but where the High Court does not have supervisory jurisdiction over a tribunal but only has a narrower jurisdiction conferred under statute, then a subsequent transfer of that jurisdiction to the tribunal meant that the tribunal would not be bound by the decisions of the High Court previously made in exercise of the limited jurisdiction).

[206] Cf. *Attorney General* v. *Gardiner* [1987] HKLR 22.

[207] District Court: see *Liu Chi Cheung* v. *Tsang Wai Choi* [1958] HKDCLR 165; *Incorporated Owners of Tropicana Gardens* v. *Tropicana Gardens Management Ltd* [2001] 4 HKC 90, at 95.

[208] *Wells* v. *Derwent Plastics Ltd* [1978] ICR 424; *Anandarajah* v. *Lord Chancellor's Department* (1984) IRLR 131.

[209] *Tsang Shiu Tim* v. *Hang Fong* [1959] HKLR 308; and see *Incorporated Owners of Tropicana Gardens* v. *Tropicana Gardens Management Ltd* [2001] 4 HKC 90, at 95.

The Standing Committee of the National People's Congress

The NPCSC has the power to interpret the provisions of the Basic Law, pursuant to article 158. While the NPCSC is not a court, interpretations of the Basic Law given by the NPCSC in accordance with article 158 are binding on all the courts in Hong Kong, including the CFA.[210]

Avoiding Precedents

Although a court may prima facie be bound by the earlier decisions of another court (pursuant to the principles of vertical and horizontal *stare decisis* discussed earlier), there are various grounds for the court to legitimately decline to follow the earlier decision. Situations where an earlier decision or a part of the decision is not binding include the following:

- Where the proposition of law set out in a judgment was simply assumed to be correct by the court, there not having been any argument before the court on the point.[211]
- Where the proposition of law was given by way of *obiter* and does not form part of the *ratio* of the case.[212]
- Where the decision is inconsistent with legislation that has been subsequently enacted.[213]
- Where it is clear that the court in the previous decision had wrongly interpreted the plain words of a statute.[214] This exception applies because the courts must give effect to the legislative intention, and so if there is a conflict between the meaning of a statute and a prior court's interpretation of the statute, the clear words of the statute must prevail.[215]

---

[210] *Ng Ka Ling* v. *Director of Immigration (No. 2)* (1999) 2 HKCFAR 141, [1999] 1 HKLRD 577; *Lau Kong Yung* v. *Director of Immigration* (1999) 2 HKCFAR 300, [1999] 4 HKC 731; *Yau Wai Ching* v. *Chief Executive of HKSAR* (2017) 20 HKCFAR 390, at para. 35.

[211] *Attorney General* v. *Sham Chuen* [1986] HKLR 365; *Baker* v. *R* [1975] AC 774.

[212] See Chapter 4.

[213] E.g., see *Secretary for Justice* v. *Wong Sau Fong* [1998] 3 HKC 544.

[214] *Re CKJW* (unreported, CFI, HCMP 5231/2001, 10 December 2001); *Lau Chu* v. *Lau Tang Su-ping* [1989] 2 HKLR 470, at 484; *Ogden Industries Pty Ltd* v. *Lucas* [1970] AC 113, at 127.

[215] *Bourne* v. *Keane* [1919] AC 815, at 874.

- Where the precedent can be distinguished on the facts of the instant case before the court. That is, where there is a material difference between the facts of the present case and the facts of the earlier decision such that it would be inappropriate to apply the legal principle from the earlier case, then although the earlier decision is still good law, the decision can be distinguished and would not be applicable in the present case. For example, in *Hoi Kong Container Services Co Ltd* v. *Bewise Motors Co Ltd*,[216] the defendant was a freight forwarder company which had contracted with the plaintiff to ship four motor vehicles to China. The cars were stolen from the defendant's depot on the evening before shipment. The defendant could have been liable if it was negligent in allowing the theft to occur, but it sought to rely on an exemption clause contained in its standard terms excluding liability for negligence. A quotation given by the defendant to the plaintiff prior to contracting had indicated that the contract would be subject to the standard terms, but the actual content of the terms had not been brought to the attention of the plaintiff. English cases such as *Hollier* v. *Rambler Motors (AMC) Ltd*[217] had indicated that an exemption clause which was particularly onerous would need to be specifically brought to the attention of the other party to the contract before the clause would be regarded as properly incorporated into the contract by reference or by notice. However, Bokhary PJ in the Court of Appeal, in holding that the clause was properly incorporated, distinguished those cases on the grounds of two material differences in the facts: (1) those earlier cases dealt with contracts with consumers, while in this case, the contract was between two commercial parties; and (2) the exclusion clause was common in the trade and was neither onerous nor unusual.

Status of English and Overseas Decisions under the Basic Law

Decisions of the Privy Council handed down since 1 July 1997 would not be binding in Hong Kong.[218] However, decisions of the Privy Council on

---

[216] [1997] 2 HKC 615.
[217] [1972] 2 QB 71.
[218] *A Solicitor (24/07)* v. *Law Society of Hong Kong* (2008) 11 HKCFAR 117, [2008] 2 HKC 1, at para. 17. The reason is because the Privy Council is no longer in the hierarchy of Hong

appeal from Hong Kong prior to 1 July 1997, being part of the pre-existing law of Hong Kong preserved by Basic Law articles 8 and 18,[219] continue to be binding in Hong Kong.[220] Where the Privy Council was deciding in relation to a case on appeal from another jurisdiction (e.g., New Zealand), the Privy Council decision would not have been binding in Hong Kong before 1 July 1997, and likewise would not be binding today.[221] However, if the Privy Council decision on appeal from another jurisdiction dealt with a matter that was not peculiar to that particular jurisdiction and there are no real grounds for distinction between the law of that jurisdiction and the law in Hong Kong, then the Privy Council decision would have such a strong persuasive authority that the courts in Hong Kong would have invariably followed it before 1 July 1997.[222]

The Court of Final Appeal is not bound by any of the Privy Council decisions on the basis that the highest appeal court is not bound by its own decisions or those of its predecessor (the Privy Council).[223]

Prior to 1 July 1997, decisions of the House of Lords were not strictly binding on the courts in Hong Kong as cases in Hong Kong have never gone to the House of Lords, with the House of Lords being in a different hierarchy of courts.[224] However, where the matter dealt with a principle of English common law that would be applicable in Hong Kong, then the Privy Council would regard itself as bound by the House of Lords, as the House of Lords is the highest court which settles the principles of

---

Kong courts and '[t]he existence of an appeal is inherent in and essential to the doctrine [of precedent]' (see *Viro* v. *R* (1978) 141 CLR 88). See further P. Wesley-Smith, 'The Common Law of England in the Special Administrative Region', in R. Wacks (ed.) *Hong Kong, China and 1997: Essays in Legal Theory* (Hong Kong: Hong Kong University Press 1993), pp. 5–40.

[219] See Chapter 4.
[220] *A Solicitor (24/07)* v. *Law Society of Hong Kong* (2008) 11 HKCFAR 117, [2008] 2 HKC 1, at paras. 7–8.
[221] *A Solicitor (24/07)* v. *Law Society of Hong Kong* (2008) 11 HKCFAR 117, [2008] 2 HKC 1, at paras. 6–11. This is because the Privy Council in these situations is sitting as the final appellate court in a different hierarchy of courts and not that of Hong Kong.
[222] Ibid., at para. 14. See also *Fatuma Binti Mohhamed Bin Salim Bakhshuwen* v. *Mohamed Bin Salim Bakhshuwen* [1952] AC 1.
[223] Ibid., at para. 18.
[224] *De Lasala* v. *De Lasala* [1980] AC 546; *Australian Consolidated Press Ltd* v. *Uren* [1969] 1 AC 590; *Invercargill City Council* v. *Hamlin* [1996] 1 All ER 756.

English common law.²²⁵ Thus, decisions of the House of Lords would invariably be applied in Hong Kong on the basis of their strong persuasive authority,²²⁶ unless there were reasons for a particular principle of the common law to develop differently in Hong Kong compared with England by reason of particular conditions or policy concerns specific to Hong Kong. House of Lords decisions handed down after 1 July 1997 would no longer be automatically applied in that way.²²⁷ With the establishment of the Supreme Court of the United Kingdom,²²⁸ which took over the appellate jurisdiction of the House of Lords from 1 October 2009, decisions of the Supreme Court should be treated in the same way in Hong Kong as post-1 July 1997 decisions of the House of Lords.

Persuasive Authorities

Although a case is not strictly binding on a particular court, the court may regard the prior decision as being of persuasive authority and take into account the approach adopted in that earlier case. An authority which is persuasive but not binding need not be followed by the court, but the court can choose to follow that decision depending on the strength of the arguments supporting the principles enunciated in that decision and depending on the status of the court (or particular judge) that handed down the earlier decision. A lower court might, for instance, give great weight to the *obiter* statements of the highest appeal court, even though those statements are not strictly binding.

---

²²⁵ *Tai Hing Cotton Mill Ltd* v. *Liu Chong Hing Bank Ltd* [1985] 2 All ER 947; *Invercargill City Council* v. *Hamlin* [1996] 1 All ER 756.
²²⁶ *A Solicitor (24/07)* v. *Law Society of Hong Kong* (2008) 11 HKCFAR 117, [2008] 2 HKC 1, at para. 15.
²²⁷ Ibid., at para. 17.
²²⁸ Established under the Constitutional Reform Act 2005 (UK). On the background to the establishment of the Supreme Court, see Department for Constitutional Affairs (UK), *Constitutional Reform: A Supreme Court for the United Kingdom – Consultation Paper* (Department for Constitutional Affairs July 2003); Department for Constitutional Affairs (UK), *Constitutional Reform: A Supreme Court for the United Kingdom – Summary of Responses to the Consultation Paper* (Department for Constitutional Affairs January 2004).

In the absence of any relevant Court of Final Appeal authority, decisions of the Privy Council or House of Lords handed down after 1 July 1997 would still command great respect. It is likely that decisions of the Supreme Court of the United Kingdom will have strong persuasive authority similar to that previously accorded to the House of Lords. Decisions of the English Court of Appeal and the High Court of Justice in England have never been binding on Hong Kong courts[229]; however, they will be regarded as being of persuasive authority[230] and will be followed in Hong Kong unless there are good reasons for the law in Hong Kong to diverge.[231] Nonetheless, the persuasive effect of English decisions after 1 July 1997 would depend on all the relevant circumstances, including the nature of the issue and the similarity of any relevant statutory or constitutional provision; and at the end of the day, the courts in Hong Kong must decide for themselves what is appropriate for their own jurisdiction.[232]

Cases decided by courts in other common law jurisdictions, such as Australia, Canada and New Zealand, can also be of persuasive authority. Article 84 of the Basic Law confirms that Hong Kong courts can refer to precedents of other common law jurisdictions.[233] As jurisdictions such as Australia and Canada have abolished appeals to the Privy Council for a longer period of time than Hong Kong, there has been greater divergence from England in the development of some areas of the common law in those jurisdictions than is the case in Hong Kong. However, it may be that Hong Kong courts will be prepared in future to give greater weight to decisions in these other jurisdictions compared with the position pre-1 July 1997.

The United States is also a common law jurisdiction, and American case law can also be relevant for Hong Kong. However, there are some areas of the law where the US case law has departed significantly from the common law of England and Commonwealth countries and so cases in those areas will be of limited relevance to the common law in Hong Kong.

---

[229] *Attorney General for Hong Kong* v. *Reid* [1994] 1 AC 324.
[230] *Yeung Wing* v. *VSL Engineers (Hong Kong)* [1981] HKLR 130, at 134.
[231] *Shun Kai Finance Co Ltd* v. *Japan Leasing (HK) Ltd (in liq) (No. 2)* [2001] 1 HKC 636.
[232] *A Solicitor (24/07)* v. *Law Society of Hong Kong* (2008) 11 HKCFAR 117, [2008] 2 HKC 1, at 17. See also *China Field Ltd* v. *Appeal Tribunal (Buildings)* [2009] 5 HKC 231.
[233] See also *ZN* v. *Secretary for Justice* [2017] 1 HKC 340, at para. 190.

Review Questions

(1) Martin wishes to sue Christina for breach of contract to recover damages in the amount of $3 million. In which court should Martin commence legal proceedings?

(2) To what extent has the system of courts in Hong Kong under British rule before 1 July 1997 remained the same following the return of sovereignty to the PRC on 1 July 1997?

(3) What are vertical *stare decisis* and horizontal *stare decisis*?

(4) Critically discuss the rationales for a doctrine of precedent.

(5) What are the arguments for and against prospective overruling? Do you think it is appropriate for the court to order that its decision should only have effect prospectively?

(6) What are the ways in which a court can decline to follow a previous decision that has been handed down?

(7) You are a judge hearing a case in the Court of First Instance. Assume that the following decisions set out legal principles under the common law relevant to the case. Are you bound by any of the following decisions? If any of these decisions are not binding on you, would you be entitled to follow those decisions anyway? Give reasons for your answers.

(a) *Automatic Self-Cleansing Filter* v. *Cuninghame* [1906] 2 Ch 34 (English Court of Appeal);

(b) *Howard Smith Ltd* v. *Ampol Petroleum Ltd* [1974] AC 821 (Privy Council – on appeal from Australia, agreeing with *Automatic Self-Cleansing Filter* v. *Cuninghame* by way of *obiter*);

(c) *Broadview Commodities Pte Ltd* v. *Broadview Finance Ltd* [1983] 2 HKC 578 (High Court in Hong Kong, applying *Automatic Self-Cleansing Filter* v. *Cuninghame*);

(d) *Tang Kam-yip* v. *Yau Kung School* [1986] 1 HKLR 448 (Court of Appeal in Hong Kong disagreeing with *Automatic Self-Cleansing Filter* v. *Cuninghame* by way of *obiter*).

(8) You are a judge hearing a case in the District Court. Assume that the following decisions set out legal principles under the common law relevant to the case. Are you bound by any of the following decisions? If any of these decisions are not binding on you, would you be entitled to follow those decisions anyway? Would your answers

to the foregoing differ if you were a judge hearing the case in the Court of Final Appeal? Give reasons for your answers.

(a) *Siebe Gorman and Co Ltd* v. *Barclays Bank Ltd* [1979] 2 Lloyd's Rep 142 (English decision of a single judge of the Chancery Division);

(b) *State Bank of India* v. *Lisbellaw Ltd* [1989] 2 HKLR 604 (High Court in Hong Kong, applying *Siebe Gorman and Co Ltd* v. *Barclays Bank Ltd*);

(c) *Re Spectrum Plus Ltd (in liq)* [2005] 2 AC 680 (House of Lords, overruling *Siebe Gorman and Co Ltd* v. *Barclays Bank Ltd*).

The Process of Legislation 6

Chapter Highlights

- Why Have New Laws? 183
- The Authority to Create Legislation 185
- The Passage of Primary Legislation 191
- The Making of Subsidiary Legislation 196

Previous chapters of this book have focused on the different types of law and the jurisprudential enquiry of 'what is law?', and Chapter 4 specifically focuses on the sources of law in Hong Kong. One of these sources is statute law. This is the name traditionally given within the English legal system to law passed by the legislative branch of government (in Hong Kong, the Legislative Council). This chapter will discuss the reasons for creating laws and the authority in Hong Kong to do so, ending with the process of the passage of primary and subsidiary legislation.

Why Have New Laws?

Roman senator and historian Cornelius Tacitus observed that 'It is found by experience that admirable laws and right precedents among the good have their origin in the misdeeds of others.'[1] The process of legislation usually begins with the recognition of the need to implement some new law or to amend existing law. This could come from social events, public opinion, political promises or recommendations from the Law Reform Commission. For example, after a series of calls in Hong Kong and by international

---

[1] Cornelius Tacitus (55–117 AD).

bodies such as the United Nations Committee on the Rights of the Child to raise the age of criminal responsibility in Hong Kong (which was previously age seven), the Law Reform Commission recommended that the age of criminal responsibility be raised to ten.[2] Subsequently, the Government adopted the change, amending the age of criminal responsibility from seven to ten.[3]

The Purposes of Legislation

The major purposes of legislation are as follows.

- To Create Law

    This involves creating law on a new subject. One example is the Bill of Rights Ordinance,[4] which involved the creation of a charter of civil and political rights for the HKSAR reflecting the contemporaneous desire in the community for the creation of such a charter.

- To Codify Law

    The codification of law requires skill in interpretation and legislative drafting as it involves the creation of an exhaustive statement on a particular area of law. This involves the synthesis of statute law, common law principles and case law precedents into a 'code' of law on a particular subject upon which nothing else needs to be consulted in determining the law on that subject. An example of a Hong Kong Ordinance that is the codification of a subject of law is the Bills of Exchange Ordinance.[5] Statute law in civil law systems is all codified for reasons of certainty and consistency. Many countries following in the English legal tradition also have some codified law; for example, both the Commonwealth Government of Australia and some of the Australian State jurisdictions have a criminal code.[6]

---

[2] See Law Reform Commission of Hong Kong, *The Age of Criminal Responsibility in Hong Kong (HKLRC Report)* (Hong Kong: Law Reform Commission of Hong Kong 2000).

[3] Juvenile Offenders (Amendment) Ordinance (6 of 2003); the amendment changed Juvenile Offenders Ordinance (Cap. 226), s. 3 and Reformatory Schools Ordinance (Cap. 225), s. 2.

[4] Bill of Rights Ordinance (Cap. 383).

[5] Bills of Exchange Ordinance (Cap. 19).

[6] See Criminal Code Act 1995 (Cth); Criminal Code Act 1899 (Qld); Criminal Code Act Compilation Act 1913 (WA).

- To Consolidate Law

    This process involves the synthesis of various related laws under one new law. Unlike the codification of law, it is not the creation of an exhaustive statement of the law; it is merely the re-grouping of existing law under a new and consolidated title. An example is the Landlord and Tenant (Consolidation) Ordinance,[7] which consolidated previous laws regarding tenancies, the relationship between landlords and tenants, and rent issues.

- To Amend Existing Law

    This process reflects the dynamic requirement of law and allows the legislative body to extend or update an existing law to bring it into line with the requirements of the community. See the Employment (Amendment) Ordinance as an example.[8] This amended ordinance reflected the desire to include all wages (including commissions, allowances and tips) for calculation of statutory entitlements such as holiday pay, annual leave pay and maternity leave pay.[9]

The Authority to Create Legislation

The creation of legislation requires legitimate authority. The paramount law in Hong Kong is the Basic Law, and it plays a significant role in the creation, authorisation and legitimisation of legislation in Hong Kong. Before any legislation is created, the constitutional order of Hong Kong contemplated by the Basic Law needs to be considered. Articles 8 and 18 of the Basic Law operate so that the law in force in the HKSAR prior to the 30 June 1997 handover continues to be part of the law in Hong Kong after that date. The Basic Law thus legitimises the legislation in force in Hong Kong, though it also qualifies the application of pre-existing legislation (namely that any such laws which contravene the Basic Law would not be preserved).[10] The Basic Law also sets out how existing legislation can be altered and amended.[11]

---

[7] Landlord and Tenant (Consolidation) Ordinance (Cap. 7).
[8] Employment (Amendment) Ordinance (51 of 2000).
[9] See Labour Department, *A Concise Guide to the Employment (Amendment) Ordinance 2007* (Hong Kong: Labour Department 2007).
[10] Basic Law, art. 8.
[11] See the discussion below.

The Basic Law also vests the exclusive right to enact legislation in the Legislative Council. This right is so vested by the line 'The Legislative Council of the Hong Kong Special Administrative Region shall be the legislature of the Region.'[12] The use of the words 'shall be'[13] as opposed to 'may be', 'might be' or 'can be' makes this vesting of power an exclusive right so that no other body in the HKSAR can enact legislation. The Basic Law further describes this power in article 73(1), which empowers the Legislative Council to 'enact, amend or repeal laws in accordance with the provisions of this Law and legal procedures'.[14] Article 18 specifies that the laws enacted by the legislature of the Region also form part of the law in Hong Kong.

There are, however, practical and legal limitations on this power vested in the Legislative Council. The first of these is a very obvious territorial restriction. The Legislative Council has power only to make law with respect to the HKSAR. There are also limitations placed on the Legislative Council to create law with respect to foreign affairs arising from the division of authority between the HKSAR and the Central People's Government of China. Article 13 of the Basic Law provides that the Central People's Government is responsible for 'foreign affairs' relating to the HKSAR. The notion of foreign affairs in a constitutional sense involves the relationship between one's own and a 'foreign' sovereign. Article 13 also states that the Central People's Government authorises the Hong Kong Special Administrative Region to conduct relevant external affairs on its own in accordance with the Basic Law.

A similar restraint on the power to legislate exists in the area of national defence. Article 14 of the Basic Law provides that the Central People's Government is responsible for national defence and the expenditure of the garrison. The administration of Hong Kong is, however, able to legislate in accordance with its responsibilities to maintain public order in the region, and the Basic Law provides that the military presence of the PRC within Hong Kong will not interfere in the local affairs of Hong Kong.[15]

The limitation on legislative authority provided by the Basic Law is furthered by article 11. This article operates with article 31 of the Constitution of the People's Republic of China to ensure that any law passed will

---

[12] Basic Law, art. 66.
[13] Ibid.
[14] Basic Law, art. 73(1).
[15] Basic Law, art. 14.

not contravene the Basic Law or transgress its limitations. Such a law will be null and void.

Has This Limitation Been Tested?

From time to time, the constitutionality of particular legislation has been challenged in the courts. For example, the case of HKSAR v. *Ng Kung Siu & Another*[16] tested whether or not a law prohibiting a case of national and regional flag desecration for a protest was made within the constitutional limits of the Basic Law. This was a criminal case where charges were brought against the defendants under the National Flag Ordinance[17] and the Regional Flag Ordinance.[18] The defendants argued that the law contravened the freedom of expression provided by article 19 of the International Covenant on Civil and Political Rights.[19] It was argued that freedom of expression was one of the fundamental freedoms of civil society in Hong Kong and that the court had to give a broad reading of the constitutional guarantee of this right under article 39 of the Basic Law. In this case, the legislation was held to be valid and the defendants were convicted, as the court considered that the restriction on freedom of expression under the legislation was necessary and proportionate for the protection of public order.[20] The defendants were free to express their opinion in a number of other ways that did not threaten public order.[21] While this approach is supported by some international precedents,[22] there is also an alternative approach adopted by various overseas countries which give greater protection to freedom of expression in that even though there are more effective ways of making a point than desecrating a national flag, boorish and offensive desecration can still be tolerated as an act of expression.

---

[16] (1999) 2 HKCFAR 442, [1999] 3 HKLRD 907.
[17] National Flag and National Emblem Ordinance (No. 116 of 1997), s. 7.
[18] Regional Flag and Regional Emblem Ordinance (No. 117 of 1997), s. 7.
[19] The International Covenant on Civil and Political Rights is applied in Hong Kong by the Hong Kong Bill of Rights Ordinance (Cap. 383), as required by article 39 of the Basic Law. See article 16 of the Hong Kong Bill of Rights.
[20] The Court of Final Appeal relied on the test of necessity and proportionality from the precedent case: *Ming Pao Newspapers Ltd* v. *Attorney General* [1998] AC 906.
[21] As contemplated by art. 19(3) of the International Covenant on Civil and Political Rights.
[22] See *Texas* v. *Johnson* (1989) 491 US 397; *United States* v. *Eichman* (1990) 496 US 310; *Re Paris Renato*, Judgment No. 1218 of the Corte Suprema di Cassazione, General Registry No. 3355 of 1988; 81 *Entscheidungen des Bindesverfassungsgericht* 27 (FRG) (German Flag Desecration Case).

Another example of a case where the constitutionality of legislation was challenged is Secretary for Justice v. Yau Yuk Lung.[23] The case dealt with section 118F(1) of the Crimes Ordinance,[24] which provided that: 'A man who commits buggery with another man otherwise than in private shall be guilty of an offence.' The defendants were charged under section 118F(1) and the magistrate dismissed the charges on the basis that the provision was unconstitutional. On appeal, the Court of Final Appeal agreed. Article 25 of the Basic Law provides that all Hong Kong residents shall be equal before the law. Further, article 22 of the Hong Kong Bill of Rights[25] provides that 'the law shall prohibit any discrimination and guarantee to all persons equal and effective protection against discrimination on any ground such as race, colour, sex, language, religion, political or other opinion, national or social origin, property, birth or other status'. The Court of Final Appeal held that section 118F(1) discriminated on the ground of sexual orientation, since homosexuals alone were subject to the offence whilst heterosexuals were subject to no comparable criminal liability in relation to vaginal intercourse or buggery.[26] The court accepted that the guarantee of equality before the law does not invariably require exact equality, since differences in legal treatment might be justified for good reason.[27] However, in the present case, the differential treatment cannot be said to pursue any legitimate, and accordingly section 118F(1) was unconstitutional and invalid under both article 25 of the Basic Law and article 22 of the Bill of Rights.[28]

The Role of the Chief Executive

The Chief Executive of Hong Kong plays an important constitutional role in the validation of legislation. This role is outlined in the Basic Law and can be said to be part of the constitutional legacy of British Westminster convention.[29] For example, article 49 of the Basic Law authorises the Chief

---

[23] (2007) 10 HKCFAR 335.
[24] Crimes Ordinance (Cap. 200).
[25] Hong Kong Bill of Rights Ordinance (Cap. 383).
[26] (2007) 10 HKCFAR 335 at para. 24.
[27] (2007) 10 HKCFAR 335 at para. 20.
[28] (2007) 10 HKCFAR 335 at paras. 25–30.
[29] For a detailed description of the Westminster model and the British political conventions it requires, see W. Bagehot, *The English Constitution* (London: Fontana 1963 [1867]), p. 61.

Executive to determine that a bill passed by the Legislative Council is or is not compatible with the overall interests of the region. If the Chief Executive finds that the bill is not compatible, he/she may return it to the Legislative Council for amendment or reconsideration within three months. If the bill is again passed by a two-thirds majority of the Legislative Council, the Chief Executive may do one of two things. Firstly, in accordance with article 49, the Chief Executive may choose to sign and promulgate the bill. If the Chief Executive does not wish to do so, then there is an effectual deadlock. This deadlock is resolved by article 50, which provides that, in the instance of such a deadlock, the Chief Executive, with consultation of the Executive Council, may dissolve the Legislative Council (but this can only be done once in each term of his/her office).

The effect of these two provisions is that, in controversial legislative matters, the Chief Executive wields an ultimate power to dissolve a recalcitrant Legislative Council once in a term of office. This offers a check and balance on the legislative authority of the Legislative Council which is pertinent to the Hong Kong system of a unicameral legislature.[30]

The Chief Executive, however, is also subject to limitations. We have already mentioned that the limit on exercising the 'deadlock power' is once in each term of office. Following such dissolution, if the bill is again passed by the Legislative Council and it appears that it is the Chief Executive and not the Legislative Council being non-compliant with the will of the region, article 52(2) of the Basic Law will force the resignation of the Chief Executive. Article 52(3) of the Basic Law works much in the same way if the Legislative Council refuses to pass a budget or an important bill of the Chief Executive's initiative following dissolution. This echoes the notion of responsible government inherited from the British legal system. Responsible government under the Westminster model requires a certain degree of confidence to be maintained between the executive and the legislature.[31]

The authority of the Chief Executive is also checked in the way that it is shared among the Executive Council. Article 56 of the Basic Law requires

---

[30] For comparison, see the deadlock provision of the Australian Constitution used in 1974 for the double dissolution of the Senate and Parliament led by Gough Whitlam. The relevant Australian High Court case for this example is *Cormack* v. *Cope* (1974) 131 CLR 432. See further 'Editorial: Public Interest Litigation and Constitutional Theory' (1992), *Modern Law Review* 55, 44.

[31] See S. Ratnapala, *Australian Constitutional Law: Foundations and Theory*, 3rd ed. (Oxford: Oxford University Press 2012), chapters 1 and 2.

that, except in cases of the employment of government officers and in emergency situations, the Chief Executive should consult the Executive Council on important matters of policy, the introduction of bills, the making of subsidiary legislation and the dissolution of the Legislative Council. In this way, the Executive Council and Chief Executive can be held, to a certain degree, collectively responsible for exercise of authority in relation to legislation. Where the Chief Executive differs in opinion and action from the Executive Council, his/her specific reasons for doing so must be put on record.[32]

The Role of the Courts

It is a fundamental feature of the doctrine of the separation of powers[33] that the role of the judiciary is to interpret, rather than to create, legislation. The courts have some latitude in their independent exercise of judicial power in that legislation may be read in broad or narrow terms[34]; however, the judicial function must be limited to that only. Sir Francis Bacon pointed out that 'Judges must beware of hard constructions and strained inferences, for there is no worse torture than the torture of laws.'[35]

The courts are unable to amend legislation due to interference with this doctrine. Occasional attempts by the judiciary to do so are widely criticised as judicial activism and usurping of the legislative power.[36] It is also in violation of the Basic Law, which vests legislative power solely with the Legislative Council[37].

However, apart from authority to interpret and apply legislation in resolving disputes, the courts also have power to declare legislation to be invalid where the court finds that the legislation is contrary to the Basic Law and hence unconstitutional.[38]

---

[32] See Basic Law, art. 56.
[33] See Chapter 3.
[34] Note the rules of statutory interpretation (see Chapter 7).
[35] Sir Francis Bacon (1561–1626).
[36] See K. D. Kmeic, 'The Origins and Current Meanings of Judicial Activism' (2004), *California Law Review* 92, 1441; M. Kirby, 'Lord Denning and Judicial Activism' (1999), Denning Law Journal 14, 127; A. D. Hellman, 'Judicial Activism: The Good, the Bad and the Ugly' (2002), *Mississippi College Law Review* 21, 253.
[37] Basic Law, art. 66.
[38] For example, see Secretary for Justice v Yau Yuk Lung (2007) 10 HKCFAR 335, discussed earlier in this chapter.

This power of the courts to invalidate legislation provides one of the mechanisms for checking the powers of the executive and the legislature in enacting laws.³⁹

The Passage of Primary Legislation

As discussed in Chapter 4, legislation in Hong Kong is either primary or secondary in nature. Primary legislation is, essentially, the traditional type of statute law created by a legislative process performed by the supreme legislature. It is a general term used to describe the main laws passed by the legislative body of a place, and it is usually collected in 'statute books'. In Hong Kong, the statute book comprises the statute law of Hong Kong, which is referred to as 'Ordinances'. A quick search on the Hong Kong e-Legislation (*HKeL*) database on the world wide web will reveal all of Hong Kong's legislation in both English and Chinese. Primary legislation also incorporates some statutory provisions of the People's Republic of China that are relevant to Hong Kong.⁴⁰

Ordinances are the result of the formal process of positing law through the legislative procedure in Hong Kong. Broadly speaking, the formal process consists of seven main stages, including (1) the proposal, (2) consultation papers, (3) producing a bill, (4) reading the bill in the Legislative Council, (5) the Chief Executive's signature and promulgation, (6) publication in the *Government Gazette* and (7) reporting to the NPCSC.⁴¹

The Proposal

This is the proposition that a law should be amended, created or repealed. Most proposals come from governmental departments in charge of policy areas. An example is the 2002 proposal from the Security Bureau for

---

³⁹ On the separation of powers, see Chapter 3.
⁴⁰ See I. Dobinson and D. Roebuck, *Introduction to Law in the Hong Kong SAR*, 2nd ed. (Hong Kong: Sweet & Maxwell Asia 2001).
⁴¹ For more details on the law-making process in Hong Kong, see Legislative Council Secretariat Education Service Team, *How Laws Are Made (Legislative Council in Brief No. 7)*. (Hong Kong: Legislative Council 2017) p. 4, available at www.legco.gov.hk/education/files/english/Factsheet/Factsheet7.pdf.

implementation of article 23 of the Basic Law.[42] The Security Bureau proposed that there is a need to legislate for article 23 of the Basic Law so that Hong Kong is able, in accordance with the necessary provisions of the Basic Law, to rely on legislation to protect national security. Another example of a proposal from a government department is the Immigration (Amendment) Bill 2000. This bill proposed a DNA testing process to legitimise the claims of Hong Kong residents to the right of abode.[43]

Proposals are also made via the Law Reform Commission.[44] As an attaché to the Department of Justice, the Law Reform Commission reviews the law and recommends amendments or proposals for new law. Individual citizens are also able to propose legislation, although this is usually done through an interest group to which the citizen belongs, or through local organisations attached to government such as the District Councils or Heung Yee Kuk.[45]

Consultation Papers

A consultation process may be initiated where the proposed law is of particular importance or if it is about sensitive policy directives. A usual consultation will involve the publication of consultation papers prepared by the Law Reform Commission or the particular Government body with which the proposal is chiefly concerned, or other information papers. These publications present information to the public and interested parties about the proposed issue to be legislated. The consultation process also acts as an invitation to the general public and concerned groups to make submissions within a set consultation period. An example of a consultation paper is the Consultation Document published by the Security Bureau in September 2002, 'Proposals to Implement Article 23 of the Basic Law'. Another example is the consultation paper presented by the Home Affairs Bureau in September 2004, 'Legislating Against Racial Discrimination'. This consultation paper arose from a proposed law to fulfil Hong Kong's

---

[42] Security Bureau, *Proposals to Implement Article 23 of the Basic Law: Consultation Document* (Hong Kong: Security Bureau 2002).
[43] Dobinson and Roebuck (n. 41), p. 36.
[44] Information on the role of the Law Reform Commission may be accessed on its website at www.hkreform.gov.hk.
[45] See Heung Yee Kuk Ordinance (Cap. 1097).

international obligations under the International Convention on the Elimination of All Forms of Racial Discrimination.

Producing a Bill

Once an area to be legislated has been accepted as a proposal, it is referred for drafting into what is known as a bill. Information obtained during the consultation process, if there is one, is included in this referral. A bill is a draft law and it is prepared in Hong Kong by the Law Drafting Division of the Department of Justice. In 2016 and 2017, the Law Drafting Division released 2,186 and 2,277 drafts of legislation respectively.[46] This drafting process is the same for bills that are creating new ordinances and those that are amending existing ordinances.

Bills are either public or private in nature. Public bills affect everyone in the Hong Kong community, such as the Immigration (Amendment) Bill 2000. Private bills concern the rights, duties and interests of only one class of persons (including legal persons such as associations and corporations).[47] There is sometimes a third category of bills: special bills. These involve the appropriation of funds for the cost of running government activities.

Once a bill has been drafted it is given to the Executive Council, where a vote is cast as to whether the bill should be presented to the Legislative Council. This is in accordance with article 56 of the Basic Law, which also provides that the Chief Executive presides over this Council and has final discretion as to whether the bill moves on to the Legislative Council. There is a possibility that this process requiring Executive consent for the bill to move to the Legislative Council may be bypassed by virtue of article 74 of the Basic Law. Article 74 provides that a member of the Legislative Council may present a bill on his or her own initiative. If this process is followed, the bill is referred to as a member's bill. Restrictions exist on the type of bills that may be introduced through article 74; they cannot relate to public expenditure, government operations or the political structure of

---

[46] Department of Justice, *Statistics: Law Drafting Division* (Hong Kong: Department of Justice 2018), available at www.doj.gov.hk/eng/about/stat.html.
[47] See Private Bills Ordinance (Cap. 69), s. 2.

Table 6.1 Number of member's bills passed

	2015–2016	2016–2017	2017–2018
New bills introduced by Government	18	29	23
New bills introduced by members	1	1	1
Government bills passed	17	12	27
Members' bill passed	1	1	1

The statistics are derived from the Legislative Council's annual reports. See *Legislative Council Annual Report 2015-2016* (Hong Kong: Legislative Council 2017), p. 20; *Legislative Council Annual Report 2016-2017* (Hong Kong: Legislative Council 2018), p. 26; *Legislative Council Annual Report 2017-2018* (Hong Kong: Legislative Council 2019), p. 22.

the region.[48] If the member's bill does relate to government policy, there must still be approval by the Chief Executive.[49]

However, members of the Legislative Council introduced only twenty-nine members' bills in the period between 1998 and 2004. Only ten were allowed to be tabled. Two needed the Chief Executive's approval, which they eventually obtained. The rest were either struck out as involving government policy or public expenditure, or because the members who introduced the bill decided not to pursue them. These twelve bills represented a mere 2.6 per cent of the 456 bills that were tabled in this period (eleven of these twelve were members' bills).[50] The number of members' bills introduced and passed between 2015–2016 and 2017–2018 has remained very small (see Table 6.1 for more details).

Reading in the Legislative Council

Once a Bill has passed through the drafting process and is to move to the Legislative Council, it is published in the *Government Gazette* as notice that it will be considered. At this point, responsibility for law-making passes from the executive to the legislature, where the purpose and details of the legislation can be fine-tuned by representatives of the electorate. This is achieved through a series of readings.

---

[48] Rules of Procedure, r. 51(3).
[49] Rules of Procedure, r. 51(4).
[50] N. Ma, *Political Development in Hong Kong: State, Political Society, and Civil Society* (Hong Kong: Hong Kong University Press 2007), pp. 117–118.

1)
The first reading is effectually a notification only to the members that the bill is in existence and has started the journey through the legislative process. This is then followed, in accordance with the schedule of the Legislative Council, by the second reading, where the person who introduces the bill (either a government official or member) outlines to the Council the purposes of the bill. After the second reading, debate on the bill in the Legislative Council is adjourned and the bill is referred to the House Committee of the Legislative Council. Usually the House Committee then allocates the bill to a Bills Committee for closer scrutiny and examination of the provisions in the bill. In 2017–2018, of the twenty-three bills introduced, twenty Bills Committees were formed to scrutinise bills.[51] Once the Bills Committee has completed its scrutiny of the bill, the deliberations of the Bills Committee are reported to and considered by the House Committee. There is then resumption of second reading of the bill in the Legislative Council and the bill is then considered and debated by a committee of the whole Council. Any amendments to the Bill (referred to as committee stage amendments) are moved and voted on by members of the Council. Following the committee stage, the Council is resumed and the Bill is reported to the Council and is set down for a third reading. The third reading proceeds on a motion that the bill be read a third time. The bill is passed by the Council if the motion is agreed to. The passage of the bill turns on a vote where a simple majority must approve the passage of bills introduced by the government. For motions, bills or amendments to government bills introduced by members, a simple majority of the two groups present (functional and geographical constituencies) is needed.[52] Failing this, the bill would not be able to proceed.

Chief Executive's Signature and Promulgation

The bill as passed at the third reading is then presented to the Chief Executive for signature and promulgation.[53] The bill may take effect only after the Chief Executive finds that it is compatible with the overall interests of the region in accordance with article 49 of the Basic Law.

---

[51] *Legislative Council Annual Report 2017–2018* (Hong Kong: Legislative Council 2019), p. 51.
[52] Basic Law, Annex II.
[53] Basic Law, art. 76.

See earlier sections in this chapter for more information on the Chief Executive's role in the legislative process.

Publication in the *Government Gazette*

Once the Chief Executive signs and promulgates the bill, the law is published in the *Legal Supplement No. 1* of the *Government Gazette* and is, on the stated date or as default on the date of publication, an ordinance with legal force in Hong Kong.[54]

Report to the NPCSC

While the HKSAR is vested with legislative power, laws enacted by the Legislative Council must be reported to the NPCSC for the record. The reporting for record shall not affect the entry into force of such laws. Article 17 of the Basic Law provides that if the Standing Committee, after consultation with the Committee for the Basic Law of the Hong Kong Special Administrative Region, considers that a law enacted by the Legislative Council lacks conformity with the Basic Law regarding affairs within the responsibility of the Central Authorities (e.g., if the law relates to defence) or regarding the relationship between the Central Authorities and the Region, the Standing Committee can 'return the law' upon which it is immediately invalidated but the Standing Committee may not amend the law.

The Making of Subsidiary Legislation

Subsidiary legislation, also known as 'delegated' or 'subordinate' legislation, comprises the rules, regulations and by-laws created by delegates of the Legislative Council such as those from the executive branch of government who have been delegated with legislative authority.[55] The reason behind this is that the Legislative Council cannot enact all laws, and subsidiary legislation provides details to their 'parent' ordinances.

---

[54] See Interpretation and General Clauses Ordinance (Cap. 1) s. 20(2) about commencement of legislation.

[55] See Chapter 4.

Subsidiary legislation includes traffic regulations and the intricate rules relating to court procedure. An example of a parent ordinance and its subsidiary is the Mass Transit Railway Ordinance (Cap. 556) and the Regulations (Cap. 556A) and By-laws (Cap. 556B). The Mass Transit Railway Corporation Limited may make both regulations and by-laws to govern its operation.[56] In many respects, these rules and regulations command obedience and can impose sanctions and guide behaviour, but they do not follow the formal process of law-making by the legislature.

It is not difficult to see how the many rules that are required in a modern society to regulate the various and complex web of activities performed by persons cannot possibly be passed through the time-consuming formal process required by primary legislation. This is particularly true of the many thousands of simple guidelines that comprise subsidiary legislation. Subsidiary legislation covers such broad areas as the assessment rules for the pneumoconiosis compensation policy,[57] the fees chargeable by a coroner[58] and the licensing of estate agents.[59]

The pragmatism of subsidiary legislation is responsible for the efficacy of modern government. However, it is interesting to note some of the international litigation which, while recognising the pragmatic value of subsidiary legislation, challenges the constitutionality of the practice.

In Australia, the Constitution of Australia vests the legislative power solely in the legislature.[60] The Australian case of *Victorian Stevedoring & General Contracting Co Pty Ltd v. Dignan (Dignan's Case)*[61] challenged the validity of some employment regulations on the basis that they were made by the executive (a government department), which does not have legislative power, according to the Constitution. *Dignan's Case*[62] found that in Australia, a delegation of legislative power could be made to the executive so long as it did not amount to a total abdication of power.[63]

---

[56] See Mass Transit Railway Ordinance (Cap. 556), s. 33 and s. 34.
[57] Pneumoconiosis and Mesothelioma (Compensation) (Assessment of Levy) Regulations (Cap 360A).
[58] Coroners (Fees) Rules (Cap. 504D).
[59] Estate Agents (Licensing) Regulation (Cap. 511A).
[60] Commonwealth of Australia Constitution Act, Part V.
[61] (1931) 46 CLR 73.
[62] Ibid.
[63] Much of this turns on the unique federal constitutional history of Australia. For further inquiry, see F. Wheeler, 'Original Intent and the Doctrine of the Separation of Powers in

That judgment had much to do with the federal nature of the Australian system, yet the case raises an interesting point.

Recall article 66 of the Basic Law, which vests legislative power solely in the Legislative Council. Recall also the use of the words 'shall be', which indicate that it is the exclusive repository of the legislative power. How then can law made by the executive (through government departments) be valid legislation?

Subsidiary legislation is included in the law of Hong Kong in article 8 of the Basic Law, so it is clear that subsidiary legislation is intended to be valid. The answer to this question is provided by the ultra vires doctrine. Subsidiary legislation must stay within the strict bounds of the parent ordinance from which it derives its authority. Subsidiary legislation which transgresses those limits will be invalid and struck down as ultra vires.[64]

The passage of subsidiary legislation usually involves the preparation of a draft, which may or may not be subject to a consultation process before being submitted to the members of the executive branch of government and, very often, to the Chief Executive in Council.[65] If approved, the rules, regulations and by-laws are tabled in the Legislative Council and unless there is a motion in the Council to amend or reject them, they will automatically become law on the day it is published in the *Gazette* (or alternatively the subsidiary legislation may contain a provision stating another date for commencement of the subsidiary legislation). According to the positive vetting procedure, the Legislative Council has the power to approve and amend any subsidiary legislation which requires the Council's approval.[66] Under the negative vetting procedure, subsidiary legislation which is published the *Gazette* may be amended by a resolution passed at a Legislative Council meeting held not later than twenty-eight days after the meeting at which it was laid on the table of the Council. The vetting period, which refers to the period of scrutinising and amending subsidiary legislation, may also be extended by a resolution passed at the Council meeting before its expiry.[67]

Australia' (1996), *Public Law Review* 7, 96; D. Meyerson, 'Re-thinking the Constitutionality of Delegated Legislation' (2003), *Australian Journal of Administrative Law* 11(1), 45.

[64] P. Wesley-Smith, *An Introduction to the Hong Kong Legal System* (3rd ed.) (Hong Kong: Oxford University Press 1998), p. 50.

[65] Law Drafting Division, Department of Justice, *How Legislation is Made in Hong Kong: A Drafter's View of the Process* (Hong Kong: Department of Justice 2012) p. 6.

[66] Interpretation and General Clauses Ordinance (Cap. 1), s. 35.

[67] Ibid., s. 34.

Express and Implied Repeal

Legislation is subject to express repeal by the Legislative Council. This occurs when statutory provisions, duly passed, declare the repeal of a part or the whole of a piece of legislation.

The doctrine of implied repeal also applies, in clear cases, so that legislative provisions that supersede existing provisions to the extent that they are 'so inconsistent or repugnant of the earlier one so that the two cannot stand together'.[68] For examples concerning the doctrine of implied repeal, see *Mita Kogyo Kabushiki Kaishi* v. *Mitac Inc.*[69] and also *Kutner v. Phillips*.[70]

Review Questions

(1) How essential is subsidiary legislation as a compliment to primary legislation?
(2) Why do laws need to be constantly created or amended?
(3) Do you think the limitations imposed by the Basic Law on legislative authority are a good thing? Explain.
(4) Do the restrictions on the types of bills that members can introduce diminish the Legislative Council's ability as lawmaker?

---

[68] *Kutner* v. *Phillips*. [1891] 2 QBD 267, at 272, cited in *Mita Kogyo Kabushiki Kaishi* v. *Mitac Inc* [1993] 1 HKC 207, at 212.
[69] [1993] 1 HKC 207.
[70] [1891] 2 QBD 267, 272.

7 Statutory Interpretation

Chapter Highlights

- General Approach to Interpretation: Legislative Intention — 201
- Common Law Background to Statutory Interpretation — 202
- Common Law Approaches to Statutory Interpretation — 203
- Interpretation and General Clauses Ordinance Section 19 — 206
- Modern Approach to Statutory Interpretation — 207
- Aids to Interpretation within an Ordinance — 212
- External Aids to Interpretation — 220
- Presumptions Which Protect Basic Values — 224
- Case Study: The Balancing of Different Interpretative Considerations — 226
- Interpretation of the Basic Law — 228
- Bilingual Legislation — 230

While legislation is enacted by the Legislative Council (or under its authority), the courts have a role in the interpretation of legislation. The question of whether a legislative provision is applicable to a particular fact situation depends on the meaning of the provision. Yet there might be uncertainties or disputes about the correct meaning of words used in a legislative provision.

For example, the case of *Leung Sai Lun Robert* v. *Leung May Ling*[1] involved a dispute about the correct meaning and scope of section 13(1) of the Wills Ordinance (Cap. 30). In that case, the deceased man had four children by his first wife. After the wife died, the man married his second wife under a Chinese customary marriage. In 1967, the man executed a will, giving his property to the four children from his first marriage. In 1985, the man and his second wife contracted a second marriage ceremony

---

[1] (1999) 2 HKCFAR 94, [1999] 1 HKLRD 649.

at a marriage registry pursuant to section 38 of the Marriage Ordinance (Cap. 181). After the man passed away, there was a dispute between the second wife and the children from the second marriage (the respondents) on the one hand, and the children from the first marriage (the appellants) on the other hand. The respondents relied on Wills Ordinance section 13 to argue that the will executed in 1967 had been revoked by the marriage in 1985. Section 13(1), at the relevant time, stated:

A will shall be revoked by the subsequent marriage of the testator except a will expressed to be made in contemplation of that marriage.

The issue was whether the section applied to a registry marriage where the parties were already married under a customary marriage. If it did, then the 1967 will would be revoked, and the respondents would be entitled to the property of the deceased. If it did not, then the will would remain effective, and the appellants would be entitled to the property. The question then depended on the correct interpretation of the words 'subsequent marriage'. The Court of Final Appeal ultimately held that marriage in section 13(1) covered all registry marriages (whether or not the persons were previously married under a customary marriage). Accordingly, section 13(1) did apply to the 1985 marriage such that the 1967 will was revoked. The principles of interpretation that a court needs to adopt to resolve such issues are the subject of this chapter.

Where a dispute arises as to the meaning and scope of legislation, it is generally for the courts to resolve the dispute under the common law. The courts' adjudicatory function, namely the courts' role in applying the law to settle disputes, encompasses the interpretation of legislation,[2] and so the courts generally have the power to decide authoritatively on the correct meaning of legislative provisions.

General Approach to Interpretation: Legislative Intention

The basic principle of statutory interpretation is that the courts must ascertain the intention of the legislature.[3] The legislative intention is ascertained

---

[2] For example, *Black-Clawson International Ltd* v. *Papierwerke Waldhof-Aschaffenburg AG* [1975] 1 All ER 810, at 828.

[3] For example, see *Viscountess Rhondda's Claim* [1922] 2 AC 339, at 397 (HL); *Jade City International Ltd* v. *Director of Lands* [2002] 3 HKLRD 33, at 39 (CA); *T* v. *Commissioner of Police* (2014) 17 HKCFAR 593, at para. 195.

by reference to the actual words used in the legislation. As stated by Donaldson J, 'The duty of the courts is to ascertain and give effect to the will of Parliament as expressed in its enactments.'[4] This approach emphasises that while at a basic level the courts are giving effect to the intentions of the legislature, such intention is essentially derived from the words which the legislature chose to use. Accordingly, the courts are not attempting to ascertain the subjective intentions of the legislators, but are focusing on the legislative intention as inferred from the legislation itself.

Common Law Background to Statutory Interpretation

In ascertaining the legislative intention, the courts have developed various 'rules' or aids to construction. It is often said that such 'rules' are not, strictly speaking, rules or principles of law which have binding force, but are simply different approaches which a court can choose to apply or not to apply.[5] This is true to some extent, but as a broad generalisation, it must be qualified. Certainly many of the so-called 'rules' applied by the courts are simply aids to construction, or factors to be weighed and taken into account. However, at a fundamental level, there must be some rules of statutory interpretation which the courts must follow.[6] If the courts are absolutely free to pick and choose which approach to adopt, the courts would be open to the criticism that decisions are made not in accordance with the rules of law but only on the basis of what the particular judge feels is right. The better view is that there are some basic approaches to interpretation which amount to rules in the strict sense, which courts are bound to apply. There are, in addition, a number of 'aids to construction, presumptions or pointers'[7] which must be weighed and evaluated in

---

[4] *Corocraft Ltd* v. *Pan American Airways Inc* [1969] 1 QB 622, at 638. See also *Black-Clawson International Ltd* v. *Papierwerke Waldhof-Aschaffenburg AG* [1975] AC 591, at 613, per Lord Reid; *Amalgamated Society of Engineers* v. *Adelaide Steamship Co Ltd* (1920) 28 CLR 129, at 161–162.

[5] For example, C. Manchester, D. Salter and P. Moodie, *Exploring the Law: The Dynamics of Precedent and Statutory Interpretation*, 2nd ed. (London: Sweet and Maxwell 2000), p. 40.

[6] See D. Bailey and L. Norbury, *Bennion on Statutory Interpretation*, 7th ed. (London: LexisNexis 2017), p. 314.

[7] *Maunsell* v. *Olins* [1974] 3 WLR 835, at 837.

accordance with the general rules. While the judgments do not always reveal the rule that the court applied in interpreting the particular statutory provision, and the cases might not all exhibit a uniform approach, an attempt is made in this chapter to elucidate the general trend of the courts and to provide guidance for students in understanding the likely approach that courts in Hong Kong will take in interpreting legislation.

Common Law Approaches to Statutory Interpretation

Three important common law approaches to statutory interpretation will be outlined in this section as background to the following discussion of the likely approach of courts today in light of statutory requirements.[8]

Literal Approach

The literal approach looks at the literal or plain meaning of the words in the legislative provision. That is, the courts are to apply the ordinary or natural meaning of the words. As stated by Lord Atkin, 'If the language of a statute be plain, admitting of only one meaning, the legislature must be taken to have meant and intended what it has plainly expressed, and whatever it has in clear terms enacted must be enforced though it should lead to absurd or mischievous results.'[9] A strict application of this approach means that the court disregards the outcome of applying the literal meaning of the words. Even though one might think that the result of applying the plain meaning of the words leads to an undesirable result, it is not the function of the courts to judicially create law to remedy the perceived defects in the legislation; rather, it is up to the legislature to enact new legislation.[10]

---

[8] Interpretation and General Clauses Ordinance (Cap. 1), s. 19.
[9] *Vacher & Sons Ltd* v. *London Society of Compositors* [1913] AC 107, at 121. See also *Liu Sing Lee* v. *Luk Fong Chun Richard* [1995] 1 HKC 499; *Leung Sai Lun Robert* v. *Leung May Ling* [1998] 1 HKC 26 (CA), affirmed on appeal: (1999) 2 HKCFAR 94, [1999] 1 HKLRD 649.
[10] *Victoria Sporting Club Ltd* v. *Hannam* [1970] AC 55, at 72.

Golden Rule

Despite the strictness of Lord Atkin's statement, the courts have qualified the literal approach under a rule which is often referred to as the 'golden rule'. In *Grey* v. *Pearson*,[11] Lord Wensleydale said that the 'grammatical and ordinary sense of the words is to be adhered to, unless that would lead to some absurdity, or some repugnance or inconsistency with the rest of the instrument, in which case the grammatical and ordinary sense of the words may be modified, so as to avoid that absurdity and inconsistency, but no farther'. A good example of this situation is the original wording of section 61B(3) of the Wills, Probate and Administration Act 1898 of New South Wales, which provided that:

> If the intestate leaves a husband or wife and also leaves issue, then if the value of the assets ... does not exceed the prescribed amount the whole estate shall be held in trust for the husband and wife.

It is clear that for the section to make sense, 'husband and wife' should be read as 'husband or wife', and a judge could well have applied the golden rule if the matter had arisen in court.[12]

However, the precise scope of the rule is not entirely clear. Some take the view that the rule can only be invoked in situations where there is some error or inconsistency in the legislation itself, as shown by the previous example. Under this approach, the rule cannot be invoked simply where there is an unjust outcome on the facts of the case. Yet a different view is that the rule can be applied whenever there is absurdity or inconvenience. Some formulations of the principle have been expressed widely in this way;[13] however, it seems that the courts have generally refrained from applying this principle liberally to any situation where it might be said that there is an unjust outcome.[14]

---

[11] (1857) 10 ER 1216 at 1234. See also *Medical Council of Hong Kong* v. *Chow Siu Shek David* (2000) 3 HKCFAR 144, [2000] 2 HKLRD 674, [2000] 2 HKC 428, at 437.
[12] C. Cook et al., *Laying Down the Law*, 5th ed. (Sydney, NSW: Butterworths 2001) p. 211.
[13] See *Matteson* v. *Hart* (1854) 14 CB 357, at 385; *Medical Council of Hong Kong* v. *Chow Siu Shek David* (2000) 3 HKCFAR 144, [2000] 2 HKLRD 674, [2000] 2 HKC 428, at 437.
[14] See *Thompson* v. *Goold & Co* [1910] AC 409, at 420.

Purposive Approach

Under the purposive approach, the courts attempt to give a meaning to the legislation which achieves the legislature's purpose[15] in enacting the law. This approach can be said to have originated from the mischief rule as set out in *Heydon's Case*.[16] The idea of the mischief rule is that legislation is enacted to remedy some mischief or problem which existed under the common law. The legislation should accordingly be interpreted in a way so as to achieve the legislative purpose of remedying the defect.[17]

The use of the mischief rule is illustrated by the case of *Kong Kam-Piu v. R*.[18] In this case, two police constables threatened to break up a dance at a church hall, but refrained from carrying out the threat after accepting HK$20 from the organiser of the party. The constables were later charged under section 4(2) of the Prevention of Bribery Ordinance (Cap. 201) which provided that:

Any public servant who, without lawful authority or reasonable excuse, solicits or accepts any advantage as an inducement to or reward for or otherwise on account of his ... performing or abstaining from performing or having performed or abstained from performing any act in his capacity as a public servant ... shall be guilty of an offence.

The constables argued that what they did on the facts did not come within section 4(2). Their argument was that the dance party had actually been lawful, and so they did not have any authority as police officers to break up the dance. Accordingly, their demand for the money was not made while acting in their capacity as public servants. The court, however, rejected this argument. The court essentially took the view that the mischief of the ordinance is of police officers obtaining bribes from the public, whether the officers are threatening to use their powers lawfully or not. To avoid this mischief, the word 'capacity' could not be interpreted in the narrow way argued by the constables. Rather, the court considered that it

---

[15] Sometimes the term 'purpose' is used interchangeably with the word 'intention'; however, the better view is that the two words are different. Thus it has been said that purpose is different to intention in that the former relates to what the statute is intended to achieve, while the latter relates to the legal meaning of the statute; see Bennion (n. 6), at 279.
[16] (1584) 76 ER 637.
[17] See *Ho Choi Wan v. Hong Kong Housing Authority* (2005) 8 HKCFAR 628, [2005] 4 HKLRD 706, at 739.
[18] [1973] HKLR 120.

was necessary to interpret the word 'capacity' widely to mean 'power', 'ability', 'capability' or 'position'. Since the constables were able to demand the bribe because of their position as police constables, they obtained the advantage in their capacity as constables and so were within section 4(2).

While the purposive approach might have as its origins the mischief rule, the two approaches might not be regarded as entirely equivalent, depending on how the concept of mischief is understood. In a narrow sense, mischief refers to some defect in the existing law, in that the existing legal principles lead to some unjust or otherwise undesirable result. Not all legislation is directed towards remedying some mischief in the existing law, but rather towards achieving some particular social or economic goal.[19] Thus, the mischief rule (in the narrow sense) is only applicable to legislation aimed at remedying some mischief in the existing law, while the purposive approach is of general application to all legislation, since every piece of legislation must have some purpose. Understood in this way, the mischief rule is simply a particular application of the wider purposive approach.

However, it is also possible to see the concept of mischief in a wider way, to include what might be termed 'social mischiefs'[20] rather than simply defects in the law. Seen in this way, the mischief rule is the same as a general purposive approach, as all legislation is viewed as being directed towards achieving some result which remedies some legal or social mischief.

Interpretation and General Clauses Ordinance Section 19

Section 19 of the Interpretation and General Clauses Ordinance (Cap. 1) states:

An Ordinance shall be deemed to be remedial and shall receive such fair, large and liberal construction and interpretation as will best ensure the attainment of the object of the Ordinance according to its true intent, meaning and spirit.

While courts have not always referred to this section when engaging in statutory interpretation, the existence of this provision surely means that

---

[19] See also Manchester, Salter and Moodie (n. 5), at 43.
[20] Bennion (n. 6), at 331.

courts must follow the approach set out in that section in interpreting legislation.[21] The section states that legislation shall be treated as being remedial. A remedial statute is one which remedies or fixes a problem in the law or which gives a remedy to an aggrieved person.[22] Thus, it might be said that section 19 is consistent with the purposive approach under the common law.[23] However, the courts have not simply treated section 19 as imposing an obligation on courts to apply a purposive rule to the exclusion of other common law aids to interpretation. Rather, while section 19 requires courts to adopt a liberal as opposed to a strict or narrow approach to interpretation so as to achieve the object and purpose of the statute as far as possible, section 19 does not displace the common law aids to interpretation. In *Medical Council of Hong Kong* v. *Chow Siu Shek David*,[24] Bokhary PJ observed that beyond stating that legislation is to be interpreted as being remedial, section 19 really only deals with 'what is to be done rather than how to do it'.[25]

Modern Approach to Statutory Interpretation

The courts have accepted in Hong Kong that the modern approach to statutory interpretation is to have regard to the various aids to interpretation or interpretative considerations when ascertaining the intention of the legislature.[26]

---

[21] See *R* v. *Soo Fat-ho* [1992] 2 HKCLR 114, at 120 (CA); *Attorney General* v. *George Wimpey International Ltd* [1986] HKLR 325, at 333; D. A. S. Ward, 'A Criticism of the Interpretation of Statutes in the New Zealand Courts' (1963), *New Zealand Law Review* 293.

[22] P. Wesley-Smith, *The Sources of Hong Kong Law* (Hong Kong: Hong Kong University Press 1994), p. 239.

[23] See, e.g., *Jade City International Ltd* v. *Director of Lands* [2002] 3 HKLRD 33, at 40 (CA); *Auburntown Ltd* v. *Town Planning Board* [1994] 2 HKLR 272.

[24] (2000) 3 HKCFAR 144, [2000] 2 HKLRD 674, [2000] 2 HKC 428, at 438.

[25] The emphasis on adopting a purposive construction under s. 19 could be said to reflect the modern approach of courts under the common law as well: see, e.g., *Medical Council of Hong Kong* v. *Chow Siu Shek David* (2000) 3 HKCFAR 144, [2000] 2 HKLRD 674, [2000] 2 HKC 428, at 437–438; *Chan Pun Chung* v. *HKSAR* (2000) 3 HKCFAR 392, [2000] 3 HKLRD 498, at 512. Thus courts have sometimes expressed the view that s. 19 has not altered the common law.

[26] See *Medical Council of Hong Kong* v. *Chow Siu Shek David* (2000) 3 HKCFAR 144, [2000] 2 HKLRD 674; *HKSAR* v. *Lam Kwong Wai* [2006] 3 HKLRD 808, at 832 (CFA). See also Bennion (n. 6), pp. 284–286.

One is to look at the natural and ordinary meaning of the words in the legislation and to construe the statutory language having regard to its context and purpose.[27] Context and purpose must be considered in the first instance, and not merely at some later stage when ambiguity may be thought to arise.[28] This rule takes into account the purposive approach and section 19 of the Interpretation and General Clauses Ordinance (Cap. 1) and is not simply an application of the literal approach. It recognises that words, especially general words, take their meaning from their context. In determining whether there is ambiguity in the ordinary or grammatical meaning of the words, the court is to look not only at the particular words in the section which is being interpreted, but also at the words in the context of the piece of legislation as a whole, as well as the wider context of the existing state of the law.[29] As stated by Bokhary PJ:

> It is necessary to read all of the relevant provisions together and in the context of the whole statute as a purposive unity in its appropriate legal and social setting.[30]

If the plain meaning of the words, interpreted in context, is not ambiguous and the interpretative considerations do not raise any real doubt as to whether that meaning is the one intended by the legislator, then the plain meaning applies.[31] If there is ambiguity or doubt (such as where the expression is capable of having more than one meaning, as a matter of language), then the various interpretative considerations are to be taken into account via a pluralistic approach.[32] The application of the different interpretative considerations may lead to opposing outcomes, but here the

---

[27] See *HKSAR* v. *Cheung Kwun Yin* (2009) 12 HKCFAR 568, at para. 12; *T* v. *Commissioner of Police* (2014) 17 HKCFAR 593, at para. 194; *HKSAR* v. *Tse Yee Ping* (2016) 19 HKCFAR 427, at para. 37. The approach outlined in this and the ensuing paragraph below might appropriately be said to constitute 'rules' of statutory interpretation in the strict sense of the word 'rule'. In other words, such an approach is binding on the courts. The weight to be given to the different interpretative considerations or aids to interpretation depends on the circumstances of the case though, and so it is those interpretative considerations which are not 'rules' in the strict sense.

[28] *Vallejos* v. *Commissioner of Registration* (2013) 16 HKCFAR 45, at paras. 75–78.

[29] *HKSAR* v. *Cheung Kwun Yin* (2009) 12 HKCFAR 568, at para. 13.

[30] *Medical Council of Hong Kong* v. *Chow Siu Shek David* (2000) 3 HKCFAR 144, [2000] 2 HKLRD 674, [2000] 2 HKC 428, at 437. See also *Jade City International Ltd* v. *Director of Lands* [2002] 3 HKLRD 33, at 40–42; *Attorney General* v. *Prince Ernest Augustus of Hanover* [1957] AC 436, at 461–463.

[31] *Jade City International Ltd* v. *Director of Lands* [2002] 3 HKLRD 33.

[32] *Lee Fred (Trustee in Bankruptcy of the Property of Leung Chin Yeung)* v. *Leung Chin Yeung* [2007] 1 HKC 164.

court is required to undertake a balancing exercise to consider and weigh the interpretative considerations in an attempt to ascertain the intention of the legislature.³³

The above approach, which requires context and purpose to be taken into account in the first instance, is illustrated by the case of *Jade City International Ltd* v. *Director of Lands*,³⁴ where the meaning of the word 'land' in section 12(1) of the Sewage Tunnels (Statutory Easements) Ordinance (Cap. 438) was in dispute. The section provided that:

Subject to this section, the Government shall be liable to pay compensation to any person who has suffered loss or damage to land (including any diminution in the value of the land) or property situated on land as a result of the creation of rights, or the exercise of rights created, under this Ordinance.

Jade City was the owner of property adjacent to land under which the government was constructing a sewage tunnel. It sought compensation under section 12, on the basis that there was damage to its land caused by the government's construction works carried out in exercise of rights created under the ordinance. Jade City argued that section 12 did not qualify the meaning of 'land', and thus, on the plain meaning of the word, any owner of land could seek compensation under the section for damage caused by the government's works done pursuant to the ordinance. The court, however, looked at section 12 in the context of the other provisions of the ordinance, and considered that there was ambiguity, since the ordinance as a whole dealt with land in relation to which the government acquired easement rights.³⁵ It was possible then to construe section 12 as being restricted to land which was subject to the easements acquired under the ordinance. On this interpretation, Jade City would not be entitled to seek compensation under section 12, since its land was not subject to those easements.

---

³³ *Medical Council of Hong Kong* v. *Chow Siu Shek David* (2000) 3 HKCFAR 144, [2000] 2 HKLRD 674, [2000] 2 HKC 428, at 438; *Lee Fred (Trustee in Bankruptcy of the Property of Leung Chin Yeung)* v. *Leung Chin Yeung* [2007] 1 HKC 164.
³⁴ [2002] 3 HKLRD 33.
³⁵ An easement is a right which a person has over the land of another person, such as a right of way: *Wan Yuk Wing* v. *Wong Kwok Hing Patrick* [2010] 4 HKC 151. For example, where an owner of one parcel of land can only access a road by walking across an adjacent owner's land, the first-mentioned owner might seek to obtain from the latter an easement for a right of way over the latter's land.

Another example is *Vallejos* v. *Commissioner of Registration*,[36] which dealt with the constitutionality of restrictions on the eligibility of foreign domestic helpers in becoming permanent residents in Hong Kong under the Immigration Ordinance (Cap. 115). Article 24(2) of the Basic Law lists the permanent residents of Hong Kong. One of the categories is:

(4) Persons not of Chinese nationality who have entered Hong Kong with valid travel documents, have ordinarily resided in Hong Kong for a continuous period of not less than seven years and have taken Hong Kong as their place of permanent residence ...

Under section 2(4)(a)(vi) of the Immigration Ordinance, a person is not to be treated as 'ordinarily resident' in Hong Kong (for the purposes of acquiring eligibility for permanent residence status under the Ordinance) during any period in which the person remains in Hong Kong 'while employed as a domestic helper who is from outside Hong Kong'.[37]

The appellants argued that section 2(4)(a)(vi) was inconsistent with article 24(2)(4) of the Basic Law and therefore unconstitutional. This was on the basis that the natural and ordinary meaning of the words 'ordinarily resided' in article 24(2)(4) refers to the situation where a person is in Hong Kong, 'living lawfully, voluntarily and for a settled purpose, as part of the regular order of life for the time being'. A foreign domestic helper working and living in Hong Kong comes within this meaning, just as any other foreign person coming to live in Hong Kong for business, education or employment purposes (and who would be treated as ordinarily resident in Hong Kong).[38]

The Court of Final Appeal rejected the view that there is a single natural or ordinary meaning of 'ordinary residence'. Taking note of examples from the case law on different meanings of the expression 'ordinary residence' in the context of different legislation, the court stated that the term is 'open-textured as a matter of language and inherently capable of assuming different meanings in different contexts'.[39] The court observed

---

[36] (2013) 16 HKCFAR 45.
[37] There are also other categories of persons deemed not to be ordinarily resident in Hong Kong. These include persons landing unlawfully in Hong Kong, refugees, contract workers from outside Hong Kong employed under a Government importation of labour scheme, a member of a consular post and a member of the Hong Kong Garrison.
[38] *Vallejos* v. *Commissioner of Registration* (2013) 16 HKCFAR 45, at paras. 20–21.
[39] Ibid., at paras. 27, 78.

that, where words have some flexibility of meaning, it would be inappropriate to assign to the words a priori some 'natural and ordinary meaning' and to then assess whether there are justifications for adopting some different or 'special' meaning.

The court emphasised that, under the modern approach to interpretation, the context and purpose of the statutory provision must be taken into account at the initial stage of ascertaining meaning.[40] According to the court, the words used in article 24(2)(4) make it clear that the immigration status of persons claiming to come within that category must be taken into account in determining whether they satisfy the seven-year ordinary residence status.[41] Also, the provision implicitly makes immigration control a feature in the process of building up eligibility when it stipulates a seven-year qualifying period.[42] The court did not attempt to lay down any definition of 'ordinarily resided' for the purposes of article 24(2)(4), but the court's approach meant that the notion of 'ordinarily resided' in the article must take into account the immigration status of the person, including the controls and restrictions on the person's status in Hong Kong.

In the case of foreign domestic helpers, the court noted the special features of their working in Hong Kong. Firstly, their permission to enter Hong Kong is tied to employment solely as a domestic helper with a specific employer (in whose home the helper is obliged to reside) under a specified contract. Secondly, helpers are obliged to return to their country of origin at the end of each contract. Thirdly, they are told from the outset that admission is not for the purposes of settlement and that dependants cannot be brought to reside in Hong Kong. In the court's view, these controls and restrictions were sufficiently significant to affect the qualitative nature of their living or stay in Hong Kong such that they could justifiably be regarded as being outside the meaning of 'ordinarily resident' in the context of article 24(2)(4).[43]

Although the modern approach to interpretation requires the context and purpose of a statutory provision to be foremost in the mind of the

---

[40] Ibid., at paras. 76–78.
[41] Ibid., at paras. 83–84.
[42] Ibid., at para. 85.
[43] Ibid., at paras. 81, 88–89.

court when interpreting the provision, it is impermissible for the court to ignore the actual words used in a statute in order to construe its effect.[44] The court cannot attribute to a statutory provision a meaning which the language cannot bear.[45] This is, however, subject to an exception where the courts may, in appropriate circumstances, adopt a remedial construction of the legislation. This involves an interpretation that rectifies defects in the wording of the legislation (including reading in words if necessary) so as to give effect to the purpose of the legislation.[46] A remedial construction was adopted by the Court of Final Appeal in *Chan Pun Chung* v. *HKSAR*.[47] The court accepted that it is possible to add words to, omit words from or substitute words in an ordinance so as to preserve the purpose of the ordinance, provided that (1) the intended purpose is clear, (2) the legislature failed to give effect to that purpose because of inadvertence, (3) the substance of the provision that the legislature would have made is clear and (4) the alteration in language is not too far-reaching.

Aids to Interpretation within an Ordinance

When attempting to interpret a particular section in an ordinance, it is also necessary to look at other parts of the ordinance, as there may be other provisions which assist in interpretation of the particular section under investigation.

---

[44] *Yung Chi Keung* v. *Protection of Wages on Insolvency Board* (2016) 19 HKCFAR 469, at para. 22.
[45] *T* v. *Commissioner of Police* (2014) 17 HKCFAR 593, at para. 195.
[46] There is also a more radical version of remedial construction where an interpretation is given to preserve the constitutional validity of a piece of legislation although that interpretation is not one that the legislation is capable of bearing as a matter of ordinary common law interpretation: see *HKSAR* v. *Lam Kwong Wai* (2006) 9 HKCFAR 574, [2006] 3 HKLRD 808; *HKSAR* v. *Ng Po On* (2008) 11 HKCFAR 91, [2008] 4 HKLRD 176; *W* v. *Registrar of Marriages* [2013] 3 HKLRD 90 (CFA).
[47] (2000) 3 HKCFAR 392, [2000] 3 HKLRD 498. But the courts need to be cautious in not being overzealous in applying such remedial or rectifying constructions: see *China Field Ltd* v. *Appeal Tribunal (Buildings) (No. 2)* (2009) 12 HKCFAR 342, [2009] 5 HKLRD 662, at 675; and see also *Akai Holdings Ltd* v. *Ernst & Young* (2009) 12 HKCFAR 376, [2009] 5 HKLRD 804.

Definitions Section

In every ordinance, there is usually a section containing definitions of words used in the ordinance. Often the definitions section is found at the beginning of the ordinance. Unless stated otherwise, the definitions would generally only be applicable to that ordinance.[48] However, where subsidiary legislation is made under the ordinance, terms used in the subsidiary legislation have the same meaning as they are used in the empowering ordinance.[49]

> **Example 1**
>
> Domestic and Cohabitation Relationships Violence Ordinance (Cap. 189) s. 2:
>
> 2. Interpretation and application
> (1) In this Ordinance, unless the context otherwise requires, 'matrimonial home' includes a home in which the parties to a marriage ordinarily reside together whether or not it is occupied at the same time by other persons; 'minor' means a person under the age of 18 years ...

The definitions section in Example 1 states that the definitions are to apply 'unless the context otherwise requires'. This means that the way in which a term is used in a particular section of the ordinance could lead to the conclusion that the definition is not to be applied for that particular section.[50] Whether that conclusion should be drawn depends on general principles of interpretation such as interpreting a provision in context and weighing up interpretative considerations.[51]

If the ordinance is large and is divided into parts, then there may be a separate definitions section at the beginning of each part. The definitions here might only be applicable for the terms when they are used in that part.

---

[48] *Hong Kong Racing Pigeon Association Ltd* v. *Attorney General* [1995] 2 HKC 201 (CA).
[49] Interpretation and General Clauses Ordinance (Cap. 1), s. 31.
[50] Even where the words 'unless the context otherwise requires' are not used, the court may still imply these words into the statute: *In the Matter of the Fourth South Melbourne Building Society* (1883) 9 VLR (Eq) 54.
[51] See *Lisbeth Enterprises Ltd* v. *Mandy Luk* (2006) 9 HKCFAR 131, [2006] 1 HKLRD 1005.

> **Example 2**
>
> Securities and Futures Ordinance (Cap 571) Pt XIII s. 245:
>
> 245. Interpretation of Part XIII
> (1) In this Part, unless the context otherwise requires – 'associate', in relation to a person, means:
> (a) the person's spouse or reputed spouse, any person cohabiting with the person as a spouse, the person's brother, sister, parent, step-parent, child (natural or adopted) or step-child ...

Definitions can also be scattered throughout an ordinance. The section being interpreted might itself, for example, contain a subsection which defines a term used in that section.

Closed and Open Definitions

The definitions of 'minor' and 'matrimonial home' in Example 1 illustrate the uses of closed and open definitions respectively. Where the definition uses the word 'means', it is a closed definition. This means that the term is defined exhaustively by that definitions section. Where the definition is an open definition (where the word 'includes' is used), it is not exhaustive and only provides examples of matters coming within the meaning of the term.[52]

For instance, say that a section defines the word 'animals' in an ordinance. If the section states that '"animals" means cats and dogs', then the definition is exhaustive so that even though the ordinary meaning of 'animals' includes birds and other animals which are not cats and dogs, these other animals are not to be treated as 'animals' for the purposes of that ordinance. If, however, the section states that '"animals" includes cats and dogs', then the definition is not exhaustive, and so other animals within the ordinary meaning of the term could still be treated as animals for the purposes of the ordinance.

---

[52] *Kwong Kwan-Nang Louis* v. *Commissioner of Inland Revenue* [1989] 2 HKLR 326 (CA); *Tyrone Crystal Ltd* v. *European Asian Bank* [1985] 2 HKC 762, at 771. In exceptional circumstances, the context of the definition could lead to a conclusion that although the word 'include' was used, the definition was intended to cut down the meaning of the term: see *Attorney General* v. *Ng Kwan* [1987] 1 HKC 183 (CA); *Hemens* v. *Whitsbury Farm and Stud Ltd* [1988] 1 AC 601 (HL).

Interpretation in Context

It is a fundamental principle of statutory interpretation that words in a section are not interpreted in isolation but must be interpreted in the context of other words in the section and in the context of the ordinance as a whole (i.e., with reference to other parts of the ordinance).[53] The case of *Jade City International Ltd* v. *Director of Lands*,[54] discussed earlier, illustrates the importance of the context of the whole ordinance in interpretation.

A number of presumptions have been applied by the courts which reflect the principle of interpreting in context. These presumptions are not strict rules but are simply aids to construction, and so might not be applied depending on the particular circumstances.

Noscitur a Sociis

This Latin phrase essentially means 'a thing is known by its associates',[55] and application of this principle means that the court interprets a word or phrase in light of the surrounding words.[56]

Ejusdem Generis

This term means 'of the same kind'. The principle is that where words of a particular meaning are followed by words of general meaning, the general words are limited to the same kind as the particular words.[57]

For example, section 17 of the Summary Offences Ordinance (Cap. 228) provides that:

Any person who has in his possession any offensive weapon, or any crowbar, picklock, skeleton-key or other instrument fit for unlawful purpose, or is unable to give a satisfactory account of his possession thereof, shall be liable to a fine of five thousand dollars or to imprisonment for two years.

---

[53] *Medical Council of HK* v. *Chow Siu Shek* (2000) 3 HKCFAR 144, [2000] 2 HKLRD 674 at 683; *Ho Choi Wan* v. *Hong Kong Housing Authority* (2005) 8 HKCFAR 628, [2005] 4 HKLRD 706, at 737–738 (CFA).
[54] [2002] 3 HKLRD 33.
[55] *London Transport Executive* v. *Betts (Valuation Officer)* [1959] AC 213.
[56] For example, *Peart* v. *Stewart* [1983] 2 AC 109, at 117.
[57] See, e.g., *R* v. *Edmundson* (1859) 28 LJ (MC) 213, at 215; *Quazi* v. *Quazi* [1980] AC 744, at 807–808.

The Court of Appeal has held that the words 'other instrument fit for unlawful purpose' should be interpreted *ejusdem generis* with the more specific words 'crowbar', 'picklock' and 'skeleton-key'.[58] That is, the type of instrument fit for unlawful purpose within section 17 must be an instrument used for the commission of the kinds of offences for which crowbars, picklocks and skeleton-keys might be used (i.e., breaking offences). Accordingly, it is likely that a pair of handcuffs would not be an instrument within section 17.[59]

However, the particular context can displace the principle. For example, in *HKSAR* v. *Luk Kin Peter Joseph*,[60] the Court of Final Appeal considered section 9(3) of the Prevention of Bribery Ordinance (Cap. 201), which provides that:

Any agent who, with intent to deceive his principal, uses any receipt, account or other document:

(a) in respect of which the principal is interested; and

(b) which contains any statement which is false or erroneous or defective in any material particular; and

(c) which to his knowledge is intended to mislead the principal

shall be guilty of an offence.

The court held that 'other document' need not be read down with reference to the words 'receipt' or 'account', and that minutes of a meeting of a company's board of directors can be a 'document' within section 9(3). In the court's view, what was critical for establishing the nature of the types of documents that are within section 9 were the elements in paragraphs (a)–(c). Documents within the section must be documents in respect of which the principal is interested and which contains a false or erroneous statement intended to mislead. As long as those elements are established, there is no need to read down 'document' on the basis of the references to receipts and accounts.[61]

---

[58] *Tsoi Shun-hing* v. *R* [1977] HKLR 408.

[59] The parties accepted this point in the case, and so the court did not need to decide the issue.

[60] (2016) 19 HKCFAR 619.

[61] (2016) 19 HKCFAR 619, at [37]. For another example where the *ejusdem generis* principle was not applied, see *Director of Lands and Survey and Universal Patents* v. *Industrial Designs Ltd* [1977] HKLTLR 81.

Expressio Unius Est Exclusio Alterius

This phrase means 'to express one thing is impliedly to exclude another'.[62] For example, the court has held that the *expressio unius* maxim applies to section 4(1) of the Town Planning Ordinance (Cap. 131).[63] Section 4(1) states that:

> The Board's draft plans for the layout of any such area may show or make provision for –
>
> (a) streets, railways and other main communications;
> (b) zones or districts set apart for use for residential, commercial, industrial or other specified uses;
> (c) reserves for Government purposes;
> (d) parks, recreation grounds and similar open space;
> (e) zones or districts set apart for undetermined uses.

It was held that the express matters mentioned in each of the five paragraphs excluded the possibility of including other matters (not mentioned in the section) in the draft plans.

It must be borne in mind, though, that this principle must be applied with caution, as the context of the statutory provisions may well indicate that the provisions were not meant to be exhaustive so that matters not expressly mentioned could still be within the provision.[64] Additionally, the exclusion might be the result of inadvertence or accident, and the maxim should not be applied where it would lead to inconsistency or injustice.[65]

Generalia Specialibus Non Derogant *Or* Generalibus Specialia Derogant

Generalia specialibus non derogant means 'general things do not derogate from special things'; that is, general provisions in an ordinance do not override specific provisions. Another way of stating this is that specific provisions override general ones (*generalibus specialia derogant*).

---

[62] *Matheson PFC Ltd* v. *Jansen* [1994] 2 HKC 250, at 257 (CA).
[63] *Singway Ltd* v. *Attorney General* [1974] HKLR 275, at 295.
[64] For example, *R* v. *Kwong Lung Co Ltd* [1986] 1 HKC 199.
[65] *Colquhoun* v. *Brooks* (1887) 19 QBD 400, at 404; *Matheson PFC Ltd* v. *Jansen* [1994] 2 HKC 250, at 257.

This principle was applied in *Secretary for Justice* v. *Tang Bun*[66] in relation to various provisions of the Costs in Criminal Cases Ordinance (Cap. 492). In this case, the defendant was acquitted by a magistrate in relation to certain offences. The prosecution applied for a review of the magistrate's decision, and following the dismissal of that application, the magistrate awarded costs to the defendant. The prosecution appealed the costs order on the basis that the magistrate did not have the power to award costs.

Section 3(1)(c) of the ordinance gave magistrates the power to award costs to a defendant where the 'magistrate dealing with a summary offence or any offence summarily dismisses the information or complaint or acquits the defendant'.

Section 3(1)(d), at the time of the case, allowed the award of costs where the 'magistrate, under section 104 of the Magistrates Ordinance (Cap. 227), on the application of the defendant or on his own initiative reviews his decision, and on that review, reverses or varies his decision'.

In this case, since the prosecution had applied for the review, section 3(1)(d) could not apply so as to give the magistrate the power to award costs to the defendant.[67] In addition, the court held that section 3(1)(c) did not apply either. This was because section 3(1)(d) was a specific provision (dealing with costs on reviews) which overrode the general provision in section 3(1)(c) (dealing with costs in summary offences generally). As the case here dealt with a review, which was covered by the specific provision in section 3(1)(d), the defendant could not rely on the general provision in section 3(1)(c).

The maxim was not, however, applied in *Secretary for Justice* v. *Lau Suk Han*.[68] The context of the provisions in the Dangerous Drugs Ordinance (Cap. 134), in particular the history of the legislation, led the court to consider that the more specific offence in section 14 (of importing a dangerous drug in transit) did not override the more general offence in section 4 (of trafficking in dangerous drugs). Thus the prosecution could elect to prosecute under section 4 instead of section 14, even though the conduct was also within section 14.

---

[66] [1999] 3 HKC 647.
[67] Note that s. 3(1)(d) has since been amended to allow an order of costs in the kind of situation which arose in this case.
[68] [1998] 2 HKC 263 (CA).

Examples of Other Presumptions

Other presumptions applied by the courts which might be seen as illustrations of the general principle of interpreting words or a provision within the context of other provisions in the ordinance include the following:

- Consistent use of words. There is a presumption that words used in one part of an ordinance have the same meaning when used elsewhere in the ordinance.[69]
- Every word has a meaning. There is a presumption that every word in a provision was used by the legislature for a reason, that is, words should not be regarded as superfluous if it is possible for the courts to give a meaning to the words which is useful and appropriate.[70]

Use of Different Components of a Statute

Interpretation in context requires that a provision be interpreted in light of other sections in the ordinance. Apart from the text of other sections, the long title[71] and preamble[72] can also be used to assist in interpretation on the basis that they are regarded as being part of the ordinance with legislative effect. However, where the words of a section are plainly inconsistent with the long title or preamble, then the clear words of the section will prevail.[73]

Marginal notes and section headings are, however, not parts of the ordinance having legislative effect, and under section 18(3) of the Interpretation and General Clauses Ordinance cannot be used to vary, limit or extend the interpretation of the ordinance.[74]

---

[69] *Courtauld v. Legh* (1869) LR 4 Ex 126; for an example where the context requires otherwise, see *Whitley* v. *Stumbles* [1930] AC 544.

[70] *Medical Council of Hong Kong* v. *Chow Siu Shek David* (2000) 3 HKCFAR 144, [2000] 2 HKLRD 674, [2000] 2 HKC 428, at 442.

[71] *Fielding* v. *Morley Corporation* [1899] 1 Ch 1, at 34; *Fisher* v. *Raven* [1964] AC 210. For an example where the court has referred to the long title to ascertain the purpose of the statute, see *Secretary for Justice* v. *To Kan Chi* (2000) 3 HKCFAR 481, [2000] 3 HKLRD 756.

[72] *HKSAR* v. *Wong Ping Shui* [2001] 1 HKC 600; *A-G* v. *Prince Ernest Augustus of Hanover* [1957] AC 436, at 467; *Siu Yin Kwan* v. *Eastern Insurance Co Ltd* [1994] 1 All ER 213; *Pun Jong-sau* v. *Poon Wing-kong* [1979] HKLR 662, at 670.

[73] As to long title, see *R* v. *Bates* [1952] 2 All ER 842 at 844. As to the preamble, see *HKSAR* v. *Wong Ping Shui* [2001] 1 HKC 600.

[74] See also *Re An Application by the Official Solicitor (No. 1)* [1983] 2 HKC 259, at 268, 274.

External Aids to Interpretation

Interpretation and General Clauses Ordinance

The Interpretation and General Clauses Ordinance (Cap. 1) contains a number of provisions which define terms that are used in other pieces of legislation. These definitions will apply to any ordinance (and instrument made under any ordinance) unless a contrary intention appears from either the Interpretation and General Clauses Ordinance or the context of the particular ordinance or instrument in question: see section 2. For example, section 3 defines terms which are commonly used in different ordinances, such as 'minor', 'oath', 'person', 'prescribed', 'property', 'public', 'publication', 'statutory declaration', 'road', etc. Other provisions which assist in interpretation include those set out in sections 3–10E, for example, provisions for gender and number (section 7) and meaning of service by post (section 8), and sections 67–72, dealing with calculation of time – relevant, for instance, where an ordinance states that certain matters must be done within a certain period of time.

Legislative History

The principle of interpretation in context extends not only to the context as derived from within the provisions of an ordinance itself, but also the context derived from the history of the ordinance. Importantly, examination of this history can involve looking at previous versions of the ordinance and comparing the changes which have been made to the ordinance by the legislature. This could, for instance, involve examination of amendments to the ordinance made by the legislature following particular court decisions interpreting the previous versions of the ordinance. Such analysis might shed light on what the legislature intended by the current provisions: see, for example, the analysis of the legislative history of the Limitation Ordinance (Cap. 347) by Litton PJ in the Court of Final Appeal in *Bank of East Asia Ltd* v. *Tsien Wui Marble Factory Ltd.*[75]

---

[75] (1999) 2 HKCFAR 349, [2000] 1 HKLRD 268. However, considerations from legislative history cannot override the words of an ordinance where the meaning of those words is clear and unambiguous: see *Attorney General* v. *Ngan Kam Ming* [1996] 2 HKC 176 (CA).

Subsequent Legislation

In addition to looking at the prior changes to an ordinance where a provision is ambiguous, it is also permissible to look at the way in which the ordinance has been subsequently amended.[76] For example, in *Matheson PFC Ltd* v. *Jansen*,[77] in concluding that the jurisdiction of the Labour Tribunal was limited to the specific matters set out in the Labour Tribunal Ordinance (Cap. 25), Penlington JA noted that the ordinance had subsequently been amended to extend the jurisdiction of the Labour Tribunal in relation to certain matters. The fact that it had been necessary to amend the ordinance to extend the tribunal's jurisdiction indicated that the pre-existing matters specified in the legislation were the only matters within the tribunal's jurisdiction.

Similar Legislation

The context in which an ordinance is to be interpreted includes other ordinances in *pari materia* (i.e., other legislation dealing with comparable matters).[78] This is so because it is important to look at the particular ordinance in the context of the wider legislative scheme. For example, in interpreting the Medical Registration Ordinance (Cap. 161), the Court of Final Appeal has looked at the Dentists Registration Ordinance (Cap. 156) and the Legal Practitioners Ordinance (Cap. 159), since these ordinances all deal with the registration of professionals.[79]

Where the ordinances are not in *pari materia*, the meaning that a court has given to a particular term in one ordinance could still be used to assist in the interpretation of the same term used in a different ordinance. There is a presumption that the legislature intends that the language used by it in a subsequent ordinance should be given the meaning which has been judicially attributed to it.[80] The context could, however, require that the

---

[76] *Matheson PFC Ltd* v. *Jansen* [1994] 2 HKC 250 (CA); *Lam Woo Shang (No. 2)* v. *Commissioner of Inland Revenue* [1961] HKLR 609, at 630–631 (CA); *Ormond Investment Ltd* v. *Betts* [1928] AC 143.
[77] [1994] 2 HKC 250.
[78] *Medical Council of Hong Kong* v. *Chow Siu Shek David* (2000) 3 HKCFAR 144, [2000] 2 HKLRD 674, [2000] 2 HKC 428, at 440–441.
[79] Ibid.
[80] *Barras* v. *Aberdeen Steam Trawling and Fishing Co Ltd* [1933] AC 402; *R* v. *Edgehill* [1963] 1 QB 593.

terms be interpreted differently, as the same words or phrases used in different ordinances may have different meanings, and an interpretation of the term in one ordinance is not binding in relation to another ordinance.[81]

Extrinsic Materials

In ascertaining legislative intent or legislative purpose, an issue arises as to whether the courts are entitled to consult other extrinsic materials, or materials external to the statute, such as law reform reports or Hansard (i.e., records of proceedings in the Legislative Council at which the bill was introduced and debated).[82]

Hansard/Parliamentary Materials

Prima facie, the exclusionary rule applies such that it is not permissible to look to reports of proceedings which took place in the legislature during the passage of the bill for assistance in construing a piece of legislation.[83] However, in *Pepper (Inspector of Taxes) v. Hart*,[84] the House of Lords held that the court can rely on parliamentary (Legislative Council) material if:

(a) the legislation is ambiguous or obscure or leads to an absurdity; (b) the material relied upon consists of statements by a minister or other promoter of the bill, together if necessary with such other parliamentary material as is necessary to understand such statements and their effect; and (c) the statements relied upon are clear.

This principle has been applied in Hong Kong: see, for example, the Court of Final Appeal decision in *Commissioner of Rating and Valuation*

---

[81] *Dewhurst v. Feilden* (1845) 7 M & G 182.
[82] On reforms previously proposed in Hong Kong in relation to the use of extrinsic materials, see Law Reform Commission of Hong Kong, *Report on Extrinsic Materials as an Aid to Statutory Interpretation* (Hong Kong: Law Reform Commission of Hong Kong 1997).
[83] *Millar v. Taylor* (1769) 4 Burr 2303, 98 ER 201.
[84] [1993] AC 593; and see Lord Steyn, '*Pepper v. Hart*: A Re-Examination' (2001), *Oxford Journal of Legal Studies* 21, 59; S. Vogenauer, 'A Retreat from *Pepper v. Hart*? A Reply to Lord Steyn' (2005), *Oxford Journal of Legal Studies* 25, 629.

v. *Agrila Ltd*.⁸⁵ For a case where the elements of the test in *Pepper* v. *Hart* were not satisfied, see *Hong Kong Clays & Kaolin Co Ltd* v. *Director of Lands*.⁸⁶ In that case, Nazareth VP in the Court of Appeal held that the legislation would be ambiguous under paragraph (a) of the test only if the term was ambiguous in the context of the provision being interpreted or in the context of the ordinance as a whole.⁸⁷ It is not permissible to refer to the extraneous material to create ambiguity, since the ambiguity must exist first before resort to the external material.

The principle in *Pepper* v. *Hart* applies not only to Hansard but also to explanatory memoranda or explanatory notes which accompany a bill when the bill is presented in the Legislative Council: see the approach of Penlington JA in the Court of Appeal in *Matheson* v. *Jansen*.⁸⁸

Other Extrinsic Materials

Apart from Hansard or parliamentary material, courts might also wish to resort to other extrinsic material such as Law Reform Commission reports or reports of other advisory bodies which were made prior to the enactment of the legislation. For example, the Court of First Instance has held that the principle in *Pepper* v. *Hart* is applicable to the use of law reform reports in ascertaining the intention of the legislature and the mischief that the legislative provision intended to remedy.⁸⁹ On the other hand, the Court of Final Appeal took the view in the later decision of *PCCW-HKT Telephone Ltd* v. *The Telecommunications Authority*⁹⁰ that papers of Legislative Council bills committees would not be within *Pepper* v. *Hart* where the statements relied on in the papers were not made by persons who

---

⁸⁵ (2001) 4 HKCFAR 83, [2001] 2 HKLRD 36, at 55. See also *HKSAR* v. *Yau Mee Kwan* [2004] 1 HKLRD A6 (CA). However, although cases such as these have assumed that the rule applies in Hong Kong, the Court of Final Appeal has kept open the question whether and the extent to which that approach is applicable in Hong Kong: *PCCW-HKT Telephone Ltd* v. *Telecommunications Authority* (2005) 8 HKCFAR 337, [2005] 3 HKLRD 235, at 248; *HKSAR* v. *Cheung Kwun Yin* (2009) 12 HKCFAR 568, at para. 17.
⁸⁶ [1999] 1 HKLRD 527 (CA).
⁸⁷ *Hong Kong Clays & Kaolin Co Ltd* v. *Director of Lands* [1999] 1 HKLRD 527, at 536.
⁸⁸ [1994] 2 HKC 250, at 258–259.
⁸⁹ *Nanyang Commercial Bank Ltd* v. *Lam Man Ki* [2003] 2 HKLRD 432.
⁹⁰ (2005) 8 HKCFAR 337, [2005] 3 HKLRD 235, at 248.

were promoters of the bill or statements made to the legislature. Also, drafting instructions[91] are not in practice included in the papers placed before the Legislative Council and would accordingly not be within the scope of materials to which *Pepper* v. *Hart* applies.[92]

To the extent that certain other extrinsic material is within *Pepper* v. *Hart*, traditionally the courts have only allowed such material to be referred to in order to ascertain the mischief intended to be remedied by the legislation. A distinction had been made by the courts between the use of materials to identify the mischief in the pre-existing state of the law on the one hand, and the use of materials to determine the actual meaning of the statutory words – the latter being impermissible.[93] Despite this traditional approach, there is at least some judicial support for the view that the materials can be used to identify both the mischief and the actual meaning of the legislation.[94]

Presumptions Which Protect Basic Values

In interpreting legislation, the courts also apply presumptions which are aimed at protecting values or rights which the courts consider to be fundamental. The approach of the courts is that since these values are fundamental and important under the common law, the legislature cannot be taken to have intended to override or abrogate these values or rights without the use of clear and unambiguous language in the legislation to the contrary.

---

[91] These are instructions on the policy intention given by the relevant Government bureau or department to the law draftsman for the drafting of a bill.
[92] See *Wan* v. *Director of Agriculture, Fisheries and Conservation* [2017] 5 HKLRD 141, at para. 22.
[93] *Assam Railways and Trading Co* v. *Commissioners of Inland Revenue* [1935] AC 445; *R* v. *Allen* [1985] AC 1029, [1985] 2 All ER 641. The courts allowed an exception for reports of the Law Commissions: *R* v. *Horseferry Road Metropolitan Stipendiary Magistrate ex parte Siadatan* [1991] 1 All ER 324.
[94] *Black-Clawson International Ltd* v. *Papierwerke Waldhof-Aschaffenburg AG* [1975] 1 All ER 810 per Lord Simon and Viscount Dilhorne (and Lord Diplock by way of obiter); however, Lord Reid and Lord Wilberforce affirmed the traditional approach.

These presumptions include the following:

- presumption that the legislature did not intend to interfere with fundamental rights[95] (including property rights[96] and individual liberties[97]);
- presumption that the legislation was not intended to have retrospective operation[98]; and
- strict and narrow construction of penal provisions[99] (such that a person should not be penalised except under clear law).[100]

Penal provisions impose a penalty (either a criminal or civil penalty) in relation to the proscribed conduct. The common law presumption is that where there is ambiguity, the provision is interpreted in favour of the person against whom the penalty is sought to be imposed. As section 19 of the Interpretation and General Clauses Ordinance deems ordinances to be remedial and requires ordinances to receive a large and liberal construction, it has been said that the presumption cannot displace the requirement under section 19 to take a purposive approach.[101] It is perhaps more accurate to say, however, that the common law presumption is not inconsistent with section 19, since the presumption only applies where there is real doubt[102] about the meaning of the provision.

---

[95] *Vo Thi Do* v. *Director of Immigration* [1998] 1 HKLRD 729, at 751 (CA); *T* v. *Commissioner of Police* (2014) 17 HKCFAR 593, at para. 196. Note also the effect of the Hong Kong Bill of Rights on interpretation of other legislation: see, e.g., *Secretary for Justice* v. *Oriental Press Group Ltd* [1998] 2 HKC 627, at 672. There is also a presumption for legislative provisions to be interpreted consistently with international obligations where the provision is otherwise ambiguous: see *Hung Chan Wa* v. *HKSAR* [2005] 3 HKLRD 291 (CA).
[96] *Secretary of State for Defence* v. *Guardian Newspapers Ltd* [1985] AC 339, at 363.
[97] For example, *R* v. *Hallstrom, ex parte W (No. 2)* [1986] QB 1090, 1104; *Collins* v. *Wilcock* [1984] 3 All ER 374.
[98] See, e.g., *Re Setaffa Investments Ltd* [1998] 2 HKLRD 236; *Yew Bon Tew* v. *Kenderaan Bas Mara* [1982] 3 All ER 833 (Privy Council); *L'Office Chérifien des Phosphates* v. *Yamashita-Shinnihon Steamship Co Ltd* [1994] 1 All ER 20 (HL). For an example of where the presumption was displaced, see *Antonelli* v. *Secretary of State for Trade and Industry* [1998] 1 All ER 997. The presumption does not apply in relation to legislative provisions dealing with procedural or evidential matters: *Wong Yu Hing* v. *Tong Pak Wing* [1995] 1 HKC 160.
[99] *DPP* v. *Ottewell* [1970] AC 642, at 649; *R* v. *Allen* [1985] AC 1029, [1985] 2 All ER 641.
[100] *T* v. *Commissioner of Police* (2014) 17 HKCFAR 593, at para. 196.
[101] *HKSAR* v. *Tang Hoi On Barry* [2003] 3 HKC 123 (CA).
[102] *DPP* v. *Ottewell* [1970] AC 642. See also Wesley-Smith (n. 22), at 240.

Case Study: The Balancing of Different Interpretative Considerations

With the basic principles and examples of presumptions outlined, the facts of *Medical Council of Hong Kong* v. *Chow Siu Shek David*[103] and the reasoning of the Court of Final Appeal will now be discussed to illustrate the approach to be taken in balancing the various interpretative considerations. The case dealt with the Medical Registration Ordinance. Under section 21, the Medical Council had the power to de-register a medical practitioner on the basis of various types of misconduct either for an indefinite period or for a specified period. Section 25 allowed a person removed from the register to apply for reinstatement as a registered medical practitioner. The provisions were as follows:

Section 21(1)
If ... the Council is satisfied that any registered medical practitioner –

(a) has been convicted in Hong Kong or elsewhere of any offence punishable with imprisonment;
(b) has been guilty of misconduct in any professional respect; ...

the Council may, in its discretion –

(i) order the name of the registered medical practitioner to be removed from the General Register; or
(ii) order the name of the registered medical practitioner to be removed from the General Register for such period as it may think fit ...

Section 25(3)
Any person whose name has been removed from the General Register under the provisions of this Ordinance ... may apply to the Council for the restoration of his name to the General Register and the Council in its absolute discretion and after such inquiry and subject to the submission of evidence that he has not been convicted in Hong Kong or elsewhere of any offence punishable with imprisonment and has not been guilty of misconduct in a professional respect while practising in Hong Kong or elsewhere and to such conditions, as it may consider desirable, may either allow or refuse the application, and if it allows the same, shall order the Registrar on payment by the applicant of the prescribed fee to restore the name of the applicant to the General Register, and thereupon the Registrar shall restore the name accordingly.

---

[103] (2000) 3 HKCFAR 144, [2000] 2 HKLRD 674.

The respondent was a doctor who had been removed from the register for a period of three years. The issue in the case was, under the proper construction of the above provisions, whether the respondent should have been automatically restored to the register after the expiry of the three-year period, or whether he was required to make an application under section 25. This issue depended on whether section 25 only applies where the medical practitioner was removed indefinitely and where the specified period had not yet expired, or whether the provision also applies where the specified period had already expired.

The Court of Final Appeal held that there was no automatic restoration. The court reasoned as follows. First of all, it was not possible to apply a literal interpretation of the provisions, since a literal reading of each of the two provisions separately would lead to conflicting outcomes. The court then ascertained the purpose of the ordinance by reference to the long title and the provisions of the ordinance dealing with the register. This purpose was to protect the public by enabling the exclusion of persons who might be regarded as unfit for practice though they may otherwise be competent and qualified for practice. In light of that purpose, the court then looked at five relevant interpretative considerations:

1. Striking a balance between the purpose of the ordinance to protect the public and the tendency of the law to frown on restraints of trade. On balance, the court felt that this consideration militated to some extent against automatic restoration.
2. Interpretation in the context of other similar ordinances. The court looked at ordinances dealing with the registration of dentists and legal practitioners, which indicate that there is a distinction between suspension and removal. Suspension entails automatic restoration of the name following the expiry of the period of suspension, but it is not the case with removal, which requires a positive act to restore the name.
3. Avoiding circularity. Here, it would be circular to allow automatic restoration, since the Council could seek fresh dismissal on the same grounds.
4. According meaning and substance to every provision.[104] Here, to allow automatic restoration meant that section 25 would only have very

---

[104] For another example of application of this interpretative consideration to avoid a provision being rendered otiose, see *Re China Star Enterprise Hong Kong Ltd* [2013] 5 HKLRD 271.

limited application, as it would only apply when removal was for an indefinite period (which was rare) or where the person applied for restoration before the specified period expired (which is unlikely to occur). The Court of Appeal had initially decided in favour of the respondent on the basis that otherwise there would not be any practical distinction in section 21 between removal indefinitely and removal for a specified period. The Court of Final Appeal, however, rejected that view on the basis that, where removal had been made for a specified period, the person would generally be entitled to restoration after the period unless there were further convictions or misconduct during the period of removal; whereas, in the situation where removal was for an indefinite period or where the specified period had not yet expired, the factors leading to the original order might still be taken into account on application for restoration to the register.

5 Reluctance to find a radical change by a side-wind.[105] Here, the legislation as originally enacted would not have led to automatic restoration. This was because in section 21, the wording used for removal for an indefinite period was 'erase' while the word 'remove' was used in relation to removal for a specified period; and section 25 referred to the need for an application both where a person's name had been 'removed' and 'erased'. The court felt that amendments subsequently made to sections 21 and 25 in replacing the word 'erased' with 'removed' were 'unremarkable' and were not intended to change the operation of section 25. Accepting the respondent's argument on this issue would involve a radical change to the law by a side-wind.

The above considerations accordingly led the court to reject the respondent's argument for automatic entitlement to restoration.

Interpretation of the Basic Law

Broadly, the principles for interpreting legislation generally can also apply to the interpretation of written constitutions such as the Basic Law. However, there are some particular points to note in relation to the

---

[105] As to this interpretative consideration, see also *Town Planning Board* v. *Town Planning Appeal Board* (2017) 20 HKCFAR 196, at paras. 47–49.

interpretation of constitutions. First, it is generally accepted in common law jurisdictions that a purposive approach is to be applied, since a constitution states general principles and uses ample and general language. The Court of Final Appeal has held that this approach is applicable to the interpretation of the Basic Law: see *Ng Ka Ling* v. *Director of Immigration*.[106] Second, in relation to the use of extrinsic materials, courts in common law jurisdictions have traditionally been more prepared to rely on such materials in the interpretation of constitutions. A similar approach has also been adopted in the interpretation of the Basic Law, where the Court of Final Appeal has stated that relevant extrinsic materials including the Joint Declaration can be used to ascertain the purpose of particular provisions of the Basic Law.[107]

Particular issues arise in relation to the interpretation of the Basic Law, which are unique to Hong Kong, since the Basic Law is itself a statute of the PRC and power is given under article 158 to the NPCSC to give interpretations of the Basic Law.[108] One issue of controversy has been whether PRC principles of statutory interpretation should be used or whether common law principles should be used in interpreting the Basic Law. On this point, the Court of Final Appeal has held that when Hong Kong courts interpret the Basic Law, they are to apply the common law principles of interpretation.[109] However, the court has also accepted that the NPCSC functions under a system which is different from the system in Hong Kong and that legislative interpretation by the NPCSC can clarify and supplement laws (in a way which would not be permissible under the

---

[106] (1999) 2 HKCFAR 4, [1999] 1 HKLRD 315. See also *Director of Immigration* v. *Chong Fung Yuen* (2001) 4 HKCFAR 211, [2001] 2 HKLRD 533; and see further Y. Ghai, 'Litigating the Basic Law: Jurisdiction, Interpretation and Procedure' in J. Chan, H. L. Fu and Y. Ghai (eds.), *Hong Kong's Constitutional Debate: Conflict Over Interpretation* (Hong Kong: Hong Kong University Press 2000).

[107] *Ng Ka Lai* v. *Director of Immigration* (1999) 2 HKCFAR 4, [1999] 1 HKLRD 315. See also *Director of Immigration* v. *Chong Fung Yuen* (2001) 4 HKCFAR 211, [2001] 2 HKLRD 533.

[108] See generally Y. Ghai, *Hong Kong's New Constitutional Order: The Resumption of Chinese Sovereignty and the Basic Law*, 2nd ed. (Hong Kong: Hong Kong University Press 1999), pp. 190–230; A. H. Y. Chen, 'The Interpretation of the Basic Law – Common Law and Mainland Chinese Perspectives' (2000), *Hong Kong Law Journal* 30, 380; A. H. Y. Chen, 'Constitutional Adjudication in Post-1997 Hong Kong' (2006), *Pacific Rim Law and Policy Journal* 15, 627; P. J. Yap, 'Constitutional Review under the Basic Law; The Rise, Retreat and Resurgence of Judicial Power in Hong Kong' (2007), *Hong Kong Law Journal* 37, 449.

[109] *Director of Immigration* v. *Chong Fung Yuen* (2001) 4 HKCFAR 211, [2001] 2 HKLRD 533; *Tam Nga Yin* v. *Director of Immigration* (2001) 4 HKCFAR 251, [2001] 2 HKLRD 644.

common law).¹¹⁰ Where the NPCSC interprets any provision of the Basic Law pursuant to its powers under article 158 and pursuant to the principles of interpretation under the Mainland, those interpretations would be binding in Hong Kong.¹¹¹

Bilingual Legislation

Where legislation is enacted in both official languages (i.e., English and Chinese),¹¹² or where the legislation was originally enacted in English but an authentic Chinese text has been published,¹¹³ both the English and Chinese versions are regarded as equally authentic.¹¹⁴ Difficulties might arise, though, where there is conflict in meaning between the two versions – which meaning is correct? Section 10B(2) of the Interpretation and General Clauses Ordinance has the effect that the provisions in a piece of legislation are presumed to have the same meaning in each authentic text, and accordingly the courts must first of all strive to give an interpretation that is consistent with both versions.¹¹⁵ Where it is not possible to do so, then the ordinary rules of statutory interpretation should be applied to resolve the differences in meaning.¹¹⁶ If this still does not enable the two versions to be reconciled, then the courts must adopt a meaning which best reconciles the two versions, having regard to the object and purpose of the legislation.¹¹⁷

---

¹¹⁰ *Director of Immigration* v. *Chong Fung Yuen* (2001) 4 HKCFAR 211, [2001] 2 HKLRD 533, at 554–555; *Yau Wai Ching* v. *Chief Executive of HKSAR* (2017) 20 HKCFAR 390, at para. 35. But cf. B. Y. T. Tai, 'A Tale of the Unexpected: Tung's Resignation and the Ensuing Constitutional Controversy' (2005), *Hong Kong Law Journal* 35, 7, at 11.
¹¹¹ *Lau Kong Yung* v. *Director of Immigration* (1999) 2 HKCFAR 300, [1999] 3 HKLRD 778; *Director of Immigration* v. *Chong Fung Yuen* (2001) 4 HKCFAR 211, [2001] 2 HKLRD 533; *Yau Wai Ching* v. *Chief Executive of HKSAR* (2017) 20 HKCFAR 390, at para. 35.
¹¹² Official Languages Ordinance (Cap. 5).
¹¹³ Ibid., s. 4B.
¹¹⁴ Interpretation and General Clauses Ordinance (Cap. 1), ss. 10A, 10B.
¹¹⁵ *HKSAR* v. *Tam Yuk Ha* [1997] HKLRD 1031, at 1036, 1037 (CA).
¹¹⁶ Interpretation and General Clauses Ordinance s. 10B(3); *HKSAR* v. *Lau San Ching* [2004] 1 HKLRD 683, at 699.
¹¹⁷ Interpretation and General Clauses Ordinance s 10B(3); *HKSAR* v. *Lau San Ching* [2004] 1 HKLRD 683, at 699. See also S. Y. C. Fung, 'Interpreting the Bilingual Legislation of Hong Kong' (1997), *Hong Kong Law Journal* 27, 206; and see A. S. Y. Cheung, 'Hong Kong and the Unprecedented Transfer of Sovereignty: Towards a Bilingual Legal System – the

Where the conflict in meaning arises in relation to legislation that had originally been enacted in English and where the Chinese version was a subsequent translation which came into effect following declaration as an authentic text, it appears that it would be incorrect to simply give pre-eminence to the English text on the grounds that it was the original version – as the approach under section 10B(3) of the Interpretation and General Clauses Ordinance is to use the rules of statutory interpretation and to ascertain the object and purpose of the legislation.[118] However, where the ordinary rules of statutory interpretation do not assist, and where there is no other indication of what the object and purpose of the legislation are, then it may be that the fact that the English text was the original version enacted can be decisive in showing the legislature's intent at the time the legislation was originally enacted.[119]

Review Questions

(1) What are the advantages and disadvantages of adopting a purposive approach to interpretation?

(2) Section 17B(2) of the Public Order Ordinance (Cap. 245) provides that

> (3) Any person who in any public place behaves in a noisy or disorderly manner, or uses, or distributes or displays any writing containing, threatening, abusive or insulting words, with intent to provoke a breach of the peace, or whereby a breach of the peace is likely to be caused, shall be guilty of an offence and shall be liable on conviction to a fine of $5000 and to imprisonment for 12 months.

X is the tenant of a first-floor room in a building adjacent to a public street. From the window of the room overlooking the street, X uses a loudspeaker to incite passers-by to revolt against the government. X has also placed a sign on the window containing abusive words aimed towards the government. A crowd of people supporting X has

---

Development of Chinese Legal Language' (1997), *Loyola of Los Angeles International and Comparative Law Review* 19, 315; *Re Madam L* [2004] 4 HKC 115.
[118] See Fung (above 119); and see, e.g., *Chan Fung Lan* v. *Lai Wai Chuen* [1997] 1 HKC 1.
[119] Cf. *HKSAR* v. *Lau San Ching* [2004] 1 HKLRD 683, at 699.

gathered in the street outside his window and is growing restless. X is arrested and charged under s 17B(2). Can he be convicted?

(3) Section 28 of the Summary Offences Ordinance (Cap. 228) provides that:

> (2) Any person who is found drunk while in charge of any vehicle (other than a motor vehicle) or of any horse, in any public road or street shall be liable to a fine of $250 or to imprisonment for 2 months.

Y is charged under section 28 after she is found pushing her bicycle along the road while in a drunken state. Can she be convicted?

(4) An ordinance states that 'If a person shall hit, punch, stab or otherwise injure any person', he or she will be guilty of an offence. Does the ordinance apply to a person who puts out his foot and trips another person?

(5) What are the advantages and disadvantages of using parliamentary (Legislative Council) materials and other extrinsic materials as an aid to interpretation?

To answer Questions 6 and 7, refer to the Interpretation and General Clauses Ordinance (Cap. 1).

(6) Section 4 of the Noise Control Ordinance (Cap. 400) provides that:
  (1) Any person who between the hours of 11 p.m. and 7 a.m., or at any time on a general holiday in any domestic premises or public place makes or causes to be made any noise which is a source of annoyance to any person commits an offence.
  (2) Any person being the owner, tenant, occupier or person in charge of any domestic premises who between the hours of 11 p.m. and 7 a.m., or at any time on a general holiday knowingly permits or suffers noise which is a source of annoyance to any person to emanate from those domestic premises commits an offence.
  (3) Any person who commits an offence under this section shall be liable to a fine of $10,000.

A is the tenant of domestic premises and holds a New Year's Eve party there which continues into the early hours of the morning. Noise from the party can be heard quite noticeably in the surrounding apartments. A's apartment is owned by A's employer, XYZ Ltd (a company). Can XYZ Ltd be convicted under section 4(2)?

(7) Section 15(1) of the Karaoke Establishments Ordinance (Cap. 573) provides that:

(1) The licensing authority may, in respect of any karaoke establishment in respect of which a permit or a licence has been granted or issued, by notice in writing, give such directions as appear to him to be required to secure that –
  (a) the conditions of the permit or the licence, as the case may be, are complied with; or
  (b) the provisions of this Ordinance are complied with.

If the licensing authority serves a notice on a karaoke establishment containing only a single direction requiring compliance with a particular safety requirement set out in the conditions of the licence, can the karaoke establishment argue that the single direction cannot be valid as section 14(1) refers to more than one direction ('directions')?

(8) The Labour Tribunal Ordinance (Cap. 25) contains the following provisions:

Section 2(1)
'contract of employment' means –
  (a) an agreement, whether express or implied by law, whereby one person agrees to employ another and that other agrees to serve its employer as an employee whether payment is to be on a price, task or time basis and wherever the services are to be rendered; and
  (b) a contract of apprenticeship ...

Section 7(1)
The Tribunal shall have jurisdiction to enquire into, hear and determine the claims specified in the Schedule.

Schedule
1 A claim for a sum of money which arises from –
  (a) the breach of a term, whether express or implied, of a contract of employment, whether for performance in Hong Kong or under a contract to which the Contracts for Employment Outside Hong Kong Ordinance (Cap. 78) applies;
    (aa) the breach of a term, whether express or implied, of a contract of apprenticeship; or ...

The Labour Tribunal Ordinance was enacted in 1972. Clause (1)(aa) of the Schedule was inserted into the ordinance as an amendment in 1976.

Chan wishes to sue for a sum owing under a contract of employment performed in Indonesia. The contract is not a contract to which Cap. 78 applies. Is Chan entitled to bring the action in the Labour Tribunal?

8 Criminal Justice System

Chapter Highlights

- Hong Kong Police Force   235
- Independent Commission Against Corruption   244
- The Prosecution   247
- Criminal Court Proceedings   251
- Sentencing   259

The criminal justice system is the part of the legal system that tackles crime and maintains law and order. The aim is to prohibit and sanction behaviour that represents a serious wrong in society, i.e. criminal behaviour. But it is equally important to note that the aim of the criminal justice system is to not only convict the guilty but also to acquit the innocent. As will be discussed below, on the one hand, criminal justice agencies such as the police and prosecution possess significant powers that are used to lead to the conviction and sentencing of offenders. On the other hand, the criminal justice system places limits on these powers and affords individuals with due process rights. The criminal justice system is comprised of various agencies, including law enforcement and legal practitioners, and extensive procedures ranging from the reporting and investigation of crime, the adjudication and sentencing of offenders, to reintegration and prevention of further crimes. This chapter will highlight the key criminal justice agencies in Hong Kong and take readers through the key stages of the criminal justice process.[1]

---

[1] For more details on the criminal procedure in Hong Kong, see C. Knight and T. Upham, *Criminal Litigation in Hong Kong*, 3rd ed. (Hong Kong: Sweet & Maxwell 2011).

Hong Kong Police Force

The police are perhaps the most visible criminal justice agency. After all, it is usual for ordinary citizens to see police officers on duty. Nowadays, Hong Kong has one of the world's largest urban police forces with around 30,000 trained police officers supported by approximately 4,500 civilian officers.[2] The Hong Kong Police Force (HKPF) headquarters is organised into five departments: operations and support; crime and security, personnel and training; management and services; and finance, administration and planning. There are also six regional headquarters (Hong Kong Island, Kowloon West, Kowloon East, New Territories North, New Territories South and Marine) that are tasked with frontline policing, and each region is divided into further districts and divisions. The police perform an array of different duties such as:

- regulating processions and assemblies,
- detecting and preventing crime,
- controlling traffic,
- enforcing port and maritime regulation,
- executing court orders such as summonses and warrants,
- escorting prisoners,
- impounding stray animals, and
- finding the owners of lost or unclaimed property.[3]

The HKPF today, dubbed as 'Asia's finest', has certainly evolved since the early colonial period. The Colonial Police Force in Hong Kong, officially established in 1844, began as a paramilitary force that resembled the classic colonial paramilitary model. Ho and Chu identified four key characteristics of Hong Kong's first police force: (1) the police was a paramilitary organisation where officers conducted armed patrols to protect the ruling class; (2) police command was centralised under the police chief; (3) the police force was a multi-ethnic force that drew mainly from Europeans and Indians with a small number of Chinese (this was based on the principle of policing strangers by strangers and the recognition of a hostile indigenous population); and (4) policing was conducted through

---

[2] Hong Kong Police Force, 'Organization Structure' (Hong Kong: Hong Kong Police Force 2016), available at www.police.gov.hk/ppp_en/01_about_us/os_chart.html.
[3] Police Force Ordinance (Cap. 232), s. 10.

coercion.⁴ The main priority of the HKPF was devoted to public order maintenance, with law enforcement (combatting crime) and other services (e.g. traffic regulations) given lower priorities. This model of policing remained virtually consistent up until the 1970s.

The HKPF before the 1970s was, and was known to be, corrupt and abusive. There were common local sayings that referred to the police as 'rascals with a licence' and that 'the good boy does not join the police'.⁵ The HKPF came to be modernised and professionalised from the 1970s, when the anti-crime function of the police gained much more prominence. Hong Kong's police was rewarded with the title of 'Royal' and held the name of the Royal Hong Kong Police Force until Hong Kong's return of sovereignty to China. Furthermore, Governor Murray MacLehose set up the Independent Commission Against Corruption (ICAC) in 1974 (see below) and implemented reforms to improve police–public relations. By the mid-1980s, the HKPF became much more professionalised, although still retaining its paramilitary capabilities, and law enforcement was given equal priority to maintaining public order.⁶ Further transformation of the HKPF came in the 1990s. The last colonial governor of Hong Kong, Chris Patten, implemented reforms to transform the public service into a customer service. In 1994, a Service Quality Wing was established in the HKPF with a mission to transform the police force into a 'service of quality'.⁷ This customer-service reorientation continued after the change of sovereignty. For instance, in 2001, the police adopted the motto 'We Serve with Pride and Care.'⁸ In recent years, events in Hong Kong have presented challenges to the police. This is evident in the Occupy Central movement that occurred from September to December 2014.⁹ In the

---

⁴ L. Ho and Y. K. Chu, *Policing Hong Kong 1842–1969: Insiders' Stories* (Hong Kong: City University of Hong Kong Press 2012), p. 3. Many police officers in the early Hong Kong Police Force were former soldiers who left the British garrison. British and European nationals held management positions, whereas Indians and Chinese were restricted in their promotions and remuneration. This reflected the mistrust of the colonial government towards the local Chinese population as well as mistrust towards Chinese police officers.

⁵ W. W. L. Chan and R. W. K. Lau, 'The Police Force' in W. H. Chui and T. W. Lo (eds.), *Understanding Criminal Justice in Hong Kong*, 2nd ed. (Abingdon: Routledge 2017), p. 141.

⁶ Ibid., 144.

⁷ Ibid., 145.

⁸ Ibid.

⁹ For a more detailed account of the Occupy Central movement, see S. S. H. Lo, *The Politics of Policing in Greater China* (New York, NY: Palgrave Macmillan 2016), chapter 7.

foreseeable future, the HKPF is likely to face further challenges, as David Ng observes: 'Under the current political environment, the Hong Kong Police are often standing in between the Hong Kong Government and the people challenging the governance of Hong Kong.'[10]

Police Powers

Police officers in Hong Kong possess wide law enforcement powers under the law.[11] These include:

- stopping and searching a person or premises,
- checking for identification,
- arresting a suspect, and
- questioning a person at a police station.

These basic powers are mainly derived from the Police Force Ordinance (Cap. 232), but can come from other legislation as well, such as the Immigration Ordinance (Cap. 115), Public Order Ordinance (Cap. 245), Dangerous Drugs Ordinance (Cap. 134) and the Road Traffic Ordinance (Cap. 374).

Stop and Search

The power to stop and search members of the public is a vital power conferred on the police and may be viewed with contempt by those being stopped (and searched) given its intrusive nature. The Basic Law guarantees that 'Arbitrary or unlawful search of the body of any resident or deprivation or restriction of the freedom of the person shall be prohibited.'[12] Within the scope of what is constitutionally permissible, the law grants police officers a considerable amount of power in conducting stop and searches.

If an individual is found to be acting in a 'suspicious manner' by a police officer or is a person whom the police officer reasonably suspects of having committed, or being about to commit, an offence, it is lawful for the police

---

[10] D. K. S. Ng, 'Police Powers' in W. H. Chui and T. W. Lo (eds.), *Understanding Criminal Justice in Hong Kong*, 2nd ed. (Abingdon: Routledge 2017), p. 159.
[11] K. Wong, 'Police Powers and Control in Hong Kong' (2010), *International Journal of Comparative and Applied Criminal Justice* 34, 1.
[12] Art. 28; see also art. 29.

officer to stop that person and demand proof of identification[13] and detain that person for a reasonable period of time so that the officer can enquire as to whether the suspected person has committed any criminal offence at any time.[14] There is no objective requirement that the police officer's suspicion is reasonable, and the individual may be lawfully stopped and searched if there is an intuitive suspicion, but the search is limited to anything that might present a danger to the police officer and it does not permit a detailed search.[15] However, for a police officer to form a subjective judgment about someone acting suspiciously, the officer must rely on some objective facts such as the time, location and circumstances of the scene, and the demeanour, conduct and acts of the individual as the basis of such judgment.[16] If a police officer 'reasonably suspects' that the individual is about to or is intending to commit a criminal offence, then the police officer can stop the individual to demand that he/she produce proof of identity for inspection, detain the person for a reasonable period while the officer enquires whether the individual is suspected of committed any criminal offence at any time, search the individual for anything that is likely to be of value to the investigation, and detain the person for such period as is reasonably required for the purpose of the search.[17] The reasonableness of the suspicion must be determined by reference to the objective facts at the material time.[18]

Where a police officer reasonably believes that an unlawful assembly or riot has occurred, is occurring or is about to occur, and that offensive weapons are involved, then the officer may search the vicinity and stop and search persons in the public place to see if anyone has committed the offence of possession of offensive weapons.[19]

A broader power can be found in the police's authority to perform random identification checks. Police officers have the power to demand anyone who is over the age of fifteen to produce proof of identity, such as a valid identity

---

[13] For the meaning of proof of identity, see Immigration Ordinance (Cap. 115), s. 17B.
[14] Police Force Ordinance (Cap. 232), s. 54(1).
[15] AG v. Kong Chung-Shing [1980] HKLR 533.
[16] Wong Tze Yam v. Commissioner of Police [2009] 5 HKLRD, at para. 13.
[17] Police Force Ordinance (Cap. 232), s. 54(2).
[18] The objective facts include the time, location and circumstances of the scene, and the demeanour, conduct and acts of the individual, Wong Tze Yam v. Commissioner of Police [2009] 5 HKLRD, at para. 14.
[19] Public Order Ordinance (Cap. 245), s. 33(6).

or travel document, for inspection. Anyone who fails to do so without reasonable excuse would be liable for a criminal conviction.[20] The police's power to check for identification can be exercised at random and without the requirement of reasonable suspicion. Similarly, a police officer may require anyone who is driving a motor vehicle on a road to produce their driving licence for examination without reasonable suspicion.[21] The Law Reform Commission has raised concern that 'the ID check provisions of the Immigration Ordinance when used in conjunction with some of the broader existing stop and search powers . . . might give rise to the conclusion that the police can justify any stop and search (*ex post facto* if necessary)'.[22]

For entering and searching any premises, the police will generally need a warrant that is issued by a magistrate. With a warrant, the police have the authority to, if necessary, break into or forcibly enter the building, vessel or place to search for and seize any materials considered of value to the investigation. During the search, the police may also detain individuals so that the search can be conducted. When seeking a warrant, the police officer must demonstrate to the magistrate on oath that there is reasonable cause that materials on the premises have likely value to the investigation of a criminal offence.[23] A warrant is not required if a police officer has reason to believe that an individual to be arrested has entered into any premises. In such a situation, the police officer can enter and search the premises for the person. If the officer is unable to gain entry after notifying the officer's authority, purpose and demand of admittance, and if a warrant cannot be obtained without giving the person to be arrested an opportunity to escape, the police officer may break any door or window of the premise in order to gain entry.[24]

Arrests

Figure 8.1 illustrates the flow of criminal procedure in Hong Kong, beginning with the police's power to make arrests. It is vital for arrests to be lawful as the Basic Law states that 'No Hong Kong resident shall be

---

[20] Immigration Ordinance (Cap. 115), s. 17C.
[21] Roads Traffic Ordinance (Cap. 374), s. 43.
[22] Law Reform Commission of Hong Kong, 'Report on Arrest' (Hong Kong: Law Reform Commission of Hong Kong 1992).
[23] Police Force Ordinance (Cap 232), s. 50(7).
[24] Police Force Ordinance (Cap. 232), ss. 50(3) and 50(4).

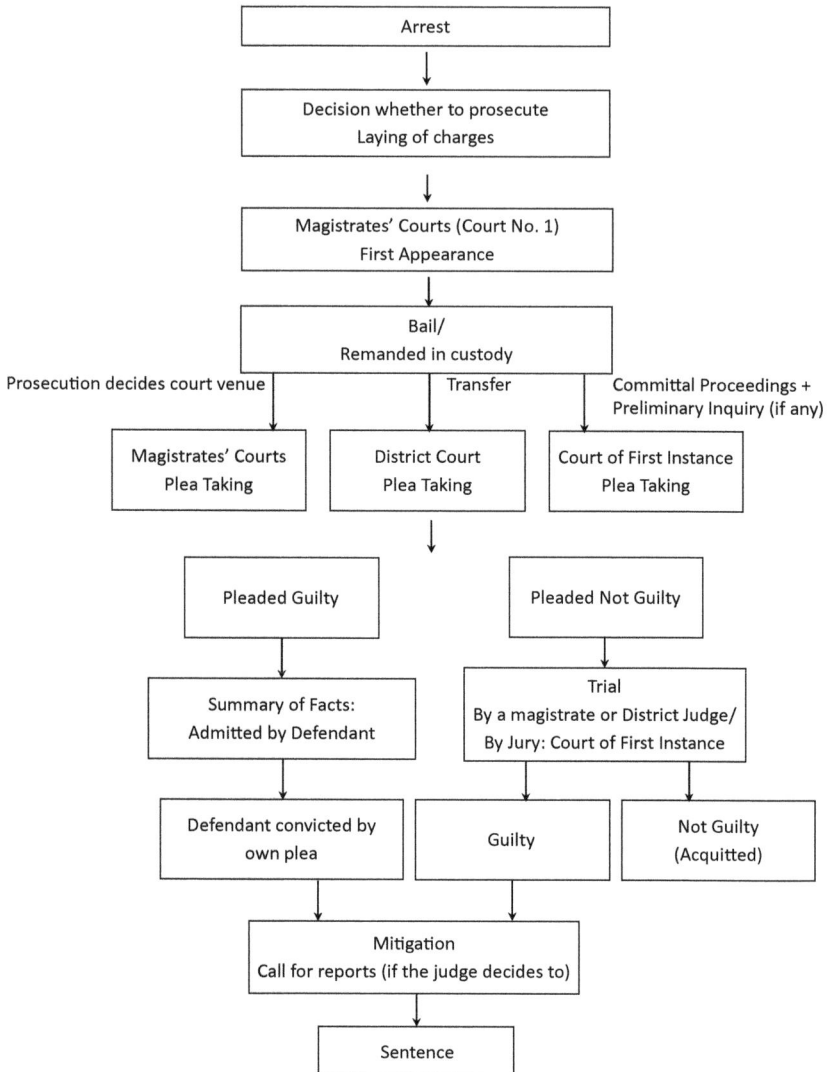

Figure 8.1 Criminal procedure in Hong Kong

subjected to arbitrary or unlawful arrest, detention or imprisonment',[25] and the Hong Kong Bill of Rights Ordinance similarly stipulates 'No one shall be subjected to arbitrary arrest or detention. No one shall be deprived of his liberty except on such grounds and in accordance with such

---

[25] Art. 28.

procedure as are established by law.²⁶ When making arrests, the police may or may not need a warrant. A police officer may execute a warrant issued by a magistrate to apprehend (i.e. arrest) a defendant. In a warrant that is directed to all Hong Kong police officers, it is lawful for any police officer to execute the warrant as if it was specifically directed at him/her.²⁷ A police officer may arrest without a warrant a person he/she reasonably believes is suspected of being guilty of a criminal offence or is liable to deportation from Hong Kong.²⁸ But suspicion by itself is not enough to justify an arrest without objective evidence to support such a belief or suspicion.²⁹

If the person to be arrested tries to evade or forcibly resists the arrest, then the police officer may use all means necessary to effect the arrest.³⁰ In the lawful arrest of suspects, reasonable force may be used.³¹ It is not necessary for the police officer to directly state 'you are under arrest'.³² It is enough for an arrest to be constituted when the police officer uses any form of words in the circumstances of the case to bring to the arrestee's notice that he/she was under compulsion and the arrestee submitted to that compulsion.³³ An arrestee must be informed, at the time of the arrest, the reasons for the arrest and be promptly informed of any charges against him/her.³⁴

Questioning

The Rules and Directions for the Questioning of Suspects and the Taking of Statements, issued by the Secretary for Security in 1992, deal with the questioning of suspects and the treatment of individuals in police custody. Although these are not legal rules, breach of the Rules and Directions may

---

²⁶ Art. 5(1).
²⁷ Magistrates Ordinance (Cap. 227), s. 31.
²⁸ Police Force Ordinance (Cap 232), s. 50(1).
²⁹ See *HKSAR* v. *Li Tai Kam and Others* [2010] HKCU 293, at paras. 71–73, and *Yeung May Wan and Others* v. *HKSAR* [2005] HKCU 551.
³⁰ Police Force Ordinance (Cap 232), s. 50(2).
³¹ Criminal Procedure Ordinance (Cap 221), s. 101A. What is reasonable force will depend on the circumstances. See *Lindley* v. *Rutter* [1981] QB 128; *Crawley* v. *Attorney General* [1987] HKCU 160.
³² *R* v. *Brosch* [1988] Crim LR 734.
³³ *Alderson* v. *Booth* [1969] 2 QB 216, pp. 220–221.
³⁴ Hong Kong Bill of Rights Ordinance (Cap 383), art. 5(2). See also *Christie* v. *Leachinsky* [1947] AC 573.

lead to an exclusion of a statement by the defendant from being admitted as evidence in court.[35]

Once a police officer has enough evidence on reasonable grounds to suspect that an individual has committed a criminal offence, the officer must caution the suspect before further questioning in the following terms: 'You are not obliged to say anything unless you wish to do so but whatever you say will be put into writing and may be given in evidence.'[36] The suspect may choose to answer questions or not, as individuals have the right to remain silent.[37] The police should also allow the suspect to speak on the telephone and in person with a solicitor or barrister in private. During the interview, the suspect may have a solicitor or barrister to advise him/her. Upon request, the police will provide the suspect with a current list of practising solicitors with the Law Society.[38] It should be noted however, that free legal services are not provided at this stage.

Answers to questions are contemporaneously recorded in full, and such record is then signed by the interviewee or by the interrogating officer if the suspect refuses. Interviews are either recorded in writing or if equipment is available by mechanical means.[39] The time and place of the interview should also be recorded as well as when intervals and refreshments were taken. When questioning, reasonable arrangements should be made for the comfort and refreshment of the individual being questioned.[40] Interviews with young persons under the age of sixteen should be conducted in the presence of a parent or guardian.[41]

If the suspect elects to make a written statement, the statement may be written on his/her own without any prompting aside from indications of what matters are material. If the suspect chooses to, a police officer can take the written statement. The police officer must write out the

---

[35] But see *HKSAR* v. *Chiu Kwok Ho* [2004] HKEC 179.
[36] Rules and Directions for the Questioning of Suspects and the Taking of Statements, r. II.
[37] Hong Kong Bill of Rights Ordinance (Cap. 383), art. 11(2)(g). See *Lee Fuk Hing* v. *HKSAR* (2004) 7 HKCFAR 600, at para. 56.
[38] Rules and Directions (n. 36), Directions 8.
[39] Rules and Directions (n. 36), r. V; See *HKSAR* v. *Chan Yuk Ling* [2013] 1 HKLRD 1093, at 18, where the Court of Appeal stressed the importance of video recording of interviews with suspects.
[40] Ibid., Directions 4.
[41] Ibid., Directions 5. In the absence of a parent or guardian, the young person should be interviewed in the presence of someone who is not a police officer and is of the same sex as them.

statement verbatim without putting any questions except to make the statement coherent, intelligible and relevant to the case. After the written statement has been taken, the suspect would be asked to read it, make any corrections if desired and sign it. If the suspect cannot read or refuses to do so, then the interrogating officer must read the statement over to the suspect.[42] The courts must exclude a confession if it was made involuntarily.[43] An individual detained in custody by the police should be brought before a magistrate as soon as possible, generally within forty-eight hours from the time of the arrest (seventy-two hours for deportation cases). If the police wish to extend the time of detention, they must make an application before a magistrate.[44]

Complaints against Police

Members of the public who wish to make a complaint against the police may do so by lodging a complaint with the Complaints Against Police Office (CAPO) for handling and investigation. These include complaints against the conduct of police officers on duty or in the execution of official duties or any practice adopted by the police.[45] Traffic complaints are referred to the Central Traffic Prosecutions Division (CTPD). It should be noted that CAPO is part of the HKPF. Those who do not wish to make a formal complaint can lodge an 'expression of dissatisfaction', where a CAPO officer will offer suggestions of possible ways to resolve the grievance. For formal complaints, a complaint form along with the summary of the incident must be filled out. Formal complaints can be addressed by informal resolution if agreed, where a police officer will address the complainant's grievances. Otherwise a full investigation will commence.

After CAPO has completed its investigation of reportable complaints,[46] the report and relevant materials will be submitted to the Independent Police Complaints Council (IPCC) for review. The IPCC is an independent

---

[42] Ibid., r. IV.
[43] See *Ibrahim* v. *R* [1914] AC 599; *DPP* v. *Ping Lin* [1976] AC 574; *Secretary for Justice* v. *Lam Tat Ming* [2000] 2 HKLRD 431; *Nauthum Chau Ching Kay* v. *HKSAR* (2002) 5 HKCFAR 540, at para. 30.
[44] Police Force Ordinance (Cap. 232), s. 52(1).
[45] Independent Police Complaints Council Ordinance (Cap. 604), s. 3.
[46] For the meaning of reportable complaint, see Independent Police Complaints Council Ordinance (Cap. 604), s. 11.

statutory body that monitors complaints against the police. The IPCC may ask CAPO for further clarification or further investigation. Under the Observers Scheme,[47] IPCC observers may attend interviews and collection of evidence by CAPO without prior arrangements.[48] When IPCC agrees that the complaint has been properly handled, it will endorse CAPO's report. Although the IPCC serves as an oversight to CAPO, it has limited monitoring powers. Furthermore, all investigators in CAPO are police officers and their impartiality could be questioned.

Independent Commission Against Corruption

Prior to the 1970s, corruption was rampant in Hong Kong. Within the police force, there were known elements that extracted protection money from triads operating in the vice and drug trade, and whistle-blowers were deterred through the fear of reprisals.[49] For many decades, corruption was investigated by branches and offices within the police force. This arrangement proved to be ineffective. A turning point came in 1973, when a Chief Police Superintendent, Peter Godber, managed to slip out of Hong Kong undetected when he was under investigation for corruption.[50] This led to public outcry for the government to tackle corruption.[51] As a result, The Independent Commission Against Corruption (ICAC) headed by the Commissioner of the ICAC was established in 1974 with the enactment of the Independent Commission Against Corruption Ordinance (Cap. 204). But the ICAC tackling of police corruption in the mid to late 1970s led to arrests and resignations of police officers, as well as mass rallies by police officers and their families, including a march to the ICAC Headquarters where a scuffle took place. In response, the Governor announced a partial amnesty for corrupt police officers in 1977.[52]

---

[47] Independent Police Complaints Council Ordinance (Cap. 604), part 4.
[48] Independent Police Complaints Council Ordinance (Cap. 604), s. 37.
[49] C. Jones and J. Vagg, *Criminal Justice in Hong Kong* (London: Routledge-Cavendish 2007), p. 437.
[50] Godber was subsequently extradited back to Hong Kong and sentenced to imprisonment.
[51] Jones and Vagg (n. 49), p. 439.
[52] The partial amnesty announced that the ICAC would not normally take action against any complaints or evidence for offences committed before 1 January 1977. See Jones and Vagg (n. 49), pp. 443–445.

The ICAC is an independent institution separate from the police and is accountable to the Chief Executive.[53] It is divided into three departments: the Operations Department, which acts as the ICAC's investigative arm; the Corruption Prevention Department, which advises government departments, public bodies and private organisations on preventing corruption; and the Community Relations Department, which educates and garners public support in combatting corruption. The Operations Department is the largest department in the ICAC and is headed by the Deputy Commissioner of the ICAC. ICAC investigators carry out investigations and enforce the law against individuals suspected of offences under three specific ordinances, namely the Independent Commission Against Corruption Ordinance, the Prevention of Bribery Ordinance[54] and the Elections (Corrupt and Illegal Conduct) Ordinance.[55]

ICAC Powers

ICAC investigators also have the legal power to:

- conduct search and seizure,
- make arrests,
- question suspects, and
- grant bail.

For instance, an ICAC officer may search and arrest an individual without a warrant if there is reasonable suspicion that the individual is guilty of an offence under any of the above ordinances or if there is reasonable suspicion that a 'prescribed officer',[56] such as a person holding an office of remuneration under the Hong Kong Government, or any principal official or judicial officer, is guilty of blackmail through the misuse of office. Moreover, reasonable force may be used in effecting the arrest.[57] The ICAC can also search the premises or place where the arrest was made and seize any evidence that is believed to be relevant to the offence.[58] After the

---

[53] Basic Law, art. 57; Independent Commission Against Corruption Ordinance (Cap. 204), s. 5.
[54] Prevention of Bribery Ordinance (Cap. 201).
[55] Elections (Corrupt and Illegal Conduct) Ordinance (Cap. 554).
[56] For the meaning of prescribed officer, see Independent Commission Against Corruption Ordinance (Cap. 204), s. 2.
[57] Independent Commission Against Corruption Ordinance (Cap. 204), ss. 10 and 10C.
[58] Independent Commission Against Corruption Ordinance (Cap. 204), s. 10C.

arrest, the suspect may be brought to a police station or be detained in the offices of the ICAC for further questioning. An officer of the rank of Senior Commission Against Corruption Officer or above may release the suspect from custody with conditions such as depositing a sum of money and entering into recognisance.[59]

The ICAC is also granted special powers beyond other law enforcement agencies. The argument in favour of this is that corruption is a difficult crime to investigate given its inherent secrecy, therefore special powers of investigation are needed.[60] For example, the Commissioner of the ICAC may authorise any investigating officer to inspect and require production of a suspect's bank, shares, and trust (or similar) accounts and relevant financial records if there is reasonable suspicion by the Commissioner that an offence has been committed in breach of the Prevention of Bribery Ordinance.[61] The ICAC can also make an application to the Court of First Instance for an order to demand disclosure of a suspect's property, expenditure and liabilities, including living expenses incurred by the suspect's spouse, children or parents.[62]

Individuals can report suspected corruption cases to the ICAC without full evidence. Known facts of the suspected case will suffice. Complaints can be made in person at the ICAC Report Centre or regional offices, where identities of complainants are kept in strict confidence, by twenty-four-hour hotline or by mail. The ICAC will assess the report and follow up with investigation if necessary and present their findings to the Department of Justice to decide whether prosecution should be initiated.

Other Agencies

Other agencies also possess law enforcement powers. The Customs and Excise Department is the primary agency that deals with anti-smuggling activities and is the frontline agency in preventing the importation and exportation of any articles prohibited by law. It is also responsible for detecting and deterring drug trafficking with customs officers stationed in

---

[59] Independent Commission Against Corruption Ordinance (Cap. 204), s. 10A.
[60] I. McWalters and A. Carver, 'Independent Commission Against Corruption' in M. S. Gaylord, D. Gittings and H. Traver (eds.), *Introduction to Crime, Law and Justice in Hong Kong* (Hong Kong: Hong Kong University Press 2009), p. 105.
[61] Prevention of Bribery Ordinance (Cap. 201), s. 13.
[62] Prevention of Bribery Ordinance (Cap. 201), s. 14.

entry/exit points having the power, for example, to board and search vehicles, ships and aircraft, and to examine cargoes, articles and baggage.[63] It is also the only agency responsible for taking criminal sanctions against copyright and trademark infringements in Hong Kong. Members of the Customs and Excise Service can stop and search and arrest without warrant any individual who he/she reasonably suspects of having committed an offence under the Customs and Excise Service Ordinance (Cap. 342) or an Ordinance listed in Schedule 2 of the Customs and Excise Service Ordinance.[64]

Immigration officers and immigration assistants from the Immigration Department also have law enforcement powers under the law. They may for instance arrest or detain any individual if there is reason to suspect that the person has committed an offence under the Immigration Ordinance or that he/she has landed in Hong Kong unlawfully and has not been authorised by the Director of Immigration to remain in Hong Kong.[65]

The Prosecution

Prosecutorial independence is a vital aspect of Hong Kong's legal system. Article 63 of the Basic Law guarantees that 'The Department of Justice of the Hong Kong Special Administrative Region shall control criminal prosecutions, free from any interference.' Although criminal cases in Hong Kong operate on the basis of the adversarial and accusatorial litigation system, the role of the prosecutor is to exclude any notions of winning or losing. In other words, the purpose of a criminal prosecution is not to obtain a conviction at all costs.[66] The prosecutor acts on behalf of the public good as a 'minister of justice'.[67]

---

[63] Custom and Excise Ordinance (Cap. 342), s. 17BA.
[64] Custom and Excise Ordinance (Cap. 342), s. 17A. The Ordinances in Schedule 2 include: Import and Export Ordinance (Cap. 60), Dutiable Commodities Ordinance (Cap. 98), Dangerous Drugs Ordinance (Cap. 134), Pharmacy and Poisons Ordinance (Cap. 138), Firearms and Ammunition Ordinance (Cap. 238) and Chinese Medicine Ordinance (Cap. 549).
[65] Immigration Ordinance (Cap. 115), s. 56(1A)(b). See also Immigration Service Ordinance (Cap. 331), ss. 12 to 13D.
[66] Department of Justice, Prosecution Code (2013), paras. 3.2–3.3. See also *Randall* v. *R* [2002] 1 WLR 2237, at 2241–2242.
[67] Ibid., para. 1.1.

A prosecutor must act fairly and objectively on the basis of the law, the facts and any other information of the case, and other applicable policy and guidelines, and must not be influenced by personal feelings or beliefs (these include the race, ethnic or national origins, sex, religion or political affiliations of the defendant or victim or other persons associated with the case), possible media reaction, possible effects that the decision may have on the government or other parties or individuals, and any possible effects that the decision may have on personal or professional circumstances of those who are involved with the case.[68]

The overall responsibility for the decision whether to prosecute or not and for the conduct of prosecutions in Hong Kong rests with the Secretary for Justice and those who prosecute on the Secretary for Justice's behalf. It is important to stress that there is a separation between the functions of investigation and prosecution. The police or other investigative agencies should in no way be considered as 'clients' of the prosecution and, likewise, prosecutors should not direct investigations but may request that further investigations be conducted. However, it is expected that because the prosecution relies on materials gathered by investigative agencies, there would be continuous dialogue and a co-operative relationship between the two where the views of each will be taken into account by the other. The prosecution may provide legal advice to investigators on matters such as the admissibility of evidence, the present state of relevant laws and the appropriate venue for trial.[69]

The Prosecutions Division is the largest division in the Department of Justice, and it is headed by the Director of Public Prosecutions. The Director of Public Prosecutions is responsible for directing public prosecutions, advising the Secretary for Justice on matters relating to the criminal law, advising law enforcement agencies on prosecutions (including matters regarding prosecutions more generally or more specific matters in particular investigations), developing and promoting prosecution policy and advising the government on the criminal law.[70] Lawyers from the Prosecutions Division prosecute the majority of cases in the District Court and Court of First Instance. They may also appear in the magistrates'

---

[68] Ibid., para. 1.2.
[69] Ibid., paras. 4.1–4.3.
[70] Ibid., paras. 2.1–2.2.

courts if a case involves difficult points of law or is considered to be an important case. Most cases in the magistrates' courts are handled by Court Prosecutors. Barristers and solicitors in private practice are also often briefed to prosecute on behalf of the Prosecutions Division at all levels of courts. This is referred to as prosecutions 'on fiat'.

Decision to Prosecute

The decision whether to initiate prosecutions against an individual is significant, as it has profound implications not only for the potential accused but for how the public views the criminal justice system as well.[71] When determining whether to prosecute or not, the prosecution must satisfy a two-tiered test. The first test is whether there is legally sufficient evidence to demonstrate a reasonable prospect of conviction. In assessing this, a prosecutor must take into account and make prospective judgments about the following: the evidence available; any challenges that may be made with respect to the admissibility or reliability of the state's evidence; the availability and credibility of witnesses (such as suggestions of exaggeration, their association with the accused, and motivations to not disclose the whole truth); likely defences that may be raised by the defendant; and how the court is likely to act on all of the evidence. Resources required to prosecute must be used reasonably, and therefore prosecution should only be used for cases that are likely to be effective.[72]

Even when the sufficiency of evidence test is satisfied, the prosecutor must be satisfied of the second test of public interest. There is no precise definition of what the public interest entails nor an exhaustive list of considerations, but a variety of considerations ought to be taken into account. They include: the nature and circumstances of the offence (any aggravating or extenuating circumstances); the seriousness of the offence; the effect on law enforcement priorities; the level of the suspect's culpability; co-operation of the suspect with law enforcement; criminal history of the suspect; the attitude, age, physical and psychological condition of the

---

[71] See M. McConville, 'Politicians and Prosecutorial Accountability in Hong Kong' (2007), *Common Law World Review* 36, 355.
[72] Prosecution Code, paras. 5.4–5.7.

suspect, witnesses and victim; likely disposition of the case; the prevalence of the offence; circumstances that may affect the fairness of the proceedings; and any alternatives to prosecution.[73]

In the Courtroom

As noted above, prosecutors should not focus on 'winning' a case by way of conviction. In litigation, prosecutors have a duty to lay before the court credible evidence and present legal proof of the facts, assist the court to ensure that the law is applied correctly to the facts of the case and, in the event where it is apparent that the prosecution cannot discharge its burden of proof, invite the court to cease the proceedings against the defendant. As a rule of thumb, the prosecution should present all its evidence during the case proceedings. Prosecutors must identify materials that may not be admissible evidence, including materials that may be excluded on the grounds that it was illegally obtained. The prosecution may decline to adduce such materials but must inform the defence of such unused material. If the prosecution decides to use such material as evidence in court, the defence must also be informed. If the defence objects to the admissibility of such evidence, its admissibility may be determined by the court.[74]

Prosecutors are required to present their case firmly but at the same time act temperately and advocate courteously. This means that prosecutors must not use language that may inflame or bias the court against the defendant or other witnesses nor use sarcasm against the defence. Similarly, prosecutors need to refrain from expressing personal opinions, particularly as to the guilt of the defendant. A prosecutor must also not argue any point of fact or law which he/she does not reasonably believe carries weight in contributing to the court's decision. Prosecutors must also assist the court to correct any errors of fact or law that become apparent in the court proceedings to avoid appealable error.[75]

---

[73] Ibid., paras. 5.8–5.9.
[74] Ibid., para. 3.10. For the prosecution's duty of disclosure, see ibid., paras. 12.1–12.7.
[75] Ibid., paras. 3.5–3.8.

Criminal Court Proceedings

Bail

One of the key decisions that criminal justice agencies must make in the criminal process is bail. The police will most likely discharge the defendant upon a cash deposit and entering into recognisance (a promise to pay all or part of a stated sum if a specified event occurs) for a reasonable amount, unless the police considers the offence to be serious or reasonably considers that the person ought to be detained.[76] If the police deny the defendant bail, then the police will need to bring the defendant before a magistrate as soon as practicable where the defendant may apply to the magistrate for bail. Prima facie, an accused person has a right to be admitted bail by the court.[77] However, bail may be denied by the court if it appears to the court that there are substantial grounds to believe that the defendant would abscond, commit another offence if granted bail, or interfere with witnesses or obstruct the course of justice.[78] Objections to bail are raised by the prosecution. Defendants who are refused bail in Court No. 1 of the Magistrates' Courts are brought up every eight days (unless the defendant waives this right), when a subsequent bail application can be made.[79] The defendant may also apply to a Court of First Instance judge for bail if bail is denied by a magistrate or District Court judge.[80] Defendants denied bail are remanded in one of the detention centres operated by the Correctional Services Department.

Even when bail is granted, there may be one or more conditions. Typical conditions involve the defendant surrendering any passport or travel document; promising not to leave Hong Kong; reporting periodically to a police station as specified; residing at a stated address; not going within a certain distance of a place or premises; not contacting directly or indirectly any person specified by the court; and depositing a sum into court which is liable to be forfeited if the conditions of bail are not met or if the defendant absconds.[81] A third party may act as a surety. If the defendant does not

---

[76] Police Force Ordinance (Cap. 232), s. 52.
[77] Criminal Procedure Ordinance (Cap. 221), s. 9D.
[78] Criminal Procedure Ordinance (Cap. 221), s. 9G(1).
[79] Magistrates Ordinance (Cap. 227), s. 79.
[80] Criminal Procedure Ordinance (Cap. 221), s. 9J.
[81] Criminal Procedure Ordinance (Cap. 221), s. 9D(3).

meet the conditions of bail or absconds, the surety will lose the amount of cash that is deposited or the amount that is pledged by their recognisance. There is no fixed amount of money that is to be deposited with the court as a condition of bail, only that it should be a 'reasonable sum.' The court will take into account the defendant's financial resources, history (such as criminal history), the prosecution's case and the seriousness of the offence.

Court Venue

All criminal cases begin and most cases end in the Magistrates' Courts, even though a case may be eventually tried in a higher court. Some offences must be tried in the Magistrates' Courts. Defendants are called to Court No. 1 in the magistracy in which they are due to appear in first. Court No. 1 is also known as the Principal Magistrate's Court or the Plea Court. In this court, the Principal Magistrate sits alone. The court rarely hears criminal trials; rather it is tasked with case processing duties such as bail hearings, plea arraignments, transfers to higher courts and sentencing. Court No. 1 must go through the usually long daily court list. The daily court lists for the various courts are accessible on the Hong Kong Judiciary's website.

The prosecution is the only party that may apply to transfer a case to the District Court[82] or the Court of First Instance for it to be tried on indictment.[83] There are some serious offences, such as murder and rape, which can only be heard in the Court of First Instance. For offences triable either summarily or on indictment, it is the prosecution that applies to have the case either transferred to the District Court or committed to the Court of First Instance. In other words, a defendant cannot elect to have his/her case heard in a higher court.

Where the prosecution applies for a case to be committed to the Court of First Instance, the accused may request the magistrate to conduct a preliminary inquiry. In the preliminary inquiry, the magistrate will consider whether there is sufficient evidence for the accused to be put on trial before a jury. If the defendant does not request a preliminary inquiry, the case will be committed to the Court of First Instance for trial immediately. If the

---

[82] Magistrates Ordinance (Cap. 227), ss. 88–90.
[83] Magistrates Ordinance (Cap. 227), ss. 71A–87B.

accused person pleads guilty, then the sentencing will be conducted in the Court of First Instance.[84]

Taking the Plea

The defendant's[85] name is called to go to the stand behind the bar table facing the magistrate or judge. Often the plea is taken in Court No. 1 for cases in the Magistrates' Courts. For cases that are transferred to the District Court, a Plea Day will be set. For defendants in pre-trial detention, the defendant is taken from the cells into the dock. For defendants on bail, they walk from the public gallery in the courtroom. The language of the defendant is ascertained. Most proceedings in the Magistrates' Courts are conducted orally in Cantonese. In certain instances, an interpreter may be required. The charge(s) is read to the defendant and the defendant is asked if he/she understands the charge(s). If the defendant understands, then the magistrate or judge asks whether the defendant pleads guilty or not guilty. The defendant must clearly state the plea by saying 'guilty' or 'not guilty'. A nod or a shake of the head or attempts at an explanation will not be accepted.[86] The plea decision must be voluntarily made by the defendant.[87] Indeed, many criminal cases in Hong Kong are disposed of by way of guilty pleas (see Table 8.1).

If the defendant enters a plea of guilty, the prosecution's Summary of Facts (also known as the Brief Facts of the Case in the Magistrates' Courts) is read. The defendant is asked whether the facts are understood and, if so, whether the facts are admitted. The magistrate or judge will announce that the defendant is convicted on the defendant's own plea and acceptance of the facts. Brief particulars of the criminal history of the defendant are read. The defence lawyer or the unrepresented defendant provides mitigating factors to the court with the aim for the court to impose a

---

[84] Magistrates Ordinance (Cap. 227), s. 81B(1).
[85] The person charged is called the accused person in the District Court or Court of First Instance and is normally referred to as the defendant in the Magistrates' Courts. For convenience, the term defendant is usually used here.
[86] Knight and Upham (n. 1), p. 144.
[87] *R* v. *Turner* [1970] 2 WLR 1093; see A. Sanders, R. Young, and M. Burton, *Criminal Justice*, 4th ed. (Oxford: Oxford University Press 2010), p. 2109; see also K. Cheng, 'Pressures to Plead Guilty: Factors Affecting Plea Decisions in Hong Kong's Magistrates' Courts' (2013), *British Journal of Criminology* 53, 257.

Table 8.1 Conviction and guilty plea rates, 2014–2017

Magistrates' courts

Year	Defendants convicted of own plea	Defendants convicted after trial	Defendants acquitted after trial	Total defendants	Guilty plea rate[a]	Conviction rate including guilty pleas
2014	4,490	2,358	2,330	9,178	48.9%	74.6%
2015	4,038	2,357	2,180	8,575	47.1%	74.6%
2016	3,944	2,061	2,114	8,119	48.6%	74.0%
2017	1,766	1,909	1,543	5,218	33.8%	70.4%

District court

Year	Defendants convicted of own plea	Defendants convicted after trial	Defendants acquitted after trial	Total defendants	Guilty plea rate	Conviction rate including guilty pleas
2014	930	229	28	1,187	78.3%	97.6%
2015	952	191	81	1,224	77.8%	93.4%
2016	1,012	182	68	1,262	80.2%	94.6%
2017	888	227	62	1,177	75.4%	94.7%

	Court of first instance				
Year	Defendants convicted of own plea	Defendants convicted after trial	Defendants acquitted after trial	Total defendants	Guilty plea rate	Conviction rate including guilty pleas
2014	439	77	43	559	78.5%	92.3%
2015	430	77	35	542	79.3%	93.5%
2016	419	61	47	527	79.5%	91.1%
2017	412	75	31	518	79.5%	94.0%

Source: Department of Justice (2016, 2017, 2018)

[a] In the figures adopted from the Department of Justice, binding over orders are included as acquittals.

more lenient sentence. However, the court may call for further reports, such as a probation officer's report, and hold off mitigation until the reports are concluded. The magistrate or judge passes sentence immediately or adjourns pending the reports.[88]

It is the policy of the courts to encourage guilty pleas by guilty persons.[89] In September 2016, the Court of Appeal revised the sentencing guidelines for sentence reductions with respect to guilty pleas. A plea of guilty at the first available opportunity will customarily entail a one-third sentence discount. For example, if the defendant would receive nine months' imprisonment post-conviction at trial, by pleading guilty, the defendant would instead receive six months' imprisonment. But if the defendant enters a guilty plea after a trial date has been set, the discount is reduced to 20–25 per cent. If the guilty plea is entered on the first day of trial, then the discount would be reduced further to 20 per cent. If the defendant enters a guilty plea during the trial, then the sentence discount would normally be reduced to less than 20 per cent depending on the circumstances in which the guilty plea was made. Nonetheless, the court retains an overriding discretion in sentencing.[90] The previous example illustrated sentence reductions in terms of months of imprisonment. If the defendant for instance was facing twenty-one years of imprisonment, then an early plea would equate to a seven-year sentence discount. The decision to plead guilty or not, and to plead sooner rather than later, is life-changing.

If the defendant enters a plea of not guilty, then a trial date will be fixed. The court will ask the prosecution how many witnesses will be called and the estimated length of the trial. The court may also ask the defence the same. It is normal for a trial date to be scheduled earlier for detained defendants compared with defendants who are granted bail.

Burden and Standard of Proof (Criminal Trials)

The burden is on the prosecution to prove the state's case beyond a reasonable doubt. The defendant has the right to remain silent and there

---

[88] Knight and Upham (n. 1), chapter 10.
[89] *R* v. *Yu Man Wu* [1995] 2 HKCLR 202.
[90] *HKSAR* v. *Ngo Van Nam* [2016] HKCA 396 and *HKSAR* v. *Abdou Maikido Abdoulkarim* [2016] HKCA 397.

is no legal requirement for the defendant to give evidence in court. The standard of proof in criminal trials has been described this way:

> That degree is well settled. It need not reach certainty, but it must carry a high degree of probability. Proof beyond reasonable doubt does not mean proof beyond the shadow of a doubt. The law would fail to protect the community if it admitted fanciful possibilities to deflect the course of justice. If the evidence is so strong against a man as to leave only a remote possibility in his favour which can be dismissed with the sentence 'of course it is possible, but not in the least probable', the case is proved beyond reasonable doubt, but nothing short of that will suffice.[91]

It is clear that the standard of proof for criminal trials is higher than that for civil trials.

Presumption of Innocence

A fundamental aspect of criminal proceedings is the presumption of innocence, meaning that the defendant is presumed to be innocent until he/she is convicted by a court of law. The presumption of innocence is enshrined in the Basic Law, which states that 'Anyone who is lawfully arrested shall have the right to a fair trial by the judicial organs without delay and shall be presumed innocent until convicted by the judicial organs'[92]; and in the Bill of Rights Ordinance, which similarly states that 'Everyone charged with a criminal offence shall have the right to be presumed innocent until proved guilty according to law.'[93] The presumption of innocence also arises pursuant to the common law. In the classic case of *Woolmington* v. *DPP*, the House of Lords provided the famous 'golden thread' quote, stating that:

> Throughout the web of the English criminal law one golden thread is always to be seen, that is the duty of the prosecution to prove the guilt ... No matter what the charge or where the trial, the principle that the prosecution must prove the guilt of the [defendant] is part of the common law of England and no attempt to whittle it down can be entertained ...[94]

---

[91] *Miller* v. *Minister of Pensions* [1947] 2 All ER 372, at 372.
[92] Basic Law, art. 87.
[93] Hong Kong Bill of Rights Ordinance (Cap. 383), art. 11(1).
[94] [1935] A.C. 462, at 481–482.

It needs to be highlighted that there are exceptions which result in a 'reverse onus' of proof where the burden of proof is placed on the defendant to disprove some element of the offence. For example, under the Firearms and Ammunition Ordinance, a person who is in possession of an imitation firearm commits an offence unless the person in question satisfies the court that the possession is not for an unlawful purpose.[95] At face value, this contradicts the presumption of innocence by imposing a persuasive burden of proof on the defendant regarding an essential element of the offence. But the Court of Final Appeal has held that a reverse burden might be justified if it had a rational connection with the pursuit of a legitimate aim and if it was no more than necessary for the achievement of that legitimate aim. If the provision on reverse burden does not satisfy both these requirements, the court could adopt a remedial interpretation[96] and impose a mere evidential burden on the defendant instead of a persuasive burden (as was held for the above offence).[97] An evidential burden only requires the defendant to adduce sufficient evidence at trial to raise an issue as to the existence of a fact but does not require the defendant to meet the burden of proving the existence of the fact.

Right to Silence

In Hong Kong, defendants have a right to silence and are not to be compelled to testify against themselves.[98] A failure to testify should not be construed as an admission of guilt. The trial judge should direct the jury that:

[The defendant] is not bound to give evidence, that he can sit back and see if the prosecution have proved their case, and that while the jury have been deprived of the opportunity of hearing his story tested in the cross-examination, the one thing that they must not do is to assume that he is guilty because he has not gone into the witness box.[99]

The prosecution must not make any comment against a defendant who has elected not to testify.[100]

---

[95] Firearms and Ammunition Ordinance (Cap. 238), s. 20(3).
[96] See Chapter 7.
[97] *HKSAR* v. *Lam Kwong Wai* (2006) 9 HKCFAR 574; [2006] 3 HKLRD 808.
[98] Hong Kong Bill of Rights Ordinance (Cap. 383), art. 11(2)(g).
[99] *R* v. *Bathurst* [1968] 2 QB 99, at 107–108.
[100] Criminal Procedure Ordinance (Cap. 221), s. 54(1)(b).

Sentencing

After a defendant has been convicted, the court will impose a sentence. The sentencing options that the court can impose as punishment can be broadly categorised as custodial sentences and community sentences. Community sentences mean any sentence that is non-custodial. Sentencing is one of the most important aspects of criminal justice and, indeed, this is the area where the public is likely to pay most attention to, as the sentences imposed on convicted offenders sometimes receive comment and debate in the media. Errors made with respect to sentencing can result in dire consequences such as disproportionate punishment of individuals, the premature release of dangerous offenders, or the victim and public perceiving that justice was not served. It is therefore important for magistrates and judges to strike a balance when sentencing.[101]

The appellate courts periodically provide sentencing guidelines for certain offences with certain factual characteristics.[102] But the courts have often stressed that sentencing is 'not a mathematical exercise', and the courts have wide discretion in imposing a sentence.[103] The court would also need to consider aggravating factors (factors that may enhance the sentence) and mitigating factors (factors that may reduce the sentence) when sentencing. Examples of aggravating factors would be commission of the offence while on bail and premeditation by the offender. Examples of mitigating factors would be remorse on the part of the offender and the age of the offender. In cases of multiple offences, the court would also need to consider the 'totality principle' to ensure that the sentences passed in aggregate are just and proportionate in reflecting the criminality involved and that an offender is not punished twice for the same offence.[104]

---

[101] S. N. M. Young, 'Sentencing', in W. H. Chui and T. W. Lo (eds.), *Understanding Criminal Justice in Hong Kong*, 2nd ed. (Abingdon: Routledge 2017).

[102] In *Secretary for Justice v. Wong Chi-fung and Others* [2018] 2 HKC 50, the Court of Final Appeal noted that the Court of Appeal is the appropriate court to set sentencing guidelines.

[103] G. Cross and P. W. S. Cheung, *Sentencing in Hong Kong*, 8th ed. (Hong Kong: LexisNexis 2018), p. 338.

[104] *HKSAR v. Ngai Yiu Ching* [2011] 5 HKLRD 690, at 22.

Imprisonment

The most serious sentence that the court can impose is imprisonment, particularly life imprisonment.[105] The only offence that carries a minimum life sentence is murder.[106] Other serious offences, such as manslaughter and rape, can carry discretionary life sentences where the judge must specify the minimum number of years that the offender must serve before release.[107] For other offences, the term of imprisonment can vary widely.[108]

Imprisonment can be immediate, or the court can impose a suspended sentence in appropriate cases. A suspended sentence may provide that for a period from one to three years the offender must not commit another offence that is punishable by imprisonment. If the offender commits another offence, then he/she will not only be sentenced for the new offence but will serve the original sentence that was suspended as well. However, a suspended sentence can only be used when the court imposes a prison term of two years or less. Certain offences such as manslaughter, drug trafficking, and rape or attempted rape cannot result in a suspended sentence even if the actual sentence is less than two years.[109]

Correctional facilities in Hong Kong are run by the Correctional Services Department (CSD). Currently CSD operates twenty-nine correctional facilities, including correctional institutions, halfway houses and custodial wards in hospitals. Prisons are divided into three levels of security: minimum, medium and maximum. The largest maximum-security prison in Hong Kong is Stanley Prison, which houses adult male offenders serving life or long-term prison sentences. Young offenders aged fourteen to twenty are separated from adults, and male and female inmates are separated as well.

Other Custodial Sentences

Besides prisons, CSD runs drug addiction treatment centres for convicted drug abusers. Inmates must undergo compulsory drug treatment, which

---

[105] Capital punishment was officially abolished in Hong Kong in 1993.
[106] Offences Against the Person Ordinance (Cap. 212), s. 2; see also *HKSAR* v. *Lau Cheong* [2002] 5 HKCFAR 415, where the constitutionality of this penalty was upheld by the Court of Final Appeal.
[107] Young (n. 101), p. 270. See Criminal Procedure Ordinance (Cap. 221), s. 67B; *R* v. *Whittaker* [1996] Crim LR 917.
[108] See Cross and Cheung (n. 103).
[109] See Criminal Procedure Ordinance (Cap. 221), sch. 3.

may last from two to twelve months, depending on the progress of the individual.[110] The treatment focuses on discipline training, outdoor activities, counselling and therapy, with the purpose of dissuading offenders from drug dependency. After release, offenders must stay in a halfway house for six to eight weeks and be subjected to one year's post-release statutory supervision.[111]

There are also correctional facilities that target young offenders. The detention centre is a US-style boot camp where sentenced offenders endure physical training and labour. Male offenders between the ages of fourteen and twenty are detained for between one and six months, whereas older male offenders between the ages of twenty-one and twenty-four are detained from between three months and a year.[112] Offenders who are deemed to be not physically fit enough to go through the detention centre may be sent to a rehabilitation centre instead. Offenders are sentenced to between three and nine months, and they attend work skills and educational training along with counselling.[113] Training centres are for offenders aged between fourteen and twenty, and inmates receive educational and vocational training. There are other activities, such as volunteer services and outdoor training.[114]

Non-Custodial Sentences

The most common form of non-custodial sentence is a fine. The court can impose a fine on its own or in addition to other sentences. The court will take into account the offenders' means when deciding on the amount of the fine. The court may agree for a fine to be paid by instalments. If the offender fails to pay a fine, he/she may be sent to prison for a period of up to twelve months.[115]

---

[110] Drug Addiction Treatment Centres Ordinance (Cap. 244), s. 4.
[111] Drug Addiction Treatment Centres Ordinance (Cap. 244), s. 5; see also T. W. Lo, 'Prison and Correctional Services' in W. H. Chui and T. W. Lo (eds.), *Understanding Criminal Justice in Hong Kong*, 2nd ed. (Abingdon: Routledge 2017).
[112] Detention Centres Ordinance (Cap. 239), s. 4.
[113] Rehabilitation Centres Ordinance (Cap. 567), s. 4.
[114] Training Centres Ordinance (Cap. 280), s. 4. See also Lo (n. 111).
[115] Criminal Procedure Ordinance (Cap. 221) s. 113A; Magistrates Ordinance (Cap. 227) s. 97; see also Young (n. 101), pp. 270–271.

Another form of non-custodial sentence is a probation order, where an offender is sentenced to be under the supervision of a probation officer and is required to abide by various conditions, such as keeping up with the probation officer regularly, providing urine samples for drug testing, working and residing as directed, abiding by curfews and attending counselling or psychiatric programmes. The probation period ranges from one year up to three years.[116] Probation orders are determined by the court on the basis of the offender's background, the circumstances leading up to the offence and the nature of the offence itself, and the recommendation by the probation officer. Probations in Hong Kong are operated by the Social Welfare Department (SWD), and an assigned probation officer is required to 'advise, assist and befriend the probationer'.[117]

A community service order may be given for offenders aged fourteen and above and who have been convicted of an offence punishable by imprisonment. Such an order requires the offender to perform unpaid work in the community up to a maximum of 240 hours within twelve months. The offender must consent to a community service order, and a probation officer recommends that the person is suitable for work under the order before it can be imposed.[118] Community service may include work such as carpentry, painting, gardening and visiting elderly homes.[119]

There are other sentencing options as well, such as disqualifications, for example, when an offender has his/her driver's licence disqualified.[120] A hospital order can be imposed for an offender who is a mentally disordered person, and the nature or degree of the mental disorder warrants the offender's detention in a mental hospital for treatment.[121]

---

[116] Probation of Offenders Ordinance (Cap. 298), s. 3.
[117] Probation of Offenders Rules (Cap. 298A), r. 19.
[118] Community Service Orders Ordinance (Cap. 378), s. 4. See also *HKSAR* v. *Chow Chak Man* [1999] 3 HKLRD 37, where the Court of Appeal approved the guidance as to the characteristics of offenders who was best suited for a community service order.
[119] W. H. Chui, 'Probation and Community Services Orders' in W. H. Chui and T. W. Lo (eds.), *Understanding Criminal Justice in Hong Kong*, 2nd ed. (Oxon: Routledge 2017), p. 303.
[120] Road Traffic Ordinance (Cap. 374) s. 69.
[121] Mental Health Ordinance (Cap. 136), s. 54(3).

Review Questions

(1) How has the Hong Kong Police Force transformed since its establishment in 1844 up to today?
(2) Compare the powers of police officers with ICAC officers. What are the similarities and differences?
(3) What tests must be satisfied before the prosecution decides to prosecute?
(4) What is the presumption of innocence and why is it so important?
(5) Do you agree with the current sentencing guidelines with respect to sentence reductions for guilty pleas? Explain.
(6) Rank the various sentence options in order of severity. Explain your choices.

9 Civil Justice System

Chapter Highlights

- Civil Litigation 264
- Drawbacks to Civil Litigation 277
- Civil Justice Reform 280

The civil justice system is the part of the legal system that allows individuals and businesses to resolve their legal grievances and enforce their legal rights. It may involve the suing for money or the recovery of damages caused by the wrongdoing, negligence or malpractice of another party. This can be done through civil litigation, which this chapter deals with, or alternative dispute resolution procedures, which is the subject of Chapter 10. Hong Kong's civil justice system has undergone a major change through the Civil Justice Reform. This chapter will take readers through the key stages of civil procedure in terms of civil litigation. It also discusses the drawbacks of civil litigation to the legal system and to society, and introduces readers to the Civil Justice Reform, highlighting the reforms that have been implemented to improve 'access to justice' and to enhance efficiency, cost-effectiveness and fairness for individuals going through the civil justice system in Hong Kong.

Civil Litigation

An aggrieved party, the plaintiff, can bring a lawsuit against the alleged wrongdoer, the defendant, for an injury/loss suffered because of the wrongdoing of the defendant. The 'causes of action'[1] include breach of contract, tort (e.g. personal injuries), matrimonial matters, recovery of land and premises, employees' compensation and claims in equity (e.g. administration of trusts and estates of a deceased person). For example, the defendant has failed to fulfil a contractual obligation, such as providing goods or services on time, and the plaintiff has suffered loss as a result; or a bus driver has been driving negligently, and passengers are injured because of the driver's actions.

The courts that have jurisdiction over civil proceedings are the District Court, the High Court, the Court of Final Appeal and various tribunals. The District Court has limited civil jurisdiction and can hear matters on contract, quasi-contract and tort where the plaintiff's claim does not exceed HK$3,000,000.[2] It can also hear actions dealing with the recovery of land where the annual rent, rateable value of the land or annual value of the land does not exceed HK$320,000[3] and other claims in equity.[4] This also applies to the defendant's counterclaims (claims by a defendant against the plaintiff in the same action).[5] The High Court has unlimited civil jurisdiction, meaning that there is not a financial limit on the value of claims that can be heard in the High Court.[6] However, there are certain cases that must be brought in the High Court (Court of First Instance). These include judicial review, admiralty actions,[7] bankruptcy and company winding-up.

If the plaintiff abandons the excess of a claim over HK$3,000,000, the matter can be brought under the jurisdiction of the District Court.[8] This is useful in situations where the excess is small, because the costs of proceedings in the District Court are generally lower than in the High Court. A claim, however, cannot be split up into smaller claims to bring them into the District Court's jurisdiction.[9] Neither the District Court nor

---

[1] This has been defined as 'those facts which a plaintiff must prove to support his right to judgment in court'. See *Bank of East Asia Ltd* v. *Tsien Wui Marble Factory Ltd* (1999) 2 HKCFAR 349.
[2] District Court Ordinance (Cap. 336), s. 32(1).
[3] District Court Ordinance (Cap. 336), s. 35.
[4] See District Court Ordinance (Cap. 336), s. 37.
[5] District Court Ordinance (Cap. 336), s. 39.
[6] High Court Ordinance (Cap. 4), s. 3(2).
[7] See High Court Ordinance (Cap. 4), s. 12A.
[8] District Court Ordinance (Cap. 336), s. 34.
[9] District Court Ordinance (Cap. 336), s. 45.

Court of First Instance can preside over cases which are within the jurisdiction of certain specialist tribunals.[10]

The procedures for civil proceedings are virtually identical in the District Court and the High Court. The rules governing civil procedure in Hong Kong can be found in ordinances, subsidiary legislation, practice directions, case law and practice books, notably *Hong Kong Civil Procedure* (also known as *The Hong Kong White Book*). The White Book has been referred to as the 'litigator's bible'.[11] Figure 9.1 illustrates the flow of civil procedure in Hong Kong.

Starting an Action

Prior to starting a civil action, it is important for the plaintiff to consider whether there is a sound legal basis for the claim. Likewise, it is important to consider whether an initiation of an action would lead to the defendant bringing a counterclaim in the same action. It is not unusual for the plaintiff and defendant each to have committed some wrong with respect to the same event. Another practical consideration is the defendant's financial viability. Even if the litigation is successful, there is no guarantee that the plaintiff will be able to recover all the sums that have been awarded by the court if the defendant is unable to pay. Very simply, there is little point in suing someone who does not have the means to pay. It would be prudent to check the assets of the defendant, such as ownership of properties, which can be searched on the Land Registry. It is likewise prudent to check whether the defendant is bankrupt, or in the case of a limited company, whether it is in liquidation or winding-up. The plaintiff also needs to think through whether he/she can afford the expenses, as litigation can be very expensive. If not, the plaintiff should find out whether he/she qualifies for legal aid or other subsidised legal services.[12] Similarly, the plaintiff must keep in mind the time associated with civil litigation, as it can take months or years before a case is heard. It is also

---

[10] D. Lau, *Civil Procedure in Hong Kong: A Guide to the Main Principles*, 3rd ed. (Hong Kong: Sweet & Maxwell 2014), chapter 2.
[11] A. Leung and D. Clark, *Civil Litigation in Hong Kong*, 4th ed. (Hong Kong: Sweet & Maxwell 2012), Preface.
[12] See Chapter 11, 'Access to Justice'.

Civil Justice System 267

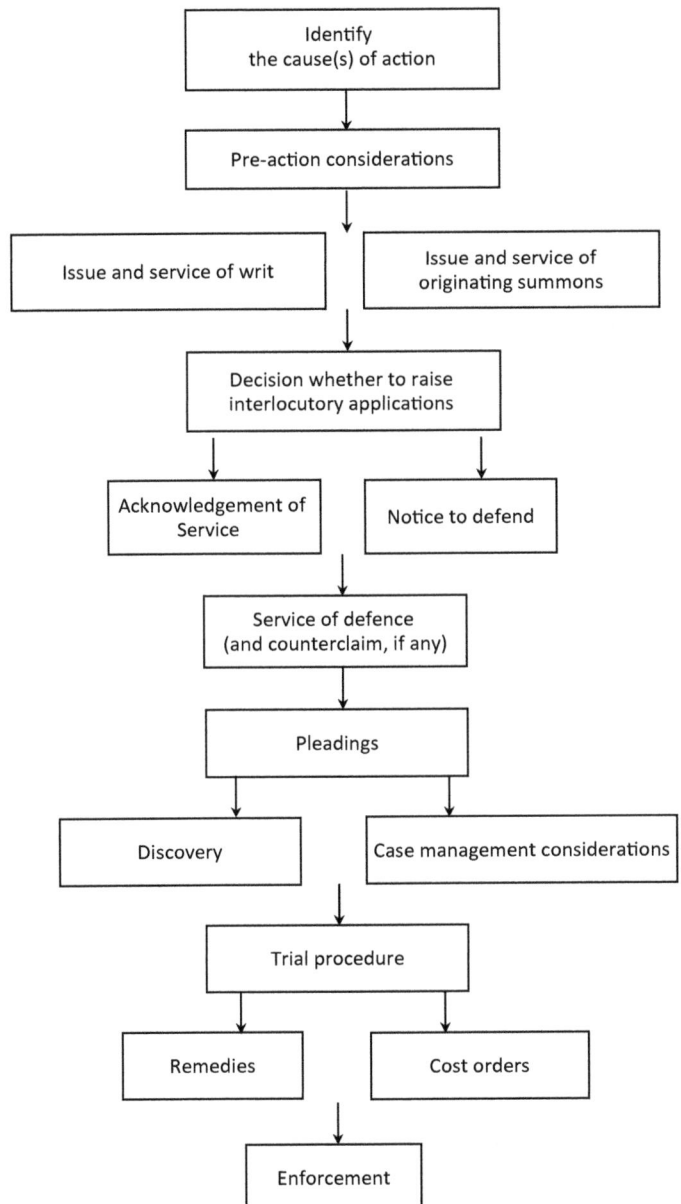

Figure 9.1 Civil litigation in Hong Kong

important to consider whether the dispute can be resolved by alternative dispute resolution.[13]

A plaintiff can start a civil action either by writ of summons or originating summons, unless any written law provides otherwise. Some proceedings may be required, or be authorised, to be begun by originating motion or petition, such as for divorce.[14] A writ of summons (referred to as a writ) is appropriate if there is a dispute of fact, whereas an originating summons is appropriate for disputes of law. Where the principal issue in a claim is likely to be about the construction of any written law or any instrument made under any written law, deed, will, contract etc., or where there is unlikely to be any substantial dispute of fact, then it is more appropriate for the plaintiff to start by originating summons.[15]

If there is a substantial dispute of fact, then the plaintiff should proceed by writ. The form of a writ must follow Form No. 1 in Appendix A of the Rules of the District Court or the Rules of the High Court. A writ must be 'indorsed' with either a statement of claim, which is a formal statement of the plaintiff's claim with the facts that will be relied upon along with the relief and remedy being claimed, or a concise statement of the nature of the claim or the relief or remedy required in the action.[16] For the purposes of service, a writ is valid for twelve months beginning from the date of its issue. Once a writ has expired, the plaintiff can either issue a new writ or apply to the court to extend the current writ. To obtain an extension from the court, the plaintiff needs to show good reason why the writ should be extended.[17]

It is important to note the limitation period for starting different types of civil actions, which is the deadline to bring a claim. An action for a breach of contract or a tort, for instance, must be instituted within six years from

---

[13] See Chapter 10, 'Alternative Methods of Resolving Disputes'.
[14] Originating motion and petition are rather specialised and are used only where written laws require or authorise.
[15] Rules of the District Court (Cap. 336H), Ord. 5, r. 4; Rules of the High Court (Cap. 4A), Ord. 5, r. 4. For the form of the originating summons and other provisions on the procedure on an originating summons, see Rules of the District Court (Cap. 336H), Ords. 7 and 28; Rules of the High Court (Cap. 4A), Ords. 7 and 28.
[16] Rules of the District Court (Cap. 336H), Ord. 6, r. 2; Rules of the High Court (Cap. 4A), Ord. 6, r. 2.
[17] Rules of the District Court (Cap. 336H), Ord. 6, r. 8(1); Rules of the High Court (Cap. 4A), Ord. 6, r. 8(1). For the two-stage test that the court will adopt for an extension, see *Chow Ching Man* v. *Sun Wah Ornament Manufactory Ltd* [1996] 2 HKC 460; *Grand Pacific Equity Ltd* v. *RSH Sports (HK) Ltd* [2006] HKCU 1816; see also *Sea Legend Holdings Ltd* v. *China Taiping Insurance (HK) Co Ltd & Ors* [2013] HKCU 2391, at para. 29.

the date on which the cause of action accrued (i.e. came into being), namely the date when the contract was broken and the day that damage was suffered, respectively.[18] In cases of personal injuries, the limitation period is three years from the date on which the cause of action accrued or, if later, the date of the plaintiff's knowledge.[19] Once the deadline is missed, the claim is 'time-barred'. Subject to certain exceptions, the expiry of the limitation period only bars the remedy (of enforcement of the claim by way of an action) and does not extinguish the underlying right.[20] Where the remedy (but not the right) is barred but the plaintiff still brings a claim out of time, it is for the defendant to plead the statute of limitations in its defence.[21] Once pleaded, the expiry of the limitation period serves as a total defence for the defendant. The time limits set out can only be extended in exceptional circumstances, such as if the plaintiff was mentally incapacitated when his/her cause of action arose or if the action is based upon the fraud of the defendant.[22]

It is a fundamental principle that a person against whom a claim is made must be given due notice so as to allow him/her to answer and defend the claim.[23] Accordingly, a writ must be served on the defendant in order for the action to proceed. A writ may be served personally on the defendant either by the plaintiff or his/her agent.[24] Personal service is achieved by leaving a copy of the document with the defendant.[25] If the defendant is a body corporate, personal service may be achieved by serving the document personally on the chairperson or president of the body, or the clerk, secretary, treasurer or other similar officer.[26] Previously, service of the writ

---

[18] Limitation Ordinance (Cap. 347), s. 4(1).
[19] Limitation Ordinance (Cap. 347), s. 27(4).
[20] *Ronex Properties Ltd* v. *John Laing Construction Ltd* [1982] 3 All ER 961. For example, a creditor could still seek payment of a statute-barred debt out of a lien or other security held over the debt even though the creditor cannot commence an action to obtain a court order for payment of the debt: *Carter* v. *White* (1883) 25 Ch D 666, at 672.
[21] Rules of the District Court (Cap. 336H), Ord. 18, r. 8(1); Rules of the High Court (Cap. 4A), Ord. 18, r. 8(1).
[22] Limitation Ordinance (Cap. 347), ss. 22 and 26.
[23] See *Craig* v. *Kanssen* [1943] 1 All ER 108 at 113.
[24] Rules of the District Court (Cap. 336H), Ord. 10, r. 1; Rules of the High Court (Cap. 4A), Ord. 10, r. 1.
[25] Rules of the District Court (Cap. 336H), Ord. 65, r. 2; Rules of the High Court (Cap. 4A), Ord. 65, r. 2.
[26] Rules of the District Court (Cap. 336H), Ord. 65, r. 3(1); Rules of the High Court (Cap. 4A), Ord. 65, r. 3(1).

on the defendant personally was required. Nowadays, a copy of the writ sent by registered post to the defendant's usual or last known address (or, for a body corporate, the registered or principal office of the body corporate)[27] or inserting a copy of the writ addressed to the defendant through the letter box for the above address would also suffice.[28] The procedure for service is largely the same for originating summons.[29]

Acknowledgement of Service and Defence

A defendant must file with the Court Registry an acknowledgement of service, and indicate whether there is an intention to defend the proceedings, within fourteen days after service of the writ (which includes the day that the writ was served).[30] The acknowledgement of service must specify the defendant's place of residence, or in the case of a body corporate, the address of the registered or principal office. If a defendant is acknowledging service by a solicitor, the solicitor's name and business address must be included as well.[31]

A defendant who intends to contest the plaintiff's claim must serve a defence on every party to the action within twenty-eight days after the time limit for acknowledging service of the writ or after a statement of claim is served, unless the court approves otherwise.[32]

Default and Summary Judgment

A default judgment may be entered against the defendant if he/she has not given a notice of intention to defend, failed to file an acknowledgement

---

[27] Rules of the District Court (Cap. 336H), Ord. 65, r. 3(2); Rules of the High Court (Cap. 4A), Ord. 65, r. 3(2).
[28] Rules of the District Court (Cap. 336H), Ord. 10, r. 2; Rules of the High Court (Cap. 4A), Ord. 10, r. 2. This applies, however, only to defendants who are in Hong Kong at the time of service.
[29] See Rules of the District Court (Cap. 336H), Ord 10, r. 5(1); Rules of the High Court (Cap. 4A), Ord 10, r. 5(1).
[30] Rules of the District Court (Cap. 336H), Ord. 12, r. 5(a); Rules of the High Court (Cap. 4A), Ord. 12, r. 5(a).
[31] Rules of the District Court (Cap. 336H), Ord. 12, r. 3; Rules of the High Court (Cap. 4A), Ord. 12, r. 3.
[32] Rules of the District Court (Cap. 336H), Ord. 18, r. 2; Rules of the High Court (Cap. 4A), Ord. 18, r. 2.

of service on time or failed to serve a defence.[33] Likewise, a judgment to dismiss the action may also be entered against the plaintiff for failure to serve the statement of claim on time.[34]

A summary judgment may be obtained by the plaintiff where it is plain that there is no defence to the claim.[35] A summary judgment is only appropriate when there was no defence and no fairly arguable point to be argued on behalf of the defendant.[36] Unlike a default judgment, the main point is not whether the defendant has served a defence but that, even though a defence is served, there are no legal grounds to resist the plaintiff's claims. The defendant can likewise apply for a summary judgment against the plaintiff on a counterclaim.[37]

Pleadings

Pleadings are the formal documents exchanged between the plaintiff and defendant which set out each party's case. They include: the plaintiff's statement of claim, reply and defence to counterclaim; the defendant's defence and counterclaim; and certain other documents used to express the parties' cases. The writ and originating summons are not pleadings. The purpose of pleadings is to give fair notice to the other party of the stance of the pleading party and to define the issues of the dispute so that proper preparations can be made against the defined issues without wasting time and expenses on other issues. It also limits the generality of the claim and the evidence, and allows each party to know what evidence they need to prepare for at trial. Well-drafted pleadings ensure that neither party is taken by surprise. Furthermore, during trial, it is important for witnesses giving evidence to know what the issues are.[38]

A pleading must state in summary form the material facts on which the party relies, preferably in chronological order, and the necessary particulars, which are the details. Omission to do so may lead the claim to be struck out either on the application of a party or the court's own motion on

---

[33] Rules of the District Court (Cap. 336H), Ord. 13; Rules of the High Court (Cap. 4A), Ord. 13.
[34] Rules of the District Court (Cap. 336H), Ord. 19; Rules of the High Court (Cap. 4A), Ord. 19.
[35] Rules of the District Court (Cap. 336H), Ord. 14, r. 5; Rules of the High Court (Cap. 4A), Ord. 14, r. 5.
[36] See *Pacific Electric Wire & Cable Co Ltd* v. *Harmutty Ltd & Ors* [2009] 2 HKC 330, para. 4.
[37] Rules of the District Court (Cap. 336H), Ord. 14; Rules of the High Court (Cap. 4A), Ord. 14.
[38] See *Wing Hang Bank Ltd* v. *Crystal Jet International Ltd* [2005] 2 HKC 638, at 643.

the ground that there is no reasonable cause of action or defence; that it is scandalous, frivolous or vexatious; that it may prejudice, embarrass or delay the fair trial of the action; or that it is otherwise an abuse of process of the court.[39] In other instances, it may lead to an application by the opposing party for an order for further and better particulars of the pleading, thereby increasing costs. Parties are bound by what has been pleaded subject to the court's allowance for amendments to pleadings or by parties' mutual consent.[40]

The evidence that is relied upon to prove the case is, however, not to be pleaded.[41] Although a party may raise a point of law in his/her pleading[42] (for example, the defence relies on contributory negligence), the point of law must not be argued in the pleading. A statement of claim must also state the relief or remedy that the plaintiff is seeking except for costs, which need not be specifically claimed.[43] In a defence, the defendant must respond to every allegation of fact by either admitting the allegation, or must 'traverse' the allegation by way of denial or by a statement of non-admission.[44] It is not enough to provide a general denial; the defendant must deal with each specific allegation that is not admitted.[45] Otherwise, the other party's pleading is deemed to be admitted.

Every pleading must be divided into paragraphs and numbered consecutively so that each allegation is contained in a separate paragraph. Dates and sums must be expressed in figures and not in words. Pleadings can be written in either English or Chinese, but not a mixture of both. Every pleading must also note the year that the writ was issued and the number

---

[39] Rules of the District Court (Cap. 336H), Ord. 18, r. 19; Rules of the High Court (Cap. 4A), Ord. 18, r. 19.

[40] See *Poon Hau Kei* v. *Hsin Cheong Construction Co Ltd* [2004] 2 HKC 235.

[41] Rules of the District Court (Cap. 336H), Ord. 18, r. 7; Rules of the High Court (Cap. 4A), Ord. 18, r. 7. Moreover, averments of an argumentative nature should not be included in pleadings; see *Excel Concrete Ltd* v. *The Concrete Producers Association of Hong Kong Ltd & Ors* [2014] HKCU 1520, at para. 13.

[42] Rules of the District Court (Cap. 336H), Ord. 18, r. 11; Rules of the High Court (Cap. 4A) Ord. 18, r. 11.

[43] Rules of the District Court (Cap. 336H), Ord. 18, r. 15(1); Rules of the High Court (Cap. 4A), Ord. 18, r. 15(1).

[44] Non-admission may be suitable when the defendant is unable to admit or deny because of lack of knowledge but wants the plaintiff to prove it at trial.

[45] Rules of the District Court (Cap. 336H), Ord. 18, r. 13; Rules of the High Court (Ca. 4A), Ord. 18, r. 13. See also *Lau Kwai Yin* v. *Tack Hsin Restaurant (London) Ltd* [2016] 4 HKC 460, at para. 4.

of the action, the title of the action, the description of the pleading and the date on which the pleading was served, and it must be signed by counsel, the party's solicitor or, if the party is unrepresented, by the party.[46] It must also be accompanied by a statement of truth.[47] The name and address of the pleader or the name or firm and business address of the representing solicitor must also be indorsed on the pleading, and the pleading must be rounded by a backsheet.

Discovery

After the close of pleadings[48] in an action begun by writ, there will be discovery, i.e. the formal exchange of documents which are or have been in each party's possession, custody or power relating to matters that are raised in the action.[49] The purpose of discovery is to enable each party to have access to relevant documents held by the other side. This avoids 'trial by ambush', where the opposing party is taken by surprise at the trial. The ability of each party to obtain access to the documents of the other can also have the effect of encouraging the parties to settle after assessing the strengths and weaknesses of each side's case.[50]

Discovery is a continuing obligation, and supplemental lists of documents must be filed from time to time.[51] While the range of documents to be included in discovery may be very wide, discovery should only be limited to documents which are relevant. Discovery should not be a 'fishing expedition' where a party requests from the other side a large volume of documents with the purpose of ascertaining whether a speculative case exists, as opposed to compelling the production of documents where there is already some evidence that a case exists.[52] Failure to comply

---

[46] Rules of the District Court (Cap. 336H), Ord. 18, r. 6; Rules of the High Court (Cap. 4A), Ord. 18, r. 6.
[47] See below.
[48] As to when pleadings are closed, see Rules of the District Court (Cap. 336H), Ord. 18, r. 20; Rules of the High Court (Cap. 4A), Ord. 18, r. 20.
[49] Rules of the District Court (Cap. 336H), Ord. 24, r. 1; Rules of the High Court (Cap. 4A), Ord. 24, r. 1.
[50] Lau (n. 10), p. 203.
[51] *Hong Lok School Ltd* v. *Chow Sai Yiu* [2003] HKCU 819, at para. 4.
[52] *Trade Practices Commission* v. *CC (NSW) Pty Ltd* (1995) 58 FCR 426, at 438; *HKFE Clearing Corp Ltd* v. *Yicko Futures Ltd* [2006] 2 HKC 233, at para. 17; *Dembele Salifou* v. *Director of Immigration* [2015] 4 HKC 294.

with discovery may lead to the dismissal of the action or the defence being struck out.[53]

Injunctions

Injunctions are court orders requiring a party to do something (mandatory injunction) or prohibiting a party from doing something (prohibitory injunction).[54] The court may grant an interlocutory or final injunction where it thinks it is just or convenient to do so.[55] Interlocutory injunctions, which are usually provisional and granted before trial, generally last until the end of the trial or until further order of the court. The purpose of interlocutory injunctions is 'is to protect the plaintiff against injury by violation of his right for which he could not be adequately compensated in damages recoverable in the action' were the plaintiff to win at trial.[56] Before granting an interlocutory injunction, the court will in principle weigh the plaintiff's need for protection with the need to protect the defendant from injury resulting from the injunction. The court will weigh the two on a 'balance of convenience'.[57]

If the defendant is likely to dispose of his/her assets improperly, then a Mareva injunction may be obtained by the plaintiff. This is an order to freeze a defendant's assets.[58] The purpose is to protect the plaintiff from receiving nothing even if judgment is made in his/her favour, where there is a real risk of the defendant dissipating his/her assets before judgment is made. If the defendant is likely to conceal or destroy documents or materials in question, then an Anton Piller order may be obtained. An Anton Piller order permits the plaintiff to enter the defendant's premises to search for certain documents and to inspect, take away or make copies of them.[59] The rationale is to prevent the destruction of evidence. However, given the

---

[53] Rules of the District Court (Cap. 336H), Ord. 24, r. 16; Rules of the High Court (Cap. 4A), Ord. 24, r. 16.
[54] Failure to comply with an injunction is a contempt of court.
[55] High Court Ordinance (Cap. 4), s. 21L(1).
[56] *American Cyanamid Co* v. *Ethicon Ltd (No 1)* [1975] AC 396, at 406.
[57] *American Cyanamid Co Appellants* v. *Ethicon Ltd* [1974] AC 396 sets out the principles for an application for an interlocutory injunction, and it has subsequently been adopted by the Hong Kong courts.
[58] This was developed in *Mareva Compania Naviera SA* v. *International Bulk Carriers SA* [1980] 1 All ER 213. See also Practice Direction 11.2.
[59] *Anton Piller KG* v. *Manufacturing Processes Ltd* [1976] Ch 55.

drastic nature of such injunctions, which have been referred to as the law's 'nuclear weapons', courts must exercise restraint in granting such orders.[60]

Burden and Standard of Proof (Civil Trials)

The burden of proof is on the plaintiff, and the standard is to prove his/her case on a balance of probabilities. The classic formulation on the standard of proof in civil trials is expressed by Lord Denning this way:

> That degree is well settled. It must carry a reasonable degree of probability, but not so high as is required in a criminal case. If the evidence is such that the tribunal can say: 'We think it more probable than not', the burden is discharged but, if the probabilities are equal, it is not.[61]

This means that the plaintiff's burden is discharged if the court is satisfied that it is more likely than not that the events occurred as the plaintiff claimed. The standard of proof in civil trials is lower than that for criminal trials.

Where the allegations are more serious (e.g., allegations of fraud), the more compelling the evidence needs to be for the plaintiff to discharge the burden of proof.[62] However, this does not mean that a different standard of proof is applied. The standard in civil trials is in all cases on the balance of probabilities. The reason why more compelling evidence is needed to prove more serious allegations is that such conduct complained of may be more inherently improbable, and hence stronger evidence is needed to satisfy the court on a balance of probabilities that the conduct did occur.

Trial Procedure

There are four modes of trial in the Court of First Instance (CFI). The usual mode is trial by judge alone. Where there is in issue a claim in respect of libel, slander, malicious prosecution, false imprisonment or seduction, then on application by a party, the trial will be conducted by a judge and jury

---

[60] *Bank Mellat* v. *Nikpour (Mohammed Ebrahim)* [1985] FSR 87 CA; See also *Ng Chun Fai Stephen & Anor* v. *Tamco Electrical & Electronics (HK) Ltd* [1993] 1 HKC 160.
[61] *Miller* v. *Minister of Pensions* [1947] 2 All ER 372, at 372.
[62] *Solicitor (24/07)* v. *Law Society of Hong Kong* (2008) 11 HKCFAR 117.

unless the court finds it to be inconvenient because there would be prolonged examination of documents or accounts or any scientific or local investigation which cannot conveniently be made with a jury.[63] The court retains discretion to order a trial by jury for cases not involving the above issues.[64] Trial may be conducted by a judge with an assessor, who is an expert appointed to assist the court.[65] Lastly, a case may, with the consent of the parties, be heard before a master, who is a more junior court officer.[66] The District Court has the same mode of trials apart from trial by judge and jury.

The trial begins with the plaintiff (plaintiff's counsel) giving the opening submissions, which provide an overview of the plaintiff's case, the issues of the case relating to both fact and law, the weaknesses of the defence's case, and the evidence that will be called. For each of the plaintiff's witnesses, the plaintiff will examine him/her first (this is called examination-in-chief). Then, the defence will have the opportunity to cross-examine that witness. Afterwards, if the plaintiff wishes, the plaintiff can re-examine the witness, mainly to clarify or elaborate on what was said in the cross-examination.

If the defence calls evidence, the defence begins with his/her opening submissions. The defence calls and examines witnesses as the plaintiff did, with the plaintiff having the opportunity to cross-examine the defence's witnesses. The defence then makes his/her closing submissions. The plaintiff makes his/her submissions in reply.[67] After hearing both parties' cases, the court can either give judgment immediately or give judgment at a later date, which is called a reserved judgment.

Remedies and Enforcement

There are a variety of remedies that may be awarded to the successful or winning party, such as damages and specific performance. If a successful party is awarded damages or other sum of money, he/she is referred to as a judgment creditor, and the losing party ordered to pay the amount is a

---

[63] High Court Ordinance (Cap. 4), s. 33A(1).
[64] High Court Ordinance (Cap. 4), s. 33A(3).
[65] Rules of the High Court (Cap. 4A), Ord. 33, r. 6.
[66] Rules of the High Court (Cap. 4A), Ord. 36, r. 1.
[67] See Rules of the District Court (Cap. 336H), Ord. 35; Rules of the High Court (Cap. 4A), Ord. 35.

judgment debtor. Although the plaintiff (or the defendant in a counter-claim) may be successful in obtaining a remedy, he/she may still need to take further action to enforce the judgment obtained. Enforcement is necessary when the court orders a payment or an injunction but the party against whom the order is made fails to comply. There are a number of ways to enforce the court's judgment. For instance, when a judgment debtor has moveable assets, the judgment creditor may seek the issue of a writ of *fieri facias* by the court. Once the writ is issued, the court bailiff executes the writ by seizing the assets, which are then sold, usually at a public auction. The assets that are liable to be sold include land, bank notes, government bonds and company shares, but not tools of trade and necessary wearing apparel and bedding not exceeding HK$10,000 in value in the whole.[68] Another method for enforcement of a judgment is to apply for a garnishee order, namely an order of the court against a third party in Hong Kong who owes a debt to the judgment debtor (such as the bank of the judgment debtor), requiring the third party to pay the judgment creditor directly.[69]

There are other orders that the court may make to help with enforcement. For instance, an application can be made by the judgment creditor for a prohibition order to prevent the judgment debtor leaving Hong Kong.[70] If the debtor does not have cash but has other assets, a charge may be imposed by way of a charging order on assets held by the debtor such as land or certain types of securities (such as shares in a company).[71]

Drawbacks to Civil Litigation

There are a number of drawbacks to civil litigation.[72] The large numbers of court proceedings and trials place pressure on the courts, and this problem is shared by Hong Kong as well as other common law jurisdictions. The

---

[68] District Court Ordinance (Cap. 336), s. 68B(1); High Court Ordinance (Cap. 4), s. 21D(1).
[69] See Rules of the District Court (Cap. 336H), Ord. 49; Rules of the High Court (Cap. 4A), Ord. 49.
[70] See District Court Ordinance (Cap. 336), s. 52E; High Court Ordinance (Cap. 4), s. 21B.
[71] District Court Ordinance (Cap. 336), s. 52AA; High Court Ordinance (Cap. 4), s. 20A.
[72] See Chief Justice's Working Party on Civil Justice Reform, *Civil Justice Reform: Interim Report and Consultative Paper* (Hong Kong 2001).

'litigation explosion'[73] and the 'culture of compensation', referring to an unreasonable eagerness of individuals to seek legal redress when things go wrong,[74] have been said to place immense strains on the court system.

Trials can be very complex and take a long time to resolve. This is especially true with social change and the advancement of industry and technology. In modern society and modern economies, commercial transactions and relationships have become increasingly complex. To keep up with such changes, the law (legislation and case law) has also become more detailed and complex. These factors in turn result in court cases becoming increasingly difficult and challenging to resolve. This is not beneficial for litigants, as the litigation process ends up being too slow, fraught with delays, incomprehensible and expensive, with costs adding up in lengthy proceedings. It may even be the case that the costs of legal proceedings is higher than the amount of the claim in the action. Aside from individuals, high costs may also have an adverse effect on business. Both local and international businesses also need to resolve their legal disputes, and legal costs become part of their overheads. If these costs are too high, then the competitiveness of Hong Kong as a place to do business or as a venue for litigation, along with its status as a leading financial centre, would erode.[75]

Litigation is slow in bringing a case to conclusion, and trials are inherently uncertain in terms not only of the outcome but also of time and eventual costs. The burden, both financial and psychological, of having a case linger should not be overlooked. This leads to inequality between the wealthy and those who are not, as the wealthy have more resources to engage in prolonged litigation. Given the expense of litigation, many members of the public are unable to enforce their rights through the civil justice system unless they receive financial assistance. Furthermore, civil proceedings are complex, with unique procedures rendering them incomprehensible for many litigants. With high legal costs, there are many litigants in person (unrepresented litigants), and the civil justice system does not do enough to facilitate their needs. At the same time,

---

[73] Ibid., para. 27.
[74] K. Williams, 'State of Fear: Britain's "Compensation Culture" Reviewed' (2005), *Legal Studies* 25, 499.
[75] Working Party on Civil Justice Reform, CJR: Interim Report and Consultative Paper, para. 41.

the phenomenon of litigants in person poses difficulties for the system.[76] This effectively undermines people's access to justice.

Litigation can also be too adversarial. The basis of the adversarial system is that it is party-driven and the court acts as a neutral adjudicator. However, given the party-driven nature, civil litigation is susceptible to manipulation and exploitation of procedural rules by the parties and their legal advisers. For example, as discussed above, the purpose of pleadings is to identify the issues clearly, ensuring that neither side is taken by surprise, thereby promoting fairness. But there are instances where the adversarial attitude of the parties leads to the raising of numerous superfluous questions. Similarly, parties misuse discovery, with one party overwhelming the other party with masses of documents that are of marginal relevance to inflate the complexity and costs for the opposing side. Parties, especially wealthier parties, may devote resources to interlocutory battles over peripheral documents as a deliberate tactic to exhaust the other party.[77] Interlocutory applications generally refer to applications made to court prior to trial. These include applications for further and better particulars, default judgment and summary judgment. The Chief Justice's Working Party on Civil Justice Reform noted that:

> the adversarial design by definition places the parties on a war footing, with each trying to secure victory on a winner-take-all basis. It is not a question of the parties going to the court simply to let an independent arbiter decide who is right, but of going to court to 'win' and to 'beat' the other side.

Moreover:

> The psychology of warfare also tends to promote disproportionate efforts and spending on interlocutory and objectively minor aspects of the case. An interlocutory application, whatever its outcome, may be likely to have little impact on the final result of the action. However, the adversarial ethic may present it as a necessary part of the general campaign to defeat and cow the enemy, justifying expenditure of both the parties' and the court's resources.[78]

---

[76] See Chapter 11, 'Access to Justice'.
[77] Working Party on Civil Justice Reform, CJR: Interim Report and Consultative Paper, paras. 34.1 and 34.2.
[78] Ibid., paras. 35.1 and 35.3.

Civil Justice Reform

In 2000, the then Chief Justice Andrew Li appointed a Working Party to review the civil justice rules procedures in the High Court with the aim of improving access to justice at reasonable cost and speed. In November 2001, an Interim Report and Consultative Paper was published. Subsequently in March 2004, the Final Report was published, setting out the Working Party's 150 recommendations for amendments. The Chief Justice announced the acceptance of the recommendations in the Final Report, and a Steering Committee on Civil Justice Reform was established to oversee its implementation. In the following years, further assessments, consultations and amendments were made, and it was decided that the reforms would apply to both the High Court and District Court. Legislation, including the High Court Ordinance, District Court Ordinance, Rules of the High Court, and Rules of the District Court were amended. The Civil Justice Reform (CJR) came into effect on 2 April 2009.

Although Hong Kong's CJR was based on the framework of the reforms in England and Wales (the Woolf Reforms), Hong Kong did not introduce an entirely new legislative code, as was done in England and Wales. The reforms in England and Wales were based on Lord Woolf's Access to Justice final report in 1996, which raised criticisms against the civil justice system. This led to the enactment of the English Civil Procedure Rules (CPR), which came into force in April 1999. The Working Party on CJR in Hong Kong decided against adopting the CPR in Hong Kong, but opted instead for amendments to existing laws and rules. Their reasoning was that while amendments would involve more effort in the initial drafting stage, it would be less disruptive and less demanding for everyone to have to master a new procedural code.[79]

Order 1A Rule 1 of the Rules of the High Court and District Court sets out the underlying objectives of the CJR:

(a) to increase the cost-effectiveness of any practice and procedure to be followed in relation to the proceedings before the court;
(b) to ensure that a case is dealt with as expeditiously as is reasonably practicable;

---

[79] Chief Justice's Working Party on Civil Justice Reform, *Civil Justice Reform: Final Report* (Hong Kong 2006), para. 22.

(c) to promote a sense of reasonable proportion and procedural economy in the conduct of proceedings;
(d) to ensure fairness between the parties;
(e) to facilitate the settlement of disputes; and
(f) to ensure that the resources of the court are distributed fairly.

As can be seen, the objectives of the CJR are a direct response to the drawbacks of civil litigation. Emphasis is placed on reducing costs and resolving disputes in a timely manner. There is a greater focus on settlements. Settlements and alternative dispute resolution, namely mediation and arbitration, are discussed in more detail in Chapter 10. Other key changes to the civil justice system are examined below.

Case Management

The court now takes a much more proactive role in managing cases after the CJR. The court is directed to give effect to the underlying objectives of the CJR stated above.[80] In the early stages of the proceedings, the court will encourage both sides to co-operate with each other and will encourage, and facilitate, the use of alternative dispute resolution and settlement of the case if deemed appropriate. It will identify the issues of the case that require investigation and trial to ensure that only the main issues to be resolved are focused on, summarily disposing of others. The court will also determine the order in which the issues are to be resolved and fix timetables and give directions to the parties to ensure the efficient progress of the case. Relatedly, the court will decide which aspects of the case can be dealt with on the same occasion and which aspects of the case can be dealt with summarily without having the parties attend court.[81] The court can exercise many case management powers including: extending or shortening the time for compliance with any rule, court order or Practice Direction; adjourning or bringing forward a hearing; consolidating proceedings; and directing a separate trial of any issue. When making an order, the court may subject it to conditions, such as a condition to pay a

---

[80] Rules of the District Court (Cap. 336H), Ord. 1A, r. 2; Rules of the High Court (Cap. 4A), Ord. 1A, r. 2.
[81] Rules of the District Court (Cap. 336H), Ord. 1A, r. 4; Rules of the High Court (Cap. 4A), Ord. 1A, r. 4.

sum of money into court and specify the consequences of failure to comply.[82]

After the close of pleadings, within twenty-eight days, each party must file a Timetabling Questionnaire for the court to give case management directions. They should consult each other but not delay in the filing of the questionnaire. The questionnaire contains a list of questions, asking each party to provide certain information and asking how each party intends to proceed with the case.[83] For example, parties are asked to confirm whether they have attempted to settle the case by alternative dispute resolution, whether more parties will be added to the case, whether pleadings will need to be amended and, if so, when the applications for amendments will be made, the number of witnesses that they intend to call at trial, whether they intend to call expert witnesses and what issues the expert witness will address, when expert reports will be ready, the estimated length of trial, and whether and why a bilingual judge is requested. The plaintiff should in light of the information provided in the Timetabling Questionnaire modify or incorporate the opposing side's directions, and the duty is on the plaintiff to communicate with the parties to agree on the directions for the progress of the case. If there is agreement, then the plaintiff is to file a consent summons containing the agreed directions and timetable for the court to consider.[84] Moreover, if a trial date is sought, then each party should give time estimates of their opening submissions, examinations-in-chief, cross-examinations and closing submissions. If there are still disagreements, the case management summons should set out the directions and timetable that can be agreed and each party's proposals on matters that cannot be agreed.[85]

The court considers the Timetabling Questionnaires and other documents submitted and gives directions. A case management conference (CMC) and/or a pre-trial review (PTR) may be held pursuant to the timetable set by the court. At the CMC, the court gives further directions, sets a timetable for further steps and may fix the trial date (or a trial period

---

[82] Rules of the District Court (Cap. 336H), Ord. 1B, r. 1; Rules of the High Court (Cap. 4A), Ord. 1B, r. 1.
[83] See Practice Direction 5.2.
[84] Ibid.
[85] Ibid. See *Faith Bright Development Ltd* v. *Ng Kwok Kuen* [2010] 5 HKLRD 425, where the court reiterated that it was the duty of solicitors to file the timetabling questionnaires on time.

within which the trial will start, if the precise trial date is not fixed). The parties will have needed to file a Listing Questionnaire not fewer than seven days before the CMC, detailing whether previous directions have been complied with and their general readiness for trial. The PTR is not an extension of the CMC, as the court expects a case to be ready for trial and late interlocutory applications may be dismissed. At the PTR, the court may vary the length of trial, fix a trial date and give further directions.[86] The dates for the CMC, PTR, trial period and trial date are 'milestone dates', meaning that these dates are immovable; for the dates to change, a party must apply to the court. Changing of milestone dates will not be granted unless there are 'exceptional circumstances justifying the variation'.[87]

Sanctioned Offers and Payments

Sanctioned offers and payments are a mechanism after the CJR that encourages parties to settle. To encourage settlement, the court may make sanctions in relation to costs and interest against a party who rejects the sanctioned settlement but fails to do better at trial.[88] One party, the offeror, makes a sanctioned payment and/or sanctioned offer into court that, if accepted by the other party (the offeree), would satisfy the claim(s) in the civil action. A sanctioned payment is an offer that is made by the defendant (or the plaintiff facing a counterclaim) which involves the payment of money into court (or the defendant in the case of a counterclaim) to settle the whole or part of the claim. A sanctioned offer is a written offer by the plaintiff, or a defendant making a counterclaim, to settle by an acceptance of a certain amount to satisfy the claim. Both sanctioned offers and sanctioned payments can only be made after the proceedings have commenced. A sanctioned offer is treated as 'without prejudice save as to costs', meaning that that the offer is not admissible as

---

[86] See n. 72.
[87] Rules of the District Court (Cap. 336H), Ord. 25, r. 3(3); Rules of the High Court (Cap. 4A) Ord. 25, r. 1B(3). See e.g. *Chan Chun Shing* v. *Chang Chen Chin* [2009] HKCU 639 (unreported, CFI, HCPI 395/2008, 4 May 2009), where the court refused to postpone the trial date for a last-minute application for legal aid by the plaintiff.
[88] See Rules of the District Court (Cap. 336H), Ord. 22; Rules of the High Court (Cap. 4A), Ord. 22.

evidence at trial except when determining costs. A sanctioned payment must also not be communicated to the court until all questions of liability and the amount to be awarded have been decided.[89] With this mechanism, there is an incentive for the offeror to make a realistic and timely sanctioned offer/payment, as the earlier the sanctioned offer/payment is made, the more likely the offeree will face greater eventual adverse sanctions from the court. This mechanism places pressure on the offeree to accept a realistic sanctioned offer/payment.

Statements of Truth

After the CJR, all pleadings, including amendments to pleadings, witness statements and expert reports, must be verified by a statement of truth and signed by the appropriate person.[90] The wording of the statement of truth is as follows: '[the (plaintiff or as may be) believes] that the facts stated in this [name document being verified] are true'.[91] A statement of truth is a statement that the party putting forth the document believes that the facts stated in the document are true, and in the case of an expert report, that the opinions expressed in it are honestly held.[92] The court may strike out a pleading if it is not verified by a statement of truth. Similarly, unverified witness statements and expert reports are not admissible as evidence unless the court orders otherwise.[93] Any false statements made may be subject to proceedings for contempt of court.[94] This helps to deter sloppy

---

[89] Rules of the District Court (Cap. 336H), Ord. 22, r. 25; Rules of the High Court (Cap. 4A), Ord. 22, r. 25.

[90] Rules of the District Court (Cap. 336H), Ord. 41A, rr. 2 and 3; Rules of the High Court (Cap. 4A), Ord. 41A, rr. 2 and 3.

[91] Rules of the District Court (Cap. 336H), Ord. 41A, r. 5; Rules of the High Court (Cap. 4A), Ord. 41A, r. 5. See also Practice Direction 19.3.

[92] Rules of the District Court (Cap. 336H), Ord. 41A, r. 4(1); Rules of the High Court (Cap. 4A), Ord. 41A, r. 4(1).

[93] Rules of the District Court (Cap. 336H), Ord. 41A, rr. 6 and 7; Rules of the High Court (Cap. 4A), Ord. 41A, rr. 6 and 7.

[94] Rules of the District Court (Cap. 336H), Ord. 41A, r. 9; Rules of the High Court (Cap. 4A), Ord. 41A, r. 9. In citing a person for contempt for making a false statement, the applicant must prove beyond a reasonable doubt (1) the falsity of the statement in question, (2) that the statement has or would have interfered with the course of justice in some material respect, and (3) that at the time it was made the maker of the statement had no honest belief in the truth of the statement and knew of the likelihood that it would interfere with the course of justice; *Numeric City Ltd v. Lau Chi Wing* [2016] 5 HKC 448, at para. 35.

and speculative pleadings and deters dishonest cases from being put forward.[95]

Costs

Prior to the CJR, the general rule was that the court would order costs to 'follow the event'. This means that the winning party would be awarded with the costs of the civil action and the losing party would not only have to pay their own costs but the costs of the winning party as well. Costs mainly refer to legal costs including solicitors' fees, barristers' fees and expenses for photocopying. Costs are in the discretion of the courts, as they decide who pays the legal costs and in what amount subject to the relevant procedural rules.[96] While the starting point now is still that costs should follow the event, the court has greater discretion in departing from this general rule and make orders 'as it sees fit'.[97] The court would take into account the parties' conduct and determine whether unnecessary costs were incurred when awarding costs. The court may make separate costs orders for different parts of the proceedings. When determining costs, the court would take into consideration the underlying objectives of the CJR.[98]

The courts can also make a wasted cost order against a solicitor or barrister if he/she, whether personally or through their employee or agent, has caused a party to incur wasted costs. Wasted costs are any costs incurred by a party as a result of an improper or unreasonable act or omission, any undue delay, or other misconduct or default on any part of the legal representative or through their employee or agent.[99] The legal representative may be directed to repay the client for costs which the client has been ordered to pay to other parties in the proceedings, or the costs as between the legal representative and his/her client may be disallowed.[100]

---

[95] *Tong Kin Hing* v. *Autron Mauritius Corp & Ors* [2010] 1 HKLRD 77.
[96] District Court Ordinance (Cap. 336), s. 53; High Court Ordinance (Cap. 4), s. 52A.
[97] Rules of the District Court (Cap. 336H), Ord. 62, r. 3(2); Rules of the High Court (Cap. 4A), Ord. 62, r. 3(2).
[98] Rules of the District Court (Cap. 336H), Ord. 62, r. 5; Rules of the High Court (Cap. 4A), Ord. 62, r. 5.
[99] District Court Ordinance (Cap. 336), s. 53(3); High Court Ordinance (Cap. 4), s. 52A(6).
[100] Rules of the District Court (Cap. 336H), Ord. 62, r. 8; Rules of the High Court (Cap. 4A), Ord. 62, r. 8.

Review Questions

(1) Imagine that you intend to sue Company A for a breach of contract. What are the considerations that you must make before starting a civil action?
(2) What are the purposes of pleadings?
(3) What is the difference between a default judgment and a summary judgment?
(4) Why is discovery important?
(5) How does each of the following further the underlying objectives of the CJR?
 (a) case management powers of the court;
 (b) sanctioned offers and sanctioned payments; and
 (c) statements of truth.

Alternative Methods of Resolving Disputes 10

Chapter Highlights

- Mediation   288
- Arbitration   294
- Advantages and Disadvantages of ADR   302

Other than litigation, either in the courts or in the tribunals, there are a number of avenues available for the resolution of disputes that are alternatives to the more adversarial judicial process. Alternative dispute resolution (ADR) is an umbrella term that covers these alternative methods of resolving disputes. The two main avenues which this chapter focuses on are mediation and arbitration.

ADR has become increasingly popular, especially since the Civil Justice Reform in 2009. As discussed in Chapter 9, one of the underlying objectives of the reform is to have the courts 'facilitate the settlement of disputes'[1]; and the new case management powers of the courts[2] even include encouragement of litigants to 'use an alternative dispute resolution procedure' if the court deems it to be appropriate and facilitation of its use.[3] But this does not mean that trial judges will be necessarily involved in the settlement procedure.

With respect to arbitration, Hong Kong has developed into one of the leading centres of international arbitration and is regarded as the leading arbitration centre in the Asia-Pacific Region. Arbitration now contributes to a large part of the legal sector's economy. But in recent years it is facing

---
[1] Rules of the High Court (Cap. 4A), Ord. 1A, r. 1(e).
[2] Rules of the High Court (Cap. 4A), Ord. 1A, r. 4(2).
[3] Rules of the High Court (Cap. 4A), Ord. 1A, r. 4(2)(e).

competition from other regional cities such as Singapore. It is therefore in the interests of Hong Kong to continue to promote arbitration and ADR.

Mediation

Mediation involves the appointment of a neutral third party, called a mediator, to assist in the negotiation process. Mediation may be court-ordered, voluntary or agreed beforehand in a contract. In Hong Kong, the model of mediation adopted is facilitative mediation, where the goal is to empower the parties to take control and solve their disputes. This is distinct from other models, such as evaluative mediation, where the mediator will assume responsibility on rendering opinions and producing a solution.[4]

The appointed mediator will facilitate the discussion of relevant issues, explore and generate options, keep communications between the disputing parties open, and assist the parties in reaching a settlement as to the whole or part of the dispute.[5] This facilitator does not have the power to impose a settlement on the disputing parties. His/her role is to assist in keeping the discussion focused and free of emotional and personal issues and interference. Unlike judges in court, mediators do not find fault, and the whole process is much less formal. Mediators do not make decisions for the parties; it is up to the parties to work out a solution and, unless the disputing parties agree, no one will force them to sign any settlement agreement.[6]

Mediation is an effective way of resolving conflicts when negotiation fails, before proceeding to litigation, because it helps the parties to focus on the live issues and re-opens basic communication where there has been a breakdown or deadlock. Mediators will most likely meet with the disputing parties separately and explore possibilities first, and perhaps multiple times, before both sides finally reach a settlement. Mediation is particularly important in solving family disputes, for example where ex-partners are mired in an emotional stalemate over the custody of children.

---

[4] See S. Sihombing, C. To and J. Chiu, *Mediation in Hong Kong: Law and Practice* (Hong Kong: Wolters Kluwer 2014), chapter 8.
[5] See Mediation Ordinance (Cap. 620), s. 4(1).
[6] But unlike a court judgment or arbitral award, a mediation settlement is only a contract, and if it is breached, a party looking to enforce the agreement would need to go through the usual steps in obtaining remedies for a breach of contract.

Since the 1980s, government bodies and voluntary organisations have used mediation as an effective way of resolving disputes in order to reduce cost and effort in litigious resolution. Mediation grew from ad hoc schemes for different industries. It is now supported by both the judiciary and the Government. Different industries continue to operate mediation services. For example, the Labour Relations Division of the Labour Department provides mediation services for employers and employees to assist them in reaching a settlement on their claims.[7] Another example is the Hong Kong Catholic Marriage Advisory Council, which provides a mediation service to both Catholic and non-Catholic couples who seek help with marital disputes or the resolution of the tumultuous issues that arise in marriage breakdown, such as maintenance, child access and property.[8]

Following the 2007–2008 Policy Address by the then Chief Executive Donald Tsang, a Working Group on Mediation chaired by the then Secretary for Justice Wong Yan Lung was set up to make mediation more extensive and effective in Hong Kong. The Working Group in its report in 2010 made forty-eight recommendations in the areas of regulatory framework, training and accreditation of mediators, and publicity and public education with respect to mediation.[9] A Mediation Task Force consisting of the Secretary for Justice, members of the judiciary and the legal profession, and mediation service providers was set up to assist in the implementation of the recommendations provided by the Working Group and take into consideration public feedback received after the report was published.[10] Among the recommendations was the introduction of legislation on mediation, which subsequently led to the enactment of a Mediation Ordinance.

Under the Civil Justice Reform, the courts openly promote the use of mediation. The courts have the power to 'stay the whole or part of any proceedings or judgment either generally or until a specified date or

---

[7] Labour Department, 'Public Services: Labour Relations Division' (Hong Kong: Labour Department 2018), available at www.labour.gov.hk/eng/labour/content1.htm.
[8] Hong Kong Catholic Marriage Advisory Council, 'Services: Marriage Mediation Counselling Service' (Hong Kong: Catholic Marriage Advisory Council 2018), available at https://cmac.org.hk/en/services_detail.php?c1id=8.
[9] Working Group on Mediation, *Report of the Working Group on Mediation* (Hong Kong: DOJ 2010).
[10] Mediation Task Force, *Membership and Terms of Reference* (Hong Kong: DOJ 2011).

event',[11] which will give parties an opportunity to engage in mediation or other forms of settlement. More noticeably, the Practice Direction on mediation[12] which came into effect on 1 January 2010 states that the courts may even penalise, by imposing adverse costs on, any party that unreasonably fails to enter into mediation or participates less than the minimal amount agreed to initially by the parties or ordered by the court.

Overall, unlike litigation and arbitration, mediation is more process-focused. It recognises that the mediation process may not necessarily lead to resolution of the dispute. But the process may help the parties learn more about themselves and provide a framework for dialogue.

Mediation Ordinance and Practice Direction 31

Despite the flexibility and voluntary nature of mediation, the Mediation Ordinance, which came into force on 1 January 2013, provides a regulatory framework for the use of mediation as an alternative dispute resolution mechanism. Such a legal framework allows for the development of mediation in Hong Kong in a proper manner and addresses areas relating to mediation where the law had been uncertain, such as the confidentiality and admissibility of information derived from the mediation process.[13] Another reason for the ordinance is that given the early stage of development of mediation in Hong Kong, legislation would serve as the Government's 'stamp of approval' and promote the acceptance of mediation by legal practitioners and the general public.[14] Indeed the objective of the Mediation Ordinance is 'to promote, encourage and facilitate the resolution of disputes by mediation' and 'to protect the confidential nature of mediation communications'.[15] The ordinance applies when at least some part of the mediation is conducted in Hong Kong or if the agreement to mediate between the disputing parties stipulates that this ordinance or the law of Hong Kong is to apply to the mediation in question.[16]

---

[11] Rules of the High Court (Cap. 4A), Ord.1B, r. 1(2)(e).
[12] Practice Direction 31.
[13] See Mediation Ordinance (Cap. 620), ss. 8 and 9.
[14] Department of Justice, *Report of the Working Group on Mediation* (Hong Kong: DOJ 2010), para. 7.22.
[15] Mediation Ordinance (Cap. 620), s. 3.
[16] Mediation Ordinance (Cap. 620), s. 5(1), but see sch. 1 for processes to which this ordinance does not apply.

Practice Direction 31 (PD31) on mediation came into effect on 1 November 2014 to assist the courts to facilitate the settlement of disputes as part of their active case management powers under the Civil Justice Reform. PD31 applies to all civil proceedings in the Court of First Instance and the District Court which commence by writ except for the proceedings set out in Appendix A of PD31.[17] It provides a mechanism for disputing parties to make credible efforts at mediation. Where the parties are legally represented, their respective solicitors must file a Mediation Certificate along with the timetable questionnaire that requires the party to confirm whether they are willing to attempt mediation and, if they are not willing, the reasons why.[18] Solicitors must also confirm that they have explained the availability of mediation. If a party wishes to attempt mediation, then he/she should as soon as practicable serve a Mediation Notice to the other party (or parties)[19] and the other party must file a Mediation Response within fourteen days.[20] The Mediation Notice sets out matters including the identity of the mediator, the venue, applicable mediation rules, time frame, costs and suggestion as to the minimum level of participation that can qualify as a sufficient attempt at mediation. The Mediation Response either agrees with the proposals or offers counterproposals. The parties are encouraged to reach consensus. If the parties are unable to agree on the proposals in the Mediation Notice and Response, then the parties may jointly apply to the court to have their differences resolved.[21] The court however, cannot appoint a mediator or set out the rules of the mediation, as this would go against the underlying principle of voluntariness of the mediation. These documents may be taken into account by the court when considering costs.

Although the disputing parties may agree upon which rules to apply in the mediation process, it may be preferable to apply commonly used rules

---

[17] This includes proceedings in the Construction and Arbitration List, Personal Injuries List and Equal Opportunities List.
[18] See Practice Direction 31 Appendix B. The burden is on the refusing party to provide a reasonable explanation; see *Golden Eagle International (Group) Ltd v. GR Investment Holdings Ltd* [2010] 5 HKC 317, at para. 44.
[19] See Practice Direction 31 Appendix C.
[20] Or as such other time that the parties may agree or as the court may direct. See Practice Direction 31 Appendix D.
[21] Practice Direction 31, Part B(2).

such as the HKIAC Mediation Rules.[22] For instance, the mediation clause in contracts can explicitly state that in the event of any disputes or differences arising out of the contract, then the matter will first be referred to the HKIAC and in accordance with its then current Mediation Rules.

Accrediting Mediators

More and more accredited and non-accredited mediators have emerged in Hong Kong. It was recommended by the Working Group on Mediation that a single system of accreditation is desirable.[23] However, at the time, the Working Group thought that the timing was not right in prescribing a standardised system of accreditation but that the focus should be on making available information about mediation for potential users that would permit them to choose competent mediators. Mediators in Hong Kong are accredited by different organisations with their own sets of requirements. The Taskforce on Mediation suggested that a single non-statutory industry-led accreditation body be supported.

The Hong Kong Bar Association, the Law Society of Hong Kong, the Hong Kong International Arbitration Centre (HKIAC) and the Hong Kong Mediation Centre are the leading providers of mediators. These four professional bodies are also the founding members of the Hong Kong Mediation Accreditation Association Limited (HKMAAL), which was incorporated in August 2012 and serves as the premier single accreditation body that accredits mediators and administers the Hong Kong Mediation Code. The objectives of the HKMAAL are to set standards for accredited mediation, to set standards on relevant mediation training courses and to promote best practices in mediation in Hong Kong. The long-term aim is to have a single accreditation body for mediators in Hong Kong. The HKMAAL maintains two panels of mediators: the General Panel and the Family Panel. The HKMAAL requires that applicants have at least three years of full-time work experience. In order to be accredited as a mediator, candidates must complete forty hours of training and successfully conduct two simulated mediation assessments. Accreditation as a Family Mediator is more stringent, as candidates must have a degree or

---

[22] HKIAC, 'HKIAC Mediation Rules', (HKIAC, Hong Kong 2018), available at www.hkiac.org/mediation/rules/hkiac-mediation-rules.

[23] Working Group on Mediation (n. 9), chapter 6.

postgraduate qualification in social work, psychology, counselling, law or other relevant qualifications in a field related to family work (such as education) and three years of work experience in family law, family welfare, family counselling or other work experience that can demonstrate the candidate's competence in human-related work (such as pastoral care). Candidates must also complete a training course on family mediation or other approved courses amounting to at least forty hours. Afterwards, candidates must participate in two live family mediations under the supervision of an approved supervisor.[24]

Accreditation ensures a level of quality assurance in terms of competency of mediators. The requirements set out above serve to filter out unqualified and unethical candidates. Another benefit of an accreditation body is that it affords a forum for dialogue for aspiring mediators, which is believed to bolster their creativity. As mediators will likely encounter different problems in their practice, this creativity allows them to test different strategies. Perhaps most importantly, accreditation legitimises the mediation profession. However, there are limits to accreditation. The skills of a mediator take months and years to hone, and possessing a certification is not always a guarantee of performance ability. Mediators would therefore need to continue to develop their skills, experience and reputation.[25]

The Mediation Code outlines the ethical standards and responsibilities of mediators. It highlights the general responsibilities of the mediator, including the need to act fairly in dealing with the parties, to have no personal interests in the terms of the settlement agreement, to be reasonably available as requested by the parties and to be certain that the parties have been informed about the mediation process. It also stresses that the mediator and his/her staff must keep all information with respect to the mediation confidential unless compelled by law or public policy grounds.[26] The Mediation Code is adopted by various professional organisations in Hong Kong.

Mediators come from a variety of backgrounds including law, commercial, medicine and social work. This diversity of backgrounds is seen as a strength of mediation, but it may also be regarded as a weakness, because mediators are not perceived as professionals on a par with, for example,

---

[24] Hong Kong Mediation Accreditation Association Limited, 'How to be a Mediator' (Hong Kong: HKMAAL 2013), available at www.hkmaal.org.hk/en/HowToBecomeAMediator.php.
[25] Sihombing, To and Chiu (n. 4), pp. 132–134.
[26] See Hong Kong Mediation Code, arts. 1 and 4.

lawyers. However, in order to avoid a conflict of interest, even when the mediator is from a legal background, no legal advice is expected to be given. The parties may wish to seek legal advice before or during the mediation, but it is not a necessary requirement for engaging in the mediation process.

Arbitration

Arbitration involves the appointment of one or more neutral third parties as in mediation; however, this third party, referred to as an arbitral tribunal and which consists of a sole arbitrator or a panel of arbitrators, has the power to impose a settlement on the disputing parties. The Arbitration Ordinance states that arbitrators should 'use procedures that are appropriate to the particular case'[27] and that it is the parties themselves that are 'free to agree on how the dispute should be resolved'.[28] A variety of legal disputes are referred to arbitration, including corporate and finance, maritime, construction and international trade.

Arbitration is usually a consensual process whereby the parties submit themselves to the process under an arbitration agreement, which can be an arbitration clause in a contract or a separate agreement. Usually, parties subject to arbitration have an arbitration clause in the disputed contract, where parties consented to the process before the dispute arose or was even contemplated. An arbitration clause in a contract would state that in the event of a dispute, the parties agree to resolve the dispute through arbitration. But even if there was no arbitration clause, the parties can subsequently agree to resolve the matter by way of arbitration instead of litigation. This consent is necessary, as the result of the arbitration may be final.

The disputing parties are also free to agree to subject themselves to a jurisdiction as the seat of arbitration. For example, if Hong Kong is chosen, then the Arbitration Ordinance would apply to the arbitration in question as well as any applicable court assistance. In the case of Hong Kong, this is handled by the Court of First Instance. Other elements of the arbitral proceedings are also determined by the parties, such as the appointment

---

[27] Arbitration Ordinance (Cap. 609), s. 46(3)(c).
[28] Arbitration Ordinance (Cap. 609), s. 3(2)(a).

of arbitrators to hear the dispute and the type of evidence to be presented in the hearings.

The courts will not usually hear matters arising from an arbitration settlement. Similarly, if one of the parties decides to commence court proceedings where there is an arbitration agreement beforehand, then the courts will likely stay the proceedings.[29] If there is already an arbitration agreement in place and an action is brought before the courts, then the court will refer the parties to arbitration unless it finds that 'the agreement is null and void, inoperative or incapable of being performed'.[30]

Similar to mediation, arbitration seeks to reach a resolution without having to resort to litigation in the courts. However, there are important differences between mediation and arbitration. One of the main differences is that arbitration resembles a court process (though it is less formal), as arbitrators hear evidence and testimony from the parties, question witnesses and make a final decision.

As the People's Republic of China is one of the signatories of the New York Convention on the Recognition and Enforcement of Foreign Arbitral Awards,[31] the arbitral awards made in Hong Kong can generally be enforced through the courts of other signatory countries. Thus, an arbitral award is not only enforceable through the local court but can be taken up through the jurisdiction of other signatory countries, of which there are currently over 150 countries.[32]

There are two types of arbitration – institutional arbitration and ad hoc arbitration. Institutional arbitrations are arbitrations that are administered by arbitral institutions such as the HKIAC. The proceedings are conducted under the arbitration rules devised by the chosen institution which effectively sets out the procedure of the arbitration. Ad hoc arbitrations, on the other hand, are arbitrations that are arranged solely between the parties and the arbitrator(s). They may choose to conduct the proceedings under rules drawn up by the parties themselves or adopt a ready-made set of rules

---

[29] See Arbitration Ordinance (Cap. 609), ss. 2(b) and 12.
[30] Arbitration Ordinance (Cap. 609), s. 20.
[31] New York Convention on the Recognition and Enforcement of Foreign Arbitral Awards (10 June 1958).
[32] Including Australia, Brazil, Belgium, Chile, Korea, Egypt, France, Germany and many others. See UNCITRAL, 'Status: Convention on the Recognition and Enforcement of Foreign Arbitral Awards (New York, 1958)' (UNCITRAL 2008), available at www.uncitral.org/uncitral/en/uncitral_texts/arbitration/NYConvention_status.html.

such as the United Nations Commission on International Trade Law Rules of Arbitration (UNCITRAL).

The Hong Kong International Arbitration Centre

The HKIAC is a home-grown body under which ADR is organised in Hong Kong. HKIAC has authority to appoint arbitrators under the Arbitration Ordinance where the parties are unable to agree.[33] It was established in 1985 by a group of leading business people and professionals to serve the growing demand for ADR in Asia. HKIAC is a not-for-profit company limited by guarantee. Initially, the business community and the government provided funding, but today HKIAC is financially self-sufficient and operates independently of the Government. It is governed by the HKIAC Council, which includes professionals and business people from around the world and has an International Advisory Board that advises it in terms of policy. Its Executive Committee is the principal body that directs the activities of the centre in accordance with the policies approved by its Council, and the HKIAC Secretariat, led by the Secretary-General, manages the day-to-day affairs.[34] Besides arbitration, HKIAC also has mediation services.

HKIAC provides state-of-the-art facilities to serve as a venue for ADR. The number of cases received by HKIAC in 2014, 2015 and 2016 was 477, 520 and 460 respectively.[35] In 2013 it opened its first overseas office in Seoul and in 2015 it set up another office in Shanghai, making it the first international arbitration institution to have a representative office in Mainland China. HKIAC is ranked as the third most preferred arbitral institution worldwide and the top-favoured arbitration institution outside of Europe, and it possesses the largest case load involving Chinese parties of all international arbitral institutions.[36]

---

[33] See Arbitration Ordinance (Cap. 609), ss. 13 and 24.
[34] Hong Kong International Arbitration Centre, 'About HKIAC' (Hong Kong: HKIAC 2018), available at www.hkiac.org/about-us.
[35] Hong Kong International Arbitration Centre, 'Statistics' (Hong Kong: HKIAC 2018), available at www.hkiac.org/about-us/statistics.
[36] Hong Kong International Arbitration Centre, 'Why HKIAC?' (Hong Kong: HKIAC 2018), available at www.hkiac.org/arbitration/why-choose-hkiac.

Other Arbitral Institutions

World-class arbitral institutions have also set up branches in Hong Kong, thereby enhancing Hong Kong's status as a leading centre for international arbitration. The International Court of Arbitration of the International Chamber of Commerce (ICC), based in Paris, is the world's leading arbitral institution. The ICC was established in the aftermath of the First World War, when its founders, believing that the private sector was best placed to set global standards for business, created the organisation to represent business everywhere. The International Court of Arbitration was established in 1923. The ICC Rules of Arbitration regulate the procedures for dispute resolution submitted to the International Court of Arbitration.[37] In 2008 it opened a branch of its Secretariat in Hong Kong.

The China International Economic and Trade Arbitration Commission (CIETAC), established in 1956, is China's oldest arbitration institution. It has administered over 10,000 arbitral cases and accepts foreign-related and international cases as well as domestic cases. The CIETAC Hong Kong Arbitration Center, which was set up in 2012, is the CIETAC's first branch outside of Mainland China.[38]

The Permanent Court of Arbitration (PCA) established by the Convention for the Pacific Settlement of International Disputes in 1899 is the first permanent intergovernmental organisation to provide a forum for international dispute resolution through arbitration.[39] Its headquarters are in The Hague. The PCA signed a host country agreement with the Central People's Government and a related memorandum of administrative arrangement with the Hong Kong SAR Government in 2015 according to which proceedings administered by the PCA can be conducted in Hong Kong on an ad hoc basis without the need for a physical presence of the PCA.

---

[37] See International Chamber of Commerce, 'Arbitration Rules' (ICC 2017), available at https://iccwbo.org/dispute-resolution-services/arbitration/rules-of-arbitration/#article_1.

[38] The China International Economic and Trade Arbitration Commission, 'Why CIETAC Hong Kong?' (Hong Kong: CIETAC Hong Kong Arbitration Center 2013), available at www.cietachk.org/portal/mainPage.do?pagePath=\en_US\chooseHK.

[39] Permanent Court of Arbitration, 'History' (The Hague: PCA 2018), available at https://pca-cpa.org/en/about/introduction/history/.

Arbitration Ordinance

In Hong Kong, the legal basis for the process of arbitration is the Arbitration Ordinance.[40] The ordinance provides the basic legal framework for the conduct of arbitrations in Hong Kong, including provision for the enforcement of local arbitrations and also enforcement in Hong Kong of international awards.[41] The current Arbitration Ordinance came into operation on 1 June 2011, replacing the previous ordinance.[42] Under the previous ordinance, there were two types of arbitration processes – one for domestic (as provided for under the Arbitration Ordinance), the other for international disputes (which followed the UNCITRAL Model Law).[43] In 1998, the HKIArb and HKIAC formed a committee to examine the reform of arbitration law in Hong Kong. The Committee on Hong Kong Arbitration Law recommended in 2003 that a unitary regime following the Model Law be adopted for both domestic and international arbitrations. In 2007, the Department of Justice launched a Consultation Paper[44] seeking public feedback on the draft Arbitration Bill. The proposal was to end this distinction and have all arbitrations follow the UNCITRAL Model Law (the Bill adopted the Model Law as its framework and entire articles of the Model Law are inserted verbatim into the relevant sections of the ordinance).[45] The thinking behind the change is to have Hong Kong operate an arbitration system that is uniform with the international community, thus making Hong Kong more appealing for businesses and an attractive venue for international arbitration. This is now implemented under the new ordinance.[46]

While the ordinance sets out the legal framework for arbitrations, the detailed procedure for arbitration is governed by arbitration rules. The various arbitral institutions have their own arbitration rules. For instance,

---

[40] Arbitration Ordinance (Cap. 609).
[41] Arbitration Ordinance (Cap. 609), s. 87.
[42] Arbitration Ordinance (Cap. 341) (now repealed). This previous ordinance was enacted in 1963 and mirrored the English Arbitration Act 1950.
[43] UNCITRAL Model Law on International Commercial Arbitration, adopted by the United Nations Commission on International Trade Law.
[44] Department of Justice, *Consultation Paper on Reform of the Arbitration Law in Hong Kong and Draft Arbitration Bill* (Hong Kong: DOJ 2007). available at www.doj.gov.hk/eng/public/pdf/2007/arbitration.pdf.
[45] The full text of the Model Law can be found in Schedule 1 of the Arbitration Ordinance, but it is for information only.
[46] Arbitration Ordinance (Cap. 609).

the HKIAC administers its arbitration cases under the HKIAC Administered Arbitration Rules, which include functions such as fixing the arbitral tribunal's fees[47] and deciding whether to consolidate two or more arbitrations.[48]

In 2017 the Arbitration Ordinance was amended to clarify that disputes over intellectual property rights may be resolved by arbitration and that it would not be contrary to public policy to do so.[49] The amendment helps to clarify Hong Kong's legal position and attract parties to resolve their intellectual property rights disputes in Hong Kong. The Ordinance was also amended with the enactment of the Arbitration and Mediation (Third Party Funding) (Amendment) Ordinance in June 2017 to allow a third party to provide arbitration funding for a disputing party under a funding agreement.[50] The third party can be any person who does not have an interest in the arbitration.[51] The funder would receive a financial benefit in return if the arbitration is successful. Previously, third-party funding was prohibited by the common law doctrines of maintenance and champerty.[52] The change will help businesses balance their financial resources and share the risks of pursuing a claim with third-party funders.

Appointing Arbitrators

Usually, the disputing parties have agreed on the number and qualifications of the arbitrators under the arbitration provisions of their commercial contract. Unlike the courts, where parties cannot pick the judge, arbitration allows the parties to choose the arbitrator(s) and the number of arbitrators[53] who will preside over their disputes. Considerations would include the expertise and language skills of the arbitrators. Typically, one arbitrator is appointed in more straightforward disputes. In more complex cases, three arbitrators are normally appointed. In these situations, each party is likely to appoint an arbitrator, and the appointed arbitrators appoint the

---

[47] HKIAC Administered Arbitration Rules, art. 10.3.
[48] HKIAC Administered Arbitration Rules, art. 28.
[49] See Arbitration Ordinance (Cap. 609), Part 11A.
[50] See Arbitration Ordinance (Cap. 609), Part 10A.
[51] Arbitration Ordinance (Cap. 609), s. 98J.
[52] Maintenance involves intermeddling of an unconnected party in encouraging a lawsuit, and champerty is a form of maintenance where the party maintaining another takes a portion of the property in dispute as his/her reward. For further discussion on how this affects access to justice, see Chapter 11, especially the section on Conditional Fees.
[53] Arbitration Ordinance (Cap. 609), s. 23.

third arbitrator. If the parties have failed to agree or have not designated an appointing authority to perform this function, then the appointment of the arbitrators would be made in accordance with the Hong Kong Arbitration Ordinance.[54] Under the Ordinance, if the parties fail to agree or to appoint a designated authority (or if the designated party has failed to carry out its function), then the HKIAC may appoint the arbitrator(s) to decide the dispute.[55] The HKIAC may, with the approval of the Chief Justice, make rules to facilitate the performance of this function.[56]

In Hong Kong, there are no formal qualifications or training required for an individual to be appointed as an arbitrator. Arbitrators are appointed on the basis of their experience and personal qualities. Arbitrators can be barristers, solicitors, engineers, surveyors or retired judges. The various arbitral institutions have arbitrators on their respective panels and provide training. Hong Kong's tertiary education institutions also provide various degrees and courses related to arbitration.

Arbitrators have the following general duties when conducting arbitral proceedings: (1) to treat the parties with equality; (2) to be independent; (3) to act fairly and impartially, giving each party a reasonable opportunity to present their case and deal with the cases of their opponents; and (4) to use procedures appropriate to the case while avoiding unnecessary delays or expenses.[57] The same strict standards that apply to judges apply to arbitrators as well.[58] Arbitral institutions have also developed ethical codes of conduct that provide ethical standards for arbitrators to abide by.[59]

If an arbitrator fails to comply with the general duties of impartiality and/or independence, then a disputing party can bring a challenge under the procedures set out by the arbitration institution's rules, under section 26 of the Arbitration Ordinance, or if an award has already been made, apply to the Court of First Instance to set aside the award.[60]

---

[54] Arbitration Ordinance (Cap. 609), s. 24.
[55] Ibid. See Arbitration Ordinance (Cap. 609), s. 13.
[56] Arbitration Ordinance (Cap. 609), s. 13(3); see Arbitration (Appointment of Arbitrators and Mediators and Decision on Number of Arbitrators) Rules (Cap. 609C).
[57] Arbitration Ordinance (Cap. 609), s. 46.
[58] G. Ma and D. Brock (eds.), *Arbitration in Hong Kong: A Practical Guide*, 4th ed. (Hong Kong: Sweet & Maxwell 2017), para. 11.024.
[59] See e.g. the HKIAC's Code of Ethical Conduct for Arbitrators.
[60] Ibid., para. 11.018.

Arbitrators' Powers and Fees

Arbitrators generally have the power to grant any remedy that may be imposed by the courts of Hong Kong,[61] but their orders are restricted to the disputing parties only (or persons claiming under them). Similar to a court, the arbitrator decides on which party is liable to pay the costs of the arbitration. Much like civil litigation, the losing side is likely to bear the costs, including the costs of the winning party.

Typically, the parties would agree with the arbitrator with respect to fees at the early stages of the arbitral proceedings. This is especially important for ad hoc arbitrations to avoid potential conflicts in the future. For institutional arbitrations, however, the arbitral institution would likely calculate arbitrators' fees using their own fee scales.[62] There are three main fee structures for arbitrators: (1) time spent, calculated by hourly or daily rates; (2) *ad valorem*, calculated by reference to the total amount of the dispute; and (3) fixed fee. If there is no agreement as to fees, then the parties are jointly and severally liable to pay the arbitral tribunal reasonable fees and expenses considering the circumstances.[63] The arbitral tribunal may refuse to deliver an award until full payment of the fees and expenses are made.[64]

Arbitral Award

The decision of the arbitrator in resolving the dispute is called an award. Unless otherwise agreed by the parties, an award made by an arbitral tribunal pursuant to an arbitration agreement is final and binding both on the parties and any person claiming through or under any of the parties (subject to certain rights of appeal, discussed below).[65] An arbitration award is enforceable in the same manner as a court judgment, but leave of the Court of First Instance is required for enforcement.[66]

---

[61] Arbitration Ordinance (Cap. 609), s. 70.
[62] See e.g. HKIAC Administered Arbitration Rules, art. 10(1).
[63] Arbitration Ordinance (Cap. 609), s. 78(1).
[64] Arbitration Ordinance (Cap. 609), s. 77(1).
[65] Arbitration Ordinance (Cap. 609), s. 73.
[66] Arbitration Ordinance (Cap. 609), s. 84.

Appealing an Arbitrators' Decision

A party to arbitral proceedings may appeal to the Court of First Instance on any question of law (but not of fact) arising out of an arbitral award following accordance with the procedures set out in section 5 of Schedule 2 of the Arbitration Ordinance. It needs to be noted that the appeal procedure is only applicable if the arbitration agreement provides so or the arbitration falls within certain specified situations where the section automatically applies, as provided for under the Arbitration Ordinance (such as arbitration agreements entered into before the commencement of the current Arbitration Ordinance stating that it is a domestic arbitration).[67] Even then, a party can only appeal with the agreement of all parties or with leave from the Court of First Instance.[68] Leave will not be granted unless: (a) the decision of the question will substantially affect the rights of one or more of the parties; (b) the question is one which the arbitral tribunal was asked to decide; and (c) on the basis of the findings of fact in the award, the decision of the arbitral tribunal on the question is obviously wrong, or the question is one of general importance and the decision of the arbitral tribunal is at least open to serious doubt.[69]

Advantages and Disadvantages of ADR

Advantages of ADR

One of the main advantages of ADR is its cost-effectiveness. Even the simplest of court-based litigation can be costly. There are, first of all, the legal costs of solicitors' fees and barristers' fees. There are court costs, which include the cost of filing documents with the court. There are also costs involved in the preparation of the matter, including costs involved in the collection of materials for the case such as affidavits and depositions. In addition, there is the cost of time lost while the litigation is prepared and carried out. Moreover, there is the overhanging threat of a costs order by the court against a party. This is very common and occurs when the losing party in a dispute is ordered to pay the cost of the proceedings, that is, not

---

[67] See Arbitration Ordinance (Cap. 609), ss. 99 to 103.
[68] Arbitration Ordinance (Cap. 609), schedule 2, s. 6(1).
[69] Arbitration Ordinance (Cap. 609), schedule 2, s. 5(4).

only to bear their own costs but also to bear the costs of the other (winning) party. The possibility of a costs order makes litigation a risky business. This is one reason why many people who have legitimate claims, for example against an employer, do not or simply cannot afford to pursue them. ADR, especially mediation, because of its informal nature, reduces these costs enormously. As well as creating an opportunity for those with standing but without resources to pursue a claim, it creates a cost- and time-effective alternative to complicated litigation, making it an attractive option to most parties who are engaged in a dispute.

Another commonly noted advantage of ADR is its confidential nature. Unlike court cases, which are typically open to the public and media, mediation and arbitration operate behind closed doors and would only involve those directly involved in the proceedings. The award made by the arbitral tribunal is also confidential. In this way, the parties can avoid bad publicity.

ADR processes provide a potential litigant with many more options. Mediation, in particular, allows the parties to explore the merits of their positions, having confidence that what they say will not be used against them in future court hearings. In this way, creative solutions can be found in resolving disputes. The strict rules of evidence do not apply and therefore it is easier for a party to enable the 'whole' side of his/her case to be put into consideration. For both mediation and arbitration, parties are free to choose the person to act as their mediator or arbitrator. The parties can take into consideration the mediator's or arbitrator's expertise, experience, language skills and fees before making their choices. When the dispute involves a technical field such as construction or engineering, parties can choose mediators or arbitrators with such expertise and can avoid time spent in explaining technical concepts in the proceedings.

Disadvantages of ADR

There are disadvantages to the use of ADR. The main concern is the effect of bypassing the protections given under the formal rules or procedures of the court, bearing in mind that there are principled reasons behind such rules and procedures. For example, rules of evidence are established to protect the overall rights of, and fairness to, both parties. If these are ignored in some matters for the sake of practicalities, it allows for the possibility of the exploitation of parties in some cases. Indeed, there are cases where the informal nature of ADR, especially mediation, would not be suitable. For example, in family cases that involve domestic violence, mediation would not be suitable given the power disparity between the parties. ADR would also not be suitable in cases where the crux of the issue is one of law and not just of facts.

Particularly in mediation, under the facilitative model, the success of mediation depends on the willingness of the parties. Unlike in civil proceedings, there is no requirement for discovery in mediation and therefore the parties need to trust each other in disclosing their respective materials.

Despite the apparent cost-effectiveness of ADR, there are costs associated with it, such as mediators' and arbitrators' fees and fees for booking venues.[70] In more complex arbitration cases, the same procedure of pleadings and examination (and cross-examination) of witnesses is often adopted, hence the time and costs of these arbitrations are comparable to court litigation. In international arbitrations, travel expenses would be incurred as well.

Review Questions

(1) Should mediation be court-compelled and mandatory for disputing parties?
(2) Why is accreditation for mediators important?
(3) Do you agree that Hong Kong should adopt a uniform regime of arbitration laws? Why?
(4) Is arbitration always more cost-effective than civil litigation?
(5) How does ADR empower the disputing parties?

---

[70] The costs of the use of court facilities and the salaries of judges are borne by the public purse.

Access to Justice 11

Chapter Highlights

- Legal Profession 306
- Legal Aid 310
- Duty Lawyer Service 318
- Conditional Fees 324
- Litigants in Person 326

The Basic Law and Hong Kong Bill of Rights guarantee that everyone is equal before the law and has a right to legal advice and representation.[1] These rights, however, lose their force in practice if access to justice is restricted because of, for example, costs and complexity of the legal and court system. As stated by Chief Justice Geoffrey Ma, 'There is little point in having a sound legal infrastructure, manned by the best judges, when there are difficulties of access to justice.'[2] The rule of law is undermined if access to justice is denied.

When thinking about access to justice, people often think about the right to legal advice and representation. Lawyers are undoubtedly important in providing their clients with sound legal advice and helping them navigate the complexity of case proceedings, in both the civil and criminal justice systems, as outlined in previous chapters. This chapter therefore begins by looking at the bifurcated legal profession in Hong Kong, namely the roles of barristers and solicitors. This chapter then goes through the

---

[1] See e.g. Basic Law, arts. 25, 35; Hong Kong Bill of Rights, art. 11(2)(d); see Hong Kong Bill of Rights Ordinance (Cap. 383), s. 8.

[2] Judiciary, 'CJ's Speech at Ceremonial Opening of the Legal Year 2015' (Hong Kong: Hong Kong Judiciary 2015), available at www.info.gov.hk/gia/general/201501/12/P201501120481.htm.

various schemes that are in place and those that have been considered to fund legal services in Hong Kong and to promote people's access to justice. The effect that litigants in persons (unrepresented litigants) have on the court system is also considered.

Legal Profession

In line with England and Wales, but differing from other common law jurisdictions such as the United States and Canada, Hong Kong continues to maintain a split legal profession after the handover. Since the enactment of the Supreme Court Ordinance in 1844, the Supreme Court of Hong Kong was conferred jurisdiction to admit persons as barristers or solicitors. This means that a person may be either a barrister or solicitor but not both at the same time. However, it is possible to switch from one profession to the other. The Legal Practitioners Ordinance regulates the administration and registration of barristers and solicitors.[3] The two professional legal bodies, namely the Hong Kong Bar Association for barristers and the Law Society of Hong Kong for solicitors, govern their members independently from the Government. This separation is important to ensure that lawyers from either profession are able to advocate for their clients forcefully, even in cases where the Government is the opposing party.

Barristers

Barristers-at-law or counsel are regarded as specialists and advocates, although this generalisation is inaccurate, since many barristers are generalists and certain solicitors may practise in a specific area of law. Nonetheless, barristers conform to the common image of lawyers as they wear a wig and gown to argue before the courts.[4] Indeed, barristers have an unlimited right of legal audience before all court levels and tribunals.[5] The effective presentation of a client's case before the courts is key to upholding the adversarial system in Hong Kong. By having the benefit of

---

[3] Legal Practitioners Ordinance (Cap. 159).
[4] Wigs and gown are only worn in the District Court, the Court of First Instance, the Court of Appeal and the Court of Final Appeal.
[5] Except for where legal representation is not allowed, such as the Small Claims Tribunal.

listening to competing arguments by legal professionals, the judge will be put in the best position to decide on the outcome of the case.

Besides advocacy, barristers provide legal opinions on a variety of matters including the legal merits of an intended claim. The profession of barristers is a referral profession, meaning that clients must first retain a solicitor who will then instruct a barrister for the client.[6] The rationale for this is that barristers can maintain their objectivity by reason of the greater detachment from the client. Barristers will then focus only on the legal merits of the case and 'promote and protect fearlessly and by all proper and lawful means the lay client's best interests'.[7] Although barristers are to act in the interests of the client, they are not to act as the 'mere mouthpiece' of the client or instructing solicitor and must exercise their professional judgment accordingly.[8]

Each barrister only practises as a sole proprietor. Barristers are not permitted to form partnerships or to incorporate themselves as a company or corporation. This is to ensure that every barrister acts independently. What barristers often do is group together to form a set of chambers (an office), in order to reduce expenses. Although forming chambers is common, individual barristers maintain their independence by sharing expenses but not profits. For attending court, a barrister's fees normally consist of a brief and a refresher. The brief fee includes the fee for the first day of court appearance and usually the preparation work as well. The refresher is the fee for each subsequent day of appearance in court. How much the barrister charges will depend on the complexity of the case, the time required and the seniority of the barrister. This is negotiable between the instructing solicitor and the barrister.[9] Barristers are not responsible for the conduct of their fellow barristers sharing the same set of chambers.

Another interesting feature of barristers is the cab-rank rule. According to paragraph 6.1 of the Code of Conduct issued by the Hong Kong Bar Association ('Bar Code'), a practising barrister must accept any brief or instruction to appear in court to provide legal services in a field of law in which the barrister professes to practise in as long as it is within the

---

[6] There are exceptions where barristers are permitted to be instructed by other professionals such as accountants, company secretaries and arbitrators. This is known as 'Direct Professional Access'. See Annex 3 – Annex 6J of the Bar Code.
[7] Bar Code, para. 10.15.
[8] Bar Code, para. 10.17(a).
[9] See Bar Code, chapter 9.

capacity, skill and experience of the barrister, the barrister is available and not committed to other engagements, and the fee offered is proper. The barrister cannot refuse irrespective of the nature of the case, the client or personal opinions formed regarding the client including beliefs about the guilt or innocence of the client.[10] The reason for the cab-rank rule is to make sure that all individuals, regardless of their background, would receive legal representation.

The Chief Justice may, after consultation with the chairman of the Bar Council and president of the Law Society of Hong Kong, appoint barristers who in the opinion of the Chief Justice have sufficient ability and standing, sufficient knowledge of the law and requisite experience of not less than ten years in aggregate, as Senior Counsel.[11] This is a recognition of the barrister's professional eminence. All other barristers, regardless of years of admission, are customarily referred to as junior counsel. There are currently around 1,400 practising barristers in Hong Kong of whom about 100 are Senior Counsel. A list of practising barristers can be found on the website of the Hong Kong Bar Association.

Solicitors

Generally, solicitors handle legal documents, advise clients and do not specialise in advocacy as barristers do. Unlike barristers, solicitors may form partnerships or operate as sole proprietors. Law firms in Hong Kong include international firms, foreign firms, large home-grown firms, smaller local law firms and boutique firms that specialise in a niche area of the law. The directory of law firms is produced by the Law Society of Hong Kong and can be accessed on its website. Given that solicitors practise in a variety of areas of law, the directory assists the public in finding the right solicitor for their legal needs. Potential clients contact solicitors directly and solicitors enter into a contract with their clients. The cab-rank rule is not applicable to solicitors. Although a solicitor is free to decide whether to accept

---

[10] The barrister must not accept any instructions that would cause him or her to be professionally embarrassed, such as if he/she lacks the experience or competence to handle the matter, there is a conflict of interest, or the barrister will not be able to complete the instructions within a reasonable time. See Bar Code, para. 6.2.

[11] Legal Practitioners Ordinance (Cap. 159), s. 31A; previously Queen's Counsel, who were appointed by Letters Patent on the advice of the Hong Kong Chief Justice before the handover.

instructions from a prospective client, the Hong Kong Solicitors' Guide to Professional Conduct ('Professional Guide') notes that refusal of instructions should not be based on the race, ethnicity or religious/political beliefs of the prospective client, nor on personal opinion of the client's guilt.[12]

Solicitors have limited rights of audience before the courts. They can act as an advocate in the Magistrates' Courts and the District Court but generally may not do so in open court in the High Court or the Court of Final Appeal. Since 2010, solicitors with the requisite experience may apply to the Higher Rights of Audience Assessment Board in order to advocate on behalf of their clients in the higher courts.[13] If approved, the solicitor obtains the higher right of audience and is referred to as a solicitor advocate. As at 2016, there are only fifty-five solicitor advocates compared with over 10,000 members of the Law Society of Hong Kong.[14]

The Professional Guide states that a solicitor owes a fiduciary duty to the client and 'must act with loyalty, openness and fairness towards the client'.[15] The solicitor must act in the best interest of his/her client and not be placed in a position where there may be a conflict of interest between the solicitor and client.[16] At the same time, solicitors like barristers, owe a duty to the court (being officers of the court). They must not knowingly attempt to deceive or participate in the deception of the court.[17] If a client admits that he/she has committed perjury or misled the court, unless the client agrees to fully disclose the conduct to the court, it is the duty of the solicitor to decline to continue to act in the proceedings.[18]

Right to Legal Assistance

Article 11(2)(d) of the Hong Kong Bill of Rights[19] provides that every person who is charged with a criminal offence is entitled, in full equality,

---

[12] Professional Guide, para. 5.01.
[13] See Legal Practitioners Ordinance (Cap. 159), s. 39I.
[14] Law Society of Hong Kong, *2016 Annual Report* (Hong Kong: Law Society of Hong Kong 2017), available at www.hklawsoc.org.hk/pub_e/about/report/AR_2016/report_2016.pdf.
[15] Professional Guide, para. 7.01.
[16] Ibid., para. 7.02.
[17] Ibid., para. 10.03.
[18] Ibid.
[19] Hong Kong Bill of Rights Ordinance (Cap. 383).

to defend himself or herself in person or through legal assistance of their own choosing and be informed of this right. Legal assistance is to be assigned where the 'interests of justice' so require, and the individual does not have to make payment for the legal assistance if he/she does not have sufficient means to pay for it. From a rights perspective, it may be argued that legal assistance should be given regardless of merits and means.[20] However, the Court of Appeal has held that legal aid in criminal trials or appellate proceedings is not an absolute right. There was 'nothing objectionable in principle' to have applicants for legal assistance be subjected to a merits and means test, and it would not violate the Bill of Rights Ordinance.[21] When determining the interests of justice criteria, each case must be examined as a whole.[22] It is appropriate to determine 'interests of justice' based on the Widgery criteria, which take into account (1) the seriousness of the offence and consequences to the defendant; (2) whether the case may involve a substantial question of law; (3) whether the defendant may be unable to understand the proceedings; (4) whether the defence involves the interviewing of witnesses; and (5) whether it is in the interests of someone else that the defendant be represented.[23] Moreover, if legal assistance was granted in all cases, the public would perceive that the public purse was being used to give legal assistance to those with substantial means. Therefore, merits and means testing is necessary to ensure that scarce public resources are used to provide help to those most in need and deserving of it. In Hong Kong, various schemes that provide legal assistance are subject to merits and means testing, and the thresholds in terms of means testing are subject to periodic review.

Legal Aid

The Legal Aid Department (LAD) established in 1970 is responsible for the provision of legal representation to eligible applicants in Hong Kong. One

---

[20] Legal Aid Services Council, *Legal Aid in Hong Kong* (Legal Aid Services Council, Hong Kong, 2006), chapter 3.
[21] *R v. Chandra Thanwardas Mirchandani* [1992] 2 HKCLR 174, at para. 32; *R v. Fu Yan* [1992] 2 HKCLR 59.
[22] *R v. Fu Yan* [1992] 2 HKCLR 59; see also *Z v. Director of Legal Aid and another* [2011] HKCU 1358.
[23] *Z v. Director of Legal Aid and another* [2011] HKCU 1358.

of the core missions of the LAD is 'to ensure that no one who qualifies for legal aid is denied access to justice because of lack of means'.[24] The administration of legal aid is governed by the Legal Aid Ordinance and the Legal Aid in Criminal Cases Rules.[25] LAD is headed by the Director of Legal Aid and has three divisions: Application and Processing, Policy and Administration, and Litigation. Legal aid is available for civil and criminal proceedings in the District Court and above and in certain tribunals, and for committal proceedings in the Magistrates' Courts. In appointing the 'return day', which is the continuation of committal proceedings, the magistrate shall inform the defendant of his/her right to apply for legal aid.[26] Regardless of whether an individual is a Hong Kong resident, he/she can apply for legal aid as long as he/she is able to satisfy the statutory requirement of the merits and means test. Three schemes are operated by the LAD: Ordinary Legal Aid, Supplementary Legal Aid and Criminal Legal Aid.

Ordinary Legal Aid

The Ordinary Legal Aid Scheme covers civil proceedings in numerous areas, including matrimonial cases, traffic accidents and employees' compensation. Besides matters heard in the District Court and above, the scheme is also applicable for tribunal hearings such as applications to the Mental Health Review Tribunal.

As noted, applicants for legal aid must satisfy a merits and means test. The merits test requires the applicant to demonstrate that there are reasonable grounds for starting or defending the proceedings. The Director of Legal Aid will make an assessment based on all relevant information, including information from the opposing party of the case, on whether the applicant has a reasonable chance of success. Even if there is a reasonable prospect of success, legal aid may still be refused in situations where the applicant would not be able to enforce judgment, for example if the opposing party has no valuable assets and is uninsured. Apart from

---

[24] Legal Aid Department, *Legal Aid Department Annual Report 2016* (Hong Kong: Legal Aid Department 2017), p. 3.
[25] Legal Aid Ordinance (Cap. 91); Legal Aid in Criminal Cases Rules (Cap. 221D).
[26] Magistrates Ordinance (Cap. 227), ss. 80A and 85A(1).

monetary outcomes, the Director will base his/her decision on the importance of the case to the applicant.[27]

In terms of the means test, the applicant's financial resources must not exceed the financial eligibility limit, which is currently set at HK$307,130.[28] Financial resources are calculated as the applicant's monthly disposable income multiplied by twelve plus the applicant's disposable capital. Monthly disposable income is calculated by taking the net monthly income after various allowable deductions have been made from the applicant's gross income. The LAD provides a statutory allowance based on the applicant's household size, namely the number of dependants. The allowance is adjusted every year. Other deductions include rent. Disposable capital includes assets such as cash, bank savings, jewellery, stocks and property, but not the house that the applicant is residing in. It also does not include household furniture, personal clothing, and tools and implements of trade. If the applicant is already aged sixty or above, the amount of capital equal to that of the limit set out in the Ordinary Legal Aid Scheme would not be counted towards the capital amount. The LAD website provides an online calculator to compute an individual's financial resources.[29] The Director of Legal Aid may waive the limit for the means test if he/she believes that there is a breach of the Bill of Rights Ordinance or an inconsistency with the International Covenant on Civil and Political Rights.[30]

If successful, the aided person is granted a legal aid certificate and may be assisted through lawyers in the LAD, or the aided person or the Director of Legal Aid may select a solicitor or barrister to provide legal assistance for the aided person. In any case, however, the Director of Legal Aid can revoke or discharge the legal aid certificate.[31] The LAD maintains a separate panel for solicitors and barristers as required under the Legal Aid Ordinance (see below). For unsuccessful applicants, the applicant can appeal the Director of Legal Aid's decision to the Registrar of the High Court within fourteen days of the decision unless the Registrar allows

---

[27] See Legal Aid Ordinance (Cap. 91), s. 10.
[28] Legal Aid Ordinance (Cap. 91), s. 5.
[29] Refer to How to Calculate Financial Resources, available at www.lad.gov.hk/eng/las/fe.html.
[30] Legal Aid Ordinance (Cap. 91), s. 5AA.
[31] Legal Aid Ordinance (Cap. 91), s. 11.

further time.[32] For Court of Final Appeal cases, the applicant can appeal to a Committee of Review composed of the chairperson, who is the Registrar of the High Court, a barrister who is eligible to be appointed as a High Court judge and a solicitor with over ten years' experience practising in a common law jurisdiction. The barrister and solicitor must be appointed by the Chairperson or President of their respective professional bodies.[33] The decision by the Registrar (although it can refer the appeal to a High Court judge in chambers) or the Committee is final.[34]

There is often a misconception that legal aid is entirely free. A successful applicant must still pay a sum by way of contribution if his/her financial resources are above a certain threshold. The cost and expenses include pre-certificate expenses, such as fees for a bank search when conducting the means test and mediation expenses. The aided person must pay the contribution before legal aid is received. The amount of the contribution is based on a sliding scale ranging from HK$0 to HK$76,780 depending on the aided person's financial resources.[35] For cases funded under the Ordinary Legal Aid Scheme, if the aided person is successful in recovering or preserving any money or property in the legal proceedings, the applicant is required to repay the LAD out of the money or property recovered or preserved. This is referred to as 'the Director of Legal Aid's first charge'. If the proceedings involve recovery of land, then the Director's first charge may be registered in the land registry without prior notice.[36] However, maintenance for children and spouse not exceeding HK$4,800 per month is exempted. The amount is reduced by the contributions that have already been paid or from any costs recovered from the opposing party.[37]

Supplementary Legal Aid

The Supplementary Legal Aid Scheme which began in 1984 targets those referred to as the 'sandwich class', namely individuals whose

---

[32] Legal Aid Ordinance (Cap. 91), s. 26(2).
[33] Legal Aid Ordinance (Cap. 91), s. 26A(1).
[34] Legal Aid Ordinance (Cap. 91), ss. 26(4) and 26A(7).
[35] Refer to the Scale of Contribution, available at www.lad.gov.hk/eng/las/lac/olascc.html.
[36] Legal Aid Ordinance (Cap. 91), s. 18A(3A).
[37] Legal Aid Department, *Contributions towards Costs of Legal Aid Case and Director of Legal Aid's First Charge: Important Information for Aided Person* (Hong Kong: Legal Aid Department 2014).

financial resources exceed the statutory limit under the Ordinary Legal Aid Scheme but below an amount where hiring private legal representation would represent financial hardship. The merits test is the same, but for the means test, the financial resources must be above the limit set by the Ordinary Legal Aid Scheme and below a certain amount, currently set at HK$1,535,650.[38] The Supplementary Legal Aid Scheme is available for claims on personal injuries or death where the claim is likely to exceed the amount of HK$60,000. Irrespective of the amount of claim, the scheme covers claims under the Employees' Compensation Ordinance[39] and appeals by employees against awards handed down by the Labour Tribunal. These are referred to as Type I proceedings. If the claim is likely to exceed HK$60,000, the scheme is also available for claims against professional negligence involving the medical, dental, accountancy, architectural, engineering and legal professions among others, negligence claims against insurers and monetary claims against vendors in the sale of first-hand residential properties, regardless of whether it is completed or not. These are referred to as Type II proceedings.

For Type 1 proceedings, the applicant must pay an initial application fee of HK$1,000, and if successful, a subsequent interim contribution. The contribution is 25 per cent of the financial eligibility limit for the Ordinary Legal Aid Scheme. If the claim is eventually successful, a final contribution is required, which ranges from 6 per cent to 10 per cent of the damages recovered. For Type II proceedings, the applicant must pay a fee of HK$5,000 and an interim contribution of 10 per cent of the financial resources of the aided person or the limit for the Ordinary Legal Aid Scheme, whichever is higher. In successful claims, the final contribution ranges from 15 per cent to 20 per cent of the damages recovered.[40] When there is change in financial resources, the person is entitled to seek assistance in another legal aid scheme. The contribution payable may thus be varied upon transfer.[41]

---

[38] Legal Aid Ordinance (Cap. 91), s. 5A.
[39] Employees' Compensation Ordinance (Cap. 282).
[40] Legal Aid Department, *Supplementary Legal Aid Fund Annual Report 2016* (Hong Kong: Legal Aid Department 2017), pp. 2–4.
[41] Legal Aid Ordinance (Cap. 91), s. 32A.

Criminal Legal Aid

The Criminal Legal Aid Scheme provides legal assistance for individuals charged with criminal offences or those engaged in criminal appeals. It does not cover matters in the Magistrates' Courts aside from committal proceedings. The means test is the same for the Ordinary Legal Aid Scheme. The Director of Legal Aid, however, may waive the limit if it is determined that it is in the interests of justice to do so and subject to contribution payments at a higher rate. For the merits test, for criminal trials, it must be deemed to be in the interests of justice for legal aid to be granted, and for criminal appeals, in addition to the interests of justice, there must be reasonable grounds for appeal.

In cases where legal aid is refused because of merits, the trial judge hearing the applicant's case may order legal aid to be granted if the means test is satisfied. If the case is one of murder, treason or piracy with violence, the trial judge may even waive the means test and subsequent contribution payments.[42] If an application for legal aid for an appeal to the Court of Final Appeal is rejected, the applicant may apply to a Review Committee, which is made up of the Registrar of the High Court and a representative from each of the Hong Kong Bar Association and Law Society of Hong Kong.

Legal Aid Panel

Practising solicitors and barristers may apply to be on the Legal Aid Panel by completing the Panel Entry Form for their respective professions. Solicitors who are not the senior partner or the sole proprietor of their firms must provide a reference letter from their senior partner or sole proprietor when making their applications. Barristers with fewer than seven years' post-qualification experience must submit two reference letters. Referees may be judges or legal practitioners with more than seven years' post-qualification experience. Applicants are asked to indicate which areas of work they would like to be considered when receiving assignments for legal aid and the number of cases that they have handled personally in each area of work in the past three years. Senior counsel are exempted from the latter requirement. The Director of Legal Aid may

---

[42] See Legal Aid in Criminal Cases Rules (Cap. 221D), s. 13.

exclude certain individuals from the Panel because of their conduct in a particular case or because of their professional conduct more generally.[43]

Legal Aid Services Council

Beginning in September 1996, the Legal Aid Services Council was established to supervise the provisions of legal aid by the LAD and to advise the Chief Executive on policy regarding legal aid.[44] The Council is made up of a Chairperson who is not a public officer or not connected directly with the practice of law, two representatives each from the solicitor and barrister professions holding a practising certificate, four other persons who in the opinion of the Chief Executive are not connected in any way with the practice of law, and the Director of Legal Aid.[45] The functions of the Legal Aid Services Council are to formulate policies with respect to the services implemented by the LAD, advise on the policy direction of the LAD, review the services provided by the LAD periodically and advise on expenditures. What the Council cannot do is direct the LAD regarding staff matters and the handling of individual cases.[46]

Independent Legal Aid Authority?

It is imperative that decisions on the funding of legal services are, and are perceived to be, made impartially. This is particularly important in cases where an individual is seeking a claim against the Government. Concerns were raised about the independence of the LAD, which is administered by civil servants under the umbrella of the Home Affairs Bureau. In other words, would decisions with respect to granting or refusing legal aid be influenced by the Government?

In October 1997, the Legal Aid Services Council appointed consultants to investigate on the desirability of establishing an independent legal aid authority. The report recommended that an Independent Legal Aid Authority be implemented by phases eventually replacing the LAD. The reasoning was that there would always be a risk of interference from the Government

---

[43] See Legal Aid Ordinance (Cap. 91), s. 4.
[44] Legal Aid Services Council Ordinance (Cap. 489), s. 3.
[45] Legal Aid Services Council Ordinance (Cap. 489), s. 5.
[46] Legal Aid Services Council Ordinance (Cap. 489), s. 4.

when legal aid is administered by civil servants; that legal aid is an integral part of the justice system and its independence is of practical reality; and that independence insulates those administering legal aid so that they can make sound decisions without Government pressure.[47] The Chief Secretary for Administration in 1999 rejected the Council's recommendation. The Government's argument was that there were already safeguards in place to ensure the independent decision-making in the LAD and that the LAD had funded many cases against the Government, showing that there was not a problem with Government influence. Moreover, disestablishment of the LAD would be costly and it would be difficult to persuade existing staff of the LAD to leave the civil service.[48]

The establishment of an Independent Legal Aid Authority was revisited in 2007, and the consultancy firm Deloitte was commissioned in 2011 by the Legal Aid Services Council to examine the issue once again. Contrary to the previous recommendation, this time the recommendation was that there was no need to set up an Independent Legal Aid Authority to replace the LAD because the level of independence of the LAD was considered sufficient. The report stated that, during the study period, there was no substantiated example of Government interference on the granting of legal aid. The report cited two examples of cases against the Government which had been granted legal aid – the domestic helpers' right of abode case and the case of the Hong Kong–Zhuhai–Macao Bridge.[49]

This recommendation did not receive the endorsement of the two legal professions. The Law Society of Hong Kong, for instance, labelled the recommendation as a U-turn compared with the Legal Aid Services Council's former position, and argued that there was no justification for this change of stance.[50] Similarly, the Hong Kong Bar Association, prior to the release of the second report, criticised the existing arrangements for legal aid as being insufficient for meeting societal demands. It is argued that access to justice is hampered, especially for those in the sandwich class. By maintaining the position where the LAD is operated as a government

---

[47] Legal Aid Services Council, *Report on the Feasibility and Desirability of the Establishment of an Independent Legal Aid Authority* (Hong Kong: Legal Aid Services Council 1998).
[48] Legal Aid Services Council (n. 19), pp. 233–236.
[49] Deloitte, *Consultancy Study on the Feasibility and Desirability of Establishing an Independent Legal Aid Authority Final Report* (Hong Kong: Deloitte 2013).
[50] The Law Society of Hong Kong, 'Independent Legal Aid Authority Submission' (Hong Kong: The Law Society of Hong Kong 2013).

department, there will continue to be resistance to raising the financial eligibility limits of legal aid to meet the needs of the public. An Independent Legal Aid Authority, on the other hand, would be able to negotiate with other departments and bring meaningful reforms.[51]

Duty Lawyer Service

The Duty Lawyer Service (formerly known as the Law Society Legal Advice and Duty Lawyer Scheme) was established in 1978 and incorporated as a company limited by guarantee in 1993. It is an organisation that is directed at providing legal assistance to individuals and complements legal aid in Hong Kong. It is subvented by the Hong Kong Government but is independently managed by the Hong Kong Bar Association and Law Society of Hong Kong through a governing council.[52] The Council of the Duty Lawyer Service consists of four members nominated by the Hong Kong Bar Association, four members nominated by the Law Society of Hong Kong, three lay members not in the legal profession and the Administrator of the Duty Lawyer Service. The Council meets monthly to discuss the operations of the Duty Lawyer Service and reviews its policies. The daily administration is handled by the Administrator.[53] The Duty Lawyer Service provides four schemes: the Duty Lawyer Scheme, the Legal Advice Scheme, the Tel-Law Scheme and the Convention Against Torture Scheme.

The Duty Lawyer Scheme

The Duty Lawyer Scheme offers legal representation to defendants in the Magistrates' Courts, the Juvenile Courts and Coroner's Inquests. The Scheme covers around 300 statutory and common law offences.[54] The scheme does not cover committal proceedings, hawking offences, traffic summons and

---

[51] The Hong Kong Bar Association, 'Statement by the Hong Kong Bar Association on the Desirability of an Independent Legal Aid Authority' (Hong Kong: The Hong Kong Bar Association 2012).
[52] The Duty Lawyer Service, *Annual Report 2017* (Hong Kong: The Duty Lawyer Service 2018), p. 2.
[53] Ibid.
[54] Refer to the Duty Lawyer Scheme's Standard List of Offences, available at www.dutylawyer.org.hk/en/doc/Standard_List_of_Offences.pdf.

departmental summonses. Since April 2014, legal representation is further available for bail applications pending trial or sentencing for Magistrates' Courts defendants in the Court of First Instance.

A Court Liaison Office is stationed in each Magistrate's Court, and a defendant who wishes to apply for the service of the Scheme should approach the Court Liaison Office in the Magistracy in which he/she is due to appear. Defendants remanded in custody are automatically contacted by the staff of the Court Liaison Office. Defendants who are charged with an offence covered by the Duty Lawyer Scheme are eligible to be represented by a duty lawyer for free without any means testing for their first court appearance. Defendants who want to continue to be represented by a duty lawyer must then pass a merits and means test. The merits test is the 'in the interests of justice' test based on the Widgery criteria. The financial eligibility limit is based on the gross annual income. The limit is periodically revised and is currently set at HK$210,600. Applicants who are successful in passing the means test must still pay a handling charge of HK$570. This is the only charge that the defendant has to pay, regardless of how long their case lasts. The charge may be waived for those in genuine financial hardship.[55]

Defendants charged in the Juvenile Court, or juveniles that must appear in adult court, are eligible for legal representation by a duty lawyer. There are no merits or means tests required for juvenile defendants but their families are encouraged to pay the handling charge. The charge can be waived for students or applicants dependent on the support of their parents or guardians. The Scheme extends to care or protection cases (under the Protection of Children and Juveniles Ordinance (Cap. 213)) as well. The Scheme also covers individuals who are at risk of criminal prosecution because of incriminating evidence given in a Coroner's Inquest, appealing to the Municipal Services Appeals Board for decisions against issuing hawker licences or facing extradition proceedings. The same means test and handling charges apply for these cases.

The Duty Lawyer Scheme draws from private practising barristers or solicitors on the List of Duty Lawyers. Lawyers are called to appear in particular Magistracies to meet and represent clients or to handle particular cases, and they are compensated by a fee. The court liaison officers are employed by the Duty Lawyer Service and assist the duty lawyers as well

---

[55] The Duty Lawyer Service (n. 52).

as taking statements and preliminary instructions from defendants. However, because duty lawyers often meet with their clients on the day of their appearance, and because of the time constraint, there are concerns that there is inadequate time to give advice fully or to build rapport. There is a general sense on the part of defendants that private lawyers are the preferred option as advocates, but those who cannot afford private lawyers must make do with legal representation from duty lawyers.[56]

Free Legal Advice Scheme

The Free Legal Advice Scheme provides members of the public with preliminary legal advice without any means testing. Volunteer lawyers on a pro bono basis give one-off legal advice without offering a full solution to the problem or subsequent follow-up. The aim is to help individuals understand their case better, including their legal rights, and to point them in the right direction for resolution. Most of the advice is on matters of civil law, including commercial and property disputes, matrimonial issues and estate administration. Around five cases are advised upon each session by each lawyer, and about twenty to thirty minutes are allocated for each case.

Individuals who want to use the Free Legal Advice Scheme may make an appointment at any one of the nine Legal Advice Centres of the Home Affairs Department where the advice scheme operates[57] or through the specified referral agencies. There are currently twenty-eight referral agencies with 153 branches across Hong Kong. These include district offices, various non-governmental organisations and the Social Welfare Department.[58] These referral agencies may also refer individuals to one of the nine Legal Advice Centres. Clerical staff at the Centres will obtain the background information of the case. The case will then be vetted by the Administration Office of the Duty Lawyer Service to determine its suitability. Suitable cases are sent to the volunteer lawyers for preparation.[59]

---

[56] See K. K. Cheng, W. H. Chui and R. Ong, 'Providing Justice for Low-Income Youths: Publicly Funded Lawyers and Youth Clients in Hong Kong' (2015), *Social & Legal Studies* 24, 577.

[57] Refer to the list and location of the Legal Advice Centres, available at www.dutylawyer.org.hk/en/free/legal.asp.

[58] Refer to the list of Referral Agencies, available at www.dutylawyer.org.hk/en/free/referral.htm.

[59] The Duty Lawyer Service (n. 52).

Beside the nine Centres, the Free Legal Advice Scheme also helps other organisations by arranging for volunteer lawyers to provide free legal advice for similar schemes set up by these organisations. These organisations include the Hong Kong Federation of Women, Hong Kong Family Welfare Society, Action for Reach Out and the Department of Professional Legal Education of the University of Hong Kong.[60] For example, under the University of Hong Kong scheme, interview sessions are first conducted by law students who take down the background information of the applicant's case, and an appointment is made for a volunteer lawyer to give preliminary legal advice. Both sessions take place on the University's campus, and the legal advice sessions are typically thirty minutes long.[61]

Tel-Law Scheme

The Tel-Law Scheme provides taped legal information for members of the public to access via two telephone hotlines. The service began in 1984 and by 1995, the system was fully computerised with a twenty-four-hour automatic answering service. Eighty introductions to a wide range of topics are available. The topics are divided into eight categories: family law; land and landlord and tenant law; criminal law; employment law; commercial, banking and sale of goods law; administrative and constitutional law; environmental and tort law; and general legal information.[62] The tapes are available in English, Cantonese and, since 1999, Putonghua. The contents of the tapes are also transcribed and can be accessed online.

Convention Against Torture Scheme

The Convention Against Torture Scheme (CAT) began in December 2009 and its purpose is to assist claimants who have made a claim under article 3 of the United Nations Convention Against Torture and Other Cruel, Inhuman or Degrading Treatment or Punishment to the Immigration Department. Article 3(1) states that 'No State Party shall expel, return

---

[60] Ibid.
[61] See the Free Legal Advice Scheme on HKU Campus, available at www.law.hku.hk/cle/.
[62] Refer to the list of topics of the Tel-Law Scheme, available at www.dutylawyer.org.hk/en/73.asp?category=tellaw/tel_law.

("refouler") or extradite a person to another State where there are substantial grounds for believing that he would be in danger of being subjected to torture.' Since March 2014, the scheme also assists claims for non-refoulement protection relating to torture, cruel, inhuman or degrading treatment, and persecution under the Hong Kong Bill of Rights Ordinance,[63] 1951 Convention relating to the Status of Refugees (Persecution) and the Immigration Ordinance.[64]

Duty lawyers assist and provide legal representation on a variety of matters including advising clients on their rights and the legal procedure, assessing merits of appeals, assisting claimants to complete and submit their claims to the Immigration Department, and representing claimants in oral hearings. Legal assistance under CAT and the Non-Refoulement Claim Scheme is free of charge, but the claimant must make a statutory declaration that he/she is without means to pay for legal representation.[65]

Pro Bono and Other Schemes

Pro bono publico, referred to simply as pro bono, means 'for the public good'. It denotes legal work for low-income individuals free of charge. Pro bono by volunteer lawyers helps to meet legal needs not met by government-funded sources. There is a longstanding culture of pro bono within the legal profession in other jurisdictions. For example, the American Bar Association's Model Rules of Professional Conduct stipulates that 'A lawyer should aspire to render at least (50) hours of pro bono publico legal services per year.'[66] While the pro bono culture in Hong Kong is not as robust as in some other jurisdictions, it is growing.[67]

The Bar Free Legal Services Scheme managed by a Management Committee of the Hong Kong Bar Association is available for applicants who have been rejected by the Legal Aid Department or who cannot afford legal assistance but whose case is determined that legal assistance should be given. Volunteer barristers are placed on a panel. However, applicants

---

[63] Art. 3 of the Hong Kong Bill of Rights, contained in s. 8 of the Hong Kong Bill of Rights Ordinance (Cap. 383).
[64] Part VIIC.
[65] The Duty Lawyer Service (n. 52).
[66] American Bar Association's Model Rules of Professional Conduct, r. 6.1.
[67] D. Papworth, 'PRO BONO: Lawyers Making a Difference', August 2014, *Hong Kong Lawyer*, available at www.hk-lawyer.org/content/pro-bono-lawyers-making-difference.

cannot request a particular barrister to assist them, and barristers are not obliged to take on a particular case under this scheme. Successful applicants are given the details of the volunteer barrister and will deal with the barrister directly.[68] The Law Society of Hong Kong supplies a list of law firms that have volunteered to provide free legal services to the public. Initial legal consultation limited to forty-five minutes is provided without charge, and individuals should contact the law firm directly.[69]

The Legal Advice Scheme for Unrepresented Litigants in Civil Procedures or the Procedural Advice Scheme aims to give litigants in person free legal advice on matters relating to civil proceedings. The scheme was launched as a pilot project in March 2013 for two years operating under the Home Affairs Bureau and has since been regularised. Its scope is limited to unrepresented litigants in the District Court, High Court, Court of Final Appeal, Lands Tribunal and Family Court but not proceedings in other tribunals. It is also limited to litigants who do not have private legal representation and who have not been granted legal aid. The litigant must not have monthly income exceeding HK$50,000 or have a gross income of over HK$600,000 in the past twelve months. This includes the income of the applicant's spouse unless they are living separately and apart or unless the spouse is the opposing party. Applications are made to the Procedural Advice Scheme Office. The scheme operates on a first-come, first-served basis. Either a Quick Advice Session of not more than fifteen minutes or an Appointment Advice Session of not more than forty-five minutes will be given to successful applicants. The sessions are provided by lawyers of the scheme or voluntary lawyers. There is a maximum of five advice sessions, including both the quick or regular advice session, every three months per each court action. Areas where advice would not be given include legal aid applications or appeals, applications for grant of probate or letters of administration, self-bankruptcy orders, foreign law, drafting legal documents, complex matters that require further research, and the seeking of advice on the same issues without providing further information. The advice will not be written and there will not be advice given via

---

[68] Hong Kong Bar Association, 'Bar Free Legal Services Scheme' (Hong Kong: Hong Kong Bar Association 2016), available at www.hkba.org/content/bar-free-legal-services-scheme.

[69] Law Society of Hong Kong, 'Free Legal Consultation' (Hong Kong: Law Society of Hong Kong 2018), available at www.choosehklawyer.org/en/search_fl_start.asp.

correspondence, including telephone or video conference. Contact between the advising lawyer and the litigant must go through the scheme.[70]

Besides schemes to provide free legal assistance to individuals, pro bono lawyers offer their services to non-governmental organisations. Examples in Hong Kong include Helpers for Domestic Helpers, which offers legal advice to domestic helpers, and Justice Centre Hong Kong, which provides legal support for refugees in Hong Kong.[71] However, there are still challenges in fostering pro bono in Hong Kong, such as instilling an ingrained culture of pro bono among the legal profession and the difficulties faced by international firms in identifying the needs of the local community.[72]

Conditional Fees

Conditional fees are an arrangement between the lawyer and individual where, if the case is lost, there would not be any legal fees; in other words, 'no win, no fee'. If the case is won, then the legal charges would be the normal legal fees, which would then be charged in addition to an 'uplift' percentage or 'success fee'. This is different from contingency fees in the United States, where lawyer fees are based on a percentage of the damages awarded in successful cases. Conditional fees are prohibited in Hong Kong. In 2007, the Law Reform Commission published a report on conditional fees and recommended against allowing conditional fees in Hong Kong, although the Commission did highlight their value with respect to access to justice.

The Law Reform Commission observed that 'The inherent characteristic of conditional fees of facilitating access to justice is probably the most valid argument in favour of the introduction of conditional fees.'[73] There is a segment of the population, namely the middle-income group, which does not qualify for legal aid because they exceed the financial eligibility limit but which would be deterred by legal costs from engaging a legal representative. Conditional fees are a way for these people to be able to retain a

---

[70] Refer to the Terms and Conditions of the Procedural Advice Scheme, available at www.admwing.gov.hk/pdf/paso/PASO_tandc_en.pdf.
[71] Papworth (n. 67).
[72] Ibid.
[73] Law Reform Commission of Hong Kong, *Report on Conditional Fees* (Hong Kong: Law Reform Commission of Hong Kong 2007), p. 148.

lawyer. This is also a means to reduce the number of cases without strong grounds, because potential litigants would be able to have their cases examined by a qualified legal practitioner who would advise against proceeding with a case without merit. This would save expenses for both the litigant and the court system. This may be contrasted with the position of litigants in person (see below), who are more likely to be emotional and have unrealistic expectations for their cases.[74]

However, a number of arguments against conditional fees have been raised. Conditional fees lead to lawyers having a direct interest in the outcome of the case, and therefore there are concerns that this inhibits them from giving impartial advice. Instead of following the client's instructions, lawyers may be tempted to persuade their clients to accept a less favourable settlement or even withhold evidence that is disadvantageous. On the other hand, the Law Reform Commission noted that safeguards can be put in place to prevent abuse.[75] There have also been concerns that lawyers would encourage their clients to raise unmerited claims against organisations with large assets in the hope that the organisation would avoid litigation and settle in order to evade bad publicity. Against these concerns, the Law Reform Commission stated that it is unrealistic to suppose that professional solicitors would take up cases with little prospect of success.[76] A related concern regarding the ban on conditional fees has to do with the old common law offences of maintenance, which involves intermeddling by an unconnected party in encouraging a lawsuit, and champerty, which is a form of maintenance where the party maintaining another takes a portion of the property in dispute as his/her reward.[77] The rationale behind these offences was to combat intermeddling in litigation that would subvert the integrity of the court process and to prevent a third party 'trafficking' and 'gambling' in the outcome of litigation.[78] It should be pointed out that, although other common law jurisdictions have abolished these old common law offences,[79] maintenance and champerty are still criminal offences and torts in Hong Kong. Although

---

[74] Ibid., p. 149.
[75] Ibid., pp. 115–116.
[76] Ibid., pp. 116–117.
[77] See *Unruh* v. *Seeberger* (2007) 10 HKCFAR 31, at paras. 84–85.
[78] *Geoffrey L. Berman* v. *SPF CDO I, Ltd. And Others* HCMP 1321/2010, at para. 24.
[79] For example, maintenance and champerty was abolished in the UK through the Criminal Law Act 1967.

the prohibitions have been relaxed, champertous arrangements (i.e. contingency fees agreements between lawyer and client) are against the law, and legal practitioners have been punished.[80]

Nonetheless, the Law Reform Commission recommended against introducing conditional fees in Hong Kong because of the lack of 'after-the-event' (ATE) insurance. ATE insurance is required to cover legal costs in cases where the client's claims are unsuccessful. This is a necessary component of a conditional fees regime. Although conditional fees would mean that, in unsuccessful cases, the litigant would not need to pay their own legal fees, in civil litigation, the losing party is often ordered to pay the winning party's legal costs. Without such insurance, these costs may prove to be unbearable for some. In Hong Kong, it appears that insurance companies are hesitant to offer ATE insurance. There is scepticism that ATE insurance could be offered at rates that are commercially viable without unduly transferring the costs to consumers.[81]

Litigants in Person

Without schemes to facilitate legal representation, there would be an increase in unrepresented litigants, or litigants in person. It should be made clear at the outset that litigants in person are not only individuals who are unable to hire private legal representation. It includes people who refuse legal aid or do not apply for legal aid because they are ignorant of its procedure and availability. It also includes those who simply want to represent themselves.[82] The judiciary operates the Resource Centre for Unrepresented Litigants, which provides assistance to litigants or prospective litigants in civil proceedings in the District Court or the High Court.[83] The assistance provided is limited to procedural matters only, and the centre does not offer legal advice. It is likely that litigants in person face

---

[80] See *Winnie Lo* v. *HKSAR* [2012] HKEC 263 and *HKSAR* v. *Mui Kwok Keung* [2013] HKEC 610.
[81] Law Reform Commission of Hong Kong (n. 73), p. 153.
[82] C. Cameron and E. Kelly, 'Litigants in Person in Civil Proceedings: Part I' (2002), *Hong Kong Law Journal* 32, 313, pp. 318–319.
[83] Matrimonial, lands, employees' compensation and probate matters are, however, not covered.

disadvantages in the complex justice system and create challenges for other actors in the justice system, such as judges and the opposing lawyers.

Litigants in person present trial judges with a conundrum. On the one hand, judges recognise that litigants in person do not have the same legal knowledge and expertise as lawyers, and that the procedures and rules of evidence may be puzzling for many. In order to achieve a fair trial, judges would need to intervene to a greater extent to explain matters. On the other hand, the adversarial trial is party-driven and requires judges to be neutral adjudicators. The need for greater intervention in cases with litigants in person may compromise that neutrality.[84]

In a similar fashion, litigants in person may also increase the costs of the opposing party and their legal representatives. Lawyers have commented that where the opposing side involved a litigant in person, the proceedings were lengthier and hence more costly. More time needs to be devoted to explaining various issues, more adjournments may be granted, and litigants in person are more likely to make procedural errors, causing more delays. Moreover, lawyers have found litigants in person to be less susceptible to negotiations and settlements, as they do not fully understand the issues in question or simply regard them as the enemy. There is also a power imbalance in such negotiations between a skilled professional lawyer and a layperson. Litigants in person may later claim that they did not understand the settlement agreement or may change their minds afterwards.[85]

There is adverse impact on other court officials as well. For instance, court administrative staff have to help provide more information to litigants in person as they are often the first point of contact. As noted, because unrepresented litigants are more likely to make proceedings longer, court administrative staff have to take more time and effort on case management tasks such as rescheduling other matters.[86] This has a domino effect because, by rescheduling hearings, other litigants face delays in having their cases put before the court. Respect for the justice

---

[84] Ibid., p. 329.
[85] See ibid.; E. Kelly and C. Cameron, 'Litigants in Person in Civil Proceedings: Part II Solicitors' Perspectives' (2003), *Hong Kong Law Journal* 33, 585; W. H. Chui, E. Kelly and C. Cameron, 'Lawyers' Perspectives on the Impacts of Self-Representation in Civil Proceedings in Hong Kong' (2007), *International Journal of the Legal Profession* 14, 195, pp. 198–200.
[86] Cameron and Kelly (n. 82), p. 339.

system may deteriorate, since litigants in person may be frustrated during the proceedings and do not possess an ability to appreciate decisions made. Overall, the court system faces more pressure owing to the increased time and costs needed when one or both parties are unrepresented.[87]

Review Questions

(1) Compare and contrast the roles of barristers and solicitors in Hong Kong.
(2) Why is access to justice important for the rule of law?
(3) Explain the merits and means tests of the various legal aid schemes.
(4) How does the Duty Lawyer Service complement legal aid?
(5) Should there be an Independent Legal Aid Authority?
(6) What are the pros and cons of conditional fees?
(7) What challenges do litigants in person pose to the justice system?

---

[87] Ibid., p. 340.

Finding and Citing Legal Materials 12

Chapter Highlights

- Primary and Secondary Sources 329
- Finding Primary Sources 330
- Finding Secondary Sources 350
- Citation of Legal Materials 359

This chapter focuses on the skills and techniques in finding the law. Legal research skills are fundamental for both lawyers and law students. The accomplished lawyer might not necessarily know every legal principle in a particular area, but he or she would at least know how to find the law quickly and accurately. Moreover, as the law constantly changes through legislative enactments and judicial development, it is imperative for lawyers and law students to have the necessary research skills so that they can inform themselves of the current state of the law in the area they are investigating.

Primary and Secondary Sources

Legal resources are divided into primary and secondary sources. Primary sources refer to the actual law, which in Hong Kong is primarily comprised of the Basic Law, legislation and judgments of the superior courts.[1] Secondary sources refer to other written (including electronic) materials on the law, such as commentaries found in legal encyclopedias, textbooks and journals, as well as government papers and publications, especially those

---

[1] See Chapter 4.

dealing with law reform. Such secondary sources may contain explanations, analyses and discussions of the law, and are hence useful for gaining an understanding of the law. However, under the common law tradition, secondary sources do not constitute the law itself. Sometimes, judges might refer to the more authoritative texts or to government papers in ascertaining the correct principles of law, but it must be borne in mind that statements of the law contained in secondary sources cannot be cited as authoritative or binding statements of the law.

For the above reason, it is important for lawyers to access and use primary sources of law rather than simply relying on secondary sources. That said, secondary sources are important and can be used, for instance,

- as a tool for gaining a better understanding of the primary sources after perusing the primary sources; or
- as a tool for gaining an overview of a particular area of law before delving into the details of the law as contained in legislation and cases.

The use of secondary sources in the second way is especially recommended where you are researching an unfamiliar area of law. In such a situation, textbooks and legal encyclopedias are particularly useful as a starting point for research, as such sources would contain an overview of the subject area, allowing you to acquire a basic understanding and to see the big picture. Once you get your bearings, it becomes easier to navigate the case law and legislation to find the specific details of the law. Moreover, secondary sources such as textbooks set out the important cases and statutory provisions, thereby providing guidance for your further research.

Finding Primary Sources

Legislation: Hard Copy

Primary and secondary legislation is published in the *Government Gazette* and reproduced in the *Laws of Hong Kong*, a set of blue loose-leaf folders containing Hong Kong legislation as published by the government.

For legislation which existed as at 31 December 1989, the official or authentic version is that contained in the 1989 Revised Edition.[2] For

---

[2] See Revised Edition of the Laws Ordinance 1965, ss. 11(2) and 15(4).

legislation after that date, the official or authentic version is that published in the *Gazette*.[3] The status of the version of legislation in the loose-leaf *Laws of Hong Kong* is regarded as one of prima facie accuracy.[4]

Private publishers might also reproduce parts or the whole of particular statutes in handbooks or other resources; however, it must be remembered that these versions are not official versions and can potentially contain inaccuracies. If, for instance, there is a grammatical error in the authentic government version of an ordinance contained in the Revised Edition or in the *Gazette*, then this error is still a part of the law. However, if there is some error, not in the authentic version but in a version of the ordinance published by a private publisher, then woe betide the lawyer who relies on that incorrect provision in court. As a matter of prudence, reliance should only be made on the loose-leaf *Laws of Hong Kong* or the *Gazette* (or the 1989 Revised Edition where necessary).[5]

The government has commenced a gradual phasing out of the loose-leaf edition of the *Laws of Hong Kong*. It is gradually being replaced with 'Hong Kong e-legislation', an electronic database of Hong Kong legislation published on the World Wide Web: see Legislation Publication Ordinance (Cap. 614) sections 3 and 5.[6] Hard copies of ordinances may be published in the form of booklets which contain the 'verified' copies of ordinances and which have the same legal status as the pre-existing loose-leaf *Laws of Hong Kong*.[7]

---

[3] Interpretation and General Clauses Ordinance, s. 98(1).

[4] Section 3 of the Laws (Loose-leaf Publication) Ordinance 1990 provides that provisions published in the loose-leaf are deemed to be correct unless the contrary is proven.

[5] For absolute accuracy on the original text, reliance would be placed on the 1989 Revised Edition or the *Gazette*, since if there is a discrepancy between the authentic copies and those in the loose-leaf edition, the versions in the authentic copies (i.e., 1989 Revised Edition and the *Gazette*) prevail: see further 'Guide to the Loose-leaf Edition of the Laws of Hong Kong' in *Laws of Hong Kong* (loose-leaf ed., Vol 1) IV/2. However, the legislation in the 1989 Revised Edition would not incorporate subsequent amendments, nor would the original versions of legislation enacted and published in the *Gazette*. The loose-leaf edition does incorporate amendments and should generally be referred to in the first instance when accessing legislation.

[6] On the Legislation Publication Ordinance (Cap. 614), see the later part of this chapter.

[7] The booklets are presumed to correctly state the ordinance as at the date of publication unless the contrary is proved: Legislation Publication Ordinance (Cap. 614) s. 8(2).

The Basic Law

A hard copy of the Basic Law can be found in the first volume of the *Laws of Hong Kong*.

Primary Legislation

Laws of Hong Kong

Ordinances are contained in the *Laws of Hong Kong*, arranged chronologically by chapter number.[8] Assistance in finding the relevant ordinance is provided in the index volume of the *Laws of Hong Kong*. The index is divided into five parts:

I. Index (in order of number of Chinese character strokes)
II. Index (titles in alphabetical order)
III. Chinese Subject Index to Ordinances
IV. English Subject Index to Ordinances
V. Chronological Table of Ordinances.

For example, if you know the title of an ordinance but not the chapter number, then Index II can be used to locate the chapter number. If you only know the year in which the ordinance was passed, then you can refer to Index V. If you do not know which particular ordinance to look for but you are interested in finding ordinances in a particular subject area, then you can refer to Index III or Index IV.

Amending Legislation

An ordinance can be amended by subsequent ordinances. For example, the Companies Ordinance (Cap. 622) was amended in 2018 by the Companies (Amendment) Ordinance (No. 3 of 2018). Note that the amending ordinance in this example was enacted purely for the purpose of amending a primary ordinance (i.e., Cap. 622) and is not incorporated into the *Laws of Hong Kong* as a chapter in its own right. A second type of situation

---

[8] Chapter numbers of ordinances in the loose-leaf follow those previously set out in the 1989 Revised Edition. New public ordinances are numbered sequentially from the last chapter number given to a public ordinance (or is given a number of a repealed ordinance). Private ordinances are numbered sequentially from 1001.

where an ordinance is amended is illustrated by the following: the Personal Data (Privacy) Ordinance (Cap. 486), which came into operation in 1996, was amended in 2003 by the Securities and Futures Ordinance (Cap. 571). In this example, the amending ordinance (Cap. 571) is itself a primary ordinance which is given a chapter number in the *Laws of Hong Kong* and included in the loose-leaf volumes in its own right. The Securities and Futures Ordinance was a new piece of legislation in the area of the securities markets, but the enactment of the main provisions of that ordinance was accompanied by various ancillary amendments made to other ordinances (such as Cap. 486).

Checking for Amendments to an Ordinance and Updating from the Loose-Leaf Laws of Hong Kong: Government Gazette Legal Supplements

The loose-leaf *Laws of Hong Kong* is generally not up to date to the present moment. This is because when an ordinance is first passed by the Legislative Council and assented to by the Chief Executive, it is initially published in *Government Gazette Legal Supplement No. 1*, and it is not until several months later that the ordinance is incorporated into the loose-leaf volumes of the *Laws of Hong Kong*. If the ordinance is a primary ordinance with a chapter number, it will subsequently be incorporated into the loose-leaf in its own right. If the ordinance only amends one or more other ordinances, then the amending ordinance will not itself be incorporated into the *Laws of Hong Kong*, but the amendments effected by it will be incorporated into the various ordinances being amended – via reprinted pages (incorporating the amendments) which replace the superseded pages in the loose-leaf volume.

Due to this time lag before inclusion in the loose-leaf, it is necessary to consult *Government Gazette Legal Supplement No. 1* (which contains the ordinances passed in the year in chronological order) in order to check for the latest legislation and most recent amendments to existing ordinances. Check the most recent cumulative index of *Legal Supplement No. 1* and then the most recent issues of the supplement following the date of the latest cumulative index.

Sometimes amendments are made by way of subsidiary legislation (pursuant to authority stipulated in an ordinance), and these can be found in *Government Gazette Legal Supplement No. 2*.

Amendments to existing legislation will not be incorporated into the *Laws of Hong Kong* until after the amending legislation has commenced operation. However, the pink page at the front of the ordinance in the loose-leaf *Laws of Hong Kong* will list any amending ordinances that are not in operation at the time of the last update to the loose-leaf.

Finding the Commencement Date of Legislation

Although an ordinance has been passed and assented to, it does not come into force and become part of the law until it has commenced operation. The ordinance itself often contains one or more sections which state the commencement date. It is possible for different sections or parts of an ordinance to have different commencement dates.[9] If the ordinance does not have any section dealing with commencement, then it commences at the beginning of the day on which it was published in the *Government Gazette*.[10]

Often the commencement provision in an ordinance states that the ordinance will commence on a date to be appointed by notice in the *Gazette*. For primary ordinances already included in the loose-leaf *Laws of Hong Kong*, the first page of the ordinance (following the contents pages) will indicate the commencement date if such a date has already been gazetted by the time of the latest update to the loose-leaf. If there is no commencement date yet at that time, it is necessary to check *Government Gazette Legal Supplement No. 2* from the time of the last update to the loose-leaf *Laws of Hong Kong* to see if a commencement date was subsequently gazetted.

For primary ordinances not yet included in the loose-leaf *Laws of Hong Kong* or for amending ordinances that would not be reproduced in the loose-leaf, it is necessary to consult *Government Gazette Legal Supplement No. 2* from the date of assent of the ordinance to check whether a commencement date has been gazetted.

Finding the Legislative History of an Ordinance

It might for a variety of reasons be necessary to ascertain what amendments were made to an ordinance in the *past*. For instance, if a lawyer is

---

[9] See Interpretation and General Clauses Ordinance (Cap. 1), s. 20(3).
[10] Interpretation and General Clauses Ordinance (Cap. 1), s. 20(2)(a).

advising a client in relation to facts that occurred two years ago, then the lawyer will need to know what the law was at that time, that is, two years ago. Thus, if the relevant ordinance had been amended since that time, the lawyer should not be advising the client on the basis of the present law but rather on the previous law that existed (unless the current law has retrospective effect). In such a situation, the lawyer would need to ascertain what the legislative provisions were prior to the amendments.

The pink sheet at the front of an ordinance in the loose-leaf *Laws of Hong Kong* sets out the legislative or enactment history of the ordinance. For example, the enactment history might read:

Originally 36 of 1987 – R. Ed. 1987, 61 of 1988, R. Ed. 1988, L.N. 23 of 1991, L.N. 295 of 1992, 54 of 1992, 3 of 1993, 4 of 1993, L.N. 411 of 1993, 98 of 1994, L.N. 66 of 1995.

In this example, the ordinance in question is Ordinance No. 36 of 1987. This number allows you to find the original version of the ordinance, in the 1987 volume of *Government Gazette Legal Supplement No. 1*. The remaining parts of the above example of the enactment history show the amending legislation by number and year. For instance, in 1994, the primary ordinance was amended by Ordinance No. 98 of 1994. It is possible to find out what amendments were made by Ordinance No. 98 of 1994 by looking up the 1994 *Government Gazette Legal Supplement No. 1* and finding Ordinance No. 98 of that year. The final amendment shown in the above example is LN 66 of 1995: to find what amendments were made by this, you can consult the 1995 *Government Gazette Legal Supplement No. 2* and find Legal Notice 66.

Legislation handbooks (e.g., LexisNexis handbooks) or other books containing the text of legislation are also useful if you wish to see what earlier versions of an ordinance looked like. For instance, if you want to know what the Companies Ordinance contained in 2015 prior to amendments made in later years, then you could consult the 2015 edition of the *Hong Kong Company Law Handbook*.

Annotations

Some private publishers reproduce legislation in hard copy, often with commentary included. These are referred to as annotations or annotated legislation. Examples are the *Annotated Ordinances of Hong Kong* and the *LexisNexis Handbook* series (e.g., the *Hong Kong Securities Handbook*, which contains the Securities and Futures Ordinance). Such products might also contain subsidiary legislation or related legislation. New editions of products like the LexisNexis handbooks might be published from time to time.

Subsidiary Legislation

Rules and regulations made pursuant to a primary ordinance are also included in the loose-leaf *Laws of Hong Kong*, following the primary ordinance under which they are made. To find the most current version of a particular piece of subsidiary legislation, it is necessary to update from the *Laws of Hong Kong*. Amendments to subsidiary legislation are found either in *Government Gazette Legal Supplement No. 2* (where the amendment is made through subsidiary legislation) or in *Legal Supplement No. 1* (where the amendment is made by an ordinance).

For any piece of subsidiary legislation which has been made recently and which is not yet incorporated into the loose-leaf *Laws of Hong Kong*, reference can be made to *Government Gazette Legal Supplement No. 2*. As for ordinances, subsidiary legislation must be published in the *Gazette* upon being made.[11] Subsidiary legislation comes into operation on the day provided for in the legislation, or if there is no such provision, then it comes into force on the day on which it was gazetted.[12] Subsidiary legislation must be tabled before the Legislative Council at its next sitting after publication in the *Gazette*, and the Legislative Council has the power to amend or disallow the subsidiary legislation within twenty-eight days after the sitting.[13] Any resolution of the Legislative Council will be published in the *Gazette* within fourteen days.[14]

Unofficial versions of subsidiary legislation can also be found in annotated works and legislation handbooks.

---

[11] Interpretation and General Clauses Ordinance (Cap. 1), s. 28(2).
[12] Interpretation and General Clauses Ordinance (Cap. 1), s. 28(3).
[13] Interpretation and General Clauses Ordinance (Cap. 1), s. 34. This is referred to as the Legislative Council's power of negative vetting of subsidiary legislation.
[14] Interpretation and General Clauses Ordinance (Cap. 1), s. 34.

Legislation: Electronic

The Basic Law

The government has a website (www.basiclaw.gov.hk) on the Basic Law, containing the full text of the Basic Law as well as related materials. An electronic copy of the Basic Law can also be found on the Hong Kong e-legislation website.

Hong Kong E-Legislation

To improve access to the law, the government has established a new online legislation database with legal status, referred to as 'Hong Kong e-Legislation' (HKeL).[15] Under the Legislation Publication Ordinance (Cap. 614), the Secretary for Justice is empowered to establish and maintain an electronic database of Hong Kong legislation, and to approve a website on which the information may be published and accessed.[16]

HKeL contains all consolidated legislation in Hong Kong. However, at the time of writing, not all the ordinances are verified copies yet. The PDF files of legislation on HKeL which contain pages marked with the words 'Verified Copy' are verified copies and are the official versions of the legislation. A verified copy of legislation is presumed, unless the contrary is proved, to correctly state the legislation as at the date specified in the copy.[17] Other copies of legislation on HKeL do not have such official status (and for the official version of these, it is still necessary to consult the hard-copy *Laws of Hong Kong* loose-leaf). It is intended that eventually all consolidated versions of ordinances on HKeL will have the status as verified copies.

HKeL contains both ordinances and subsidiary legislation. On the front page, there are search boxes enabling quick searches of legislation by either the chapter number or the short title of the legislation. The 'search' tab can be clicked on, which enables advanced searches, for example, by

---

[15] www.elegislation.gov.hk. This website replaces the former website 'Bilingual Laws Information System' (BLIS), which did not have legal status as official versions of legislation.
[16] Legislation Publication Ordinance (Cap. 614), s. 3.
[17] Legislation Publication Ordinance (Cap. 614), s. 5.

keywords. There is also a 'browse' tab, which can be clicked on to see the lists of ordinances by chapter number or in alphabetical order.

Gazette

Ordinances and subsidiary legislation as published in the *Gazette* can also be accessed electronically (see the later section on the *Gazette*).

LexisNexis and Westlaw

Legislation can also be found on the LexisNexis or Westlaw Hong Kong databases. These databases are not free to the public and subscriptions are required before they can be accessed. University libraries would generally subscribe to these electronic services, and students should check with their university library for access.

Hong Kong Legal Information Institute

The Hong Kong Legal Information Institute (HKLII) is a free website (www.hklii.org) that also contains Hong Kong legislation. While it is a useful resource, this database does not purport to provide the official versions of legislation.

Bills

Bills can be found in *Government Gazette Legal Supplement No. 3*, which is blue in colour (hence the reference to 'blue bills'). Electronic copies of bills can be accessed at the Legislative Council website (www.legco.gov.hk).

Gazette

The *Gazette* is an official journal published by the government containing legislation and government notices, etc. The legal materials in the *Gazette* are contained in the legal supplements:

- Legal Supplement No. 1, which contains ordinances passed and assented to;

- Legal Supplement No. 2, which contains subsidiary legislation and legal notices;
- Legal Supplement No. 3, which contains bills.

An electronic version of the *Gazette* is accessible from the Hong Kong e-legislation website (discussed above). The front page of the website contains a tab 'gazette', via which particular issues of the *Gazette* can be browsed online. The website also has a search function available which allows searching by gazette number or gazette title. The website only contains gazettes going back to the year 2000, and so for earlier gazettes it would be necessary to find the hard-copy versions.

Legislation: Overseas

Hard-Copy Sources

Local university libraries should generally have UK legislation. UK Acts may be found, for example, in *Current Law Statutes* and *Halsbury's Statutes*. For other overseas legislation, consult library catalogues or check with the librarians to see if they are available.

Electronic Sources

Some overseas legislation can be accessed electronically. Both LexisNexis and Westlaw contain legislation databases from the United Kingdom, the United States and various other common law and non-common law jurisdictions. The particular materials that you can access within either LexisNexis or Westlaw might differ depending on your (or your library's) particular subscription.

Some overseas governments (or private organisations) make available the legislation of their country online. Examples of overseas websites containing legislation are as follows:

- United Kingdom: the National Archives department has established an official website of UK legislation, www.legislation.gov.uk
- Australia: AustLII (Australasian Legal Information Institute), www.austlii.edu.au
- New Zealand: the New Zealand Parliamentary Counsel Office's legislation website, www.legislation.govt.nz

- Canada: the Department of Justice Laws Website, laws.justice.gc.ca
- United States: the US Government's Official Web Portal, www.usa.gov (which contains a link to US laws and regulations).

International legislation can also be accessed from the World Legal Information Institute website (www.worldlii.org).

Reported Cases: Hard Copy

The method for locating the judgment of a case differs depending on the information that you have available.

Finding a Case Using the Report Citation

Example: *Yuen Sha Sha v Tse Chi Pan* [1999] 2 HKLRD 28

The steps are as follows:

(1) Check which law report the abbreviation 'HKLRD' refers to by consulting the *Index to Legal Citations and Abbreviations*. In this example, 'HKLRD' refers to the *Hong Kong Law Reports and Digest*.
(2) Find the relevant volume (and issue) of that law report from the shelves. In the above example, the volume is designated by the year (since square brackets are used), that is, the 1999 volume, issue number 2.
(3) The judgment of the case starts at the page indicated by the page number in the citation, that is, page 28.

Finding a Case Using the Parties' Names

Example: *Pang Wai Chung v Hoi Tat Rubber Factory*

You will need to find the full citation of the case. This can be done through the use of Hong Kong case indexes or case citators. These lists report Hong Kong cases by name, in alphabetical order. Examples are as follows:

- *Consolidated Index to All Reported Hong Kong Decisions:* You should access the most recent Reissue of the *Consolidated Index* and check also for supplements to the index which are published from time to time.

- *Hong Kong Case Citator:* Check the latest Reissue of the *Case Citator* and the latest cumulative supplement to the citator which is also published from time to time.

In addition, leading cases would be contained in the 'Table of Cases' in extensive works such as *Halsbury's Laws of Hong Kong*. If you know that the case is in a particular subject area, then you can also check the 'Table of Cases' in a leading textbook in that area.

Case indexes and case citators, etc., might only be up to date to the end of a particular year (or a particular month in a particular year). If the case that you are looking for is a more recent case, then you will need to check the latest issues of the HKLRD from the date of currency of the index or case citator. For example, assume that the latest supplement to the *Hong Kong Case Citator* is current to August of *last year*.

The steps are as follows:

(1) Find the HKLRD Yearbook from the *previous year* and check the following table: 'Cases Reported and Digested – Cumulative'.
(2) If the case is not found in step 1, then look up the latest month-end issue of the HKLRD in the *current year* and check the following table: 'Cases Reported and Digested – Cumulative'. The issues of the HKLRD published in the middle of the month do not contain a cumulative table. If the most recent month-end issue of the HKLRD is not the most current issue (i.e., there is a later mid-month issue), then you will also need to check that latest (mid-month) issue.

Finding Cases on a Particular Subject

The steps are as follows:

(1) Refer to the latest Reissue of the *Consolidated Index to All Reported Hong Kong Decisions*, and find the volumes containing the 'Subject Index'. This index contains cases listed by subject.
(2) For cases handed down after the date of currency of the latest Reissue of the above *Consolidated Index*, check the latest supplements to the index (if any).
(3) For the most recent cases, refer to the HKLRD, and look up the table 'Cumulative Index for Cases', which lists cases by subject area. To see the cases in the whole of one year, refer to the cumulative index

in the HKLRD Yearbook of that year. To find the index of all the cases up to the current time in a year, refer to the cumulative index in the latest month-end issue of the HKLRD in that year.

Noting Up: Checking the Status of a Case

If you are relying on a case for a legal rule or principle, you need to know whether the case is still good law. This means that you will need to check whether any later decisions have overruled or declined to follow the primary case that you are looking at. In addition, although a case is still good law, you may wish to know how the case has been treated in later decisions, that is, in what situations the case has been applied or followed or distinguished. The process of finding out the treatment of a case in later decisions is referred to as 'noting up'.

Case indexes and case citators can be used.

Consolidated Index to All Reported Hong Kong Decisions

Example: *Balfour* v. *Balfour* [1919] 2 KB 571

The steps are as follows:

(1) Find the volume of the *Consolidated Index* which contains 'Decisions Referred To'. If the case is not listed in that table, then it means that no subsequent cases have considered the primary case (in the period covered by the index). This case can be found in the above index, which shows that the decision was considered in Hong Kong in the case with citation '[1996] 1 HKC 1'.
(2) To see if any Hong Kong decisions after the date of currency of the latest Reissue of the *Consolidated Index* have considered the primary case that you are looking at, you will need to refer to the latest supplements to the index (if any).
(3) The latest supplement (if any) might only be up to date to the end of the previous year. To check whether your primary case has been judicially considered in decisions passed in the current year (or in a year following the latest supplement to the above index), then check the HKLRD.

Hong Kong Case Citator

Example: *Balfour* v. *Balfour* [1919] 2 KB 571

The steps are as follows:

(1) Look up the case *Balfour* v. *Balfour* in the latest Reissue of the *Hong Kong Case Citator*. If this case is listed in the citator, and under the entry of this there are one or more cases listed, then it means that *Balfour* v. *Balfour* has been considered in the subsequent case(s). The citator also indicates the treatment, for example, whether applied or distinguished, etc.

(2) Look up the case in the latest cumulative supplement to the *Hong Kong Case Citator*, which works in a similar way. If there is no entry for *Balfour* v. *Balfour*, then it means that the case did not arise for consideration in any Hong Kong case during the period of coverage of the supplement.

Hong Kong Law Reports and Digest

Use of the above index or case citator is not sufficient, as they may not cover the most recent cases. Accordingly, you will need to look up recent issues of the HKLRD to cover the period from the date of the most recent edition or supplement of the index or citator that you referred to above. The relevant table in the HKLRD is 'Cases Judicially Considered – Cumulative' or 'Cases Cited – Cumulative'. To see the cases in the whole of one year, refer to the cumulative index in the HKLRD Yearbook for that year (or the 31 December issue of the HKLRD, if the Yearbook is not yet published). If the latest issue of the HKLRD in the current year is not the December issue, then to find the index of all cases up to the current time in that year, refer to the cumulative index in the latest month-end issue of the HKLRD in that year.

Example: Check whether any cases have considered *Re Barleycorn Enterprises Ltd* [1970] 2 WLR 898 in 2007.

The steps are as follows:

(1) Find the 2007 HKLRD Yearbook (or the 31 December 2007 issue of the HKLRD).

(2) Look up the 'Cases Judicially Considered – Cumulative' table.

If these steps are done, then you should see the following in the table:

Barleycorn Enterprises Ltd, Re [1970] Ch 465, [1970] 2 WLR 898, [1970] 2 All ER 15, **[1]**453.

This entry means that the *Barleycorn* case was considered in one decision in 2007. Use the reference number **[1]**453 to locate the case in which the *Barleycorn* decision was cited. The numbers in bold refer to Volume 1 of the HKLRD in 2007, page 453.

(3) Look up Volume 1 of the HKLRD in 2007, page 453. You will see the case which cited the *Barleycorn* decision is *Re Good Success Catering Group Ltd* [2007] 1 HKLRD 453.

Finding a Case Which Referred to Particular Legislation

When looking at particular provisions in some piece of legislation, it is important to see whether any courts have considered those provisions and if so how the courts have interpreted the provisions. The available hard-copy resources for conducting this research are as follows.

Consolidated Index to All Reported Hong Kong Decisions (Cumulative Supplement)

Look up the legislation table and find the ordinance that you are checking. Any cases that have considered the legislation (in the period of coverage of the supplement) would be listed under that ordinance.

Hong Kong Law Reports and Digest

(1) For coverage over the period of an entire year, refer to the HKLRD Yearbook of that year, and look up the 'Legislation Judicially Considered – Cumulative' or 'Legislation Mentioned – Cumulative' table. If you are searching in the current year, then for coverage of the entire period from January to the present, look up the latest month-end issue of the HKLRD.

(2) If an ordinance has been judicially considered in the period covered by the issue of the HKLRD that you are looking at, then there will be an entry for that ordinance in the table, next to which will be a reference,

for example, 3[218]. In this example, the reference is to Volume 3 of the HKLRD of that year, page 218, wherein you would find the case that referred to the ordinance in question.

Reported Cases: Electronic Databases

LexisNexis and Westlaw

The LexisNexis database contains the HKC (*Hong Kong Cases*) and the HKPLR (*Hong Kong Public Law Reports*) report series, while the Westlaw database contains the previous HKLR (*Hong Kong Law Reports*) and the current HKLRD (*Hong Kong Law Reports and Digest*) series. The cases can be accessed through the search templates in these databases.

Finding a Case Using the Citation or Parties' Names

Once you have logged into the Hong Kong database of either LexisNexis or Westlaw, you can access the judgments of cases through use of the search templates in the database. The look and precise functions of the templates in the two databases differ, but the broad approach to searching is the same.

Search tips:

- Both databases have a 'Quick Search' type of template, with boxes where you can type either the parties' names or the citation of the case.
- The search templates are usually not case sensitive.
- If you are entering the citation, then you must be precise in typing in the correct citation, and in the format required by the search template.

If you are typing in the parties' names, it is not always necessary to type the full name. Sometimes the search does not obtain a match if you type the full name, because of the name of the case in the database being slightly different from the name that you have. This might arise because of the use of abbreviations.

Example: *Pyrok Industries Ltd* v. *Chee Tat Engineering Company Ltd*

It is sufficient to type in the names 'Pyrok' and 'Chee Tat Engineering'. If, for instance, for the first party, you type in the full name 'Pyrok Industries Engineering Company Ltd' in the database, you might not obtain any results for your search if the database uses the abbreviation 'Co' for 'Company'.

Finding Cases on a Particular Subject

Electronic databases contain search templates which allow for the searching of documents contained in the database. If a word is entered into the search box without narrowing the search (e.g., via the use of specific fields or document segments), then the search will find any document that contains the word entered. It is advisable to initially try searching using specific fields. Common fields are 'Catchwords', 'Keywords' and 'Headnotes'.

For example, if you are searching for cases on privity of contract, then you could type 'privity of contract' in one of these fields. If the privity doctrine was an important part of the judgment, then the words 'privity of doctrine' should be in either or both the 'Catchwords'/'Keywords' and 'Headnotes' fields. If such a search does not provide many results, then you can search more widely without restricting to these fields to find other cases.

Search tips:

- Do not search using terms that cover vast areas of the law. For example, if you simply typed 'Contract' in the 'Catchwords' box, then the search is likely to pick up thousands of cases in Hong Kong. It is too inefficient to look at each of those cases to find the ones that are relevant for you. You need to be more specific in your research. For example, if you are researching promissory estoppel in the context of contract law, you might try using the following search terms together: 'contract' and 'estoppel'.
- Do not search solely by using terms that might be very specific. For example, if you are dealing with a legal problem concerning whether estoppel can be relied on in relation to a dispute over a lease in a shopping centre, then do not *only* rely on a search using the terms 'estoppel', 'lease' and 'shopping centre'. Certainly you can try a search using these terms to see if there is any existing case with similar facts to your problem. However, it might also be necessary to do a wider search if you are looking for cases dealing with general principles of estoppel that can be applied to your case, especially if your initial narrow search does not yield any results.

Make use of Boolean searching, discussed later in the chapter.

Noting Up: Checking the Status of a Case

Noting up can be done electronically using LexisNexis or Westlaw. There are different ways of noting up cases electronically, depending on the available features of the database. The following are two possibilities:

- Simply search for the case itself by typing the parties' names or the citation in the appropriate field. The database might have features which will reveal the subsequent treatment of the primary case. For example, the database might use coloured flags as symbols to indicate subsequent treatment: a red flag might be used to show that the case was reversed on appeal, overturned by a later decision, disapproved of, etc. You will need to become familiar with the particular features of the database that you are using.
- Type the name of the case or its citation in the search template of the database. This will reveal whether the case has been cited in any later judgments. In order to see how the primary case was treated (whether applied or overruled, etc.), you will need to click on each of the cases in your search results.

Finding a Case Which Referred to Particular Legislation

In the search template, type the name of the ordinance and the section number. For example, if you are researching section 465 of the Companies Ordinance, you could try searching using the following sets of search terms: 'companies ordinance' and 's 465'; 'companies ordinance' and 'section 465'.
Search tips:

- You might need to try both sets of search terms as judgments may or may not use the abbreviation of 's' for 'section'.
- Do not only search using the phrase 'companies ordinance s 465', as the text in a judgment referring to the section might not necessarily refer to the section within that exact phrase.
- Some search templates might have a field for 'Legislation referred to' (or 'Legislation cited'). If so, then type the name of the ordinance and the section number in that field. In the example of researching section 465 of the Companies Ordinance, you would type in the following: 'companies ordinance' and '465'.

Boolean Searching

Electronic legal databases often allow for the use of Boolean searching, that is, through the use of connectors referred to as Boolean operators. Using such connectors or operators allows for more accurate searching.

Some common examples are as follows:

Example: 'privity of contract'

The use of quotation marks around a phrase will involve a search for the exact phrase contained in the quotation marks.

Example: contract and estoppel

The use of the connector 'and' means that you will be searching for a document in the database (e.g., a judgment in a case database or an article in a journal database) that contains both the words 'contract' and 'estoppel'.

Example: remedies or damages

The use of the connector 'or' means that you will be searching for a document that contains either the word 'remedies' or 'damages'.

The following connectors are also useful, but the precise symbol used for the connector might differ for different databases, and you will need to check the information provided in the database as to the correct symbol to use.

Example: doctrine /s privity

The use of '/s' means that you will be searching for any document that contains the words 'doctrine' and 'privity' within the same sentence.

Example: damages /20 'economic loss'

The use of '/20' means that you will be searching for any document that contains the terms 'damages' and 'economic loss' within twenty words of each other. You can insert different numbers, so instead of searching for the terms within twenty words of each other, you could for instance use '/10' to search for the terms within ten words of each other.

Example: negli*

This will produce a search of documents containing any word that begins with 'negli', so, for example, it will yield any document that contains either the word 'negligent' or 'negligence'.

Reported Cases: Freely Available Public Websites

Hong Kong Legal Information Institute

Apart from legislation, the Hong Kong Legal Information Institute website (www.hklii.org) also contains judgments of the various courts and tribunals in Hong Kong. The HKLII database contains both judgments of the superior courts and those from a number of other courts and tribunals, including the District Court, Family Court and Lands Tribunal.

Judiciary

The website of the Hong Kong Judiciary (www.judiciary.gov.hk) also contains judgments of the superior courts as well as other courts and tribunals in Hong Kong.

Unreported Cases

For unreported cases, some law libraries might contain folders containing hard copies of the unreported judgments. However, unreported judgments can perhaps be more easily found electronically. Both LexisNexis and Westlaw contain Hong Kong case databases which cover unreported decisions. Once you have ascertained that the database that you are searching contains unreported judgments, you can search broadly via the same methods discussed earlier for reported decisions. Unreported decisions can also be found on the Judiciary or HKLII website.

International Case Law

Overseas publishers produce indexes, case citators, etc., relevant for the case law in the particular overseas jurisdiction. Check with your librarian for available resources. Law libraries should also have many of the major overseas report series, containing full judgments of reported cases. Electronic databases such as LexisNexis and Westlaw also contain overseas legal materials, including case law. Once you have accessed the relevant overseas case law database, you can adopt the same broad search techniques as discussed earlier for Hong Kong cases. The freely available public website, World Legal Information Institute website (www.worldlii.org), can also be searched for international case law.

Finding Secondary Sources

Books

You can search for textbooks and other legal books by using your university's library catalogue. Textbooks are generally written in a particular subject area that is taught as a university course, for example, contract law or tort law. There are also practitioner works which are aimed towards the practitioner market, and which also focus on a broad area of law, for example, insurance law. Other legal books are more specialised in their focus and include books that focus on a more specific or niche area of law (say, cross-border issues in securities law), books that deal with general policy issues in an area of law or those that cover more theoretical or conceptual issues related to the law.

Legal Encyclopaedias

Legal encyclopaedias contain commentary outlining the basic principles in most areas of the law. They are a useful starting point when researching an unfamiliar subject area, especially if the area is not one that is covered by any textbooks. Currently the only legal encyclopedia published on Hong Kong law is *Halsbury's Laws of Hong Kong*, which was originally based on the English edition but includes the Hong Kong authorities and appropriate changes to reflect Hong Kong law.

Halsbury's Laws of Hong Kong: Hard-Copy Version

The hard-copy *Halsbury's* is comprised of a number of volumes, ordered alphabetically by subject area. Each volume contains one or more titles, which refer to the particular subject area. Each title is given a particular number. For instance, Volume 1(1) contains [10] Administrative Law. The list of titles is contained in the 'Title Scheme' index which is found at the beginning of each volume.

Each volume contains contents tables and subject indexes to assist in locating specific topics in the particular subject area. The tables include the following:

- Table of Ordinances
- Table of Hong Kong Subsidiary Legislation
- Table of Cases.

If you are interested in looking for discussions of a particular ordinance or case, then you can use these tables to locate the particular paragraph containing such discussions.

If you do not know which volume to look up, then you should make use of the tables and index volumes (i.e., the *Consolidated Tables* and *Consolidated Index* volumes). These volumes contain tables of ordinances and other legislative and related instruments, tables of cases and a subject index. The reference given for entries in the tables and index is a reference to the paragraph number. For example, a reference to [175.065] is a reference to paragraph [175.065], which can be found in title [175] Evidence. Reference to the Title Scheme in the tables and index volumes (or any volume of *Halsbury's*) will reveal which volume contains title [175] Evidence (in this example, Volume 12).

Halsbury's Laws of Hong Kong: Electronic Version

This is available in the LexisNexis Hong Kong database. There are two main methods for accessing material in the electronic version of *Halsbury's*:

- Browsing: Click on 'Table of Contents – Halsbury's Laws of Hong Kong'. This lists the different titles (i.e., the subject areas), and you can access each title by clicking on the links in the titles. This will then lead you to a table of contents for the title, and clicking further on each link will drill down further into headings and subheadings.
- Searching: Use either the basic (quick search) template or the advanced search template. You can enter words, phrases or names of statutes or cases in the search box. The general electronic search techniques discussed earlier in the context of searching for cases, including the use of different fields and Boolean connectors, are also relevant for searching in the *Halsbury's* database.

Digests

Law digests are often published fortnightly or monthly, providing information on the latest developments in the law, such as new cases, information on bills and new statutes. The *Hong Kong Law Reports and Digest* is a digest as well as a law report series. The digest component of the HKLRD was formerly the *Hong Kong Law Digest* (from 1989 to 1994), and before that, *Hong Kong Current Law* (before 1989).

Hong Kong Law Reports and Digest

Two issues of the HKLRD are published each month (Part 1 and Part 2), with one letter assigned to the two issues of each month (i.e., A for January, B for February, C for March, etc.). The digest is contained in the second issue, which is published at the end of the month. For example, the digest for the July issue of the HKLRD is contained in G – Part 2 (published 31 July). Information contained in the digest includes the following:

(1) Subject Index for Reports: This is an index of subject topics, with entries indicating what cases have been reported in the period covered by the digest relating to the particular topic. For example, consider the following entry in the index:

Criminal law and procedure

> Homosexual buggery with or by man under 21 contrary to s 118C – s 118 unconstitutional: unequal treatment as 16 year old heterosexuals could engage in sexual intercourse – Crimes Ordinance (Cap 200) s 118C

[CA] *Leung* v. *Secretary for Justice* 211

This entry indicates that the Court of Appeal decision in *Leung v Secretary for Justice* dealing with the above subject matter was reported on page 211 of that issue of the HKLRD.

(2) Subject Index for Digest: This is an index of subject topics, with entries indicating what cases have been included in the digest in the period covered by that issue of the HKLRD relating to the particular topic. For example, the following entry might appear in this index:

Company law

Directors

> Disqualification – period of disqualification

[CFI] *Official Receiver* v. *Cheung Gin Hung* A1

Cases in the digest each have a reference number. The number in this example is 'A1', and you will find the case *Official Receiver v Cheung Gin Hung* in the A issue (January issue), at A1 in the section 'Digests – Cases'.

(3) Reports – Cases: This section contains the full judgment of cases reported in that issue of the HKLRD.

(4) Digests – Cases: This section contains digested cases, ordered alphabetically by subject. The case digest contains basic details of the case, including catchwords, brief facts and the decision of the court.
(5) Digests – Legislation: This contains information on the latest bills, ordinances and subsidiary legislation. The entries include both the subject topics and names of ordinances, listed in alphabetical order. Brief details are provided in relation to the legislation, including brief summaries, date of assent and commencement date (if available).
(6) Law Reports and Digest – Indices: The tables contained here are as follows:
    - Legislation (Including Commencement Dates) – Cumulative: This lists ordinances and subsidiary legislation contained in the 'Digests – Legislation' section of the issues of the HKLRD of that year. The reference number given allows you to find the issue and section number. For example, consider this entry in the index:

    Airport Authority (Amendment) Ordinance (No 10 of 2004) – 11 June 2004, G21

    This means that the ordinance is digested in the G issue (31 July issue), at G21 in the section 'Digests – Legislation'.
    - Amended Legislation – Cumulative: This lists ordinances and subsidiary legislation which have been affected by amending legislation in the year to date. For example:

    Chinese Medicine Ordinance (Cap 549) ss 2, 98(5)(b), 404, H19

    This entry in the table means that sections 2, 98(5)(b) and 404 of the Chinese Medicine Ordinance have been amended by certain legislation. The details of the amending legislation can be found in the following issue of the HKLRD of the year (i.e., 31 August, H – Part 2), at H19 in the 'Digests – Legislation' section.
    - Cumulative Index for Legislation: This is an index of information contained in the 'Digests – Legislation' section of each issue of the HKLRD in the year to date. The entries include both subject topics and names of ordinances, listed in alphabetical order. For example:

    Dangerous drugs,

    Prescribed hospitals and institutions, K21

This entry in the index indicates that there has been legislation in relation to the topic mentioned in the entry. To see what the legislation is, you need to find issue K of the HKLRD of that year (i.e., 30 November, K – Part 2), and look up K21 in the 'Digests – Legislation' section of that issue. There would be information contained in that section setting out details of the relevant legislation.

- Cases Reported and Digested – Cumulative: This lists the cases decided in the year to date, that is, cases either reported (i.e., with full text of judgment) or digested (i.e., containing the summary only) in the HKLRD in the year to date.
- Legislation Mentioned – Cumulative (or Legislation Judicially Considered – Cumulative): This lists legislation that has been referred to in cases decided in the year to date.
- Cases Cited – Cumulative (or Cases Judicially Considered – Cumulative): This lists cases that have been referred to in judgments handed down in the year to date.

Cumulative Index for Cases: This lists by subject cases reported or digested in the year to date.

Journals/Periodicals/Law Reviews

Legal journals (also referred to as periodicals or law reviews) contain articles or essays written by law academics, practising lawyers and other scholars, focusing on particular issues or aspects of the law. The subject matter of journal articles is diverse, and coverage of the many overseas and international journals extends to all areas of law and policy. Many journals are refereed or peer reviewed, which means that articles submitted for publication are reviewed by one or more experts before acceptance for publication. This is intended to ensure that published material is of high quality. Journals are an important source of secondary legal material and it is important for students to learn to find and use journal sources for their own studies and research.

An issue of a journal might be published once every few months. At the end of each year (or perhaps once every few years), the issues published in the particular period are bound together in a hardback volume.

Finding a Journal Article from Its Citation

The aspects of a journal article citation are discussed here. If you know the citation of an article, then you can use the information in the citation to locate the article.

Example: (2003) 33 HKLJ 139

The article with this citation can be found in Volume 33 of the HKLJ (*Hong Kong Law Journal*) at page 139.

If a citation contains only an abbreviation of the journal name, then you can ascertain what the abbreviation stands for by consulting the *Index to Legal Citations and Abbreviations*.

The full text of many journal articles can also be found in electronic databases, for example LexisNexis, Westlaw and HeinOnline. Check with your university library to access such databases. There are also some journals which are freely accessible to the public on the World Wide Web without the need for subscription.

Search templates in databases such as LexisNexis and Westlaw would contain fields including 'Author' and 'Title'. Thus, if you know the author or title of the article that you are looking for, then you can type the name of the author or the title of the article in the appropriate field. Suppose that you have the following citation and wish to access an electronic copy of the article:

David J Harland, 'The Statutory Prohibition of Misleading or Deceptive Conduct in Australia and Its Impact on the Law of Contract' (1995) 111 LQR 100.

Search tips:

- If searching by author, type the following in the 'Author' field: david and harland. Note the use of the Boolean connector 'and'. Note also that it is probably not necessary to type in the full name 'David J Harland', as the electronic database might not necessarily include the abbreviated middle name in the database. If the author's name in the database is simply 'David Harland', then typing in the full name will mean there is no exact match, and hence no result will be obtained from the search.
- If searching by title, type the following in the 'Title' field: "statutory prohibition of misleading". Note the use of quotation marks to indicate a

search of the exact phrase. Note also that it is not necessary to type in the full title. Simply type in a sufficient part of the title that should reasonably identify the article.

If the search does not yield any result, one reason might be that the database does not contain the journal you are looking for. Each database should contain information on which journals are contained in the database, and so you may need to check the coverage of the particular database in which you are searching.

Finding Journal Articles on a Particular Subject: Electronic

There are two broad ways of using electronic resources to search for journal articles in a particular subject area:

(1) Searching in journal databases such as the following:
   o LexisNexis
   o Westlaw
   o Social Science Research Network (SSRN) www.ssrn.com
   o Google Scholar scholar.google.com.

   These databases contain the full text of a huge number of journals originating from both Hong Kong and overseas countries.

(2) Searching using index databases such as the following:
   o Wilson Index to Legal Periodicals
   o Westlaw Legal Journals Index.

   These databases do not contain the full text of journal articles. However, they operate as indexes, containing brief information on published articles (including the citation). The search function of such databases allows you to search for relevant articles, and with the citation details provided, you can then look up the article either in a hard-copy volume in a library or through a full text database.

The search tips and techniques discussed earlier in the context of searching for cases electronically are also applicable for searching for journal articles. Generally, Boolean searching should be utilised.

The following examples illustrate a suggested approach to searching. You will first need to access the relevant database; this will involve, for example, deciding which jurisdictions to search across. The number of Hong Kong law journals is small compared with journals published overseas, and for research on the common law, it is useful not only to search Hong Kong journals but also overseas journals, including those in the United Kingdom, other Commonwealth countries as well as the United States.

Example: Find journal articles on the doctrine of collateral contracts.

Search tips:

- Start by attempting to find the most relevant articles on collateral contracts. This could be done by typing in the 'Title' field the following: 'collateral contract'. Note the use of quotation marks for a search on the exact phrase.
- If this search does not yield sufficient results, then see if there are any fields such as 'Summary' or 'Abstract'. If an article is focused on collateral contracts, then the words 'collateral' and 'contract' should appear in the summary or abstract of the article, and hence search of those words in the 'Summary' or 'Abstract' fields should pick up matches (if any).
- As a last resort, search across the full text of the database (i.e., without the use of specific fields) using the following words: 'collateral contract'.

Example: Find journal articles relating to tort liability where there is more than one tortfeasor who caused injury to the victim.

Search tips:

- Use appropriate fields and Boolean searching similar to that in the first example.
- Make sure that your search terms are not too broad. For example, you should not simply search using the word 'tort' across the full text of the database, as this would produce thousands of results. If your search results number in the hundreds or more, you should attempt to narrow down your search, since it would be too inefficient to look at each of those results to find items relevant to your topic of research. The search can be narrowed down, for instance, by using the following search terms: 'multiple tortfeasor'.
- Often you will need to think of different words or phrases to use in your search, as the one concept or idea can be expressed in different ways, and different authors might use different terminology. In order to obtain a match for as many relevant articles as possible, it is important to be able to think of different search terms to use. In this example,

the following alternative search terms could be used: 'joint tortfeasor' or 'joint torts' or 'concurrent tortfeasor' or 'several tortfeasor'.

Government Publications

Government publications can also be useful when researching particular areas of law. Examples are as follows:

Hansard

Hansard (i.e., the *Official Report of Proceedings in the Legislative Council*) is a record of the proceedings and debates of LegCo members in relation to bills put before the Legislative Council. They are a useful source of information when ascertaining the background of particular legislation, including the concerns of legislators when the bill was debated in the Council. An issue for each LegCo sitting is published weekly and an index is included in the annual bound volume. On the spine of each volume, the volume number and the year are shown.

Also useful on the background to the passage of bills is information relating to the proceedings of bills committees of the Legislative Council: see the Legislative Council website (www.legco.gov.hk).

Consultation and Policy Papers

Various government departments or bodies responsible for particular sectors or laws may publish consultation or policy papers when seeking to implement law reform in a particular area. Such papers and reports typically set out the problems in the area and proposals for reform of the law in the area. Consultation papers are issued for the purpose of inviting the public to make submissions to the government in response to the government proposals. These government papers are useful for looking at the latest developments in a particular area, or when researching specifically on law reform in particular areas. In addition, if legislation was subsequently enacted, then it might be useful to refer back to the consultation papers for background on the enactment of the laws.

Such government papers are accessible from the government website, including the specific websites of government departments and organisations. The websites of the various government departments can be found at www.gov.hk.

The Law Reform Commission

The Law Reform Commission is an independent body of the government, entrusted with the task of investigating areas that might require law reform in Hong Kong and making proposals as to whether reform is recommended, and if so, the suggested changes to the law. The Commission was established in 1980, and its members (legal experts and others of appropriate background) are appointed by the Chief Executive on the advice of the Secretary for Justice. The Commission issues consultation papers inviting comments from the public before making its recommendations in a final report.

The papers and reports are useful for researching law reform in a particular area, and as background to reform where legislation is enacted to implement recommendations of the Commission. Information about the Commission and electronic copies of the Commission's documents can be found at its website (www.hkreform.gov.hk).

Loose-Leaf Services

Loose-leaf services are publications that are in loose-leaf format, that is, where the pages of the published work are contained in a folder in a format where individual pages can be removed and replaced (for ease of updating, without the need to republish the entire work).

The *Laws of Hong Kong* is an example of a loose-leaf publication. There is a wide range of other loose-leaf works produced by private publishers on particular areas of the law. Commonly, such loose-leaf publications contain legislation or commentary and perhaps also common forms (or precedents) used by practitioners in the area, and are updated periodically. Although such loose-leaf products are aimed at the practitioner market, they are also a useful reference source for students.

Citation of Legal Materials

Legislation

It is common to cite ordinances by their short title. Section 13 of the Interpretation and General Clauses Ordinance (Cap. 1) provides that an ordinance can be cited either by (1) the title or short title, (2) its number among the ordinances of the year in which it was enacted, or (3) its chapter number in the *Laws of Hong Kong*.

Examples of citations of ordinances in a written work are as follows:
Copyright Ordinance
Dangerous Drugs Ordinance
For completeness, the chapter number can also be included in the citation:
Copyright Ordinance (Cap. 39)
Dangerous Drugs Ordinance (Cap. 134)

Sections and subsections of an ordinance can be cited as follows, using the example of section 247 of the Securities and Futures Ordinance in Figure 4.2 in Chapter 4.

Citing in a Written Work	Citing the Provision Orally
s 247	section 247
s 247(1)	section 247, subsection (1)
s 247(1)(a)	section 247, subsection (1), paragraph (a)
s 247(1)(c)(i)	section 247, subsection (1), paragraph (c), subparagraph (i)
s 247(1)(c)(i)(A)	section 247, subsection (1), paragraph (c), subparagraph (i), subsubparagraph (A)

Thus section 247, subsection (1) can be cited as follows:

Securities and Futures Ordinance s 247(1)

Subsidiary legislation can be cited as per the following examples:
Companies (Forms) Regulations
Bankruptcy Rules

Cases

Reported Cases

The case shown in Figure 4.5 in Chapter 4 is cited as follows:

Loyal Luck Trading Ltd v. *Tam Chun Wah* [2007] 4 HKLRD 917

A case citation shows the following:

- Parties' names: The following points should be noted regarding the parties' names:
  - Where the party/litigant is a natural person, the practice in citing cases in Hong Kong law reports is to provide the full name (as illustrated in the citation given). However, the practice in citing law reports from overseas jurisdictions is to only use the surname (e.g., *Smith v Brown* instead of *John Smith v Kylie Brown*).
  - The parties' names are italicised in the citation.
  - The letter 'v' separates the parties' names. For civil cases, the 'v' is stated verbally as 'and' (i.e., the case would be referred to verbally as 'Loyal Luck Trading Limited and Tam Chun Wah'); while for criminal cases, the 'v'. is stated verbally as 'against' (e.g., 'HKSAR against Wong Po Lam').
  - Some cases have more than two parties, for example, where the plaintiff is suing more than one defendant. For the citation of the case, it is usually sufficient to cite the first plaintiff/appellant named and the first defendant/respondent named in the judgment. Alternatively, the use of the words 'Another' or 'Others' can be used in the citation, for example, *Secretary for Justice* v. *Yau Yuk Lung and Another* [2006] 4 HKLRD 196. This indicates that the action was brought against Yau Yuk Lung and another defendant.
  - There are cases where the judgment only contains the one name. For example, in winding-up proceedings, the name of the company being wound up is named rather than the parties who bring the petition for the winding-up proceedings to be commenced. For instance, *Re Tourmaline Ltd* [2000] 4 HKC 348.
- The report series: The earlier example 'HKLRD' refers to the *Hong Kong Law Reports and Digest*.
- The volume number of the report in which the case appears:
  - Some reports, such as the HKLRD, use the year to designate the volume. In this situation, the year usually appears in square brackets, that is, [2007]. Where more than one volume is produced for that particular year, then numbers are used after the year to refer to the specific volume. In this example, the volume is the first volume in the year 2007.
  - Other law reports do not use the year to designate the volume. For example, the case *Ng Siu Tung* v. *Director of Immigration (No. 3)*

(2004) 7 HKCFAR 24. Here, the law report series is simply numbered consecutively, and the case appears in Volume 7. The year does not designate the volume as such but is simply the year in which the decision was handed down. Here, the year appears in parentheses or round brackets.
- The page number where the report of the case commences: In the example of the Loyal Luck case, the case report commences on page 917 of the particular HKLRD volume.

Where a case is reported in more than one law report, it is preferable to cite the case using the authorised law reports. Authorised law reports are those where the text of the judgments are verified by the relevant court before being published. The authorised reports in Hong Kong are the *Hong Kong Court of Final Appeal Reports* and the *Hong Kong Law Reports and Digest*.

For Hong Kong cases handed down from 1 January 2018, 'neutral citations' are provided by the Judiciary.[18] Judgments with neutral citations should be cited with both that citation and the citation for the law report. The neutral citation should follow the law report citation. For example:

Banco De Chile v. *Boruida Trading Co Ltd* [2018] 5 HKLRD 154, [2018] HKCFI 2294

Unreported Cases

For unreported cases handed down from 1 January 2018, the case should be cited using the neutral citation (see further the discussion below). For example:

Ng Shek Wai v. *Independent Commission Against Corruption* [2019] HKCA 343

For earlier unreported cases, how they are cited in written works often depends on the particular style of the publisher. Whatever style is adopted, it is important to maintain consistency in the one piece of work. An example of a possibility for citing unreported judgments is as follows:

Marblesum Ltd v. *Poon Shu Pang* (unreported, CFI, HCCW 628/2001, 10 Jun 2005)

---

[18] See the discussion below on neutral citations.

This mode of citation shows information as to the following: the court which heard the matter, the matter number for the case and the date on which judgment was given.

Westlaw and LexisNexis also have their own citation methods for unreported cases which are accessed from their electronic databases.

- Westlaw uses the abbreviation HKEC (Hong Kong Electronic Cases), for example, *Hing Sheung Fung Investment Co Ltd* v. *Incorporated Owners of Man Kee Mansion* [2008] HKEC 217.
- LexisNexis uses the abbreviation HKCU (Hong Kong Cases Unreported), for example, *Hing Sheung Fung Investment Co Ltd* v. *Incorporated Owners of Man Kee Mansion* [2008] HKCU 205.

Neutral Citations

A form of citation that is now used by the judiciary (following similar developments in some overseas jurisdictions) is referred to as 'neutral citations' or 'media neutral citations'. Such a citation provides the names of the parties, the year of the judgment, an abbreviation for the court in which the decision was handed down and a unique number denoting that case in that court for the particular year. For example:

Chang Wa Shan v. *Esther Chan Pui Kwan* [2018] HKCFA 29

'HKCFA' is the abbreviation for 'Hong Kong Court of Final Appeal'.

Other abbreviations include: 'HKCA' (Court of Appeal) and 'HKCFI' (Court of First Instance).

Neutral citations were introduced by the Judiciary for all Hong Kong judgments from 1 January 2018. Such cases should accordingly be cited with the neutral citation. If the case is reported, then the neutral citation should follow the law report citation.[19]

Secondary Sources

There are different accepted citation styles for secondary sources, but again what is important is to adopt a consistent style for the one piece of work. For legal journals, the usual method of citation in Hong Kong and Commonwealth jurisdictions is as follows:

---

[19] See Practice Direction 5.5 (1 December 2017).

Paul Spink and Stephen Chan, 'The Hong Kong Company Director's Duty of Care and Skill: A Standard for the 21st Century?' (2003) 33 HKLJ 139.

The order of information in the citation is as follows:

- Name(s) of the author(s).
- Title of the journal article. The title should be placed within quotation marks.
- Year in which the article was published, placed in parentheses or round brackets.
- The volume number of the journal in which the article appears: here it is Volume 33.
- The name of the journal (or its abbreviation). In the example given, the abbreviation is used. This can be done where the journal is a well-known one in the particular jurisdiction. However, often it is preferable to provide the full name of the journal, so that readers can easily ascertain what the journal is without needing to consult an index if they are unfamiliar with the abbreviation. The full name of the journal here is the *Hong Kong Law Journal*.
- The page number where the article commences in the particular volume: here the article commences on page 139.

Books can be cited, for example, as follows:

Roy Goode, *Commercial Law* (3rd edn, Penguin, London 2004).

The citation provides the following information:

- Name(s) of the author(s).
- Title of the book, in italics.
- If the book is a second or later edition, then this should be shown in the citation.
- Publisher: here, Penguin.
- Place of publication: here, London.
- Year of publication: here, 2004.

Where a specific chapter in an edited book is to be cited, this can be done in the following fashion:

Yash Ghai, 'The NPC Interpretation and Its Consequences' in J Chan, H L Fu and Y Ghai (eds), *Hong Kong's Constitutional Debate: Conflict Over Interpretation* (Hong Kong University Press, Hong Kong 2000).

For a more complete discussion of citations of different sources, see, for example, the University of Oxford Faculty of Law's *Oxford Standard for Citation of Legal Authorities* (available at www.law.ox.ac.uk/publications/oscola.php).

Review Questions

Unless otherwise indicated, conduct the following exercises using both hard-copy and electronic resources.

(1) Find the Gambling Ordinance and answer the following:
   (a) What is the commencement date of the ordinance?
   (b) What ordinances have amended the Gambling Ordinance?
   (c) Have all the amending ordinances commenced operation?
(2) Find the full judgment of the following cases:
   (a) *Re Fan Ling Theatre Ltd* [1991] 1 HKC 362
   (b) *Kan Wing-yau* v. *Hong Kong Housing Society* [1988] 2 HKLR 187
   (c) *Kirby* v. *Wilkins* [1929] 2 Ch 444.
(3) Find the complete citation for the following cases:
   (a) *Goodway Ltd* v. *Pirelli Cables Ltd*
   (b) [1978] HKLR 374
   (c) (1875) 10 Ch App 606.
(4) Find whether any cases in Hong Kong have considered the following cases:
   (a) *Mui Po Chu* v. *HKSAR* [1997] 3 HKC 12
   (b) *Edwards* v. *Halliwell* [1950] 2 All ER 1064.
(5) Find whether any cases in Hong Kong have considered section 725 of the Companies Ordinance (Cap. 622).
(6) Find the following:
   (a) relevant legislation in Hong Kong concerned with privacy
   (b) cases in Hong Kong dealing with the topic of privacy from media intrusion or media surveillance.
(7) Find relevant commentary in *Halsbury's Laws of Hong Kong* dealing with the topic of sexual harassment.
(8) Using electronic resources, find relevant articles in Hong Kong, the United Kingdom and Australia dealing with the topic of sexual harassment in the workplace.

13 Interface between Hong Kong and International and Chinese Law

Chapter Highlights

- International Legal Personality and International Law — 368
- International Law in Hong Kong — 369
- Mutual Legal Assistance with the Mainland — 375
- Closer Economic Partnership Arrangement (CEPA) — 382
- Cross-Border Crime — 385

Previous chapters in this book have focused on domestic (or municipal) law within Hong Kong. Mainland China has its own domestic laws, as do other countries or states. There is also a system of 'public international law', which governs the relationship between states.[1] This chapter deals with the interaction, first, between Hong Kong's legal system and public international law and, second, between Hong Kong's legal system and Chinese law (the law of Mainland China).

The distinct international legal personality of Hong Kong is a unique feature of its status. As previously discussed, under the Basic Law, the Central People's Government is responsible for foreign affairs relating to Hong Kong, but at the same time, it authorises the Government of

---

[1] Public international law is distinguished from what is referred to as 'private international law' (also referred to as 'conflict of laws'), the latter being the (domestic) legal rules applied by each state or territory to determine matters which have a connection with the legal system of more than one jurisdiction. For example, say that a contract is made between a party in Hong Kong and another party in the United States via email for a sale of goods, with the goods to be delivered from the United States to Australia. The law of contract may differ in these three jurisdictions. Whose law is to apply to govern the parties' contractual relationship – Hong Kong law, United States law or Australian law? These issues are resolved by the rules of 'private international law' or 'conflicts of law'. See generally G. Johnston, *The Conflict of Laws in Hong Kong*, 3rd ed. (Hong Kong: Sweet & Maxwell 2017).

the Hong Kong Special Administrative Region (HKSAR) to conduct relevant external affairs.² Although ambiguities persist regarding the meaning of external affairs, Hong Kong's membership in international organisations and its being party to multilateral and bilateral treaties pre- and post-handover demonstrate that it is a recognised, and respected, member of the international community under international law.³ Hong Kong possesses a distinct international legal personality despite not being a sovereign state.⁴

Interestingly, the interaction between Hong Kong and the Mainland's legal system operates less smoothly compared with Hong Kong's interaction with international entities even though Hong Kong and the Mainland are part of the one country. Co-operation relating to legal issues between Hong Kong and the Mainland is still developing and, as will be shown, there is a reliance on administrative and informal arrangements. Moreover, the interface between the Hong Kong and Mainland legal systems has led to various controversies. Given their reunification and social and economic interconnectedness, there is a need for Hong Kong and the Mainland to resolve vital matters such as cross-border civil and commercial proceedings, cross-border crime and issues relating to economic integration.

Interface with the International System

Being a world-class international financial centre, there are areas where it is imperative for 'Asia's World City' to interact with international entities including foreign states and international organisations. Hong Kong's situation is unique in the sense that it is not a state, yet in the eyes of the international community, it can be rightly said that Hong Kong possesses a separate international legal personality that distinguishes it from the People's Republic of China (PRC) (and previously from the United Kingdom). Indeed, Hong Kong has extensive agreements with

---

² Basic Law, chapter VII.
³ See C. L. Lim and R. Mushkat, 'External Affairs Powers', in J. Chan and C. L. Lim (eds.), *Law of the Hong Kong Constitution*, 2nd ed. (Hong Kong: Sweet & Maxwell 2015).
⁴ R. Mushkat, *One Country, Two International Legal Personalities* (Hong Kong: Hong Kong University Press 1997), chapter 1.

international entities and participation in a range of international and regional organisations.

International Legal Personality and International Law

Possessing an international legal personality means having the ability to act, both exercising rights and bearing obligations, within the system of international law.[5] Public international law traditionally governs the relationship between sovereign states as states are considered the primary actors in international relations. The scope of international law has expanded to include international organisations, non-governmental organisations and even groups of individuals who increasingly contribute to the international community. Sources of international law include international treaties or conventions and customary international law.

Although not a state itself, Hong Kong has stately attributes such as a population of permanent inhabitants, a physical territory with defined frontiers, and a local government that effectively exercises jurisdiction over its populace and territory. It has been conferred powers that give it a separate international personality, such as the conclusion and implementation of agreements with international and regional actors, issuing its own passports and travel documents,[6] and establishing official and semi-official economic and trade missions overseas.[7] Hong Kong is also recognised by other international actors through its extensive involvement in international activities. For instance, under the name 'Hong Kong, China', Hong Kong is admitted to important international organisations not limited to states, including the Asian Development Bank, the Asian Infrastructure Investment Bank and the World Trade Organisation.[8] Additionally, Hong Kong can claim 'international legitimacy' because of its adherence to international norms. Although not a democracy, Hong Kong inhabitants possess rights and freedoms protected by law, it operates an independent judiciary, has a vigorous free press, and continues to uphold the rule of law.[9]

---

[5] Ibid., p. 1.
[6] Basic Law, art. 154.
[7] Basic Law, art. 156.
[8] Refer to the list of international intergovernmental organisations not limited to states available at www.cmab.gov.hk/en/issues/external2.htm.
[9] Mushkat (n. 4).

Monism and Dualism

When thinking about the relationship between international law and domestic (or municipal) law, it is useful to distinguish between the theories of 'monism' and 'dualism'. In its most radical form, monism contends that there exists only one legal order where international law and domestic law are different aspects. International law, according to monism, is automatically part of a state's domestic legal order. In terms of hierarchy, domestic law derives its authority from international law, and when there are inconsistencies between the two, international law shall prevail. Monism is associated with civil law jurisdictions and natural law theorists.

Dualism, on the other hand, draws a distinction between international law and domestic law, viewing each with its own legal orders and sources of law. International law, including treaties signed by the state in question, does not automatically become part of the domestic legal order of that state. For international law to become part of the domestic legal order, it needs to be transformed, for instance through legislation, into domestic law. Dualism is associated with common law jurisdictions and legal positivism.[10]

International Law in Hong Kong

Hong Kong, being a common law jurisdiction, adheres to dualism with respect to the applicability of international law in its domestic legal system. In examining the interface between Hong Kong law and international law, the discussion below examines the role of (1) international treaties and (2) customary international law in the Hong Kong context.

International Treaties

There are a multitude of treaties that are in force and applicable to Hong Kong which cover a variety of subjects. Treaties are legally binding agreements between two or more states or international organisations where the parties agree to be regulated by their terms. As of July 2018, there are

---

[10] S. Hall, *Foundations of International Law*, 3rd ed. (Hong Kong: LexisNexis 2016), p. 176.

263 multilateral treaties that are applicable to Hong Kong.[11] There is also a host of bilateral agreements that have been concluded by Hong Kong with other states and regions, and they cover a broad range of areas including air services agreements, mutual legal assistance agreements and double taxation avoidance agreements. Treaties applicable to and in force in Hong Kong can be divided into the following categories: (1) treaties to which the PRC is a party; (2) extension of treaties previously applied to Hong Kong where the PRC is not a party; and (3) treaties entered by into by Hong Kong upon authorisation.

For treaties to which the PRC is a party, the Central People's Government may decide to apply the treaty to Hong Kong after considering the circumstances and needs of Hong Kong and after seeking the views of the HKSAR Government.[12] This means that not all treaties to which the PRC is a party are applied to Hong Kong. Generally, treaties dealing with foreign affairs and defence (which are areas within the responsibilities of the Central People's Government under the Basic Law) would be applied to the entirety of the State, including Hong Kong.[13] Examples of such treaties include treaties on diplomatic and consular relations and armed conflict.[14] Likewise, reservations and declarations made by the PRC on treaties applicable to Hong Kong also extend to Hong Kong. An example is the reservations and declarations regarding the compulsory jurisdiction of the International Court of Justice.[15]

Treaties to which the PRC is not a party but which were previously implemented in Hong Kong before 1 July 1997 may continue to be applied in Hong Kong.[16] There were over 300 multilateral treaties that were applicable to Hong Kong prior to the handover. To ensure the smooth transition of sovereignty, the PRC and the United Kingdom reached a consensus for

---

[11] Refer to the List of Treaties in Force and Applicable to the Hong Kong Special Administrative Region, available at www.doj.gov.hk/eng/laws/interlaw.html.

[12] Basic Law, art. 153.

[13] W. P. Lung, 'Application and Conclusion of Treaties in the Hong Kong Special Administrative Region of the People's Republic of China: Sixteen Years of Practice' (2013), *Chinese Journal of International Law* 12, 589.

[14] E.g. the Vienna Convention on Diplomatic Relations 1961, the Vienna Convention on Consular Relations 1963, bilateral consular agreements concluded by the PRC with other states that expressly provide for their application to Hong Kong, and the four Geneva Conventions of 1949.

[15] Lung (n. 13), p. 596.

[16] Basic Law, art. 153.

the continued application of such treaties, even treaties where the PRC is not a party.[17] Accordingly, there are many treaties today that are applied to Hong Kong which do not apply to Mainland China. These treaties cover a wide range of subjects, such as international crimes,[18] customs,[19] science and technology[20] and civil aviation.[21] In addition, the Central People's Government may, as necessary, authorise or assist the HKSAR Government to make appropriate arrangements for the application to Hong Kong of other relevant international agreements.[22]

Hong Kong can also conclude international agreements with the authorisation of the Central People's Government. Under a general authorisation, Hong Kong may on its own, using the name 'Hong Kong, China', conclude and implement multilateral and bilateral agreements with foreign states and regions and international organisations in the appropriate fields, including the economic, trade, financial and monetary, shipping, communications, tourism, cultural and sports fields.[23] As these areas fall under the autonomy of Hong Kong, there is no a need to obtain further authorisation when concluding such agreements unless they impinge on the areas within the responsibilities of the Central People's Government.[24] Hong Kong may also conclude international agreements, even those involving foreign affairs and defence, with specific authorisation from the Central People's Government.[25] For instance, as stated under article 133 of the Basic Law, the HKSAR Government may, acting under specific authorisation from the Central People's Government, renew or amend air service agreements and arrangements previously in force, negotiate and conclude new air service agreements, and negotiate and conclude provisional arrangements with foreign states and regions where no air service agreements existed before.

---

[17] Lung (n. 13), pp. 598–599.
[18] E.g. Convention on the Marking of Plastic Explosives for the Purpose of Detection, Montreal 1991.
[19] E.g. International Convention relating to the Simplification of Customs Formalities, and Protocol of Signature, Geneva 1923.
[20] E.g. Convention on Third Party Liability in the Field of Nuclear Energy, Paris 1960, as amended in 1964 and 1982.
[21] E.g. International Air Services Transit Agreement, Chicago 1944.
[22] Basic Law, art. 153.
[23] Basic Law, art. 151.
[24] Lung (n. 13), p. 602.
[25] Ibid.

Furthermore, representatives of the HKSAR Government may, as members of delegations of the PRC Government, participate in negotiations conducted by the Central People's Government at the diplomatic level if the negotiations directly affect Hong Kong.[26] Likewise, Hong Kong representatives may be incorporated in the PRC delegation to participate in international organisations and conferences in appropriate fields. This method for Hong Kong to take part in international matters that are open to states only allows for the furthering of Hong Kong's interests.[27] On the basis of the above, Hong Kong has access to major international organisations such as the Group of Twenty (G20), the International Monetary Fund, the World Bank and the World Health Organization.[28]

With respect to the applicability of international treaties in domestic law, consistent with the dualist approach, it is a longstanding common law position that international treaties do not have an effect on the domestic legal system unless it is done so formally through 'transformation', such as by way of legislation. A prime illustration of this is the Hong Kong Bill of Rights Ordinance[29] that incorporates the provisions of the International Covenant on Civil and Political Rights into Hong Kong's domestic legal system by way of domestic legislation. The rationale for dualism is related to the doctrine of separation of powers.[30] Under English law, it is the Crown that is responsible for concluding treaties and it is Parliament that has the power to enact or authorise legislation which affects the rights and obligations of individuals domestically. If international treaties can directly affect the domestic legal order, then law-making power is given to the executive. This would upset the constitutional arrangements that, for centuries, have provided a balance between the powers of the branches of government.[31]

Hong Kong, following English law, has adopted the same dualist approach. Unless international treaties are made part of Hong Kong law, they would not impose rights and obligations on individual citizens.[32] When interpreting statutes that incorporate or implement provisions in

---

[26] Basic Law, art. 150.
[27] Lim and Mushkat (n. 3), p. 90.
[28] Refer to the list of international intergovernmental organisations limited to states available at www.cmab.gov.hk/en/issues/external1.htm.
[29] Hong Kong Bill of Rights Ordinance (Cap. 383).
[30] See discussion on separation of powers in Chapter 3.
[31] Hall (n. 10), p. 218.
[32] *Ubamaka Edward Wilson* v. *Secretary for Security & Another* [2013] 2 HKC 75, para. 43.

international treaties in domestic law, it is important to note that where the domestic legislation is ambiguous, the courts will presume that the legislature intended to enact the statute in accordance with the treaty's obligations; but when the statute is clear, then it is the duty of the courts to give effect to the statute whether or not that would involve a breach of a treaty obligation.[33]

Customary International Law

Customary international law is a source of international law and has been described 'as evidence of a general practice accepted as law'.[34] It refers to the established, widespread and generally accepted customary rules and principles of international law. For a practice to be deemed as customary international law, there must be an objective and a subjective element. The objective element is the constant and uniform practice of states and the subjective aspect, *opinio juris* (an opinion of law), is a state's belief to act in accordance with the custom because they consider themselves legally bound by it.[35]

Although common law jurisdictions adopt the dualist approach when applying international treaties domestically, there is a difference with respect to customary international law. English courts have at times adopted the more liberal view of automatic 'incorporation' instead of the need for transformation as discussed above. Incorporation means that international law is incorporated into English law as long as it conforms with domestic statutes. Moreover, once a rule of customary international law is adopted or incorporated by a competent court, it becomes part of the common law. This means that, as with other common law rules, it is subject to *stare decisis* and must not be inconsistent with domestic legislation even if the rule of customary international law subsequently changes at the international level.[36]

---

[33] Ibid. See also Chapter 7, Statutory Interpretation.
[34] Statute of the International Court of Justice, art. 38.
[35] *North Sea Continental Shelf* cases (*Germany* v. *Demark, Germany* v. *the Netherlands*), ICJ Rep (1969) 3, para. 74.
[36] Hall (n. 10), p. 183; J. Shen, 'The Status of Customary International Law in the Municipal Law of the HKSAR', in R. Wacks (ed.) *The New Legal Order in Hong Kong* (Hong Kong: Hong Kong University Press 1999), p. 224.

This position is expressed in the case of *Chung Chi Cheung* v. *R*,[37] which is a Privy Council case on appeal from Hong Kong. Lord Atkin stated:

> It must be always remembered that, so far, at any rate, as the Courts of this country are concerned, international law has no validity save in so far as its principles are accepted and adopted by our own domestic law. There is no external power that imposes its rules upon our own code of substantive law or procedure. The Courts acknowledge the existence of a body of rules which nations accept amongst themselves. On any judicial issue they seek to ascertain what the relevant rule is, and, having found it, they will treat it as incorporated into the domestic law, so far as it is not inconsistent with rules enacted by statutes or finally declared by their tribunals.[38]

Here, the Privy Council affirms that the common law acknowledges customary international law and that it is available to be incorporated into the common law.[39]

In the case of Hong Kong, customary international law can thus be said to form part of Hong Kong's legal system. The incorporation approach adopted by English courts under the common law was received into Hong Kong's legal system as part of the common law applicable to Hong Kong[40] (as demonstrated by the Privy Council decision in *Chung Chi Cheung* v. *R*, above). In addition, since Hong Kong is accepted as a distinct international legal entity, it has a duty to observe international law and, as such, it is suggested that incorporation of customary international law into Hong Kong's legal system is mandated.[41] The Hong Kong courts have, consistent with *Chung Chi Cheung* v. *R*, above, acknowledged and applied customary international law. For example, the courts have recognised the customary norm of non-refoulement, which is the prohibition against the returning of asylum seekers to a country if there is risk of persecution or human rights abuse.[42]

---

[37] *Chung Chi Cheung* v. *R* [1939] AC 160, pp. 167–168.

[38] Ibid., pp. 167–168.

[39] Hall (n. 10), p. 186; see also *FG Hemisphere Associates LLC* v. *Democratic Republic of the Congo* [2010] 2 HKC 487, para. 55.

[40] Mushkat (n. 4), pp. 167–168. On reception of English common law in Hong Kong, see Chapter 1, and on preservation of the common law system in Hong Kong, see Chapter 4.

[41] Mushkat (n. 4), p. 168.

[42] *C and Others* v. *Director of Immigration* [2008] 2 HKC 165; see also M. Ramsden, 'Using International Law in Hong Kong Courts: An Examination of Non-Refoulement Litigation', (2013), *Common Law World Review* 42, 351.

Interface with Mainland China

With the resumption of sovereignty and the increasing interconnectedness between Hong Kong and Mainland China, legal issues involving both jurisdictions often arise. Examples include disputes involving parties from both Hong Kong and the Mainland, and crimes committed across both jurisdictions. Therefore, mechanisms need to be in place to enable smooth interaction between these two very different legal systems and for co-operation between legal institutions and authorities from each jurisdiction. Other points of interaction between the two systems, such as the applicability of national laws in Hong Kong and the Standing Committee of the National People's Congress (NPCSC) interpretations, have been discussed in other parts of this book. This discussion below focuses on mutual legal assistance, cross-border crime and areas of economic integration.

Mutual Legal Assistance with the Mainland

Article 95 of the Basic Law stipulates that 'The Hong Kong Special Administrative Region may, through consultations and in accordance with law, maintain juridical relations with the judicial organs of other parts of the country, and they may render assistance to each other.' To provide mutual legal assistance, arrangements, which are essentially agreements between Mainland China or parts of the Mainland such as with certain provinces (or with Macao) are made.[43] Arrangements are non-binding and are reliant on the goodwill of the contracting parties.[44] These arrangements cover a variety of areas such as air services, taxation and recognition of educational degrees. With respect to mutual legal assistance however, cross-border litigation is thus far limited to commercial and civil matters with the exclusion of criminal justice.

---

[43] Hong Kong also has arrangements with Macao, which operates a different legal system from Hong Kong and the PRC. This chapter is limited to discussing the interface between Hong Kong and Mainland China.

[44] E. C. Ip, *Law and Justice in Hong Kong*, 2nd ed. (Hong Kong: Sweet & Maxwell 2016), p. 424.

Arrangement for Mutual Service of Judicial Documents

With increasing cross-border disputes involving parties from Hong Kong and Mainland China, situations would arise, for example, where one party in Hong Kong proceedings is from the Mainland and documents generated in Hong Kong would need to be served on the Mainland party. Before the handover, the service of judicial documents between Hong Kong and Mainland China was governed by the Convention on the Service Abroad of Judicial and Extrajudicial Documents in Civil or Commercial Matters, which was concluded and signed at The Hague in November 1965. The Convention provides for channels of transmission of judicial and extrajudicial documents from one signatory state to another. Although the Convention continues to apply to Hong Kong after the handover, it is no longer applicable to the service of documents between Hong Kong and the Mainland given that they are now unified as one country.

On 14 January 1999, after consultations between the High Court of the Hong Kong Special Administrative Region and the Supreme People's Court, the Arrangement for Mutual Service of Judicial Documents in Civil and Commercial Proceedings between the Mainland and Hong Kong Courts was signed. The arrangement allows for various types of judicial documents to be entrusted for service between the Mainland and Hong Kong courts. Requests for the service of judicial documents can be made through the High Court of the HKSAR and the Higher People's Courts in the Mainland. Judicial documents in the case of Hong Kong include the following: 'copy of originating process, copy of notice of appeal, summons, pleading, affidavit, judgment, decision or ruling, notice, court order, certificate of service or non-service'. In the case of the Mainland, the following are included: 'copy of originating process, copy of motion of appeal, letter of authorization or entrustment, summons, judgment, mediation decision, ruling, decision, notice, certificate, return form on service'.[45] The Rules of the High Court (Amendment) Rules 1999 were put in place to amend the relevant provisions in the Rules of the High Court in order to implement this arrangement.[46] Similarly, the Supreme People's Court promulgated the

---

[45] Arrangement for Mutual Service of Judicial Documents in Civil and Commercial Proceedings between the Mainland and Hong Kong Courts art. 9, available at www.doj.gov.hk/eng/mainland/pdf/mainlandmutual1e.pdf.

[46] Rules of the High Court (Cap. 4A), Ords. 11 and 69.

arrangement by way of judicial interpretation. The arrangement was put into effect on 30 March 1999.

Arrangement on Reciprocal Enforcement of Judgments

On 14 July 2006, the Arrangement on Reciprocal Recognition and Enforcement of Judgments in Civil and Commercial Matters by the Courts of the Mainland and of the Hong Kong SAR Pursuant to Choice of Court Agreements between Parties Concerned was signed by the Hong Kong Secretary for Justice and the Vice President of the Supreme People's Court. Prior to this arrangement, there was no reciprocal enforcement on court judgments between Hong Kong and the Mainland. Foreign judgments were enforced in Hong Kong through the Foreign Judgments (Reciprocal Enforcement) Ordinance,[47] but this excludes Mainland China. This meant that a judgment debtor who had assets on the Mainland might escape enforcement.[48] Likewise, a party who had obtained a judgment from a Mainland court could only enforce it by starting fresh proceedings in Hong Kong under the common law, which is time-consuming and costly. The arrangement permits enforceable judgments requiring payment of money made by designated courts in Hong Kong and the Mainland pursuant to a written choice of court agreement[49] by the parties, to be recognised and enforced in the other jurisdiction.[50] The Mainland Judgments (Reciprocal Enforcement) Ordinance[51] was enacted to give effect to the arrangement and came into force in August 2008. In July 2014, the list of Basic People's Courts

---

[47] Foreign Judgments (Reciprocal Enforcement) Ordinance (Cap. 319).
[48] S. K. Wong, 'Reciprocal Enforcement of Court Judgments in Civil and Commercial Matters Between Hong Kong SAR and the Mainland', in J. Oliveira and P. Cardinal (eds.), *One Country, Two Systems, Three Legal Orders: Perspectives of Evolution* (Berlin: Springer 2009).
[49] This is an agreement by the parties that expressly designates a court of the HKSAR or people's court of the Mainland as the court having sole jurisdiction for resolving any dispute which has arisen or may arise in respect of a 'particular legal relationship' (which is defined as civil and commercial contracts between the parties concerned, excluding employment contracts). See Arrangement on Reciprocal Recognition and Enforcement of Judgments in Civil and Commercial Matters by the Courts of the Mainland and of the Hong Kong SAR Pursuant to Choice of Court Agreements between Parties Concerned, art. 3, available at www.doj.gov.hk/eng/mainland/pdf/mainlandrej20060719e.pdf.
[50] Ibid., art. 1.
[51] Mainland Judgments (Reciprocal Enforcement) Ordinance (Cap. 597).

authorised to exercise jurisdiction in commercial and civil cases involving Hong Kong judgments was updated.[52]

However, the arrangement is limited.[53] First, the arrangement only covers money judgments and not for sums payable for taxes, fines or other penalties. Not all the courts in Mainland China are covered, but only courts specified in Schedule 1 of the Mainland Judgments (Reciprocal Enforcement) Ordinance. As noted, the arrangement is only applicable where the parties expressly agreed to submit to the sole jurisdiction of either the courts of Mainland China or the Hong Kong Special Administrative Region. For Hong Kong courts, only final judgments of Mainland courts satisfying the common law requirement of finality will be recognised and enforced in Hong Kong.[54] Under the common law, to show finality, it must be demonstrated that the court where the judgment was pronounced, conclusively and finally established the existence of the debt in question.

In what is believed to be the first reported case relating to the application of the Mainland Judgments (Reciprocal Enforcement) Ordinance, the Court of First Instance (CFI) dismissed an application by the defendants to set aside an order of a Mainland judgment in Hong Kong. In *Chan Sang v. Chan Kwok and others*,[55] there was a loan agreement between the plaintiff and the defendants. The first defendant defaulted in repayment, and the parties attended conciliation sessions at the Shenzhen Immediate People's Court, where a Reconciliation Statement outlined the terms of the settlement for the first defendant to repay the loan by instalments and for the plaintiff to apply to discharge a freezing order on the defendants' assets. The same court subsequently issued an enforcement order, because the settlement was not adhered to. The plaintiff later obtained a certificate from the Shenzhen court certifying that the Mainland judgment was final and enforceable in the Mainland, and an order to register parts of the Mainland judgment in Hong Kong's CFI. The defendants applied to set aside the registration order. The defendants argued that the Mainland

---

[52] Refer to www.doj.gov.hk/eng/topical/pdf/egn201418304289.pdf.
[53] Wong (n. 48). See also X. Zhang and P. Smart, 'Development of Regional Conflict of Laws: On the Arrangement of Mutual Recognition and Enforcement of Judgments in Civil and Commercial Matters between Mainland China and Hong Kong SAR' (2006), *Hong Kong Law Journal* 36, 553.
[54] Wong (n. 48), p. 376. See Mainland Judgments (Reciprocal Enforcement) Ordinance (Cap. 597), s. 6.
[55] [2016] HKCU 401.

judgment was not enforceable and should be set aside. The CFI disagreed, noting that since the plaintiff had produced a certificate from the Shenzhen Immediate People's Court showing the finality of the judgment, the onus shifted onto the defendants to prove the contrary, which they had failed to do. The defendants also argued that no active enforcement was taken by the plaintiff in the Mainland, and the CFI held that there was no requirement for a judgment creditor to show active enforcement in the Mainland prior to pursuing registration in the Hong Kong courts.

Arrangement on Mutual Taking of Evidence

Another arrangement, the Arrangement on Mutual Taking of Evidence in Civil and Commercial Matters between the Courts of the Mainland and the Hong Kong Special Administrative Region, was signed between the Hong Kong Secretary for Justice and the Vice President of the Supreme People's Court on 29 December 2016 and came into force on 1 March 2017. With this arrangement, disputing parties can make requests through the respective designated liaison authorities to obtain evidence in civil and commercial matters in the two jurisdictions.[56] On the Mainland, the designated liaison authority is the Higher People's Court, whereas in Hong Kong, it is the Administration Wing of the Chief Secretary for Administration's Office. The scope of assistance however, is not identical. A Mainland People's Court can request, through a letter of request, the taking of evidence by Hong Kong courts including the following: examination of witnesses; obtaining documents; the inspection, photographing, preservation, custody or detention of any property; taking samples of any property or carrying out of any experiments on any property; and medical examination of any person. A Hong Kong court can only request Mainland courts to do the following: obtain statements from parties concerned and testimonies from witnesses; provide documentary evidence, real evidence, audio-visual information and electronic data; and conduct site examination and authentication.[57] Overall, this arrangement seeks to assist litigants and bolster the efficiency and certainty of court cases.

---

[56] Arrangement on Mutual Taking of Evidence in Civil and Commercial Matters between the Courts of the Mainland and the Hong Kong Special Administrative Region, art. 1, available at www.doj.gov.hk/eng/topical/pdf/mainlandmutual4e.pdf.
[57] Ibid., art. 6.

Arrangement Concerning Mutual Enforcement of Arbitral Awards

As discussed in Chapter 10, international arbitral awards can be enforced in other countries under the New York Convention on the Recognition and Enforcement of Foreign Arbitral Awards. However, this framework is inapplicable after the handover between Hong Kong and Mainland China as they are part of the one country. For over two years after the handover, there existed a legal vacuum, where Mainland arbitral awards were unenforceable in Hong Kong and vice versa.[58] To remedy this, the Arrangement Concerning Mutual Enforcement of Arbitral Awards between the Mainland and the Hong Kong Special Administrative Region was signed by Hong Kong's Department of Justice and the Supreme People's Court in Mainland China on 21 June 1999 and took effect on 1 February 2000. The Arbitration Ordinance was amended accordingly.[59] Under the arrangement, Hong Kong courts agree to enforce arbitral awards made pursuant to the Arbitration Law of the People's Republic of China by the arbitral authorities in the Mainland, and the People's Courts of the Mainland agree to enforce the awards made in Hong Kong pursuant to the Arbitration Ordinance.[60] This arrangement restored mutual enforcement of arbitral awards between the two jurisdictions along the lines of the pre-Handover situation.

When a party fails to comply with an arbitral award made in Mainland China or Hong Kong, the other party (the applicant) may apply to the relevant court for enforcement in the place where the respondent is domiciled or in the place where the respondent's property is located.[61] In Hong Kong, the relevant court is the Court of First Instance, and in Mainland China it is the Intermediate People's Court.[62] Applicants must submit a written application for enforcement, the arbitral award and the arbitration agreement.[63] The Arbitration Ordinance defines a 'Mainland award' as an arbitral award made in the Mainland by a 'recognised

---

[58] See *Ng Fung Hong Ltd* v. *ABC* [1998] 1 HKC 213.
[59] See now Pt. 10 Div. 3 of the Arbitration Ordinance (Cap. 609).
[60] Arrangement Concerning Mutual Enforcement of Arbitral Awards between the Mainland and the Hong Kong Special Administrative Region, available at www.doj.gov.hk/eng/topical/pdf/mainlandmutual2e.pdf.
[61] Ibid., art. 1.
[62] Ibid., art. 2.
[63] Ibid., art. 3.

Mainland arbitral authority in accordance with the Arbitration Law of the People's Republic of China'.⁶⁴ Therefore not all arbitral awards are eligible for enforcement in Hong Kong. The list of recognised arbitration organisations is provided by the Legislative Affairs of the State Council, and the Secretary for Justice from time to time publishes a list of the recognised Mainland arbitral organisations in the Gazette.⁶⁵

The courts however, may refuse to enforce the arbitral award.⁶⁶ Of interest, an Intermediate People's Court may refuse to enforce the arbitral award if it holds that it would be 'contrary to the public interests of the Mainland'. In Hong Kong, the High Court may refuse enforcement if it decides that enforcement would be 'contrary to the public policy of the HKSAR'.⁶⁷ Although the two terms seem to be similar, there are important distinctions. The term 'social public interest' is defined much more broadly, and ambiguously, in Mainland China. It is said to include economic and social consequences, adopted rules, expressed state commitments, social morality, and other state interests and short-term policies.⁶⁸ Local Mainland courts have been found to apply public policy flexibly, thereby rejecting enforcement, but errors have been corrected by the Supreme People's Court.⁶⁹ On the other hand, in Hong Kong, 'public policy' is construed by the Hong Kong courts narrowly when refusing enforcement of foreign arbitral awards. The Hong Kong Court of Final Appeal has held that Hong Kong courts should recognise the validity of foreign arbitral decisions unless doing so would 'violate the most basic notions of morality and justice'.⁷⁰

---

⁶⁴ Arbitration Ordinance (Cap. 609), s. 2.
⁶⁵ Refer to www.gld.gov.hk/egazette/pdf/20111521/egn201115213248.pdf.
⁶⁶ See Arrangement Concerning Mutual Enforcement of Arbitral Awards (n. 60), art. 7.
⁶⁷ Ibid., art. 7(5).
⁶⁸ Li Hu, 'Enforcement of the International Commercial Arbitration Award in the People's Republic of China' (1999), *Journal of International Arbitration* 16, 1, p. 21; X. C. Zhang, 'The Agreement between Mainland China and the Hong Kong SAR on Mutual Enforcement of Arbitral Awards: Problems and Prospects' (1999), *Hong Kong Law Journal* 463, 29, pp. 476–477.
⁶⁹ The Supreme People's Court has held that infringement of the interests of state-owned enterprises does not necessarily lead to the diminishing of the public interest. See L. Fei, 'Enforcement of Arbitral Awards between Hong Kong and Mainland China: A Successful Model?' (2009), *Chinese Journal of International Law* 8, 621, para. 24.
⁷⁰ *Hebei Import and Export Corp. v. Polytek Engineering Co. Ltd.* (1999) 2 HKCFAR 111, at 118.

Another important difference between the two jurisdictions relates to limitation periods.⁷¹ The arrangement states that the time limit for an applicant to apply to the relevant court shall be governed by the law on limitation periods of the place of enforcement.⁷² In the case of the
→ Mainland, if both parties are natural persons then the limitation period is one year from the date of default, and for legal persons it is six months.
→ In Hong Kong, the application would generally need to be submitted within six years from the date when the arbitral award is dishonoured.⁷³ Moreover, an applicant cannot file simultaneous applications in both Hong Kong and the Mainland.⁷⁴ This means that an applicant must be careful to decide where to initiate the application for enforcement, which will depend on knowledge of the whereabouts of the respondent's assets.⁷⁵

The arrangement has facilitated cross-border arbitration between Hong Kong and the Mainland although there are still notable differences between the two systems and practical considerations for applicants seeking to enforce arbitral awards.⁷⁶

Closer Economic Partnership Arrangement (CEPA)

The Mainland and Hong Kong Closer Economic Partnership Arrangement (CEPA) is the first free trade agreement between the Central People's Government and the HKSAR Government with the aim of opening the Mainland market to allow greater access for Hong Kong businesses. At the same time, Hong Kong serves to act as a springboard for Mainland enterprises entering the global market.⁷⁷ The main text of CEPA was

---

⁷¹ For a wider comparison between the arbitration systems in Hong Kong and Mainland China, see X. Xu and G.D. Wilson, 'One Country, Two – International Commercial Arbitration – Systems' (2000), *Journal of International Arbitration* 17, 47.
⁷² Arrangement Concerning Mutual Enforcement of Arbitral Awards (n. 60), art. 5.
⁷³ G. Ma and D. Brock (eds.), *Arbitration in Hong Kong: A Practical Guide*, 4th ed. (Hong Kong: Sweet & Maxwell 2017), para. 19.047; Limitation Ordinance (Cap. 347) s. 4(1)(c).
⁷⁴ Arrangement Concerning Mutual Enforcement of Arbitral Awards (n. 60), art. 2.
⁷⁵ Ma and Brock (n. 73), para. 19.046.
⁷⁶ See W. Gu, '15 Years of the Handover: The Rise, Discontent, and Positive Interaction of Cross-border Arbitration in Hong Kong with Mainland China' (2013), *University of Pennsylvania East Asia Law Review* 9, 42.
⁷⁷ Trade and Industry Department, *CEPA* (Hong Kong: TID 2018), available at www.tid.gov.hk/english/cepa/cepa_overview.html.

signed on 29 June 2003, and ten annual Supplements have been signed in subsequent years to further foster integration between Hong Kong and Mainland China. CEPA covers four broad areas: trade in goods, trade in services, investment, and economic and technical co-operation.

With respect to the legal sector, there have been various liberalisation measures to permit easier access for the Hong Kong legal profession to gain entry into the Mainland legal services market. CEPA permits Hong Kong permanent residents of Chinese citizenship to sit the National Legal Professional Qualification Examination (previously the National Judicial Examination), which otherwise may not be taken by foreign lawyers. Sites have been set up in Hong Kong and Shenzhen for Hong Kong residents to sit the examination. This allows Hong Kong residents to obtain a licence to practice law (but not litigation work) in the Mainland after completing the required internship, training and assessments.[78] China considers that litigation belongs to its internal affairs and should not be opened for foreign lawyers, including lawyers from Hong Kong.[79] This has been relaxed somewhat, as Hong Kong residents who have acquired Mainland legal professional qualifications and hold a Mainland lawyer's practice certificate may carry out activities as agents in matrimonial or succession cases involving Hong Kong parties in the capacity of Mainland lawyers and in civil litigation cases on the Mainland relating to Hong Kong parties for designated categories including family issues, disputes about contracts and intellectual property rights, and applications for enforcement of civil judgments and arbitral awards from Hong Kong courts.[80] The number of candidates sitting the National Legal Professional Qualification Examination, however, remains low. For instance, in 2016, 139 Hong Kong residents sat the exam and only five passed.[81]

---

[78] Supplement VI to CEPA.
[79] P. Y. W. Chiu, 'CEPA: A Milestone in the Economic Integration between Hong Kong and Mainland China' (2006), *Journal of Contemporary China* 15, 275, p. 282.
[80] Supplements III and VIII to CEPA. See Ministry of Justice, 'Notice on the Scope of Businesses of Hong Kong/Macao Residents Having Mainland Legal Professional Qualification and Holding a Mainland Lawyer's Practice Certificate in Acting as Agents in Civil Litigation Cases Relating to Hong Kong/Macao in People's Courts' (Circular of the Ministry of Justice No. 136, Aug 2013) (in Chinese), available at www.mofcom.gov.cn/article/b/g/201310/20131000359888.shtml.
[81] A. Tsang, 'Legal Services Industry in Hong Kong' (Hong Kong: HTDC Research 2018), available at http://hong-kong-economy-research.hktdc.com/business-news/article/

Hong Kong law firms may set up representative offices in the Mainland and can operate in association with up to three Mainland law firms. A Hong Kong law firm may operate in the form of a partnership with a Mainland law firm in Shenzhen, Guangzhou and Zhuhai. The previous minimum stay requirement for Hong Kong representatives working in representative offices has been waived, allowing for more flexibility in working in both jurisdictions.[82] But the scope of practice is restricted, as these representative offices are not allowed to advise on PRC law. Representative offices set up by Hong Kong law firms can engage in businesses including the following: advising clients on Hong Kong law, on foreign law (if the law firm has such expertise and approval has been given) and on international conventions and practices; engaging on behalf of Hong Kong clients a Mainland law firm to handle affairs relating to PRC law; handling legal matters relating to laws of other regions (not PRC law) with respect to which the law firm has been approved to practise; keeping a long-term clientele with Mainland law firms through the conclusion of contracts to handle legal affairs; and providing information on the Mainland legal environment.[83]

The Agreement between the Mainland and Hong Kong on Achieving Basic Liberalisation of Trade in Services in Guangdong signed in December 2014 and the Agreement on Trade in Services (ATIS) signed in November 2015[84] consolidate and extend commitments relating to the liberalisation of trade services under CEPA, including legal services from Hong Kong. For example, under ATIS, Hong Kong law firms can second Hong Kong lawyers to Mainland law firms as consultants to advise on Hong Kong law or cross-border laws. Since 2014, Mainland lawyers can be seconded as consultants to work in Mainland representative offices set up by Hong Kong law firms established in Guangdong Province, where they can advise on PRC law.[85] This has been subsequently extended under the ATIS to apply to the rest of the Mainland.

Hong-Kong-Industry-Profiles/Legal-Services-Industry-in-Hong-Kong/hkip/en/1/1X000000/1X003UYK.htm.

[82] Supplement III to CEPA.

[83] G. H. Y. Tsang and D. L. H. Leung, 'Opportunities Flowing from CEPA and other Trade Developments in the Guangdong Province for Hong Kong Legal Service Providers', (May 2015), *Hong Kong Lawyer*.

[84] The ATIS extends the coverage of the preceding Guangdong agreement to the rest of Mainland China.

[85] Supplement X to CEPA.

Cross-Border Crime

Cross-border crime between Hong Kong and the Mainland is unfortunately nothing new. In the nineteenth century, the British East India Company exported opium to southern China. Notwithstanding the prohibition issued by the Qing dynasty, this contraband made its way into China. As discussed in the first chapter, the Opium War led to the eventual ceding of Hong Kong to Britain. Mark Gaylord points out that 'Colonial Hong Kong was thus founded, quite literally, on cross-border crime.'[86]

With further economic and social integration pre- and post-handover, there is an increase in cross-border crime between Hong Kong and the Mainland. Immigration offences are the most common offences committed by Mainland visitors, including breaches of conditions of stay, using counterfeit travel documents and illegal immigration. Undertaking illegal employment and engaging in prostitution are two other prevalent offences, as well as property offences such as theft and forgery. In the 1990s, there were sensational cases of armed robberies, kidnapping of tycoons and murders committed by offenders originating from the Mainland. On the other hand, Hong Kong residents are frequently caught in the Mainland for financial crimes, fraud, drug trafficking and smuggling goods.[87] There is therefore a need for mutual legal assistance between the two jurisdictions, but the mechanisms so far remain a work-in-progress.

Mutual Care Assistance Scheme

An arrangement for mutual legal assistance regarding cross-border crimes is the Mutual Case Assistance Scheme (MCAS), which was established prior to the Handover in 1988. This is an arrangement between the Independent Commission Against Corruption (ICAC) and the Guangdong Procuratorate. The Summary of Review on Mutual Case Assistance was signed by the two parties in 1996, providing a written agreement setting out the underlying principles and implementation of the MCAS. The MCAS facilitates the

---

[86] M. S. Gaylord, 'Cross-border Crime and Legal Jurisdiction in Post-Colonial Hong Kong' (1999), *Crime, Law & Social Change* 31, 31, p. 31.
[87] Ibid.; D. W. Choy and H. Fu, 'Cross-Border Relations in Criminal Matters', in M. S. Gaylord, D. Gittings and H. Traver (eds.), *Introduction to Crime, Law and Justice in Hong Kong* (Hong Kong: HKU Press 2009) 223, pp. 225–226.

cross-border taking of evidence in corruption cases, including the searching for witnesses, interviewing witnesses, arranging for witnesses to testify in court on a voluntary basis, and the checking of public records. Through this arrangement, Hong Kong or Guangdong officers can be sent to the other's jurisdiction to interview witnesses, but not suspects. In 2000, the MCAS was extended with the help of the Supreme People's Procuratorate to other Mainland procuratorate offices.[88] Since the MCAS was established, there have been around 500 occasions where ICAC officers have travelled to the Mainland where 900 witnesses were interviewed. At the same time, there have been nearly 750 visits to Hong Kong by Mainland procuratorate officials where over 1,100 witnesses were interviewed.[89]

Police Joint Operations

Cross-border police co-operation operates predominately on an informal and contingent basis.[90] Assistance can be requested by law enforcement authorities of both jurisdictions. The PRC joined the International Criminal Police Organization (Interpol) in 1984, and three years later the Guangdong Public Security Bureau established an Interpol liaison office that regularly communicates with the Hong Kong police. To further enhance co-operation, in 1992 it was agreed that a permanent official from the PRC's Ministry of Public Security would be stationed in Hong Kong to facilitate the gathering and transmission of information. In 1994, it was reiterated that police forces from both jurisdictions should seek assistance from each other in accordance with the method set forth by Interpol.[91] When one police force is seeking assistance, it must provide prior notification about the nature of the case and what assistance is being sought. Upon acceptance of the request, investigation will be conducted by law enforcement of the requested party in accordance with the laws of its jurisdiction. Police officers from the other jurisdiction may interview

---

[88] Ibid.
[89] C. G. Claytor, 'Face to Face with Simon Peh, Commissioner, Independent Commission Against Corruption' (October 2015), *Hong Kong Lawyer*; ICAC, *Annual Report 2016* (Hong Kong: ICAC 2016); ICAC, *Annual Report 2017* (Hong Kong: ICAC 2017).
[90] K. C. Wong, 'Fighting Cross-Border Crimes between China and Hong Kong' (2004), *Asian Policing* 1, 1.
[91] Choy and Fu (n. 87), p. 228.

witnesses in the other jurisdiction, but this must be conducted under the supervision of police officers from the other jurisdiction.[92]

Nowadays, there are regular police joint operations between Hong Kong and Mainland China, along with Macao. The annual joint operation, codenamed 'Thunderbolt', which typically lasts for months, tackles organised crime in the three jurisdictions. For example, the first phase of 'Thunderbolt 17', conducted from March to June 2017, resulted in the arrests of over 3,500 people in Hong Kong, including Hong Kong residents, Mainlanders and non-ethnic Chinese for a variety of offences including drug trafficking and money laundering. Over 2,200 suspects were arrested by officers in Guangdong Province, and over 5,000 individuals were brought in for questioning in Macao.[93]

Rendition of Suspected Offenders

There is an absence of a formal rendition agreement between Hong Kong and the PRC for the rendition of suspected or fugitive offenders. A pre-handover informal administrative arrangement is still used today, according to which some suspected offenders may be returned from the Mainland to Hong Kong. In seeking the rendition of suspects to Hong Kong, Hong Kong's Secretary for Security would make a request if the following conditions are met: the offence was committed entirely in Hong Kong; the person is a Hong Kong resident; and the person was not accused of having committed a crime in the Mainland.[94]

The arrangement does not, however, provide for transfers from Hong Kong to the Mainland, leading to resentment by Mainland authorities of its unilateral nature.[95] From Hong Kong's perspective, one of the main reasons for why Hong Kong refuses to transfer suspected offenders to Mainland China, and for the lack of any rendition agreement, is the Mainland's widespread use of the death penalty. Whereas capital punishment was formally abolished in Hong Kong in 1993, it is the maximum

---

[92] Ibid., pp. 228–229.
[93] C. Lo, 'Huge police crackdown not linked to Hong Kong handover events, officials claim', (16 June 2017), *South China Morning Post*.
[94] Choy and Fu (n. 87), p. 236.
[95] H. Fu, 'The Relevance of Chinese Criminal Law to Hong Kong and Its Residents', (1997), *Hong Kong Law Journal* 27, 229.

punishment for many criminal offences in the Mainland.⁹⁶ There is fear that the returning of offenders to the Mainland would violate Hong Kong's commitment to the rule of law and human rights.⁹⁷

The lack of a formal rendition agreement, and of criminal jurisdiction issues, leads to controversies about jurisdiction when both Hong Kong and the Mainland may have jurisdiction over the same crime. Such controversy is illustrated in the 'Big Spender' case, which marked the first time that a Hong Kong resident was tried, and executed, under PRC law for criminal acts largely perpetrated in Hong Kong.⁹⁸ Cheung Tze-keung, nicknamed Big Spender, and thirty-five of his associates went on trial in Mainland China for a series of criminal charges committed in Hong Kong and on the Mainland between 1991 and 1997. Cheung, a Hong Kong resident, and his associates were arrested on 20 July 1998 and prosecuted in the Guangzhou Intermediate People's Court on 29 September 1998. The flamboyant nature of the case attracted considerable media attention as Cheung obtained HK$1.38 billion for the kidnapping of Cheung Kong Company's deputy chairman Victor Li and another HK$0.6 billion for the kidnapping of Sun Hung Kai Company's chairman Walter Kwok.⁹⁹ It was argued by some at the time that Cheung should be sent back to Hong Kong because the kidnappings and armed robbery had been committed in Hong Kong and the Mainland's prosecution raised issues about Hong Kong's autonomy. The preparatory offences of the smuggling of arms and ammunition, the illegal trading of explosives and conspiracy to kidnap were committed in the Mainland.¹⁰⁰ Hong Kong authorities, however, had shown no intention to repatriate Cheung to Hong Kong to stand trial because the crimes involved were wholly or partially committed within the Mainland and the crimes were not reported by the victims in Hong Kong, so there was insufficient evidence to request Cheung's rendition.¹⁰¹ Cheung was subsequently executed in December 1998. The Big Spender cases underline the need for Hong Kong and Mainland China to negotiate agreements in resolving cross-border matters.¹⁰²

---

⁹⁶ Ibid.
⁹⁷ Wong (n. 90), p. 133.
⁹⁸ K. C. Wong, *One Country Two Systems: Cross-Border Crime between Hong Kong and China* (New Brunswick, NJ: Transaction Publishers 2012) 1.
⁹⁹ Ibid.
¹⁰⁰ Ibid., p. 152.
¹⁰¹ H. Fu, 'The Battle of Criminal Jurisdictions' (1998), *Hong Kong Law Journal* 28, 273.
¹⁰² Ibid.

Notification Mechanism

There are concerns over occurrences of Hong Kong residents being caught up in the PRC's criminal justice system and how the Hong Kong Government can monitor its own residents and render assistance to them and their families in such circumstances. On 1 January 2001, the Arrangement on the Establishment of a Reciprocal Notification Mechanism between the Mainland Public Security Authorities and the Hong Kong Police came into effect. Under the mechanism, the Liaison Officer of the Ministry of Public Security (the Mainland Notification Unit) should notify the Liaison Bureau of the Hong Kong Police (the Hong Kong Notification Unit)[103] when there are impositions of criminal compulsory measures, such as arrests, detention or prosecution, on Hong Kong residents and unnatural deaths of Hong Kong residents in the Mainland. The notification should include information on the date of detention, the suspected offence, the type of compulsory measures, the place where the measures are taken and the Mainland enforcement agency concerned; and for unnatural deaths, the time and place of death, and the cause of death. The Hong Kong Notification Unit should notify the public security authorities of criminal prosecutions instigated against Mainland residents and unnatural deaths of Mainland residents in Hong Kong. But no notifications will be made for offences regarding landing and remaining in Hong Kong without permission or contravening the conditions of stay.[104]

New arrangements on the notification mechanism, the Arrangements on the Reciprocal Notification Mechanism between the Mainland and the Hong Kong Special Administrative Region Relating to Situations Including the Imposition of Criminal Compulsory Measures or the Institution of Criminal Prosecution, were signed between the Hong Kong Secretary for Security and the Director of the Office of Hong Kong, Macao and Taiwan Affairs of the Ministry of Public Security on 14 December 2017 and came into force on 1 February 2018. The new agreement enhances the timeframe and transparency of notifications.

---

[103] For smuggling cases, notifications should be made by the Smuggling Activities Investigation Bureau of the General Administration of Customs as assigned by the Ministry of Public Security.
[104] Arrangement on the Establishment of a Reciprocal Notification Mechanism between the Mainland Public Security Authorities and the Hong Kong Police, available at www.doj.gov.hk/eng/topical/pdf/mainlandmutual3e.pdf.

Upon imposing criminal compulsory measures, initiating criminal prosecution or the confirmation of the person's identity in unnatural deaths, notification should be made within seven working days. For serious and complicated criminal cases, notification should be made within fourteen working days. For cases involving terrorist activities or suspected offences endangering national security, notification should be made within thirty working days. The contents of the notifications will now be standardised and will include details such as the suspected offence and the legal basis, where detention is taking place, and the officer-in-charge. The new mechanism now requires all Mainland agencies who are authorised to impose criminal compulsory measures on Hong Kong residents to make notifications.[105] The Mainland Notification Unit is now the Office of Hong Kong, Macao and Taiwan Affairs of the Ministry of Public Security; and the Anti-smuggling Bureau of the General Administration of Customs, the Shanghai Municipal Bureau of Public Security, the Guangdong Provincial Public Security Department are authorised to make direct notifications to the Hong Kong Notification Unit. Notifications from Mainland prosecution authorities are made by the Office of Hong Kong and Macao Affairs of the Supreme People's Procuratorate.[106]

Review Questions

(1) Discuss the features that contribute to Hong Kong having a distinct international legal personality.
(2) How can Hong Kong participate in international organisations that are not limited to states? What about international organisations that are limited to states?
(3) How can international treaties be applied in Hong Kong's domestic legal system?
(4) How can customary law be applied in Hong Kong's domestic legal system?

---

[105] These are the public security authorities, the state security authorities, the customs and anti-smuggling departments and the prosecution authorities.
[106] The Government of HKSAR, 'HKSAR and Mainland Sign New Arrangements on Notification Mechanism', available at www.info.gov.hk/gia/general/201712/14/P2017121400516.htm.

(5) How do you enforce a judgment made in the Mainland in Hong Kong?
(6) In what ways does CEPA allow for Hong Kong law firms to have access to the Mainland market? What are its limitations?
(7) What are the reasons for the lack of a rendition agreement of suspected offenders between Hong Kong and Mainland China?

Glossary

abscond	– When a defendant/accused person fails to appear before the court as required.
accused person	– An individual who is charged with a criminal offence.
acquittal	– A judgment by a court that a defendant/accused person is not guilty for the offence(s) for which he/she is charged.
adjournment	– The postponement of a court hearing.
aggravating factors	– Information presented to the court that may enhance the offender's sentence.
annotated legislation	– Legislation that is reproduced by private publishers, with commentary included.
Anton Piller order	– A court order to permit the plaintiff to enter the defendant's premises to search for certain documents and to inspect, take away or make copies of them.
appeal	– The application to a higher court for a review of a decision made by a lower court.
appellant	– The person who appeals a decision of a court or tribunal to a higher court.
arbitration	– A form of alternative dispute resolution involving the appointment of a neutral third party, called an arbitral tribunal, to impose a settlement on the disputing parties.
arrest	– The taking of an individual into custody in a manner that is authorised by the law.
bail	– The conditional release of an individual by the police or the courts held in legal custody while awaiting appearance in court.

bailiff	– An officer of the court who is concerned with the enforcement of the court's orders and the service of court processes.
bill	– Draft law that has yet to become law.
cab-rank rule	– A rule where a barrister is bound to accept any brief to appear before a court in the field in which he/she professes to practise at his/her usual fee having regard to the type, nature, length and difficulty of the case.
cause of action	– The reason that entitles a party to sue another; the facts giving rise to a legal claim.
chambers	– The offices of barristers. Also refers to a judge's private office.
champerty	– A form of maintenance where the party who finances another to institute a lawsuit takes a portion of the property in dispute or other recovery in the proceedings as his/her reward.
civil law system	– A legal system based on Roman law. Civil law systems are based on codified law.
Closer Economic Partnership Arrangement (CEPA)	– A free trade agreement between the Central People's Government and the HKSAR Government signed on 29 June 2003. It covers four broad areas: trade in goods, trade in services, investment, and economic and technical cooperation.
co-location arrangement	– The Hong Kong and Mainland customs, immigration and quarantine arrangements of the Hong Kong section of the Guangzhou–Shenzhen–Hong Kong Express Rail Link where part of the West Kowloon Station is leased to Mainland authorities.
common law system	– A legal system derived from England that places great weight on judicial decisions where laws are not only made by the Legislature/Parliament but can also develop from previous decisions by the courts.
community service order	– A court order that requires the offender to perform unpaid work in the community (up to 240 hours).

conditional fees	– An arrangement between the lawyer and his/her client providing that if the case is lost, there would not be any legal fees.
confession	– An admission by an individual in part or in whole of his/her guilt.
conviction	– A judgment by a court that a defendant/accused person is guilty for the offence(s) for which he/she is charged.
cross-examination	– The questioning of a witness on the other side in a trial.
customary international law	– A source of international law that arises from the established, widespread and generally accepted customary rules and principles of state practice. It is established by showing state practice and *opinio juris*.
default judgment	– A judgment entered against the defendant in a civil action if he/she has not given a notice of intention to defend, failed to file the Acknowledgment of Service on time or failed to serve the defence.
defendant	– The party against whom court proceedings are brought.
discovery	– The formal exchange of documents which are or have been in each party's possession, custody or power relating to matters that are raised in a civil action.
examination-in-chief	– The questioning of one's own witnesses in a trial.
fine	– A sum of money that the offender is ordered to pay to the court after conviction as a penalty.
garnishee order	– A court order against a third party in Hong Kong who owes a debt to the judgment debtor to pay the judgment creditor directly.
Gazette	– The official journal published by the government containing legislation and government notices, etc.
golden rule	– A rule of statutory interpretation where the ordinary and natural meaning of the words is to be adhered to, unless that would lead to some

	absurdity, or some repugnancy or inconsistency with the rest of the instrument.
guilty plea	– An admission by a defendant/accused person in court that he/she has committed the offence charged against him/her.
Hansard	– A record of the proceedings and debates of Legislative Council members in relation to bills put before the Legislative Council.
horizontal stare decisis	– The requirement that for decisions of courts at the same level or standing in a court hierarchy, earlier decisions of the courts bind later decisions of the same court or another court of equal standing.
interlocutory injunctions	– Court orders before the trial commences for a party to do something or to refrain from doing something.
inferior courts	– Courts that have limited jurisdiction and are subject to the supervision of superior courts, e.g. the Magistrates' Courts.
judgment	– Decision of the court in legal proceedings.
jury	– A body of jurors who have been sworn in to reach a verdict based on the evidence heard in court.
law enforcement agencies	– Agencies that enforce the law with the aim of maintaining law and order in society.
law report	– report of a case by legal publishers which contains the judgment of a case.
legal aid	– The financial assistance provided for individuals towards the cost of legal representation.
limitation period	– The deadline for bringing a civil action as imposed in limitations statutes.
literal approach	– A rule of statutory interpretation where the ordinary and natural meaning of the words is applied.
litigant in person	– An individual, company or organisation that is not legally represented by a solicitor or a barrister but instead represents themselves in court.
maintenance	– Intermeddling of an unconnected party in encouraging a lawsuit.
Mareva injunction	– A court order to freeze a defendant's assets.

mediation	– A form of alternative dispute resolution involving the appointment of a neutral third party, called mediators, to assist the disputing parties in the negotiation process with the aim of reaching a mutually acceptable resolution.
member's bills	– bills that are introduced by members of the Legislative Council.
milestone dates	– Dates that the court has fixed for a case management conference, a pre-trial review, the trial or the period in which a trial is to take place.
mischief rule	– A rule of statutory interpretation where legislation is regarded as being enacted to remedy some mischief or problem which existed under the common law.
mitigating factors	– Information presented to the court which may reduce the offender's sentence.
notification mechanism	– Mechanism where Mainland and Hong Kong authorities notify each other when there are impositions of criminal compulsory measures (and criminal prosecutions) and unnatural deaths of its residents in the other's jurisdiction.
opinio juris	– In Latin meaning 'an opinion of law'; it is the second element in establishing customary international law; it is a state's belief to act in accordance with custom because they consider themselves legally bound by it.
obiter dictum (or *dicta*)	– In Latin, 'a remark in passing'; a judge's opinion in a written judgment that does not form part of the decision and is therefore not legally binding as precedent. But it may be regarded as having persuasive authority.
originating summons	– A legal document that commences legal proceedings that concern primarily a dispute of law.
per incuriam	– In Latin, 'through lack of care'; a court decision is given *per incuriam* if it was made in ignorance of some statutory provision or of some binding precedent.

petition	– A legal document for initiating certain actions in court, such as in bankruptcy or winding up.
plaintiff	– In civil proceedings, the party that brings an action against the defendant in a court of law.
plea arraignment	– The procedure in court where the charge(s) are read out and the defendant/accused person is asked to plead guilty or not guilty.
pleadings	– In civil proceedings, these are the formal documents that are exchanged between the plaintiff and the defendant which define the issues to be decided in the action.
prima facie	– In Latin, 'at first appearance'.
probation order	– A court order that places an offender under the supervision of a probation officer for a period of time (ranging from one year up to three years) and subject to certain conditions.
pro bono publico	– In Latin, 'for the public good'; denotes free legal work that is conducted for the benefit of the general community.
prosecutor	– The individual that initiates criminal proceedings and prosecutes trials and appeals on behalf of the HKSAR.
private bills	– Bills that concern the rights, duties and interests of only one class of persons.
public bills	– Bills that affect everyone in the community.
purposive approach	– A rule of statutory interpretation where the courts attempt to give a meaning to the legislation which achieves the legislature's purpose in enacting the law.
ratio decidendi	– In Latin, 'the reason for the decision'; the principles of law on which the court reaches its decision. It is the part of a judgment that creates binding precedent.
recognisance	– An undertaking by an individual to a court to do something that the court requires and which failure to do would lead to a payment of a sum to the court.
remanded in custody	– The holding of an individual in legal custody while he/she is awaiting appearance in court. This is as opposed to being granted bail.

respondent	– A party to court proceedings against whom a claim is made by an applicant, petitioner or appellant.
sanctioned offer	– A written offer by the plaintiff (or a defendant making a counterclaim) to settle by an acceptance of a certain amount to satisfy the claim.
sanctioned payment	– An offer that is made by the defendant (or the plaintiff facing a counterclaim) which involves the payment of money to the plaintiff (or the defendant in the case of a counterclaim) to settle the whole or part of the claim.
sentence discount	– Reduction of the sentence by the court because of the defendant's/accused person's guilty plea.
solicitor advocate	– The title used by a solicitor who has been granted a higher right of audience in the higher courts.
stare decisis	– In Latin, 'to keep to what has been decided previously'; it is the basis of the doctrine of precedent.
statement of claim	– A pleading in which the plaintiff sets out the facts giving rise to the plaintiff's cause of action.
statement of truth	– A statement where the party putting forth the document believes that the facts are true, and in the case of an expert report, that the opinions expressed are honestly held.
summary judgment	– A judgment obtained by the plaintiff without a full trial where it is plain that there is no defence to the claim.
superior courts	– Courts that have unlimited jurisdiction, e.g. the Court of Final Appeal and the High Court.
suspended sentence	– A custodial sentence that does not take effect unless the offender is convicted of a subsequent offence that is punishable by imprisonment within a specified period of time.
tort	– In old French, 'harm and wrong'; in Latin, 'twisted or crooked'; a wrongful act or omission that harms someone else which may result in damages being claimed in a civil action.

totality principle	– A common law principle that applies when a court is determining sentence for multiple offences at the same time, the court is seeking to ensure that the total sentence is just and proportionate, meaning a sentence which reflects the overall seriousness of the crimes and the overall effect that the sentence will have on the offender.
treaties	– Agreements between two or more states or international organisations where the parties agree to be regulated by its terms.
ultra vires	– In Latin, 'beyond the powers'.
vertical *stare decisis*	– The requirement for lower courts to follow the decisions of higher courts in the same court hierarchy.
writ of summons	– Referred to as a writ, a legal document that commences legal proceedings which mainly concern a dispute of facts.

Index

abuse of official powers, 42–43
academic personnel, in legal systems, 16
access to justice. *See also* legal aid
  under Basic Law, 305
  conditional fees and, 324–326
    Law Reform Commission on, 324–326
  through Duty Lawyer Service, 318–322
    Convention Against Torture Scheme, 321–322
    Duty Lawyer Scheme, 318–320
    Free Legal Advice Scheme, 320–321
    Tel-Law Scheme, 321
    Widgery criteria in, 319
  under Hong Kong Bill of Rights, 305, 309–310
  litigants in person and, 326–328
  through *pro bono publico*, 322
    Bar Free Legal Services Scheme, 322–323
    Legal Advice Scheme for Unrepresented Litigants in Civil Procedures, 323–324
    Procedural Advice Scheme, 323–324
  right to legal assistance and, 309–310
accreditation of mediators, 292–294
ad hoc arbitration, 295–296
ADR. *See* alternative dispute resolution
Agreement on Trade in Services (ATIS), 384
alternative dispute resolution (ADR). *See also* arbitration; awards; payments; remedies
  advantages of, 302–303
  confidentiality, 303
  cost-effectiveness, 302–303
  in CJR, 287–290
  disadvantages of, 303–304
  through mediation, 288–294
    accreditation of mediators, 292–294
    as contract, 288
    facilitative, 288
    function and purpose of, 288–289
    under Mediation Code, 293
    under Mediation Ordinance, 290–292
    under Practice Direction 31, 290–292
amendments, to legislation, 103
appeals systems, before July 1, 1997, 144–145
Aquinas. *See* Thomas Aquinas
arbitral awards, enforcement of, 380–382
arbitration, 294–302
  ad hoc, 295–296
  under Arbitration Ordinance, 294, 298–299
  arbitrators, 299–302
    appointment of, 299–300
    arbitral awards by, 301
    decisions by, appeals of, 302
    duties of, 300
    fee structure for, 301
    power of, 301
  champerty and, 299
  through China International Economic and Trade Arbitration Commission, 297
  through Hong Kong International Arbitration Centre, 296
  institutional, 295
  through International Court of Arbitration of the International Chamber of Commerce, 297
  maintenance of, 299
  under New York Convention on the Recognition and Enforcement of Foreign Arbitral Awards, 295
  through Permanent Court of Arbitration, 297
  purpose and function of, 294–295
  under UNCITRAL, 295–296
Aristotle, 37
  on separation of powers doctrine, 76
arrangement on mutual taking of evidence, 379

arrangement on reciprocal enforcement of judgments, 377–379
arrests, by HKPF, 239–241
ATIS. *See* Agreement on Trade in Services
Austin, John, 46–47
Australia, subsidiary legislation in, 197–198
authority, in legislative process, 185–191
  of Chief Executive, 188–190
  of courts, 190–191
  limitations of, 187–188
autonomy, in governance, 67–71
  under Basic Law, 68–71
  under Joint Declaration, 67–68
awards, in civil litigation, 276–277

bail, in criminal court proceedings, 251–252
Bar Free Legal Services Scheme, 322–323
barristers, 15–16, 306–308
  cab-rank rule, 307–308
  Direct Professional Access for, 307
barristers and solicitors, 15–16
  legal training for, 15–16
Basic Law (Hong Kong), 90–98. *See also* Hong Kong Special Administrative Region Government
  access to justice under, 305
  Chief Executive authority under, 188–190
  Chinese customary law and, 134
  constitutional elements of, 90–91
  contents of, 92–93
  Court of Final Appeal under, 9–10
  court systems under, 137
  electronic copies of, 337
  English case law decisions under, 177–179
  governance structure under
    autonomy, 68–71
    Chief Executive position under, 72–74
    Legislative Council, 74–75
    'one country, two systems' concept, 64–67
  in HKSAR Government, 68–71
  independent judiciary under, 7
  international case law decisions under, 177–179
  interpretation of, 93–98
    consistency of, 98–99
    hybrid system in, 94
    by NPCSC, 94–98
  judicial review in, 38
  legal validity of, 91
  Legislative Council and, 3–4, 8–9, 13
  legislative process and, 185–190

political order in, 37–38
under PRC sovereignty, 25
public order in, 37
rule of recognition in, 47
and Standing Committee of the National People's Congress, 7
statutory interpretation of, 228–230
battered women syndrome, 56
Bentham, Jeremy, 46
bilingual judgments, 133
bilingual legislation, 102
  statutory interpretation of, 230–231
bills
  electronic copies of, 338
  in primary legislation, 193–194
  private, 193
  public, 193
books, as secondary source for legal materials, 350
Boolean searching, 348
burden of proof. *See also* standards of proof
  in civil litigation, 275
business transactions, law and, 42

cab-rank rule, 307–308
capitalism, in 'one country, two systems' concept, 65
CAPO. *See* Complaints Against Police Office
case law
  court judgments and, 120
  definition of, 107
  English, under Basic Law, 177–179
  international, under Basic Law, 177–179
  law reports, 113–120
    parts of reported cases, 114–120
    reporting procedures, 113
    unreported cases, 113
  legal systems and, 4
CEPA. *See* Closer Economic Partnership Arrangement
CFA. *See* Court of Final Appeal
champerty, 299
Chief Executive, 72–74
  authority of, in legislative process, 188–190
  primary legislation and, 195–196
China. *See also* colonial Hong Kong; People's Republic of China
  leasing agreement with Great Britain, 17
  Opium Wars, 17
  Second Convention of Peking 1898, 17
  Treaty of Nanking 1842, 17, 63

Index

China International Economic and Trade Arbitration Commission (CIETAC), 297
Chinese customary law, 134
CIETAC. *See* China International Economic and Trade Arbitration Commission
citations, 359-365
  of cases, 360-363
    for reported cases, 360-362
    for unreported cases, 362-363
  in legal journals, 355-356
  of legislation, 359-360
  neutral, 363
  in secondary sources, 355-356, 362-365
Civil Justice Reform (CJR), 280-285
  ADR in, 287-290
  case management in, 281-283
    documents in, 282-283
  costs of, 285
  CPR and, 280
  English influences on, 280
  objectives of, 280-281
  payments as part of, 283-284
  sanctioned offers in, 283-284
  statements of truth in, 284-285
civil justice system. *See* civil litigation
civil law, 57-58, 60-61
  common law and, 107-108
  origins of, 57-58
civil litigation, 264-279
  acknowledgment of service, 270
  burden of proof, 275
  court jurisdictions for, 265-266
  in Court of First Instance, 275-276
  'culture of compensation' and, 277-278
  default judgments, 270-271
  defence against, 270
  discovery in, 273-274
  in District Court, 265-266
  drawbacks to, 277-279
  enforcement of awards in, 276-277
  explosion of, 277-278
  initiating an action, 266-270
    due notice for, 269-270
    limitation period for, 268-269
    by plaintiffs, 266-268
  injunctions in, 274-275
    interlocutory, 274
    mandatory, 274
    Mareva, 274-275
    prohibitory, 274
  pleadings in, 271-273
  remedies as awards in, 276-277
  standards of proof, 275
  summary judgments, 270-271
  trial procedures, 275-276
CJR. *See* Civil Justice Reform
Closer Economic Partnership Arrangement (CEPA), 382-384
codification of legislation, 100
colonial Hong Kong, 17-18
  law in, 21-24
    under Application of English Law Ordinance, 22-23
    Chinese, 23-24
    under Supreme Court Ordinances, 21-22
  legal institutions during, 18-21
    Legislative Council, 19
    as tools of political control, 20
  legal systems during, development of, 16-18
  rule of law during, 18-21
  after Second Convention of Peking 1898, 17
  separation of powers doctrine in, 81-82
    Legislative Council, 81-82
  though leasing agreement, 17
  for trade, 18
command theory of law, 47
common law, 57-58
  civil law and, 107-108
  court judgments, 120
  development of, in England, 108-111
    Court of Chancery, 109-111
  equity and, 57, 109-111
  fairness and, 110
  fact and law in, distinctions between, 120-123
  judicial reasoning and, 129-133
    declaratory theory and, limitations of, 129-131
    development of law and, 131-132
    under separation of powers doctrine, 129-131
  law reports under, 113-120
    parts of reported cases, 114-120
    reporting procedures, 113
    unreported cases, 113
  meanings of, variety in, 108
  obiter dicta in, 57, 124-129
  ratio decidendi in, 57, 124-129
  as source of law, in Hong Kong, 111-112
  statute law and, 108

statutes under
  components of, 104–107
  consolidation of, 100
  interpretation of, 123–124
  statutory interpretation of, 202–206
    background of, 202–203
    'golden rule' in, 204
    literal approach in, 203
    purposive approach in, 205–206
  under Supreme Court of Judicature Acts, 110–111
community service orders, 262
Competition Tribunal, 140, 157–158
Complaints Against Police Office (CAPO), 243–244
conditional fees, 324–326
  Law Reform Commission on, 324–326
confidentiality, in ADR, 303
consensus model, of law, 50–51
consolidated index of reported decisions, 342
Constitution, U.S., separation of powers doctrine in, 77
consultation papers, 358
Consumer Goods Safety Ordinance (Cap 456), 38–39
contract law, critical legal theory and, 54
Convention Against Torture Scheme, 321–322
court judgments, 120
Court of Appeal, 10, 141, 148–149
  doctrine of judicial precedent, 168–172
    horizontal *stare decisis*, 168–172
    vertical *stare decisis*, 168
Court of Chancery, 109–111
Court of Final Appeal (CFA), 9–10, 141, 146
  doctrine of judicial precedent and, 164, 168–172
    horizontal *stare decisis*, 166–168
    vertical *stare decisis*, 165–166
  establishment of, 145–147
  resident criteria in, 210
Court of First Instance, 10, 141, 146, 148
  civil litigation in, 275–276
  doctrine of judicial precedent in, 172–174
    horizontal *stare decisis*, 173–174
    vertical *stare decisis*, 172–173
court systems. *See also* tribunals; *specific courts*
  authority of, in legislative process, 190–191
  under Basic Law, 137
  doctrine of judicial precedent and, 160

hierarchy in, 160
inferior, 140–141
before July 1, 1997, 141–145
  appeals systems, 144–145
  District Court, 143
  Magistrates' Courts, 143–144
  Privy Council, 144–145, 177–179
  Supreme Court, 142–143
  tribunals, 144
after July 1, 1997, 145–159. *See also specific courts*
  District Court, 149–150
  Magistrates' Courts, 150–151
  tribunals, 151–159
judicial power of, 138–139
  basic functions of, 138
  limitations of, 139
jurisdiction of, 139
  of superior courts, 140
persuasive authorities in, 179–180
superior, 140–141
  Competition Tribunal, 140
  jurisdiction of, 140
court venue, 252–253
CPR. *See* Civil Procedure Rules
criminal court proceedings, 251–262
  bail, 251–252
  court venue, 252–253
  pleas in, 253–256
    conviction rates for, 254–255
    of guilt, 253–256
    of not guilty, 256
  presumption of innocence in, 257–258
  right to silence, 258
  sentencing, 259–262
    community service orders, 262
    custodial, 260–261
    errors in, 259
    imprisonment in, 260
    mitigating factors for, 259
    non-custodial, 261–262
    probation orders, 262
  standard of proof, in criminal trials, 256–257
criminal justice system. *See also* Hong Kong Police Force
  prosecutions in, 247–250
    in courtrooms, 250
    decision-making about, 248–250
    prosecutorial independence and, 247–248
  scope of, 234

criminal law, 60-61
Criminal Legal Aid Scheme, 315
critical legal theory, 52-55
    contract law and, 54
    feminist perspectives of, 55-56
        battered women syndrome and, 56
    legitimation problem in, 53-54
    Marxist perspectives of, 55
    oppression problem in, 53-54
    political choice in, 52-53
    property rights in, 52-53
    schools of, development of, 54-55
'culture of compensation,' 277-278
Cumulative Supplement, 344
custodial sentencing, 260-261
customary international law, 373-374
Customs and Excise Department, 246-247

Declaration of the Rights of Man, 77
declaratory theory, limitations of, 129-131
default judgments, 270-271
delegated legislation, 99. See also subsidiary legislation
Deng Xiaoping, 83-84
digests. See legal digests
Direct Professional Access, for barristers, 307
discovery, in civil litigation, 273-274
District Court, 10, 141
    civil litigation in, 265-266
    before July 1, 1997, 143
    after July 1, 1997, 149-150
    doctrine of judicial precedent. See judicial precedent
dualism, public international law and, 369
Duty Lawyer Scheme, 318-320
Duty Lawyer Service, 318-322
    Convention Against Torture Scheme, 321-322
    Duty Lawyer Scheme, 318-320
    Free Legal Advice Scheme, 320-321
    Tel-Law Scheme, 321
    Widgery criteria in, 319

economic order, through law, 39
ejusdem generis (of the same kind), 215-216
Elliot, Charles, 17
England
    Act of Settlement, 6-7
    CJR in Hong Kong influenced by, 280
    common law in, development of, 108-111
    Court of Chancery, 109-111
    Supreme Court in, 166-167

equity, in law, 38
    common law and, 57, 109-111
    fairness and, 110
executive branch, in governance structure, 71-74
    authorities as part of, 71-72
    Chief Executive, 72-74
    Executive Council, 72
    powers of, 71-72
    selection criteria in, 72-74
    under separation of powers doctrine, 85-86
Executive Council, 72
expiration and lapses of legislation, 104
expressio unius est exclusio alterius (to express one thing is implied to exclude another), 217

facilitative mediation, 288
facts, law as distinct from, 120-123
fairness, equity and, 110
feminism, in critical legal theory, 55-56
    battered women syndrome and, 56
Finnis, John, 45
Frank, Jerome, 51
Free Legal Advice Scheme, 320-321
Fuller, Lon L., 45-46
functional separation of powers, 79

G-20. See Group of Twenty
generalia specialibus non derogant (general things do not derogate from special things), 217-218
Godber, Peter, 244
governance structure, in Hong Kong. See also separation of powers doctrine
    autonomy levels in, 67-71
        under Basic Law, 68-71
        under Joint Declaration, 67-68
    under Basic Law
        autonomy, 68-71
        Chief Executive position under, 72-74
        Legislative Council, 74-75
        'one country, two systems' concept, 64-67
    executive branch, 71-74
        authorities as part of, 71-72
        Chief Executive, 72-74
        Executive Council, 72
        powers of, 71-72
        selection criteria in, 72-74
    judiciary, 75-76

legislative branch, 74-75
  Legislative Council, 74-75
  under 'one country, two systems' concept, 53-54
  under Basic Law, 64-67
  capitalism in, 65
  'one country' in, 63-64
  'two systems' in, 64-67
Government Gazette Legal Supplement No 1, 331, 333-334, 336-339
government publications, as secondary source, 358
Group of Twenty (G-20), 372
guilty pleas, 253-256

Halsbury's Laws of Hong Kong, 330-334, 336, 350-351
  electronic version of, 351
  hard copy of, 350-351
Hansard materials, 358
  in statutory interpretation, 222-223
Hart, H. L. A., 47
Heung Yee Kuk, 192
High Court of Hong Kong Special Administrative Region, 147-149
Hindu legal system, 58
HKeL. *See* Hong Kong e-legislation
HKIAC. *See* Hong Kong International Arbitration Centre
HKPF. *See* Hong Kong Police Force
HKSAR. *See* Hong Kong Special Administrative Region Government
Hobbes, Thomas, 46
Holmes, Oliver, 51
Hong Kong. *See also* Basic Law; colonial Hong Kong; court systems; governance structure; Hong Kong Special Administrative Region Government; legal systems
  ATIS, 384
  bilingual judgments in, 133
  CEPA and, 382-384
  common law in, as source of law, 111-112
  cross-border crime and, with PRC, 385-390
    Mutual Care Assistance Scheme, 385-386
    notification mechanisms for, 389-390
    police joint operations for, 386-387
    rendition agreements, 387-388
  international law in, 58-59
  national law in, 58-59

  during Opium Wars, 17
  under PRC sovereignty, 24-27, 63-64
    Basic Law in, establishment of, 25
    HKSAR established under, 25-26
    under Joint Declaration, with UK, 24-25
    NPC, 25-26
    Second Convention of Peking and, 24
    resident criteria for, 210
  under Treaty of Nanking 1842, 17
Hong Kong Bar Association, 317
Hong Kong Bill of Righfs, 305, 309-310
Hong Kong Case Citator, 342-343
Hong Kong e-legislation (HKeL), 337-338
Hong Kong International Arbitration Centre (HKIAC), 296
Hong Kong Law Reports and Digest, 343-345, 352-354
Hong Kong Legal Information Institute, 338
Hong Kong Police Force (HKPF), 3-4, 235-247
  CAPO and, 243-244
  criminal procedures and, 240
  historical development of, 235-237
  ICAC and, 244-246
    authority and powers of, 245-246
    operational structure of, 245
  IPCC and, 243-244
  modernization and transformation of, 236-237
  organizational structure of, 235
  police officers in, 235-244
    arrests by, 239-241
    powers of, 237-243
    stop and search authority of, 237-239
  questioning of suspects by, 241-243
Hong Kong Special Administrative Region (HKSAR) Government, 10-11. *See also* court systems; governance structure; legal personnel
  Basic Law in, 68-71
  Chief Executive in, 12
  Secretary for Justice in, 12-13
  separation of powers doctrine in, 82-88
    academic literature as influence on, 84
    for executive branch, 85-86
    through judicial courts, 84-86
    for Legislative Council, 86-87
    legislative protections in, 83

ICAC. *See* Independent Commission Against Corruption

ICC. *See* International Court of Arbitration of the International Chamber of Commerce
Immigration Department, law enforcement by, 247
imprisonment, in sentencing, 260
Independent Commission Against Corruption (ICAC), 244-246
  authority and powers of, 245-246
  operational structure of, 245
independent judiciary. *See* judiciary members
Independent Police Complaints Council (IPCC), 243-244
inferior court systems, 140-141
  doctrine of judicial precedent in, 174-175
    horizontal *stare decisis*, 175
    vertical *stare decisis*, 174-175
initiating an action, in civil litigation, 266-270
  due notice for, 269-270
  limitation period for, 268-269
  by plaintiffs, 266-268
injunctions, 274-275
  interlocutory, 274
  mandatory, 274
  Mareva, 274-275
  prohibitory, 274
institutional arbitration, 295
institutional separation of powers, 79
interlocutory injunctions, 274
International Court of Arbitration of the International Chamber of Commerce (ICC), 297
international law. *See* customary international law; private international law; public international law
international legal personality, 368
International Monetary Fund, 372
international order, through law, 39-40
IPCC. *See* Independent Police Complaints Council
Islamic law, 58

Joint Declaration, 67-68
journals, legal, 354-358
  citations in, 355-356
  electronic, 356-358
judges, as member of legal system, 13-14
judicial precedent, doctrine of, 159-165
  abolishment of, 167-168

  avoidance of, 176-177
  in CFA, 164, 168-172
    horizontal *stare decisis*, 166-168
    vertical *stare decisis*, 165-166
  in Court of Appeal, 168-172
    horizontal *stare decisis*, 168-172
    vertical *stare decisis*, 168
  in Court of First Instance, 172-174
    horizontal *stare decisis*, 173-174
    vertical *stare decisis*, 172-173
  court systems and, 160
  decisions on law as, 160
  disadvantages of, 161-163
  hierarchy of courts, 160
  in inferior courts, 174-175
    horizontal *stare decisis*, 175
    vertical *stare decisis*, 174-175
  limitations of, 161-163
  NPCSC and, 176
  prospective effect of court decisions, 163-165
    prospective overruling, 165
  rationale for, 160-161
  retrospective effect of court decisions, 163-165
    retrospective overruling, 165
  standards of proof in, 164
  in tribunals, 174-175
    horizontal *stare decisis*, 175
    vertical *stare decisis*, 174-175
judicial reasoning, in common law, 129-133
  declaratory theory and, limitations of, 129-131
  development of law and, 131-132
  under separation of powers doctrine, 129-131
judiciary
  in court systems, power of, 138-139
    basic functions of, 138
    limitations of, 139
  in governance structure, 75-76
  judiciary members. *See also* judges
    independence of, 6-8, 13-14
      under Act of Settlement, 6-7
      under Basic Law, 7
      Standing Committee of the National People's Congress and, 7
    as member of legal system, 13-14
juries, 14-15
jurisdiction
  for civil litigation, 265-266
  of court systems, 139
  of superior courts, 140

Kelsen, Hans, 48
Kwok, Walter, 388

Labour Tribunal, 144, 156–157
Lands Tribunal, 144, 154–156
lapses of legislation. *See* expiration and lapses of legislation
law. *See also* case law; common law; rule of law; *specific legal theories*
  arbitrary power as antithesis of, 5–6
  Aristotle on, 37
  civil, 60–61
  classifications of, 56–61. *See also specific types of law*
    adversarial systems, 58
    inquisitorial systems, 58
    international types, 58–59
    national types, 58–59
  in colonial Hong Kong, 21–24
    under Application of English Law Ordinance, 22–23
    Chinese law in, 23–24
    under Supreme Court Ordinances, 21–22
  command theory, 47
  consensus model of, 50–51
  criminal, 60–61
  definition of, 34–35
  equity in, 38
  fact as distinct from, 120–123
  Hindu, 58
  Islamic, 58
  legal reasoning in, 28
  legislation as source of, 100–101
    through NPCSC, 101
    for statutory law, 100–101
  macrofunctions of, 37–41
    economic order, 39
    international order, 39–40
    moral order, 40–41
    political order, 37–38
    public order, 37
    social order, 38–39
  microfunctions of, 41–43
    for business transactions, 42
    consequences for behaviors, 42
    limitations of acceptable behaviors, 41
    to prevent abuse of official powers, 42–43
    for regulatory frameworks, 42
  normative nature of, 48
  private, 60
  procedural, 59–60
  public, 60
  purpose and functions of, 1, 36–43
  Sino-Soviet system of, 58
  social context for, 29
  social control though, 50–51
  as social phenomenon, 49
  sociology of, 49–52
  statute, 108
  statutory, 4, 100–101
  study of, 27–30
    legal knowledge through, 35–36
  substantive elements of, 59–60
law enforcement. *See also* Hong Kong Police Force
  Customs and Excise Department, 246–247
  by Immigration Department, 247
Law Reform Commission, 324–326, 359
law reports, 113–120
  parts of reported cases, 114–120
  reporting procedures, 113
  unreported cases, 113
law reviews, 354
Law Society of Hong Kong, 317–318
Legal Advice Scheme for Unrepresented Litigants in Civil Procedures, 323–324
legal aid, 310–318
  application of, 311
  Criminal Legal Aid Scheme, 315
  Hong Kong Bar Association and, 317
  independent authority of, 316–318
    establishment of, 317
  Law Society of Hong Kong, 317
  Legal Aid Panel, 315–316
  Legal Aid Services Council, 316–317
  Ordinary Legal Aid Scheme, 311–313
    under Legal Aid Ordinance, 312–313
  Supplementary Legal Aid Scheme, 313–314
    Type I proceedings, 314
    Type II proceedings, 314
Legal Aid Panel, 315–316
Legal Aid Services Council, 316–317
legal assistance, as right, 309–310
legal digests, 351
legal encyclopaedias, 350
legal institutions. *See also* legislation
  in colonial Hong Kong, 18–21
    Legislative Council, 19
    as tools of political control, 20
  in legal systems, as part of, 3–4, 8–11

legal institutions. (cont.)
    executive institutions, 10–11. *See also*
        Hong Kong Special Administrative
        Region Government
    judicial institutions, 9–10
    legislative institutions, 3–4, 8–9, 13
legal journals. *See* journals
legal knowledge, through study of law,
    35–36
legal materials. *See* primary sources;
    secondary sources
legal personnel, 11–16, 306–309
    academic, 16
    barristers, 15–16, 306–308
        cab-rank rule, 307–308
        Direct Professional Access for, 307
    Chief Executive, 12
    judges and judiciary members, 13–14
    juries, 14–15
    legislators, 13
    Secretary of Justice, 12–13
    separation of, in Hong Kong legal system,
        306
    solicitors, 15–16, 308–309
        fiduciary duty to clients, 309
        limited audience for, 309
legal philosophers, 46–47
legal positivism, as legal theory, 46–49
    command theory of law and, 47
    Hart and, 47
    Kelsen on, 48
    legal philosophers and, 46–47
    natural law theory compared to, 46,
        48–49
    normative nature of law and, 48
legal realism, 51–52
legal reasoning. *See also* legislation
    in law, 28
legal systems, in Hong Kong
    case laws and, 4
    elements of, 3–4
    establishment of, 1–2
    historical development of, 16–18
        during British colonisation, 16–18
        English law in conflict with British law
            in, 17
        establishment in, 1–2
    independent judiciary as part of, 6–8,
        13–14
        under Act of Settlement, 6–7
        under Basic Law, 7
    international legitimacy of, 368

legal institutions as part of, 3–4, 8–11
    executive, 10–11. *See also* Hong Kong
        Special Administrative Region
        Government
    judicial, 9–10
    legislative, 3–4, 8–9, 13
'one country, two systems' and, 2
PRC and, interface with, 375–379
    arbitral awards, enforcement of,
        380–382
    arrangement on mutual taking of
        evidence, 379
    arrangement on reciprocal enforcement
        of judgments, 377–379
    mutual legal assistance, 375
    mutual service of judicial documents,
        376–377
public international law and, 367–374
    international treaties and, 369–373
    rules and principles for, 4–8. *See also* rule
        of law
    separation of legal personnel in, 306
    separation of powers in, 6
    under statutory laws, 4
    transfer of sovereignty as influence on,
        1–2
legal theories. *See specific legal theories*
legislation, 98–107. *See also* legislative
        process; primary legislation; statute
        law; statutes
    bilingual, 102
        statutory interpretation of, 230–231
    citations of, 359–360
    codification of, 100
    constitutional invalidity of, 101–102
    definition, 98
    delegated, 99
    operation of, 103–104
        amendments, 103
        commencement of, 103
        expiration and lapses of legislation,
            104
        repeals, 103
    primary, 99
    secondary, 99
    as source of law, 100–101
        through NPCSC, 101
        statutory law, 100–101
    statutes in
        components of, 104–107
        consolidation of, 100
    subsidiary, 99

legislative branch, in governance structure, 74–75. *See also* legislative process
Legislative Council, 74–75
Legislative Council
  under Basic Law, 3–4, 8–9, 13
  in colonial Hong Kong, 19
    separation of powers doctrine and, 81–82
  primary legislation and, 193–195
  separation of powers doctrine and
    in colonial Hong Kong, 81–82
    in HKSAR, 86–87
  subsidiary legislation and, 196–197, 199
legislative process. *See also* primary legislation
  authority in, 185–191
    of Chief Executive, 188–190
    of courts, 190–191
    limitations of, 187–188
  Basic Law and, 185–190
  for new laws, 183–184
  purposes of, 184–185
    for amendments to law, 185
    for codification of law, 184
    for consolidation of law, 185
    for law creation, 184
  separation of powers in, 190–191
  for subsidiary legislation, 196–199
    in Australia, 197–198
    Legislative Council and, 196–197, 199
    passage of, 198
    repeal of, 199
    ultra vires doctrine, 198
legislators, 13
legitimation, as legal problem, 53–54
LexisNexis, 338, 345
Li, Andrew, 280
Li, Victor, 388
litigants in person, 326–328
litigation. *See* civil litigation
'litigation explosion,' 277–278
Llewellyn, Karl, 51
Locke, John, 45
  on separation of powers doctrine, 76–77
loose-leaf services, 359

MacLehose, Murray, 236
Madison, James, 77
Magistrates' Courts, 10
  before July 1, 1997, 143–144
  after July 1, 1997, 150–151
    permanent, 150

special, 150
mainland China. *See* People's Republic of China
mandatory injunctions, 274
Mandela, Nelson, 59–60
Mareva injunctions, 274–275
Market Misconduct Tribunal, 158
Marx, Karl, 58
Marxism, in critical legal theory, 55
Mason, Anthony, 67
mediation, 288–294
  accreditation of mediators, 292–294
  as contract, 288
  facilitative, 288
  function and purpose of, 288–289
  under Practice Direction 31, 290–292
Mediation Code, 293
mediators. *See* accreditation of mediators
monism, public international law and, 369
Montesquieu, Charles de, 45
  on separation of powers doctrine, 77
moral order, though law, 40–41
morality, natural law theory and, 44
Mutual Care Assistance Scheme, 385–386
mutual legal assistance, 375
mutual service of judicial documents, 376–377

National People's Congress (NPC), 25–26
  NPCSC, 7, 26
natural law, as legal theory, 43–46
  Cicero on, 44
  Finnis on, 45
  Fuller on, 45–46
  legal positivism compared to, 46, 48–49
  morality in, 44
  in social contract theory, 44–45
neutral citations, 363
new laws, legislative process for, 183–184
New York Convention on the Recognition and Enforcement of Foreign Arbitral Awards, 295
non-custodial sentencing, 261–262
normative law, 48
noscitur a sociis (a thing known by its associates), 215
not guilty pleas, 256
NPC. *See* National People's Congress
NPCSC. *See* Standing Committee of the National People's Congress

410 Index

obiter dicta, 57, 124–129
Obscene Articles Tribunal, 159
'one country, two systems' concept, 2
  governance structure under, 53–54
    under Basic Law, 64–67
    capitalism in, 65
    'one country' in, 63–64
    'two systems' in, 64–67
Opium Wars, 17
oppression, as legal problem, 53–54
ordinances. *See also specific ordinances*
  definitions section of, 213–214
  primary sources for legal materials
    of amendments, 333–334
    legislative history of, 334–335
  statutory interpretation of, 212–219
Ordinary Legal Aid Scheme, 311–313
  under Legal Aid Ordinance, 312–313
overruling. *See* prospective overruling; retrospective overruling

parliamentary materials, in statutory interpretation, 222–223
Patten, Chris, 236
payments. *See also* awards; remedies
  in CJR, 283–284
PCA. *See* Permanent Court of Arbitration
People's Republic of China (PRC)
  ATIS, 384
  CEPA and, 382–384
  cross-border crime and, with Hong Kong, 385–390
    Mutual Care Assistance Scheme, 385–386
    notification mechanisms for, 389–390
    police joint operations for, 386–387
    rendition agreements, 387–388
  Hong Kong as part of, 24–27, 63–64. *See also* Basic Law
    Basic Law in, establishment of, 25
    HKSAR established in, 25–26
    under Joint Declaration, with UK, 24–25
    NPC and, 25–26
    Second Convention of Peking and, 24
  Hong Kong legal system and, interface with, 375–379
    arbitral awards, enforcement of, 380–382
    arrangement on mutual taking of evidence, 379
    arrangement on reciprocal enforcement of judgments, 377–379
    mutual legal assistance, 375
    mutual service of judicial documents, 376–377
  national laws created by, 58, 135–136
  NPC in, 25–26
  NPCSC and, 7, 26
periodicals, as secondary sources, 354
Permanent Court of Arbitration (PCA), 297
permanent Magistrates' Courts, 150
personnel separation of powers, 79
persuasive authorities, in court systems, 179–180
pleadings, in civil litigation, 271–273
pleas, 253–256
  conviction rates for, 254–255
  of guilt, 253–256
  of not guilty, 256
police officers, in HKPF, 235–244
  arrests by, 239–241
  cross-border crime and, joint operations for, 386–387
  powers of, 237–243
  stop and search authority of, 237–239
policy papers, 358
political choice, in critical legal theory, 52–53
political order, through law, 37–38
Pound, Roscoe, 50
Practice Direction 31, 290–292
PRC. *See* People's Republic of China
precedent. *See* judicial precedent
presumption of innocence, 257–258
primary legislation, 99, 191–196
  bills as part of, 193–194
    private, 193
    public, 193
  Chief Executive signatures as part of, 195–196
  consultation papers, 192–193
  Legislative Council, 193–195
  NPCSC reports, 196
  passage of, 195–196
  primary sources for, 332–336
    amendments of, 332–334
    annotations to, 335–336
    for commencement dates of legislation, 334
    in hard copies, 330–331
  proposals, 191–192
  publication of, 196
primary sources, for legal materials, 329–349
  in Cumulative Supplement, 344
  electronic copies of legislation, 336–338

of Basic Law, 337
of bills, 338
Hong Kong e-legislation, 337–338
Hong Kong Legal Information Institute, 338
electronic databases, 345–348
  Boolean searching, 348
  for case status, 347
  for specific legislation, 347
  for specific subjects, 346
  free public websites, 349
in *Government Gazette Legal Supplement No 1*, 331, 333–334, 336–339
Halsbury's Laws of Hong Kong, 330–334, 336
hard copies, 340–345
  for case status, 342
  in consolidated index of reported decisions, 342
  of primary legislation, 330–331
  report citations, 340–341
  for specific subjects, 341–342
Hong Kong Case Citator, 342–343
Hong Kong Law Reports and Digest, 343–345
LexisNexis, 338, 345
of ordinances
  amendments to, 333–334
  legislative history of, 334–335
of overseas legislation, 339–340
for primary legislation, 332–336
  amendments of, 332–334
  annotations to, 335–336
  commencement dates of, 334
  in hard copies, 330–331
scope of, 329
secondary sources compared to, 330
for subsidiary legislation, 336
Westlaw, 338, 345
private bills, 193
private international law, 366
private law, 60
privity of contract, 346
privity of doctrine, 346
Privy Council, 144–145, 177–179
pro bono publico, 322
  Bar Free Legal Services Scheme, 322–323
  Legal Advice Scheme for Unrepresented Litigants in Civil Procedures, 323–324
  Procedural Advice Scheme, 323–324
probation orders, 262

Procedural Advice Scheme, 323–324
procedural law, 59–60
prohibitory injunctions, 274
proof. *See* burden of proof; standards of proof
property rights, in critical legal theory, 52–53
prosecutions, prosecutors and, 247–250
  in courtrooms, 250
  decision-making about, 248–250
  prosecutorial independence and, 247–248
prospective overruling, 165
public bills, 193
public international law, 366
  customary international law and, 373–374
  dualism and, 369
  Hong Kong's legal system and, 367–374
  international treaties and, 369–373
  international legal personality and, 368
  monism and, 369
public law, 60
public order, through law, 37

questioning of suspects, by HKPF, 241–243

ratio decidendi, 57, 124–129
realism. *See* legal realism
remedies, in civil litigation, 276–277
rendition agreements, between PRC and Hong Kong, 387–388
repeals, of legislation, 103
  for subsidiary legislation, 199
retrospective overruling, 165
right to silence, 258
rights. *See* property rights
Rousseau, Jean-Jacques, 45
rule of law
  arbitrary power and, 5
  bias protections under, 5
  during colonial era, in Hong Kong, 18–21
  in colonial Hong Kong, 18–21
  effectiveness of, criteria for, 6
  equality of protection under, 5
  five basic principles of, 5–6
  societal benefits of, 6
rule of recognition, in Basic Law, 47

of the same kind. *See ejusdem generis*
sanctioned offers, in CJR, 283–284
Second Convention of Peking 1898, 17
secondary legislation, 99

secondary sources, for legal materials, 350–359
   books, 350
   citations in, 355–356, 362–365
   consultation papers, 358
   government publications, 358
   Halsbury's Laws of Hong Kong, 350–351
      electronic version of, 351
      hard copy of, 350–351
   Hansard materials, 358
   Hong Kong Law Reports and Digest, 352–354
   journals, 354–358
      citations in, 355–356
      electronic, 356–358
   Law Reform Commission, 359
   law reviews, 354
   legal digests, 351
   legal encyclopaedias, 350
   loose-leaf services, 359
   periodicals, 354
   policy papers, 358
   primary sources compared to, 330
   scope of, 329–330
Secretary of Justice, 12–13
Securities and Futures Appeals Tribunal, 158
sentencing, 259–262
   community service orders, 262
   custodial, 260–261
   errors in, 259
   imprisonment in, 260
   mitigating factors for, 259
   non-custodial, 261–262
   probation orders, 262
separation of powers doctrine, 6, 76–88, 152
   Aristotle on, 76
   through checks and balances, 79
   in colonial Hong Kong, 81–82
      Legislative Council, 81–82
   in Declaration of the Rights of Man, 77
   function of, 80
   functional, 79
   in HKSAR, 82–88
      academic literature as influence on, 84
      for executive branch, 85–86
      through judicial courts, 84–86
      for Legislative Council, 86–87
      legislative protections in, 83
   institutional, 79
   judicial reasoning under, 129–131
   in legislative process, 190–191
   Locke on, 76–77

Montesquieu on, 77
   origins of, 76–78
   personnel, 79
   political rationale of, 76–78
   scope of, 77–78
   in U.S. Constitution, 77
Sino-Soviet system, of law, 58
Small Claims Tribunal, 144, 153–154
social contract theory, 44–45
social control, through law, 50–51
social order, through law, 38–39
solicitors. *See* barristers and solicitors
sovereignty
   PRC, over Hong Kong, 24–27, 63–64
      Basic Law in, establishment of, 25
      HKSAR established under, 25–26
      under Joint Declaration, with UK, 24–25
      NPC, 25–26
      Second Convention of Peking and, 24
   transfer of, 1–2
special magistrates, 150
standards of proof, 164
   in civil litigation, 275
   in criminal trials, 256–257
Standing Committee of the National People's Congress (NPCSC), 7, 26
   doctrine of judicial precedent and, 176
   interpretation of Basic Law, 94–98
   for primary legislation, reports on, 196
   as source of legislation, 101
stare decisis. See judicial precedent
statements of truth, 284–285
statute law, 108
statutes
   components of, 104–107
   consolidation of, 100
   interpretation of, 123–124
   statutory interpretation of, 219
statutory interpretation
   of Basic Law, 228–230
   basic values protections in, 224–225
   of bilingual legislation, 230–231
   case study for, 226–228
   common law and, 202–206
      background of, 202–203
      'golden rule' in, 204
      literal approach in, 203
      purposive approach in, 205–206
   ejusdem generis, 215–216
   expressio unius est exclusio alterius, 217
   external aids to, 220–224

extrinsic materials, 222–224
Hansard materials, 222–223
legislative history as, 220–222
parliamentary materials, 222–223
generalia specialibus non derogant, 217–218
legislative intention and, 201–202
modern approach to, 207–212
noscitur a sociis, 215
of ordinances, 212–219
definitions section of, 213–214
principle of, 201–202
of statute components, 219
statutory laws, 4, 100–101
stop and search authority, of HKPF, 237–239
subordinate legislation. *See* subsidiary legislation
subsidiary legislation, 99, 196–199
in Australia, 197–198
Legislative Council and, 196–197, 199
passage of, 198
repeal of, 199
ultra vires doctrine, 198
substantive law, 59–60
summary judgments, 270–271
superior court systems, 140–141
Competition Tribunal, 140
jurisdiction of, 140
Supplementary Legal Aid Scheme, 313–314
Type I proceedings, 314
Type II proceedings, 314
Supreme Court, England, 166–167
Supreme Court, Hong Kong, 142–143. *See also* High Court of Hong Kong Special Administrative Region

Tacitus, Cornelius, 183
Tel-Law Scheme, 321
a thing known by its associates. *See noscitur a sociis*
Thomas Aquinas (Saint), 44
Treaty of Nanking 1842, 17, 63
trial procedures, in civil litigation, 275–276
tribunals
Competition Tribunal, 140, 157–158
doctrine of judicial precedent in, 174–175
horizontal *stare decisis*, 175
vertical *stare decisis*, 174–175
before July 1, 1997, 144
after July 1, 1997, 151–159
in Hong Kong, 152–153
Labour Tribunal, 144, 156–157
Lands Tribunal, 144, 154–156
Market Misconduct Tribunal, 158
Obscene Articles Tribunal, 159
Securities and Futures Appeals Tribunal, 158
Small Claims Tribunal, 144, 153–154
Tsang, Donald, 289

ultra vires doctrine, 198
UNCITRAL. *See* United Nations Commission on International Trade Law
United Nations Commission on International Trade Law (UNCITRAL), 295–296
United States (U.S.). *See also* Constitution
Joint Declaration, with China, 24–25

Weber, Max, 49–50
Westlaw, 338, 345
Widgery criteria, 319
Wong Yan Lung, 289
World Bank, 372
World Health Organisation, 372

For EU product safety concerns, contact us at Calle de José Abascal, 56–1°, 28003 Madrid, Spain or eugpsr@cambridge.org.

www.ingramcontent.com/pod-product-compliance
Ingram Content Group UK Ltd.
Pitfield, Milton Keynes, MK11 3LW, UK
UKHW020628011125
464535UK00005B/37